COLLECTED WORKS OF JOHN STUART MILL

VOLUME XXXII

The Collected Edition of the Works of John Stuart Mill has been planned and is being directed by an editorial committee appointed from the Faculty of Arts and Science of the University of Toronto, and from the University of Toronto Press. The primary aim of the edition is to present fully collated texts of those works which exist in a number of versions, both printed and manuscript, and to provide accurate texts of works previously unpublished or which have become relatively inaccessible.

Editorial Committee

J.M. ROBSON, *General Editor*

HARALD BOHNE, J.C. CAIRNS, J.B. CONACHER,

D.P. DRYER, MARION FILIPIUK, FRANCESS HALPENNY,

SAMUEL HOLLANDER, R.F. MCRAE, IAN MONTAGNES,

ANN P. ROBSON, F.E. SPARSHOTT

Additional Letters

of

John Stuart Mill

Edited by

MARION FILIPIUK
Senior Research Assistant, J.S. Mill Project,
University of Toronto

MICHAEL LAINE
Associate Professor of English,
Victoria College, University of Toronto

and

JOHN M. ROBSON
University Professor and Professor of English,
Victoria College, University of Toronto

Introduction by

MARION FILIPIUK

UNIVERSITY OF TORONTO PRESS
ROUTLEDGE

© *University of Toronto Press 1991*
Toronto and Buffalo
Printed in Canada

ISBN 0-8020-2768-7

London: Routledge
ISBN 0-415-06399-X

Printed on acid-free paper

Canadian Cataloguing in Publication Data
Mill, John Stuart, 1806–1873.
[Works]
Collected works of John Stuart Mill
Includes bibliographies and indexes.
Partial contents: v. 32. Additional Letters / edited by
Marion Filipiuk, Michael Laine, and John M. Robson.
ISBN 0–8020–3461–6 (v. 32).
1. —Collected works.
2. —Collected works.
3. —Collected works.
I. Robson, John M., 1927–
II. Title.
B1602.A2 1963   192   C65-188-2 rev.

British Library Cataloguing in Publication Data
Mill, John Stuart, 1806–1873
Additional letters of John Stuart Mill.
Introduction by Marion Filipiuk.
(Collected works of John Stuart Mill. Vol. 32).
I. Title   II. Filipiuk, Marion   III. Laine, Michael
IV. Robson, John M.   V. Series
826.8
ISBN 0-415-06399-X.

This volume has been published with the assistance of a grant
from the Social Sciences and Humanities Research Council of Canada

Contents

INTRODUCTION, by Marion Filipiuk	vii
Additional Earlier Letters: 1824 to 1848	1
Additional Later Letters: 1849 to 1873	77
Undated Letters	239

APPENDICES

Appendix A. Letters to Theodor Gomperz: Variant Readings	251
Appendix B. List of Form Letters at the India Office Library and Records	253
Appendix C. Additions and Corrections to the Check List of Mill's Indian Despatches in Volume XXX	255
Appendix D. List of Letters to Mill	256
Appendix E. Index of Correspondents	274
Appendix F. Index of Persons and Works Cited, with Variants and Notes	278
INDEX	321

Introduction

MARION FILIPIUK

EDITORS, both past and present, of Mill's correspondence have had to live with the certain knowledge that the task would remain incomplete. To the second volume of *Earlier Letters*, Professor Francis E. Mineka had to append three "Additional Letters" that had come to light after the volumes were in page proof.[1] At the conclusion of the fourth volume of *Later Letters*, he added another, much larger collection of recently discovered letters, one of which had, again, arrived too late to take its proper chronological place, even in the late additions.[2] We have been somewhat more fortunate with timing, in being able to add to this collection at the very last moment a newly arrived series of letters to M.E. Grant Duff. The ever impending problem of new acquisitions bears evidence to the continued flourishing state of Mill studies, and we cannot pretend to undue concern.

Even before the manuscript of Volumes XIV–XVII was submitted to the publisher, a misplaced fragment of a letter was sent to John M. Robson, appropriately by Professor F.A. Hayek, the originator of the project to collect and publish Mill's correspondence. The fragment appeared first in the *Mill News Letter*,[3] and was added in its proper place in Volume XIV. Six letters from Mill to Sir William Molesworth also made their first appearance in the *News Letter*,[4] and then were subsequently included in the Appendix to *Later Letters*.

Since 1972 thirty-seven more letters have been edited for publication in the *News Letter* by friends of Mill and members of the Mill Project, and seven others have been published in the *Mill Society Bulletin, Japan*. As we continued to become aware of the existence of yet other letters, and were fairly certain that in the intervening years new material would have found its way into manuscript

---

[1]*Earlier Letters*, ed. Francis E. Mineka, *Collected Works* [*CW*], XII–XIII (Toronto: University of Toronto Press, 1963), XIII, 742–3.
[2]*Later Letters*, ed. Francis E. Mineka and Dwight N. Lindley, *CW*, XIV–XVII (Toronto: University of Toronto Press, 1972), XVII, 1954–2016. Additional letters in the present volume will be referred to in the text by number, frequently in parentheses.
[3]See *Mill News Letter* [*MNL*] (Fall 1968), 29–30.
[4]William E.S. Thomas and Francis E. Mineka, eds., "New Letters of J.S. Mill to Sir William Molesworth," *MNL*, VI (Fall 1970), 1–13.

collections, we became convinced that we should initiate a new search and gather in all known correspondence as part of the *Collected Works*.

Beginning in 1985, major public and university libraries and archives in the United Kingdom, the United States, and France, historical associations, relevant special collections, and selected libraries in Europe, Australia, and New Zealand were contacted about recent acquisitions or holdings possibly overlooked, with some pleasantly surprising results. We were informed of three Mill letters in an important collection of manuscripts recently left to the Pierpont Morgan Library in New York by Gordon N. Ray; and a set of eight letters exchanged between Mill and James Fitzjames Stephen was drawn to our attention by the Librarian at Cambridge University. In the course of locating the various drafts of Mill's despatches in the India Office Library and Records for the publication of a finding list in Volume XXX of the *Collected Works*, Martin and Zawahir Moir found more than seventy letters and notes from Mill to his colleagues in the East India Company. Professor Shohken Mawatari undertook the task of checking the manuscript holdings in Japan, with resulting additions to this collection, and Professor Shigekazu Yamashita sent us copies of the letters to Theodor Gomperz, earlier believed lost, but now held at Kokugakuin University. Individual collectors, such as Professor Arnold Heertje, have also been extremely helpful and generous.

From the files of Professor Mineka (which included those of Professor Hayek), graciously passed on to us in 1985, emerged other clues to previously unpublished material, such as entries from dealers' catalogues. Though most of these letters could no longer be traced, three have subsequently been located, in the Pierpont Morgan (Ray) collection and in Japan; some, no doubt, remain in private hands. In the files was also a series of typescripts of letters from Mill to Henry Cole made by Professor James McCrimmon from manuscripts in his possession in the early 1940s. Some, but not all, of these were printed in Volumes XII–XIII; the rest appear here for the first time. We believe that the McCrimmon manuscripts, apparently sent off for inclusion in the Mill-Taylor Collection at the London School of Economics, were probably victims of enemy action while in transit during the Second World War. A letter to Professor Mineka, indicating the existence of a manuscript fragment at Manchester College, Oxford, enabled us to obtain the first part of Letter 1474A, to Mary Carpenter; and, much to our surprise, the remaining fragment appeared in the collection of the College of Law, Nihon University, Tokyo.

In all, well over 300 letters have come to light over the past eighteen years, and now take their place in the *Collected Works*. The distribution by decade is generally similar to that in the previous volumes. Three have been added to the relatively meagre number that hitherto represented the correspondence of the 1820s, and forty-three to each of the decades of the 1830s and 1840s. There are fifty-eight new letters written in the 1850s, of which forty-four derive from the

India Office Records. By far the greatest number, however, 129, belong to the decade of the 1860s, when Mill achieved the height of his fame; and thirty-three, in a roughly similar proportion, represent the first two-and-a-half years of the 1870s. They add appreciably to our knowledge of almost every stage of Mill's life.

Particularly significant is the long letter to George and Harriet Grote (8.1), which describes many of the activities of Mill's circle in 1824–25, and three early letters to John Bowring (8.2, 8.3, and 31.1) that suggest the relations between him and the Mills may not have been quite so strained as has previously been believed. A letter of condolence to J.B. Say, on the death of Mme Say (29.1), reveals the deep respect and gratitude that Mill entertained for Say and his family, as well as the depth of his feelings on the suicide of his great friend Eyton Tooke. A response to questions by J.A. Blanqui (85.1), Say's pupil and successor, about the teaching and propagation of political economy in England in 1833, illustrates Mill's boundless good will and effort in accommodating and assisting French acquaintances. A letter to the Paris bookseller Paulin (177.01) also, however, demonstrates his signal lack of success in making the *London and Westminster Review* a real vehicle for the international exchange of ideas.

The series of letters to Henry Cole, which is discussed in a separate section below, has greatly enriched the detail of the circumstances surrounding the transfer of the *Review* to him and William Hickson in 1840. Two other letters of that year (284.1 and 285.1) to John Calvert, from a Mill deeply grieved by his younger brother's death, show that relations with Calvert, John Sterling's great friend, on whom Mill relied during Henry's last days at Falmouth, were close. The second also throws light on the way in which discussions at the Sterling Club helped Mill to understand the Christian commitment of the Wilberforces, and it dates his earliest steps to revise his essays for publication, a plan not completed until the appearance in 1859 of *Dissertations and Discussions*. The correspondence with Theodor Gomperz, discussed in detail below, which began in the 1850s, illustrates another of Mill's warm, personal relations, in this case with a younger disciple who was much in need of the generosity of spirit that was shown him. A separate section is also devoted to consideration of the recently discovered internal memos from the archives of the East India Company, which add to our understanding both of the workings of the Company and of Mill's work as its employee.

Many previously unknown and interesting contacts during the decade of the 1860s came to light in the course of our search, some producing challenging questions. The second of three letters (594A, 617A, 1547A) to J.E. Thorold Rogers, Drummond Professor of Political Economy at Oxford, expresses Mill's relief at escaping "the crowd and turmoil of the present occasion," in mid-June 1863, and adds, "I should be a little ashamed, too, as well as surprised, at being thought sufficiently orthodox when Kingsley is not." No evidence has been found that Mill was, like Kingsley, nominated for the degree of Doctor of Common

Laws, but at that time Kingsley withdrew his name from the lists of candidates because of objections to his views. A letter to the botanist John Lindley, editor of the *Gardeners' Chronicle* (671B), demonstrates both Mill's active concern for conservation and his intolerance of the "selfish rapacity" of those who would collect rare plants. Three letters to James Fitzjames Stephen (690A, 833A, 1431A) illustrate the course of their relationship between 1864 and 1869.[5] Two letters to the philosopher Henry Sidgwick in the fall of 1867 (1127A, 1160A) are, like two of those to Stephen, answers to requests for advice, and demonstrate the same tact and wisdom in response to difficult questions. Five to J.M.F. Ludlow (1046A, 1046B, 1112A, 1118A, 1521B) deal with more practical matters, the administrative reforms with which Mill was concerned; they reveal that in 1867 Ludlow was very active in assisting Benjamin Scott in preparing his evidence for the Select Committee on Metropolitan Government (on which Mill served), and that Ludlow had assisted James Beal in preparing his bills on the same subject.[6] One letter is Ludlow's reward for services rendered: a warm endorsement by Mill of his candidacy for the office of Registrar of Friendly Societies, along with a keen and humorous assessment of the politician Robert Lowe. There are three letters supportive, in principle, of William Rossiter's efforts in 1867 and 1868 to launch and develop the South London Working Men's College and its accompanying school (1152B, 1239A, 1246A), and one to Elizabeth Malleson (999A) applauding her similar endeavours for a Working Women's College.

An excerpt from a letter written to the General Council of the International Working Men's Association in July 1870 (1583A) confirms that Mill had indeed some knowledge of Marx, or, specifically, of his speech on the Franco-Prussian war, which may have been sent to him for comment and which he found admirable. Other new contacts in the few years of the 1870s that remained to him continue to illustrate the constant demands made upon his time for a variety of causes. A group of letters that are held at the Palais du Roure in Avignon may also illustrate something about the way Mill's correspondence was bundled up, when, more than thirty years after his death, books and papers were disposed of at the local Librairie Roumanille. There are fourteen letters to Mill, with seven draft replies written verso and two drafts on separate sheets, most dating from the short period of August to October, 1871; the remaining pieces are a certificate dated 1858, unanswered letters of 1861, 1864, and 1865, and an envelope from 1888.[7]

[5]There is a full discussion of the eight letters in Jean O'Grady, "Mill and Fitzjames Stephen: Personal Notes," *MNL*, XXII (Winter 1987), 2–9.

[6]For Mill's introduction of Beal's bills in the House of Commons, and his questioning of Scott in Committee, see *Public and Parliamentary Speeches*, *CW*, XXVIII–XXIX (Toronto: University of Toronto Press, 1988), XXVIII, 162–5, 230–1, XXIX, 443–4, and *Miscellaneous Writings*, *CW*, XXXI (Toronto: University of Toronto Press, 1989), 390–1, 402–4.

[7]For further detail, see Marion Filipiuk, "New Letters from Avignon," *MNL*, XV (Summer 1980), 1–11.

Introduction xi

In all there are twenty items, probably representing a single lot at the sale in May, 1905.

The editorial method followed here is virtually the same as that used in the six previous volumes of correspondence. When the autograph letter has not been available, the draft has been used and is so identified. We have reproduced our sources as closely as possible, retaining vagaries of spelling in both English and French without comment. We have, however, transferred dates and addresses that appeared at the end of a letter to the beginning, and occasionally have silently added an end-of-line comma or full stop. The first footnote to each letter provides the location of the manuscript; addresses and postmarks where available; publication information for letters previously printed; information about conjectural dating; and, at first references, identification of the recipient. When possible, letters have been related to those sent to Mill.

The practice in the Appendices of *Collected Works*, Volume XVII, has been followed for the enumeration of the letters. For additional *Earlier Letters*, a decimal notation has been used: e.g., Letter 284.1 below, of 25 Apr., 1840, is next in chronological sequence after 284, of 22 Apr., 1840, in Volume XIII, pp. 429–30. An alphabetical indicator signals additions to *Later Letters*: e.g., Letter 336A below, of 29 Nov., 1858, follows 336, of 28 Nov., 1858, in Volume XV, p. 578. In eight cases, when the letter antedated one already inserted in the sequence, we were forced to resort to a further refinement; see, e.g., 171.01 and 862AA below. Letters already in *Collected Works* in incomplete form, reprinted here in full, retain their original numbers. Of fifty-two undated letters discovered, we have managed to assign dates to all but fifteen; these last have been arranged chronologically, as far as could be determined, in a separate section, and bear the prefix "No." In footnotes, letters in this volume will generally be referred to by number, letters in *Earlier* and *Later Letters*, by volume and page.[8]

---

[8]In the course of preparing this volume we have discovered that the following emendations should be made to the information provided in *Later Letters*:

The MS of Letter 513.1 below, at the Houghton Library, has enabled us to date the letter to John William Parker at *CW*, XVII, 2006, to 25 Oct., 1847.

The unidentified recipient of the letter dated [Before May 8, 1868], *ibid.*, XVI, 1397, is probably Mrs. Mary Johnson of Birmingham.

The letter to Edward Livingstone Youmans, *ibid.*, XVII, 1569, has been dated 9 Apr., 1869, from the MS at the College of Law, Nihon University, Tokyo.

The librarian at Northwestern University informs us, on the basis of both internal and external evidence, that the recipient of the letter dated 3 June, 1870, *ibid.*, 1731–2, is not Herbert Spencer; no other identification has been made.

The letter to David King dated [Oct.? 1870], *ibid.*, 1768, may now be dated 9 Nov., 1870, from information in Letter 1631A below.

See also the summary of the reordering of letters, most to Henry Cole, on xvi below.

LETTERS TO HENRY COLE

SEVERAL of the new letters to Henry Cole and one to John Mitchell Kemble throw more light on the story of Mill's divesting himself of the *London and Westminster Review* and transferring it in the spring of 1840 to Cole and William Edward Hickson.[9] Mill's determination to withdraw from the costly proprietorship and onerous editorship was evident in October 1839, when he tried to interest Thomas Wentworth Beaumont, the wealthy proprietor of the *British and Foreign Review*, in taking it on. His first tentative approach (265.1 below) was through Kemble, the editor, with whom he had only "a former slight acquaintance," but through whom he thought it prudent to make the preliminary enquiry. Since the two reviews had had the "same difficulties to struggle against," and basically the same readership to draw upon, Mill thought there might be some pecuniary advantage to Beaumont in incorporating the rival radical organ. Kemble's reply apparently indicated several issues on which the opinions of the two reviews had been at variance, and clearly suggested that he was unfavourably disposed to the merger; but he offered to write to Beaumont.[10] Mill was left dangling for months, expecting some sort of response from Beaumont, and apparently unwilling to let the silence speak for itself.

As early as August 1839, Mill began to confide his problems with the *Review* (and with John Robertson, who had been mismanaging it in his absence on the Continent) to Cole, who was obviously interested in becoming involved, but said nothing at that point.[11] He knew about Mill's offering it to Beaumont, since they discussed the matter during walks to town in October. There is no hard evidence in Cole's diary that he was pressing his suit, though VanArsdel interprets the fact that all contact with Mill ceased during Cole's illness, 7 November to 14 January, as an indication that he was perhaps putting too much pressure on Mill.[12]

Robertson apparently called on Cole on the first day of that illness to talk about the "future management of the review." A previously unpublished letter from Mill

---

[9]Cole, Mill's intimate friend since 1828, was, at this time, an assistant keeper in the Public Record Office and an active advocate of postal reform; he was extremely ambitious for influence, but rather embarrassed for money. Hickson, in contrast, was an older, more experienced radical, with solid finances and a penchant for economy. The other player in the struggle for control of the *Review* was John Robertson, Mill's sub-editor since 1837. For many of the details of the story and the references to Cole's diary in the Victoria and Albert Museum, we are indebted to Rosemary T. VanArsdel, "*The Westminster Review*: Change of Editorship, 1840," *Studies in Bibliography*, XXV (1972), 191–204. The new letters here printed, however, as will be explained, alter the chronology she suggested for those already in *Earlier Letters*.

[10]Kemble's letter is not extant, but see Mill's reply of 14 October, *CW*, XIII, 410–11.
[11]Cole's diary, entry for 16 August.
[12]VanArsdel, "*Westminster Review*," 196.

Introduction xiii

to Cole (268.1) may be dated to 12 November, the Tuesday following that meeting. Robertson must have explained some sort of "plan" that he and Cole had formulated, which possibly involved their sharing of the editorial duties in future. The letter also suggests that they were hoping Mill might be persuaded to retain the proprietorship if he were relieved of the editorial burden. Robertson appears not to have felt that his position was threatened by the proposed arrangements, as Mill says, "He seemed to me to be neither *for* nor *against* the plan, but to await my decision. Now my decision, if I consider myself only, will be, whatever becomes of the review, to withdraw myself from it." Beaumont is still his major hope; he thinks, after waiting nearly a month, that he "cannot be much longer without" an answer. If Beaumont fails, Mill says: "I should like best . . . that your schemes should proceed, with some other person than myself as the proprietor."

There is no mention of Hickson in this letter, and no indication that the discussion went any further at this point. Mill may have decided that he prefered to shelve their plans until he knew definitely where Beaumont stood. Cole, however, was not totally idle. The diary for 17 November notes that Hickson called and "promised to help in some new arrangements of the L. and W.R." This is the first entry that specifically links Hickson with the plans, though contacts between Cole and Hickson were frequent during this period.[13]

Mill continued to wait throughout December and January, and the only relevant item in Cole's diary is the unspecific comment that on 7 January, 1840 he had a chat with William Makepeace Thackeray about the *Review*. It is likely that no one wanted to push Mill, since all were aware that he had serious concerns and financial responsibilities resulting from the declining health of his brother Henry. And it is likely that Mill's procrastination and wavering were at least partly the result of his disturbed state of mind and the uncertainty about his brother's fate.[14]

On 6 February, in the midst of this turmoil, and presumably feeling the pressure of shortly having to produce the March number, Mill suddenly offered the *Review* to Cole, still "in case of Beaumont's refusal to buy it," and then, just as suddenly, the next day withdrew the offer. Letters 273 and 276, the dates of which were uncertain, can now be assigned through Cole's diary to 6 and 8 February: Cole and his brother called on Mill on the 9th to try to straighten things out. "One or two

---

[13]*Ibid.*
[14]With his mother and sister, Henry had been sent off to Falmouth, en route for Madeira, probably immediately after a party at the Mills', mentioned by Cole, on 14 January. Mill's letter to Clara (No. 274, *CW*, XIII, 420) reveals that the doctor had admitted to him after their departure that Henry's case was in fact "alarming," and that he had recommended the trip only because Mill himself "so much wished it." Caroline Fox, the new family friend in Falmouth, noted in her diary on 8 February that "Mrs. Mill with her daughters, Clara and Harriet, have been for some weeks nursing Henry Mill . . . in lodgings on the Terrace"; this letter to Clara should then be dated to 22 or 29 January, 1839. (See *Memories of Old Friends*, 2nd ed., 2 vols. [London: Smith, Elder, 1882], I, 102–3.)

friends" had, in the interval, been trying to persuade Mill that he should not allow the *Review* to continue with the name unchanged, as he would remain closely associated in people's minds with it, and that it would be more to his credit "that it should cease entirely than that it should be continued as anything else than the philosophical & political organ it was designed to be." Perhaps Mill felt guilty and embarrassed about having treated Cole badly, because, after a breathing space, contact, if not negotiations, resumed by 15 February.[15]

At the "eleventh hour," on a Thursday, probably 27 rather than 20 February, Mill wrote to Cole, again offering him the *Review* if he would carry it on under the name of *Westminster*, and adding that he would be even happier to turn it over to him and Hickson jointly, as Cole proposed, but all this still subject to a last-minute offer from Beaumont, "or from some other quarter almost as improbable."[16] Letter 277.1, here published for the first time, is obviously a second note written at "20 minutes before 6," on the same day, just as Mill was rushing off to Reynell's to oversee the printing of the March number of the *Review*.[17] It was prompted, obviously, by the fact that he had indeed had the offer from the "other quarter [he] alluded to," and he would suddenly like the matter decided, with "an announcement in the present number," but was still somewhat short of certain: "if you are willing to carry it on our agreement must be conditional on the very probable event of my refusing [the other offer]."

No such announcement appeared in the March number, though, curiously, discussion seems to have heated up among all parties almost at once. It is scarcely surprising that final arrangements failed to be made on such short notice, and other moves were apparently afoot. Cole had noted in his diary on 20 February (a Thursday) that Robertson had called on him; there is no specific mention of the *Review* at all, but on the following Friday, the 28th, Cole and Robertson dined together, and then with Mill and George Fletcher (an occasional contributor to the *Westminster*) walked to Kensington. How can all this be squared with Mill's making an offer to Cole on the 27th, which Cole not only failed to take up at once, but failed to mention in his diary?

It is possible that by 20 February Robertson could see that Mill was wanting to put the matter to rest soon, and that his job as editor was in jeopardy; so a reminder to Cole of his interest in staying on, and his difficulties, may have appeared timely. Cole's lack of response to Mill's offer may have resulted from "the force of circumstances"—an inability to reach Hickson, vagueness in their arrangements (as everything still seemed to hinge on Beaumont), or his own financial uncertainty. Whatever the reasons, or the sequence of events, it is certain that after the conversations on the 28th, Robertson was aware that the tide had definitely set

---

[15]*CW*, XIII, 419 and 421; Letter 273, headed "Thursday," must have been written on 6 February. Cf. VanArsdel, "*Westminster Review*," 196–8.
[16]No. 277, *CW*, XIII, 421–2.
[17]The advertisement in the *Examiner* of Sunday, 1 March, 1840, describes the number as "just published," making the date of 27 February likely for the letter.

against him and that he immediately mounted a campaign to save his position. It sounds, indeed, as if Robertson had made a bid to conduct the *Review* as sole editor. Cole's diary for the 29th reports:

Walked to town with John Mill who seemed to think that Robertson could not manage the Review by himself. . . . Robertson called and in a round about manner urged all sorts of reasons to influence his remaining Editor of the Review. He said he did not like J. Mill's conduct and that he had offers to write in the Edinburgh, that without him and J. Mill the character of the Review would be gone, that in fact the Review owed him £900, that he had never been able to have his own way, etc. etc.[18]

It seems likely that Robertson had had a rude shock on the 28th when he discovered that Cole and Hickson were potential co-proprietors and his editorship was in question. Cole was apparently sympathetic to his problems, and Robertson persevered. On 5 March he returned to visit Cole, and made a new proposal—that Cole "be sole propietor and he editor of the Review." Mill must have heard about this scheme from Robertson later on the same day and hoped to talk to Cole about it the next morning, but missed him. This inference dates Mill's letter of Friday to 6 March.[19]

It is here that an undated letter of Cole's must fit, in response to Mill's early morning note.[20] It is also headed "Friday." Cole had talked to Hickson on Thursday night; Hickson was unwilling to enter into a joint proprietorship with Robertson as editor. In the letter Mill is asked to decide between Cole and Hickson, or Cole and Robertson: "the decision must rest with you." Later that day, Mill replies: "The responsibility thus devolving wholly on me I must take till Monday to consider. But I will be prepared to give you an answer positively on that day." (277.2.)

Cole, however, did not wait for Mill's answer—or he knew what it would be. His diary for 6 March notes: "Wrote to John Mill abt. Robertson's editorship. . . . In the evening writing to Robertson to decline his proposition." On Saturday, the 7th, Hickson made Cole a generous offer to take a greater number of the shares, thereby lessening Cole's financial responsibility in the venture.[21]

VanArsdel's dating of Mill's letter of partial explanation to Robertson to 10 or 11 March seems correct.[22] Mill undoubtedly would have written before the formal transfer took place, as it did on Thursday, the 12th.[23] Letter 279, in reply to Robertson's answer of complaint, may thus be dated to Monday, 16 March.[24]

---

[18]Quoted in VanArsdel, "*Westminster Review*," 198.
[19]No. 275, *CW*, XIII, 420.
[20]Referred to *ibid.*, n2.
[21]Cole's finances were undoubtedly one of the problems all along. He wanted the *Review* badly, but could not quite find the money when opportunity knocked, as it did, for example, on the 27th. The fact that he does not record this problem in his diary is no surprise.
[22]No. 278, *CW*, XIII, 422.
[23]With No. 280, *ibid.*, 424.
[24]*Ibid.*, 422–3; VanArsdel, "*Westminster Review*," 201n.

Mill obviously agreed to help Cole and Hickson with the editing if they so wished, and the brief letter to Cole (287.1) can probably be dated "before 26 May," the date of publication of the June issue. "The Critical and Miscellaneous Notices" section became a feature of the *Review* under the new owners, mentioned as such in the notice of change. Though Mill clearly thought it was a poor substitute for solid articles, he went over the notices for the June number, as requested, and contributed three to the September number. This letter must have reference to the June and not the September number, because Cole withdrew in July and was no longer in charge of the section.[25]

The evidence from the three new letters to Cole printed below, Cole's diary, Caroline Fox's diary, and VanArsdel's article permits a redating and reordering of the letters from this period as listed below. (Those preceded by No. are found in *Collected Works*, Volume XIII.)[26]

268.1 [12 Nov., 1839?]	No. 275 [6 Mar., 1840]
No. 274 [22 or 29 Jan., 1840]	277.2 [6 Mar., 1840]
No. 273 [6 Feb., 1840]	No. 278 [10 or 11 Mar., 1840]
No. 276 [8 Feb., 1840]	No. 280 12 Mar., 1840
No. 277 [27 Feb., 1840]	No. 279 [16 Mar., 1840]
277.1 [27 Feb., 1840]	

LETTERS TO THEODOR GOMPERZ

THE RELATIONSHIP between Mill and his young Austrian disciple Theodor Gomperz was similar to that with the even younger Englishman, John Morley. With these two men, Mill's role was that of father figure as well as mentor, and his genuine interest in, and abundant kindness to, the rising generation of the talented and reform-minded is much in evidence in his dealings with them. But Gomperz's special problems brought out the depth of Mill's generosity of spirit for a troubled mind in a way that no other relationship called for. Mill was, in many ways, at his absolute best with Gomperz, in the honesty that accompanied the compassion and the modest reticence that avoided applying pressure to an overburdened spirit. Yet in the circumstances that accompanied Gomperz's aspirations to Helen Taylor's hand, Mill also demonstrated the naïveté bordering on blindness that was characteristic of his attitudes where his wife and her daughter were concerned. Gomperz treasured Mill's letters to him over the years, and they were used by his

---

[25]Cole's diary for 4 and 10 August reports that he wrote some notices for the September number and sent them to Hickson (VanArsdel, *"Westminster Review,"* 202).

[26]The dating of the letters in *EL* is as follows: No. 274 [Feb., 1840]; No. 273 [Feb.(?), 1840]; No. 276 [Feb. or March(?), 1840]; No. 277 [Feb. or March(?), 1840]; No. 275 [Feb.(?), 1840]; No. 278 [March(?), 1840]; No. 280, 12 Mar., 1840; No. 279 [March 1840(?)].

son Heinrich in a study of his father's life, based on his correspondence.[27] It was from this source and from drafts in the Johns Hopkins and Mill-Taylor collections that most of these letters came into *Later Letters*.

In a communication to the editor of the *New York Times* of 25 April, 1939, Heinrich Gomperz claimed to have "published all of these letters in their full English text," and then, having

put [them] to all the use they were capable of yielding, . . . sold the originals at a very modest price to a second-hand bookseller in London from whom they were purchased by Lord Stamp, who, not knowing that they had already been published, . . . wrote a lengthy article about them and, indeed, republished them in part in The Times of London on Dec. 29, 1938.

Stamp's selection in fact revealed that Gomperz had not published quite all of the letters, or "their . . . full text," as, for example, a two-sentence fragment of Letter 292 and an additional paragraph of Letter 324 below, which Stamp included, bore witness. It was subsequently assumed that the letters were destroyed in 1941, when Lord Stamp died in an air raid that demolished his home.[28] We now know that such was not the case. The collection appeared on the market in 1986 and, through the Tokyo dealers, Maruzen, was purchased by Kokugakuin University. It includes thirty-nine letters to Gomperz, a questionnaire relating to the *Logic*, and a letter to Gomperz's sister Josephine von Wertheimstein. Owing to the good offices of Professor Shigekazu Yamashita, we were able to obtain copies for collation with the versions which had already appeared in *Later Letters*.[29]

Eight letters in the collection, and the questionnaire, are previously unpublished. Four have additional paragraphs, and other differences range from as many as three-and-a-half missing sentences to a short phrase or two. We have decided to reprint those letters (including the one to Gomperz's sister) that differ by as much as, or more than, a major clause from the version published in *Later Letters*, with substantive variants noted at the foot of the page. Variants (excluding consideration of salutations and complimentary closings) between the manuscripts and the other letters in *Collected Works*, not reprinted here, are listed in Appendix A below.

The friendship between Mill and Gomperz began when the latter wrote in the summer of 1854 asking permission to translate and publish a German edition of the

---

[27]Only one volume, *Theodor Gomperz, 1832–1912: Briefe und Aufzeichnungen* [hereafter *Briefe*] (Vienna: Gerold, 1936), covering the years up to 1868, was issued in Heinrich's lifetime. A much-abridged version of the remaining typescript, at Harvard, has appeared as *Theodor Gomperz, ein Gelehrtenleben im Bürgertum der Franz-Josefs-Zeit* [hereafter *Ein Gelehrtenleben*], ed. Robert A. Kann (Vienna: Österreichischen Akademie der Wissenschaften, 1974).

[28]See Introduction to *CW*, XIV, xx, and *ibid.*, 238, n1.

[29]There is only one lacuna in the collection; the last page of the manuscript letter of 15 July, 1863, is missing. (In *CW*, XV, 865–6, the letter is incorrectly dated 5 July.)

Logic, a request which Mill readily granted.[30] Three previously unknown notes from Mill to Gomperz (262A, 262B, and 262C, below), dated almost two years later in the early fall of 1856, document the fact that Gomperz, when in England, was provided with the latest edition of the *Logic*, the fourth, and invited overnight to Blackheath to discuss the translation. It was the only occasion on which Gomperz met Harriet, and she seems to have approved of him, if one may judge from the personal revelation she made to him.[31] Her approval would surely help to account for Mill's continued loyalty to Gomperz, despite his inability, over a considerable period, to arrange for publication of the translations of Mill's works.

The friendship was thus firmly established in 1856, though there was at once to be a year's gap in their correspondence. Gomperz apparently next wrote to Mill on 30 September, 1857, telling of the death of his father earlier that year and asking a favour. Could Mill determine whether it would be possible for a medical friend of his to obtain a post in the service of the East India Company? Mill replied at once, on 5 October, as helpfully as he was able, in Letter 292 below (most of which is previously unpublished), and expressed an interest in learning more about Gomperz's own scholarly work. Yet another ten months passed before Gomperz wrote again, apparently on 21 August, 1858, telling of his publications in the *Rheinisches Museum*, and suggesting that he would like to include in his translation of the *Logic* some of Mill's controversy with Whewell. Once again, Mill's response (324 below) was immediate, on 30 August, agreeing to all Gomperz's suggestions, and in a previously unpublished paragraph saying that he needed a long "recruiting" from the "confinement of an office"; he had therefore seen fit to refuse the post on the Council of India that had been offered to him by Lord Stanley.

On 10 November, pleased to have at last, it seemed, found a publisher for the *Logic*, Weber of Leipzig, who was planning to bring it out in December and January, Gomperz replied.[32] He enclosed a pamphlet, *Die Theorie der Induktion*, by Professor Ernst Friedrich Apelt of the University of Jena, and asked Mill if he would care to answer the arguments and include his response in the translated volumes. He also asked for permission to be the translator of *On Liberty*. This letter arrived when Mill was crippled by grief at Harriet's death, but he dutifully

---

[30]Gomperz's letter of 20 July, 1854, is in the Mill-Taylor Collection, and Mill's reply of 18 August is in *CW*, XIV, 238–9. Gomperz's own philosophical and philological studies were, as Mill put it, directed to "exhibiting the speculations of the ancients from the point of view of the experience philosophy" (324 below). A first draft of the translation of the *Logic*, based on the 3rd ed., was apparently completed by the beginning of 1855; see Gomperz's letter to Heinrich Jaques of 7 January (*Briefe*, 198–9), and Adelaide Weinberg, *Theodor Gomperz and John Stuart Mill* (Geneva: Droz, 1963), 14–15.

[31]Heinrich Gomperz's account (*Briefe*, 233) suggests that Harriet Mill told Gomperz that from the time she met Mill she had been a "Seelinfreundin," but no more, both to him and to her husband.

[32]MS at Johns Hopkins.

Introduction

replied to Gomperz on 4 December,[33] suggesting that perhaps Gomperz would make some comment on the controversy himself and seeming not to have focused on the request about *On Liberty*. In his lost letter of condolence of 10 December, Gomperz apparently was enthusiastic in his praise of Harriet; Mill was pleased that "so little as [he] saw of her, should have made so true an impression." He acceded to Gomperz's request about the translation of the forthcoming work, promising to let him have "one of the earliest copies or the sheets."[34]

In January 1859, Gomperz apparently wrote again, asking another favour—that a copy of *On Liberty* be sent to a friend. Mill made the arrangements, and then, not having had any acknowledgment by 31 March, wrote volunteering to send another copy if the first had gone astray. He also made a discreet enquiry into Gomperz's "various literary projects" (381 below, previously unpublished). This letter went unanswered, and Mill wrote yet again on 16 May (392 below). He asked this time not about the book for the friend, but whether Gomperz had ever received the sheets of *On Liberty* and whether he was still wanting to do the translation, since he had had another offer from a Prussian magistrate, Eduard John, who was interested in undertaking it and seemed like "a competent person." Mill in fact directly asked Gomperz (in a sentence omitted by his son) whether he knew of John, and whether "in case the undertaking should not suit [Gomperz]," he should "close with [John's] offer." Mill was obviously anxious that *On Liberty* should make the impact and gain the recognition that the memory of Harriet deserved.

This appeal brought a response from Gomperz in late May or early June, in which he referred to "unhappy events which [had] caused [him] so much pain and disturbance of mind." Whatever the events, here was the first evidence of the emotional problems that were to plague Gomperz for the next several years and to impede progress both with his own scholarly work and with his good intentions of making Mill's writings known in German-speaking Europe. In his reply of 11 June (398 below), Mill said he was content to leave the translation of *On Liberty* with Gomperz as he wished, and he tried to remove any semblance of pressure concerning it. The relationship then lapsed into a period of silence for almost two years.

Mill's note of 18 April, 1861, and the follow-up of 3 July (487B and 494A below), were not published in *Briefe*, presumably because they underlined Gomperz's failure to fulfil his commitments. Unsure that the first note would reach Gomperz, since his address had been mislaid, Mill asked him to write and give it in full again so that a copy of *Representative Government* could be properly sent; he also mentioned his surprise at learning that a German translation of *On Liberty* had appeared. By 3 July Mill had found the address, and wrote to say that a copy of the

---

[33]*CW*, XV, 581.
[34]*Ibid.*, 589.

new work was on the way and that he was "vexed" to learn of the German version by an unknown translator (494A). Whether Gomperz received the first of these appeals is not known, but the second at least evoked a response written on 1 August, which fortunately is still extant. Gomperz had evidently been in the depths of a depression for some time. Though a considerable portion of the translation of *On Liberty* had been finished and even "*printed* long ago," his lethargy and "apathy of mind" had prevented its completion and publication. His embarrassment at his lack of performance and his immense gratitude for Mill's kindness in renewing their friendship are touching, as is Mill's response of 24 August.[35] Mill was fully able to sympathize with a "morbid affection" that sapped energy, but expressed great confidence in Gomperz's ability and encouraged him to continue with his translation of *On Liberty*. He also assured Gomperz that he did not "know anything more important or more intensely interesting than the progress and chances of the political transformation of Austria," and that he agreed, "from beginning to end," in Gomperz's analysis of the Hungarian question.

Yet another silence fell until Mill, showing great forethought, wrote again, this time from Athens, on 12 June, 1862 (538B below, previously unpublished), to say that he and Helen were planning to visit Vienna and Budapest on their return home and would like to see Gomperz in Vienna, or elsewhere in Austria, "during the month of August." He asked that Gomperz write to him, Poste Restante in Constantinople, where they hoped to be "in a month from this time, perhaps sooner." Heinrich Gomperz did not publish this note, presumably because in his view it represented merely a complication of arrangements; but Mill watchers are interested in his deliberately planning to visit Gomperz (probably motivated in part by the young man's new political concerns and connections) and his shortening his trip with Helen, reaching Constantinople by 24 June.[36] It is interesting too that they continued in the area until about 5 July, without receiving any communication from Gomperz, as Mill's note to him of 17 July, announcing their early arrival in Vienna, suggests.[37] This note, which implies no failure on the part of Gomperz,[38]

---

[35]Gomperz's letter is at Johns Hopkins: Mill's reply is in *CW*, XV, 739–40, where the date is incorrectly given as 21 August. Gomperz had apparently found some new interest in life through politics, and included copies of four articles he had written from Budapest on the history of Austro-Hungarian relations, three of which had been published in the *Neueste Nachrichten* of Vienna; the fourth had not appeared, presumably because the editor did not endorse his democratic and pro-Hungarian proposals. See Weinberg, *Gomperz and Mill*, 25–6.

[36]Letters to George Grote of 11 June and to J.E. Cairnes of 24 June (*CW*, XV, 781, 784). Helen's letter of 6 July to Fanny Stirling explains that they had hoped to take the overland route from Smyrna to Constantinople in order "to see the plains of Troy and to climb Mount Ida," but were dissuaded by the danger of fever and took the faster sea route (MS Mill-Taylor Collection).

[37]*CW*, XV, 786.

[38]He seems to have tried unsuccessfully, it being the holiday season, to make arrangements for Mill to meet his friends in Budapest (*Briefe*, 319–20).

was published by his son Heinrich; it in fact initiated a visit of several days, which was both a pleasant interlude and a prelude to further problems.

On his return to Avignon from Bad Ischel, where he and Helen had left Gomperz, Mill wrote on 17 September (554 below) to tell him of their movements in Austria after they had parted, and their activities since, in three-and-a-half sentences of interesting detail that his son chose not to include. Heinrich also made another, apparently minor, omission at the end, of two short sentences: "I have found Dr Schiel's letter; it is dated Frankfurt. Let me hear from you now and then:" The implications in the comment about Schiel, however, are rich. In 1849 J. von Schiel had published a translation of part of the *Logic*, as *Die inductive Logik*, and in 1862–63 through the same publisher, Vieweg, a complete translation of the work. Mill's brief remark suggests that Schiel had written to Gomperz to tell him that he was issuing this new edition, and that he had also written to inform Mill. It suggests too that there had probably been some discussion of the difficulties that Gomperz had had in trying to find a publisher, and also of Gomperz's position as the authorized translator of Mill's works; yet, again, the fact of a previously issued translation did not negate Mill's endorsement of Gomperz's efforts, though still unfulfilled.

Before Mill had posted this letter of 17 September, he had received a letter from Gomperz (now lost) that expressed great anxiety at not having heard about their safe return. Gomperz had apparently misread the signals of friendship that he had been receiving during their time together, and had begun to entertain romantic notions about a possibly permanent relation with Helen and her father. Mill's comment in his postscript to the letter of 17 September—"I should have written before, had I thought you would have felt any such anxiety as you mention on our account"—appears unintentionally to have fed Gomperz's hopes rather than lessened them.

The effect of these aspirations, and no doubt also of the appearance of Schiel's edition of the *Logic*, seems to have been that Gomperz was driven back to his own translation of that work, and to plans for a trip to England. He wrote to Mill in late November or early December,[39] setting out his hopes for a reunion in London in January and enclosing a questionnaire about the *Logic*, the first question of which reflects his persistent concern about his being the truly authorized translation, carried out "with the collaboration of the author" (564 below). Gomperz apparently reached London in mid-February, 1863, and Mill at once hastened to provide the new arrival with a letter of introduction, dated 20 February, to the Greek historian George Grote (589A below, previously unpublished). On that same day, Mill also took the trouble to write to the editor of the *Spectator* (589B below, also previously unpublished) to send him some information about the political situation in Austria that Gomperz had enclosed in an earlier letter. One must conclude that Mill hoped that the younger man would be pleasantly

---

[39]See Mill's reply of 14 December (*CW*, XV, 809 and n5).

surprised, and encouraged in his endeavours, by seeing that some serious notice had been taken of his activities and his writings.

Mill clearly made an effort to repay the hospitality shown to him and Helen in Austria the previous summer, unaware that his gestures of friendship might well be misconstrued by a young man with marriage on his mind. Gomperz was invited on two consecutive Sunday evenings to dinner at Blackheath, where he met William Thornton and Thomas Hare.[40] Mill also arranged for him to attend a meeting of the Political Economy Club on 6 March,[41] and the public meeting of the 26th in St. James's Hall, at which the trades unionists of London demonstrated their support for the cause of the North in the American Civil War. Mill's invitation to that meeting (603A below), at which Gomperz was to meet Henry Fawcett, is previously unpublished. The occasion for Gomperz was an extremely impressive one, both historically, as it was the first time that the working men's societies had participated in public discussion of a great public question of the day, and personally, as he accompanied Helen, while Mill sat on the platform.[42] Yet another token of Mill's friendship was the gift of a copy of *Utilitarianism*; and on Gomperz's immediate request, permission was once again granted to him to be the authorized translator.[43]

Mill and Helen apparently never mentioned to Gomperz that they were planning to leave for Avignon two days after the meeting in St. James's Hall.[44] Gomperz's letter to his sister Josephine of 29 March, describing his reception at breakfast by the Grotes at their London home on that day, suggests that he was quite unaware of the departure.[45] By the time he returned on 5 April from a weekend with the Grotes and their friends at Barrow Green, however, he had heard the news, and, despite his recent social success, he was plunged into despair, both because he had obviously failed to convey his intentions about Helen and because he felt abandoned.[46] On 18 April Gomperz wrote to suggest that he join Mill and Helen in Avignon, where he hoped to make his feelings clear.

---

[40]In a letter to his mother of 3 March, Gomperz described his various trips to Blackheath. On Sunday, 22 February, he first met Thornton, who, on their walk back to the station, pointed out to him what a rare privilege it was to be on such intimate terms with Mill, the best of men, and went on to describe the three happiest weeks of his life, spent the previous summer as a guest at Avignon. The second Sunday dinner occurred on 1 March. It appears that Gomperz also apparently called, uninvited, on Wednesday, 25 February, and again on Monday, 2 March; on the latter occasion, Mill and Helen were not at home (*Briefe*, 333–5).

[41]*Ibid.*, 335. See also *Proceedings of the Political Economy Club* (London, 1882), IV, 212.

[42]The occasion is described in a letter of 20 April (*Briefe*, 350–1).

[43]See Mill's letters to his publisher, Parker, of 14 March, and to Gomperz of 22 March (*CW*, XV, 849 and 849–50).

[44]See Mill's letter to Cairnes of 25 March (*ibid.*, 852).

[45]*Briefe*, 338–41.

[46]*Ibid.*, 341–5. See also Weinberg, *Gomperz and Mill*, 34–5.

Mill's answer of the 23rd, dissuading him from the visit, poured cold water on his hopes.[47] He sent a tormented response, to which Mill replied, on 9 May,[48] honestly, yet somewhat tentatively, since Gomperz's letter referred to "suppositions," apparently adverse to himself, which Mill was deemed to have made. Gomperz then went off to Oxford, where he did, in fact, make some progress with his plans to study and edit tracings of manuscripts from Herculaneum, before experiencing a kind of breakdown towards the end of the month. His strange behaviour caused his new friends there to send for help from home, which arrived, apparently in the first week of June, in the person of his friend Eduard Wessel, but not before Gomperz had gone missing for a short time and caused some alarm.[49] According to Weinberg's account, it was on Saturday, 6 June, as this crisis was occurring, that Mill, back from Avignon, invited him to dinner on the 7th to meet Alexander Bain.[50] Gomperz of course did not receive this invitation until he came back to London shortly thereafter with Wessel.

The next note of invitation of 11 June (617 below) suggests that Mill, receiving no reply, went to call on Gomperz; the two phrases omitted from the letter as published by his son indicate that there was apparently some intervening arrangement proposed for the 12th, a dinner at Blackheath with Louis Blanc. When Blanc proved unavailable for that date, Mill wrote to suggest that Gomperz and Wessel come on Sunday, the 14th. The restoration of what may seem trivial omissions shows clearly that Mill was making an all-out effort to see the distressed young man.[51]

Distressed he most assuredly was, however, though apparently under control at the Sunday dinner party. On the following day, it seems that he wrote to Mill, hinting again at his "wishes" with regard to Helen and communicating his paranoid fears about having been "maligned" to them. This time, Mill understood what he was aiming at, and in his reply of 16 June very kindly, but firmly, suggested that he had no chance with Helen. Mill also, however, most wisely left a course of action open to him: "If you think fit to carry the matter farther, either by speech or writing—even if only for the relief of your own feelings—you will have my truest sympathy, as you have my sincere friendship and esteem. . . . I hope that nothing that has passed will make any difference in your friendly feelings towards

---

[47]*CW*, XV, 854–5. Though Mill's tone was gentle, his protestations about not having enough time in Avignon to do justice to friends must have rung rather hollow, given Thornton's glowing account of his experience the previous summer.

[48]*Ibid.*, 858.

[49]Weinberg, *Gomperz and Mill*, 37–8.

[50]*CW*, XV, 861.

[51]Mill's letter of 16 June, to Harriet Grote, who had sent him good news about Gomperz's condition from a helpful Dr. Schlesinger, also tends to confirm the supposition that Mill had called on him, by the remark: "I have seen him twice, the last time for a whole evening" (*ibid.*, 863). The optimistic tone of this letter, 619, suggests that it was written and despatched prior to his receiving Gomperz's note, and replying to it in 618.

us, who remain unchanged to you. . . ." And Mill expressed hope that Gomperz and Wessel would come (as had probably been arranged at the earlier meeting) on the following day.[52] Mill's sympathy for such mental anguish was the product of experience, and his everlasting tolerance of Gomperz's inability to bring out German editions of his works, as undertaken, was probably born of the awareness that he had contributed, even if unknowingly — or perhaps because unknowingly — to his suffering.

After Gomperz's departure from London, which must have occurred very shortly after their last visit, Mill wrote to him on 15 July a most kind and friendly letter of encouragement,[53] expressing confidence in his great ability and in the therapeutic benefits of "real intellectual work." Gomperz apparently responded immediately, on the 18th, from the depths of unhappiness and paranoia.[54] Mill waited until the 29th to reply, presumably because Gomperz had intimated that he would write again immediately, but then failed to do so. Once more Mill's wisdom in dealing with emotional disturbance, and delusions, is greatly in evidence. He forthrightly asks Gomperz to explain to him in exactly what way he sees himself as misunderstood, so that the matter may be cleared up, and he gently reiterates the gospel of work, in proper doses, as the remedy for a great mind, greatly troubled. Nor did his active concern cease at that point. When he received no response to this encouragement, he replied on 25 August (639 below) to a letter from Gomperz's sister, apparently written earlier, on her brother's return to Austria, explaining the line of encouragement he had taken with him. In a sentence omitted by Heinrich Gomperz, Mill suggests that Wessel had, in the interim, sent him word of their friend's condition,[55] and Mill asked that he continue to do so.

It appears that Gomperz made some response himself after this second, indirect, effort, saying that he was somewhat better, and at work, but he also responded to Mill's attempt to let him clear the air. Mill's reply of 17 September (644 below) certainly suggests, however, that Gomperz was still suffering from paranoid delusions, which Mill once more dealt with directly; and once again he acceded to the request from Gomperz to be recognized as the authorized translator of *Utilitarianism*, enclosing a formal statement to that effect on a separate sheet.

At this point another silence fell, and it lasted until the summer of the following year, when Mill again wrote, on 26 June, 1864 (700 below), prompted, one might surmise from the introductory sentence (another omission of Heinrich Gomperz's), by a letter from Wessel that spoke of Gomperz's "intended publication" of Philodemus's *On Anger*. Mill yet again reaffirms his friendly feelings, as well as his genuine interest in, and the inherent value of, Gomperz's scholarly work. Gomperz apparently at once had a copy of the volume sent to Mill, without any

---

[52]Letter 618 (*CW*, XV, 862–3).
[53]*Ibid*., 865–6, incorrectly dated 5 July.
[54]The evidence is in Mill's response, *ibid*., 873–5.
[55]See the second last paragraph of Letter 639 below.

Introduction

personal communication; and Mill took the opportunity of a favourable notice in the *Saturday Review* to acknowledge and praise it, on 22 August.[56]

Gomperz's next gesture was to send Mill the first number of his Herculanean series, concerning Philodemus on induction, and Mill wrote in reply the following spring, on 30 April, 1865 (806 below). It seems that Gomperz had written to him "some months ago," and had at the time promised a longer letter, which had failed to materialize (a detail Gomperz's son excised). Mill had already sent Gomperz both the *Examination of Sir William Hamilton's Philosophy*, and the first part of his study of Comte (neither of which had apparently been acknowledged), and was planning to send shortly an advance copy of the second article on Comte. It had been two years since there had been any discussion of the projected translations of *three* of Mill's works, but never a word of question or hint of reproach had been whispered. Is such restraint possible in ordinary human nature?

And so the pattern would continue on both sides, Gomperz sending Mill yet another scholarly production, the second volume of the Herculanean series, "dedicated [to him] with reverence and love, on the occasion of his sixtieth birthday, May 20," and Mill thanking him heartily, if a trifle tardily, on 22 August, 1866, giving parliamentary business as his excuse, and trying to elicit a response from the reticent disciple by asking his opinion about the remarkable political changes in Germany.[57] There is no evidence that his opinion was ever forthcoming; perhaps for that reason Mill's direct invitation to write to him in the final paragraph did not find its way into *Briefe*. The silence descended again until the beginning of 1868, at which time a flurry of activity about a possible collected edition of Mill's works in German began.

In January of that year, Mill received a letter from Julius Grosser, proprietor of the Viennese firm of Tendler and Co., which was prepared to undertake the project, and an accompanying note from Gomperz,[58] full of enthusiasm about this new undertaking. He naturally gave explanations for previous non-performance, described in Mill's reply of 28 January as "causes of unhappiness . . . respecting which you hold out the hope that I shall hear something from Mr Wessel";[59] and Mill apparently did subsequently learn through him of the sudden death of Gomperz's nephew, Carl, and the resulting breakdown of his sister Josephine.[60] Mill probably follows Gomperz's letter in discussing the works to be included in the new edition. The *Logic* would occupy the first two volumes, and Mill volunteered to send the alterations he was making at the time for the seventh edition. He informed Gomperz that he had already given permission to Dr. Anton

---

[56]*CW*, XV, 953–4. The notice, copied in Mill's hand, is at Kokugakuin University.
[57]*CW*, XVI, 1196 and n, 1197.
[58]Both are in the Mill-Taylor Collection.
[59]*CW*, XVI, 1356, dated 27 January.
[60]In a letter, now lost, enclosed with Gomperz's of 26 March, 1868 (MS at Johns Hopkins).

Dohrn of Jena to translate the *Inaugural Address*, and suggested that Grosser get in touch with Dohrn. Mill had also referred Wilhelm Sattler to Grosser about a translation of the work on Comte. Gomperz had apparently asked Mill whether he had seen F.A. Wille's translation of *Representative Government* (1862), and Mill replied that it seemed to him to need "a good deal of correction." Gomperz had also asked about the possible inclusion of *Essays on Unsettled Questions of Political Economy*, and Mill commented that he would wish to alter the first essay considerably if they were to be reissued in English—not a very positive reply. Gomperz was sure, however, that it would be wise to keep the *Examination* back, at least at first.

Not having received any acknowledgment of the sheets of Book I of the *Logic*, Mill wrote again on 18 March, 1868 (a letter not included in *Briefe*), inquiring whether Gomperz had received them; he enclosed those for the rest of the first volume, and promised to have the sheets of volume two sent on to him "without any avoidable delay."[61] Gomperz replied apologetically on 26 March,[62] thanking Mill for the sheets of the whole work, which had arrived, and raising various issues and questions about the edition. The details are interesting, since they show that Gomperz now certainly wanted to take full charge and ensure that the translations would be of high quality. He recommended that Mill accede to Eduard Wessel's request, enclosed, to be the translator of *Dissertations and Discussions*, and that Wessel also be allowed to translate *Representative Government* again, as Wille's version was so poor. Sattler's translation of *Auguste Comte and Positivism* would be carefully scrutinized by Gomperz, who would not hesitate to correct "any material errors." (In the event it satisfied him so ill that another translation was undertaken later by Gomperz's wife, Elise.) Anton Dohrn had reported that he would have to give his translation of the *Inaugural Address* a thorough revision, but since he had no time for the task he had no objection to another's correcting it. Gomperz requested, however, that a new translation of the *Inaugural*, and that of *Utilitarianism*, be entrusted to his friend Adolph Wahrmund, an Oriental scholar, and that a formal statement of Mill's consent be forwarded, so as to give Gomperz "the advantage of a fuller control over these translations [than he] could otherwise exercise." Indeed he admitted that Wahrmund had already completed the major part of the latter task, and had "submitted without reluctance to a careful revision" by Gomperz himself.

To all this effort and enthusiasm Mill responded warmly, in a letter of 23 April;[63] but before any volumes were published, the firm of Tendler went bankrupt later that year. There was no hint of trouble, however, in Gomperz's reply of 11 May,[64] and apparently no further explanation forthcoming either of this

[61] *CW*, XVI, 1374–5.
[62] MS at Johns Hopkins.
[63] *CW*, XVI, 1391–2.
[64] MS at Johns Hopkins.

disappointment or of the later renegotiation of the project with the Fues Verlag of Leipzig.

Mill wrote again, in March of the following year (1413 below), to inquire about the edition, because he had "just received an agreeable evidence of the demand for it" in another proposal for a series of his works, which he proceeded to outline.[65] To his question, Mill seems to have had no reply, as on 15 June he gave Gomperz yet another gentle nudge, and for a similar reason. He had received several requests from aspiring translators for the recently issued *Subjection of Women*, and since it was "very desirable that this should be done immediately," he had "accepted the offer of Dr Heinemann . . . reserving [Gomperz's] right to include in the collected edition either his translation by agreement with him or a different translation."[66] Three weeks later, on 6 July, Mill responded in a similar vein (1454A below, previously unpublished) to a letter from Anton Dohrn, agreeing to Dohrn's issuing his translation of the *Inaugural*, "merely reserving the right of the publishers of the complete edition to include it (or another translation) afterwards in their series."

From Gomperz he appears to have received only an announcement of his marriage, which took place on 8 August of that year. On 23 October Mill replied with warm congratulations and a request for information, not for himself, but for an acquaintance, whose address he enclosed, who was anxious to discover how the system of secret voting actually functioned in those countries where it had been adopted. The edition was not mentioned.[67]

This is the last letter in Mill's correspondence with Gomperz, as his son Heinrich testifies, adding, in some surprise, that Mill never thanked his father for the first volume of the *Gesammelte Werke* (1869), which certainly must have been sent to him.[68] Whether it was indeed sent, or whether the outbreak of the Franco-Prussian war in July of that year had any effect upon the arrangements, it almost certainly never arrived, since it is inconceivable that Mill would not have acknowledged its appearance.

There was a hiatus of four years before the publication of Volumes II–IV of the edition which contained, at last, Gomperz's translation of the *Logic*. Heinrich Gomperz claimed that he did not know why it had taken so long.[69] It was just at the time of Mill's death that the final volume of the three was issued. In his letter of condolence to Helen Taylor of 11 May, 1873, Gomperz said he would send to her "the eight volumes of the translation of Mr. Mill's works that have just come

---

[65]Heinrich Gomperz omitted mention of the rival proposal in the typescript of Volume II of *Briefe*.
[66]*CW*, XVII, 1615–16, much abridged in *Ein Gelehrtenleben*, 45.
[67]*CW*, XVII, 1655–6; most in *Ein Gelehrtenleben*, 56.
[68]*Ein Gelehrtenleben*, 43.
[69]*Ibid.*, 42.

out."[70] It is doubtful whether this intention was ever carried out, as in his letter of 25 November, 1873, thanking Helen for a copy of the *Autobiography*, he concluded: "If you would be good enough to let me know your residence, I would send you the nine volumes which have appeared (the ninth is being published at this moment)."[71] The tenth volume, which he said was also being printed at that time, was the first of the two-volume *Dissertations and Discussions*, translated by Wessel. It appears that none of these volumes was despatched as suggested, however, and that two more years elapsed before the publication of the second volume of the collected essays, because the publisher made difficulties about some of the subject matter. It was October, 1875 before Elise Gomperz could write to Helen: "My husband hopes that you have received the *eleven* volumes of the translation he directed Mr. Reisland to send you."[72] These reached their destination, and now form part of the Somerville College collection.

Gomperz was apparently relying on his friend Wessel to complete the translation of the works to be included in the final volume of the edition, and Wessel's death in January, 1879 left him in dire need of assistance. He found it in the person of Sigmund Freud, who was recommended by his former philosophy professor, Franz Brentano, a colleague and friend of Gomperz at the University of Vienna.[73] Another year elapsed, however, before the twelfth volume appeared. When it did, Gomperz sent copies to Helen without delay,[74] and surely with a sense of relief that his commitment to making Mill's works available in German was at last fulfilled. He could now, with a clear conscience, devote all his time to

---

[70]MS, Mill-Taylor Collection. He presumably meant Volume I (1869), which contained *On Liberty*, translated by himself, and *Utilitarianism* and the *Inaugural Address*, both translated by Wahrmund; two of the three volumes of the *Logic* (Vols. II–III); three volumes of the *Political Economy* (Vols. V–VII), translated by Adolf Soetbeer; and Volume IX, *Auguste Comte and Positivism*, translated by Elise Gomperz. He was still waiting for Volume IV, in which he had incorporated, as an appendix, the changes made to the 8th ed. See Weinberg, *Gomperz and Mill*, 56–7.

[71]MS, Mill-Taylor Collection. The ninth volume was the tardy Volume IV, the third of the *Logic*. Mr. Reisland of the Fues firm asked for permission to include the *Autobiography* in the edition, but Helen declined, and accepted the offer of Mr. Vogel of Meyer and Zeller of Stuttgart (MSS, Mill-Taylor Collection).

[72]MS, Mill-Taylor Collection.

[73]An excerpt from Freud's letter to Heinrich Gomperz of 9 June, 1932 (*Ein Gelehrtenleben*, 106–7) explains the circumstances. Volume XII contained his translations of the *Enfranchisement of Women*, "Grote's Plato," "Thornton on Labour and Its Claims," and the "Chapters on Socialism." No explanation seems to exist of the fact that Harriet Mill's *Enfranchisement* was included, and Mill's *Subjection of Women* omitted. The arrangements with Dr. Heinemann for a translation of the *Subjection* had apparently fallen through, and another, by J. von Hirsch, had already been published by this time (Berlin: Berggold, 1869). Perhaps its appearance influenced the decision to issue the companion piece as part of the edition.

[74]His accompanying letter of 9 February, 1880, is in the Mill-Taylor Collection.

Introduction xxix

his own writings on classical thought,[75] which, in their own way, would continue to spread the influence of Mill's empiricism in scholarly Europe.

EAST INDIA CORRESPONDENCE

MILL'S WORK and influence at the East India Company has been the least studied area of his much explored life and thought. The record he compiled of the more than 1700 despatches that he drafted over the course of his thirty-five years in the Examiner's Office of the Company[76] is daunting, even to scholars with a Benthamite bent for lists. It is only recently, thanks to the efforts of Martin and Zawahir Moir, co-editors with John M. Robson of Mill's *Writings on India*, that his despatches have become really accessible,[77] and we anticipate that there will now be considerably more investigation of the role he played in the history of British India.

As the Moirs located the various versions of the despatches, other treasures of three kinds emerged from the collections: letters in Mill's own hand to an official in another department, supplying further information about the matters dealt with in the documents; letters in a clerk's hand, signed by Mill, as Examiner of India Correspondence, 1856–58, usually making requests to the Finance and Home Committee of the Company; and copies of letters, some with Mill's signature, written when, as Examiner, he served as Clerk to the Secret Committee of the Court of Directors and communicated their views to the Board of Control.[78] About half of the letters from that Committee are purely formal requests for the release by the Board of secret documents. These we have simply listed, in Appendix B, with a brief indication of the subject matter. The other seventy-three we are delighted to be able to include here, as they provide new insight into the nature of Mill's responsibilities at the East India House, and illustrate its complex bureaucracy.

The workings of that bureaucracy were described and commented upon by officials of the Company, including Mill, as they answered the questions of an investigating Parliamentary Select Committee in 1852;[79] and they have been further explained and analysed in Martin Moir's admirable Introduction to Volume XXX of the *Collected Works*. Some of that explanation bears repeating here, however, to give proper context to the letters below.

---

[75]His most important work was *Griechische Denker*, 3 vols. (Leipzig: Veit, 1896–1909).

[76]The manuscript is at the India Office Library and Records, MSS Eur B405.

[77]The finding list that they prepared is in Appendix A of *CW*, XXX (Toronto: University of Toronto Press, 1990).

[78]The first group of letters, dealing with political matters in the field, is in the L/P&S/6 archive series; the second is in the L/F/2 series; the third, Secret Home Correspondence, 1856–58, is in the L/P&S/3 series.

[79]See Mill's evidence in *CW*, XXX, 31–74.

The East India Company was governed by two different bodies: the Court of Directors, elected from among its Proprietors (the shareholders); and what was known as the Board of Control, composed of a number of commissioners appointed by the British government to oversee the Company's operations. The Directors served on various standing committees, responsible for specific aspects of the Company's activities;[80] and to assist them in their administration they had a great number of paid officers and clerks in several departments. The Secretary was the senior official of the Company, and next to him was the Examiner, in charge of the office that had responsibility for drafting most of the despatches to India.[81] The Board, which was in practice dominated by its chief commissioner, the President, also had a number of officials and clerks to help carry out its supervisory role. The dual nature of this administration resulted in a complex procedural ritual for the handling of the correspondence with India, in which there were as many as six stages.[82]

An abstract of each despatch received from India was made in the department and circulated to the Chairman and Deputy Chairman (the Chairs) of the Court and the members of the relevant standing committee. If the matter was purely routine, a member of the Correspondence branch of the Examiner's office, such as Mill, would prepare a draft reply, which would be submitted, with a collection of accompanying documents, for the approval of the Chairs. (In delicate or difficult matters, the officer would take instruction from them before preparing the draft.) When each draft conformed to the views of the Chairmen (stage 1), it would be passed on for the unofficial consideration of the President of the Board (stage 2) in a form known as "PC" ("previous communication"). If the President returned it unaltered, it moved directly to the departmental standing committee. If he made alterations, the draft was returned to the Chairmen (stage 3), who had discretion to "allow wholly or partially, or reject entirely, the alterations,"[83] before passing it on to the committee, which also had discretion to introduce changes (stage 4). The official draft was next discussed, possibly amended further, and passed by the Court of Directors (stage 5). Then it returned once more to the Board as a whole for its official approval (stage 6). If accepted, it was immediately despatched to India. If altered at this late stage, it was again referred to the standing committee, "upon whose report the Court decide[d], either that the alterations [should] be acquiesced in, . . . or that a remonstrance [should] be addressed to the Board against

---

[80]In 1834, when the Company's commercial operations ended, three committees were established: Finance and Home; Political and Military; Revenue, Judicial, and Legislative (XXX, xxvii n–xxviii n).
[81]For the Political, Public, Judicial, Legislative, Revenue, Separate Revenue, and Public Works Departments (*ibid.*, xxx n).
[82]Identified by Moir, *ibid.*, xxvii.
[83]From the evidence of the Secretary, James Cosmo Melvill, to the Select Committee, quoted *ibid.*, xxvi.

the alterations, in which case the draft [was] sent back until the final decision of the Board [was] communicated, and then the despatch [was] forwarded."[84]

All the opportunities for alterations to the drafts in this description suggest that changes were more common, and more substantive, than was in fact the case. It was clearly in the best interests of the Company and of its officials and employees that unnecessary hitches or confrontations not occur in a procedure that was already slow and cumbersome enough, and matters were conducted so as to ensure a smooth passage of a draft through the system. We have, unfortunately, no record of Mill's conferring with the Chairmen, or receiving their advice, prior to drafting a despatch; but there are indications that the Chairs occasionally sounded out the President in a "Pre-PC" or "official draft sent ahead of the more formal PC in order to elicit his first reactions."[85] We know, from Mill's evidence before the Commons Committee, that the Chairs rarely submitted a PC to the Board which they knew to contain opinions directly contrary to those of the President.[86] We also know, from the letters below, that disagreement occasionally occurred, and that Mill experienced the frustrations that normally result from bureaucratic delay and bungling.

In 229.02, for example, from the first group of letters, one of many addressed to William Cabell, Senior Clerk in the Political Department and Assistant Secretary to the Board of Control, we see Mill attempting to resolve a difference of opinion between the Chairs and the President concerning the affairs of Oudh: "If the President after reading the Oude P.C. should continue of his former opinion I should be much obliged to you if you would suggest to me the sort of modification which would best meet the President's views." The difficulties entailed by the pace of the process and the multiplicity of drafts is illustrated in 241.1, where Mill is writing to ask whether the PC forwarded to the Board three months earlier "is likely to be soon returned?" Several other PCs were being held up by it; so he "would venture to suggest that in case any point or points should require prolonged consideration . . . the paras relating to them might perhaps be detached & made into a separate PC & the rest proceeded with." In 290.2, Mill offers Cabell an abject apology for "a gross & untraceable blunder in this office . . . one of the absurdest pieces of official negligence I have ever known of." It had resulted in the original version of a despatch being sent to the Board a second time, "instead of a greatly altered PC which I prepared & which the Chairs sanctioned." Such errors and delays were probably not so infrequent in the Company's operation as Mill suggests.

About half of the letters below to Cabell serve to illustrate stage 2 of the complicated processing of despatches. Having received Mill's draft PC, forward-

---

[84]*Ibid.*
[85]Moir, *ibid.*, xxviii n.
[86]*Ibid.*, 54.

ed after its approval by the Chairmen for the Board's consideration, Cabell occasionally asked for more documentation or clarification of some aspect of the matter at hand; for example, in 96.2, 125.1, and 239.3 below, Mill is responding to various sorts of requests. In the first, he reports that no trace had been found of a project that was thought to have appeared in despatches some number of years earlier; in the second, he records success in locating an agreement of even more recent date than the one the Board had requested; in the third, he provides a direct answer to a question regarding the desirability of asking for an explanation from the local government. Most responses, however, are more complex than these.

In 76.1 below, for instance, Mill is replying to the Board's query whether the government in India had the legal power "to detain a civil servant in India against his will." The question was apparently referred by the Examiner (then James Mill) to the solicitor retained by the Company, and Mill is duly reporting this man's legal opinion. The context of the question, and several of Mill's comments, reveal some of the characteristic features of the problems encountered by the Home Establishment in dealing with events in the field and in the handling of the despatches.

At issue was the case of Mordaunt Ricketts, the Resident at Lucknow, who had been dismissed for taking bribes and had left India before any other punitive action could be launched against him. As was so frequently the case, the officials at home were having to judge after the fact whether a matter had been properly handled on the spot, what measures could or should have been taken to ensure a different outcome, and what recommendations ought to be made to direct policy in the future. In this instance, the Board wanted to know whether, and how, Ricketts's departure could have been prevented.

Mill's reply affirms that the Government might have applied for some sort of restraining order on Ricketts from the Supreme Court, but that the application might not have been successful, given "the presumption they could have established against him." This fact and the likelihood of his being able to get away "before process could have issued" should determine, in Mill's view, the official attitude of the Home Establishment to the Indian Government's conduct in the matter: "it is perhaps more than we could be warranted in affirming positively here that they were wrong in not making such an application." One of the functions of the despatches, to assess fairly what had been done in the field with a view to improving performance by analysis, and criticism when necessary, is demonstrated here.[87] In this case, with great tact, Mill moves on to suggest a legislative change: that power be given to the Indian Government, allowing it in future cases to detain "its servants in India until their accounts with Government are settled."

In 249.1 below, Mill himself provides a legal opinion in answer to a question directed to him by Robert Gordon, one of the two Secretaries to the Board of

---

[87]See Mill's evidence, *ibid.*, 69–70.

Introduction xxxiii

Control. The Board was considering the problem raised in the estate of the late postmaster at Ryepur by the questionable legitimacy of his children, who had been born before his marriage to their mother. Gordon had apparently been told that, since the parents were Catholics, the provision of the Canon Law, by which a subsequent marriage of the parents legitimized the children, might be applicable. Mill, "although unable to refer him at once to any authority," sounds quite certain as he explains the legal history—that the barons of England, unwilling to change the laws of the land under church pressure, had rejected this principle. Though it was relevant in Scotland and France, whose laws were of Roman origin, it was not applicable in an English jurisdiction. Mill's legal studies are not often so evidently on display.

In his capacity as drafter of political PCs, Mill was, technically, the voice of the Chairs, but it is certain that the contents of the despatches were very much of his own devising, a fact that is reflected, for example, in 308.1 below. Cabell had written to ask whether, in composing a particular paragraph, Mill had given proper weight to the opinion of James Sutherland, the Political Agent at Gujerat, which presumably was included in the collection Cabell was examining. Mill confirms that he had indeed taken Sutherland's views into consideration, but had been persuaded to come to a different conclusion based on other evidence.

The same responsibility for the opinions expressed in a PC under consideration by the Board of Control is demonstrated in a later reply (still at the second stage of the progress of the despatches through the system) to the questions of Thomas Nelson Waterfield, Cabell's successor in the Political Department. In 339.1, of 16 January, 1842, Mill explains why he draws a distinction between one division of ceded territory and the others, and the conclusion he has reached as to the Company's right to dues from it, grounding his reasons solidly on the evidence of the Resident who had negotiated the relevant treaty in 1817.[88] He also gives his interpretation of a separate treaty of the same period between two local rulers, affirming that the Company had been making a mistake, irreparable so long after the event, in paying over the dues in question to one of them. The Chairs must have concurred, but the voice is Mill's.

Three letters in the collection illustrate the third stage in the processing of despatches, the consideration by the Chairmen of any alterations to the PCs made at the Board. In the matter of treaties with native princes, discussed in 103.1 below, the President, in adding to a paragraph, had given more status to some of the Boondela chiefs and to other individuals with hereditary rights to collect rents than they merited, and Mill is writing to explain why the alteration is being

---

[88]James Rivett Carnac, son of a Company official and born in India, served in the field from 1802 to 1822, when he retired and moved to England. Elected Director in 1827, Deputy Chairman in 1835, and Chairman for two successive terms (an exception to general practice), 1836–38, he had returned to India as Governor of Bombay, 1838–41. Mill was citing a real authority.

rejected. "The Chairman has often seen them when he was in Bundelcund and says they are petty Jageerdars of no sort of consequence, and their engagements are not treaties but are constituted by Sunnuds on our part, & acknowledgments of allegiance on theirs."[89] Mill adds that "we have made several additions to this PC since it returned to us. We find that it saves much time & trouble to continue the subjects up to the latest advices." The instances in which additional information about a given matter reached the home office as the discussion was in progress were obviously frequent. In this situation, however, Mill saw no difficulty created; the Board would simply be informed of the new circumstances when the PC was sent to it a second time for final approval.

Two other letters, 294.2 and 296.1, also contain criticism of the Board's alterations in a recently returned PC. In discussing the matter at issue, however, Mill relies on his own knowledge of the local rulers in making the objection:

It strikes me that the plan suggested by the Board would never answer. *We* could manage the villages of a native prince & pay over the revenues to him, because he can trust us—besides he *must*. But they never trust one another, & there is no instance among them I believe of a joint property in which the agents of both sharers do not exercise a right of joint management. It must end therefore in our managing the villages for both governments; which neither would like.

He follows the observations with another suggestion about a change that might be implemented by a recommendation from the Board: "Would it not be better to refer to the Govt of India as a general question, the possibility of negotiating an arrangement by which the double Revenue agency might be avoided?" And in the subsequent letter to Cabell, four weeks later, he adds more argument to "the remarks which I took the liberty of privately communicating to you." A third party to the question, the Raja of Nagpur, would never be satisfied with the arrangement. "It is not the money, but the tenure, as an ancient family possession, that he is solicitous about; & no money grant would compensate him for the cession of a privilege venerated for its antiquity."

Mill's objection to another alteration by the Board, in 239.2 below, relates simply to its wording: "I do not clearly understand in what manner the Joonaghur chief is to continue his responsibility for the Babrias, when he is specifically interdicted from interfering with them. It strikes me that a clearer statement of the Board's intentions would be desirable & would facilitate the passing of the Draft through the Court." Cabell obliged immediately with a better version that clarified

---

[89]Henry St. George Tucker, the Chairman referred to, had also served in India for more than thirty years. A Director from 1826, and Chairman in 1834, he led the Directors' protest against the first Afghan War. It is occasionally assumed that the Company was governed largely by men such as James Mill, who had written a history of British India without ever having visited the place, but it is well to remember that there were Directors, such as Carnac and Tucker, and also officials, who brought a wealth of experience in India to their positions.

the matter for the benefit of the Chairmen, the members of the Political and Military Committee, and the Court, who were to consider it next, in stages 4 and 5 of the process.

The complications that could arise from the dual authority between the Board and the Court and the multiplicity of despatches are admirably illustrated in the problem created by Mr. Williams, the Resident and Commissioner at Baroda, which Mill discusses in 212.1 below. He is writing to explain why orders for Williams's dismissal are included in the PC on Baroda that he is forwarding with this letter, when similar orders incorporated by the Board in an earlier PC on the Mahi Kantha had been rejected. The Board is to understand the delicacy of choosing the proper grounds for the dismissal. It would be "more just and less embarrassing in its consequences" if Williams's removal were for

> general unfitness . . . than for specific instances of misconduct of which his superiors (the Bombay government of the time) must share the blame & which the home authorities when they first animadverted on them did not deem worthy of so serious a punishment, for you will observe that the misconduct of Mr Williams in regard to the Myhee Caunta was as fully known to the Court when they sent out their last despatch on that subject as it is now.

A little face-saving all round is recommended in this matter. Why it would also be "more just" to fire Williams for general rather than specific reasons seems to relate to the case of his assistant, Mr. Erskine, whom the Board had ordered dismissed with him in the Mahi Kantha PC. "This seems very severe treatment for an error of judgment which in *him* was comparatively venial." In Mill's view it would be "hard to ruin the entire prospects of a young man," given the circumstances of the case. The wisdom and utility of dealing with Williams through the Baroda channel as outlined is most tactfully, but at the same time forcefully, made. The Board did not seem to get the point, however, as six months later, in 233.1, Mill is once against suggesting that the Chairs want Williams's conduct criticized in a general way.

Letter 271.1 below illustrates Mill's role in the processing of the despatches in its fourth stage, the consideration of the drafts by the relevant committee of the Court. Replying to a question from the Board about the reasons for the "additional matter in para 7" of the despatch they were considering for the second time, Mill explains that

> it was inserted in the Political Committee on the proposition of a Director & I presume he cannot have adverted to the passages in the Collection, to which you have now been so obliging as to refer me. (If I had remembered their existence I would have pointed them out to him.) His object was to discourage the Government from embarrassing themselves with the domestic disputes of stipendiaries.

In this case, Mill seems to think that the Board has the better view, and one regrets not being able to report whether anything further was done in the matter. It is interesting to note, however, that Mill was in close contact with the members of the

Political Committee as they considered his despatches, presumably assisting them, as requested, in their deliberations.

From the Committee, the despatch moved on to the Court of Directors, where further changes might be introduced. Letter 287.1 illustrates this fifth stage, and the power of the Court to influence policy. Sending Cabell some advance notice of the "two material variations" that the Board would find in the recently approved despatch "which either has been or will be immediately sent to you from the Court in the official form," Mill explains the Court's changes. The first of their alterations was in support "of the proposed reform of the Jyepore Army by the substitution for the greater part of it of a force under British officers," as this was in line with "Lord Auckland's views on the subject of bringing the armies of the native states under our control as opportunities offer," to which they had recently grown "much more favourable." The second change was again related to the misconduct of an employee. In the case of Major Borthwick, the Court had decided on the evidence that the accusation by the local ruler of Borthwick's having misappropriated funds was false, and the paragraph of criticism had been removed.

The apparently persistent problem of incompetent or dishonest officials of the Company in the field is also the issue in another letter, 49.01, that again illustrates Mill's efforts to prepare for the sixth stage of the process, final approval by the Board. The Court having passed "Bengal Political Draft No 237," which contained criticism of an employee, Mill is returning it to the Board, pointing out that "explanations" from this individual had been recently received from India. In Mill's opinion, they warrant making only "verbal" alterations "in the strictures on his conduct," and not holding up the Draft altogether; but Mill defers to the possibility of a different view at the Board, suggesting various courses of action open, and leaving the matter to Cabell's discretion: "When you have decided which of these alternatives to adopt, we will act accordingly."

Mill's position as Assistant in the Correspondence Branch of the Examiner's office in the long middle period of his career, from 1828 to two years before his retirement, was clearly one of great responsibility, and there can be no doubt that he earned the respect and the admiration of his colleagues both for his drafts and for his skills as a negotiator. Though there is a little, and humorous, evidence, that they occasionally believed him to be mistaken,[90] his move upward to the senior post in the office, on the retirement of Thomas Love Peacock and David Hill in 1856, must have seemed to all concerned a normal and well-earned promotion. Then, as the new Examiner of India Correspondence, Mill naturally assumed some different duties, at least a few of which are fortunately illustrated in the other two series of letters that have recently come to light. One of these is addressed to the Finance and Home Committee of the Company, which, as its title suggests, was

---

[90]See the comments written on the manuscript at 68n below.

responsible for matters relating to the employees, the premises, and the records of the Home Establishment.

Mill's correspondence with this Committee would not have been regular in the years *before* his promotion, but one letter does survive amongst the Finance and Home Committee papers from the earlier period. It is dated 9 April, 1844 (427.1), and is a statement in support of his brother George's application for employment by the Company. The short note testifies to the superior "acquirements . . . conduct & character" of the young man, which Mill, as his chief tutor, was well qualified to know. Its success also testifies to the "high status and influence" that Mill himself enjoyed by that time in the Company, and to the fact that his own "experimental apprenticeship in the 1820s [had] provided the Company with the kind of model it later used in training other potential despatch writers," such as George, who joined the Correspondence Branch and learned the job under his brother's supervision. The nepotism that was traditional ("dynasties of family employees were quite common in the Company's history") and generally and unashamedly practised in the nineteenth century is also illustrated by this episode.[91]

The twenty-seven later letters, from Mill as Examiner 1856–58, to the Home and Finance Committee, treat of more mundane subjects, and underline the irony that is often inherent in promotion. Any alterations to, or maintenance of, the "physical plant," as we now say, had to be approved in principle, and in advance, by the Committee, as 258A, B, and D, and 286D illustrate. In the first, Mill is requesting an extra office, and suggests the necessity of providing yet another room, because "It frequently happens that permission is granted by the Chairman to gentlemen in the Honorable Company's Service or others, to consult the official records either for public or private purposes, and there is at present no place in which they can make use of such permission except the compound of the Clerks in the Office." The second is a request that "one of the two extra offices" be included in "the general order for painting." The third is to report that "the new room ordered by the Honorable Committee for Mr Kaye[92] is now completed, and to solicit that provision of the necessary furniture may be sanctioned." The last is in support of a letter from the Assistant Registrar in the Book Office, "representing the necessity of whitewashing the rooms occupied by his Department, and of effecting some minor improvements" in them. Diligently bureaucratic, Mill affirms: "I have the honor to state that from personal inspection I can confirm Mr Atkins' representations, and I beg to recommend that his proposals be carried into effect."

Changes in the accommodation of the Company's records, the payment of the

---

[91]Cf. Moir, Introduction, *CW*, XXX, xix.

[92]John William Kaye, who had earlier served in India, had just been appointed to the post of Assistant Examiner in charge of the Political Department.

workmen involved, and the destruction of "old and useless duplicate Collections" also required the Committee's approval (258E and G, 260B, 269B, and 286C). An increased volume of work in the Examiner's Office necessitated the hiring of extra staff, which was sanctioned for periods of six months at a time (258G, 262D, 269C, 283A, 293A, and 306A). Provisions for individual employees, of various kinds, also required the Committee's sanction. Leave of absence on account of illness had to be extended (269A); the death of an employee required his being replaced (258C), and his salary continued to his widow for the current quarter (258F); an official who had expended a great deal of extra time and effort on preparing a report for Parliament was entitled to special remuneration (323A); the petition from the messengers in the Book Office had to be forwarded (309B). It is not certain whether Mill actually dictated these letters or whether most were simply prepared for his signature. We do know, however, as noted above, that he personally ascertained that the Registrar's rooms needed whitewashing.

As Examiner, Mill had to deal with the bureaucratic trivia of his office, and some of the problems in his employees' lives. He was also concerned with more apparently important matters in his capacity as Clerk to the Secret Committee of the Court, which was composed of the two Chairmen and a senior Director, and handled matters relating to war, peace, and diplomacy. The third series of letters, addressed from this Committee to Waterfield or to one of the Secretaries of the Board, number forty-three, twenty-six of which are simply official requests for the release of documents, and are listed, with their subjects, in Appendix B. The other seventeen also have their touch of (secret) bureaucratic trivia, in two requests (283C and 299B) for the Board's consent to the employment in the Secret Department of particular individuals, "on their taking the prescribed oath." The remaining fifteen letters, which throw light on a variety of contemporary problems, are of considerable historical and political interest.

The first is a proposed agreement between Britain and France, apparently suggested as early as 1852, for a mutually beneficial exchange of territory in India, France seeming anxious to consolidate her possessions around Pondicherry. The terms of the exchange—that is, finding settlements of equivalent value on both sides—were difficult to arrange, however, and several different plans came under discussion. In the five letters below on the subject, 260A, 263B, 266A, 283B, and 309A, over a period of almost two years, it is clear that the chief concern both of the Secret Committee and of the Board is with matters of revenue, though the political advantage for Britain is thought to be of some interest as well. It is also evident that both bodies had to rely heavily on the assessment of the situation by the government in India.

A second problem, dealt with in six letters, was that created by the brief war with Persia from November 1856 to March 1857, the dispute centring on the fortress city of Herat. These letters demonstrate the role of the Board as a channel of communication for the British Government with the Court. In 262F, for example, the Secret Committee is responding to a letter from the Secretary for Foreign Affairs, asking whether "it might be advisable to take possession of Mohummerah for the purpose of increasing pressure upon Persia." The Committee was forwarding all the information they had that might be relevant, but refrained "from expressing any opinion on the course which it might be most expedient to adopt." The Committee had a more positive reaction to questions about "postal communication for Government purposes . . . during the present war" in 270B, agreeing with Lord Clarendon's view that "Bagdad via Constantinople" would be the best route, and notifying the government that "Lieutenant General Sir James Outram [head of the Company's army for 'the Persian Expedition'] will therefore be apprised of the arrangment and instructed to send to Her Majesty's Ambassador a short summary of any important intelligence, which could be put into cypher at the Embassy and so forwarded by telegraph."

The presence of the telegraph by this time (at least as far as Constantinople) makes it seem less odd to think that the Secret Committee in London had also to be consulted about orders for individual officers and arrangements for specific missions (262E, 286E, 321A). It was to facilitate the establishment of a more extensive telegraph system that Britain had obtained the Kuria Muria islands from the Imam of Muscat in 1854, a cession whose legality Mill questions in 270D, relative to another issue—the difficulty of protecting British citizens granted rights to exploit the guano of those islands.

Another problem in the Persian Gulf area is the subject of perhaps the most interesting of these letters from the Secret Committee, 283D below, concerning the actions of that flamboyant lieutenant in the Bombay Army, just beginning his career as an explorer of exotic places, Richard Burton. On leave late in 1854, Burton had undertaken his first trip into the interior of Somaliland (against the wishes of Outram, the Political Agent of the day at Aden), and had subsequently recommended to the Company that an agency be established at Berbera, a plan that the Governor of Bombay solidly rejected. Burton had then made the suggestion in a letter to the Royal Geographical Society, on which the Committee is commenting, readily concurring "in the observation of the Board respecting the impropriety of Lieutenant Burton's conduct in addressing to the Geographical Society criticisms on the political measures of the Government of India." An accompanying letter in the collection contains a comment to the effect that the Society ought to be discouraged from publishing Burton's letter[93]—and indeed it did not appear at that time, a fact that perhaps demonstrates the Company's power, when it so wished, to save itself embarrassment.

That the Examiner's title was "Clerk" to the Secret Committee in its communications with the Board is probably just another instance of an inadequate

---

[93]Letter of 17 Jan., 1857, from George Russell Clerk, Secretary to the Board of Control, to Edmund Hammond, Under-Secretary of State for Foreign Affairs, in L/P&S/3/54, 484.

job description. It was surely proper that only the most senior official in the Correspondence Branch should be admitted to the very highest level of deliberation in the Company, but his contribution was likely greater than merely that of a secretary. Mill himself probably exercised substantial influence in that Committee, as he had when he conferred with the Chairmen about the contents of his despatches; and he clearly enjoyed the confidence of the Court, the Board, and the government, as evidenced by his being offered a post in 1858 on the newly established Council of India. That he declined to accept it, since he disapproved of the government's assumption of control and needed "a long recruiting, not so much from work, as from the confinement of an office" (324), is no surprise.

THE DISCOVERY of Mill's letters in the archival series of the India Office Library and Records has greatly enriched our knowledge both of his career and of the East India Company's operations, and has also confirmed our collective certainty that the task of editing Mill's correspondence will not end with Volume XXXII of the *Collected Works*. It is more than probable that, as scholars continue to consult the collections of despatches, other letters will emerge, and that previously unknown items will appear in the pages of dealers' catalogues. We would be most grateful if readers continue to report their discoveries, through the University of Toronto Press, so that the record may be kept entire.

At the conclusion of this volume are six Appendices: Appendix A contains the variant readings derived from a collation of copies of the manuscript letters to Theodor Gomperz at Kokugakuin University with those letters to him in *Collected Works* not reprinted here. Appendix B provides a list of the form letters from the Clerk of the Secret Committee of the East India Company to the Board of Control requesting the release of various secret documents. Appendix C contains some additions to the finding list of Mill's Indian despatches in Volume XXX of the *Collected Works*. Appendix D provides a list of letters to Mill, compiled in response to many requests from readers over the years. Once more, we must mention our debt to Professor Mineka, who had listed the holdings at Yale and Johns Hopkins and made photocopies of the latter, thereby greatly facilitating the process of checking for accuracy. The Mill-Taylor Collection is, of course, the other principal repository of such letters.[94] We conducted a further search, using references suggested in the footnotes to Volumes XII–XVIII, and through relevant printed sources, and were thus able to locate some previously unknown correspondence. Again, we ask readers to share their knowledge, for the record, of other "In" letters that may have been overlooked. Appendix E contains an index of the recipients of the letters printed in this volume.

Since Appendix F serves as an index to persons, writings, and statutes,

---

[94]We have not listed the purely formal addresses to Mill, from the employees of the East India Company on his retirement, and from academic institutions conferring honours.

references to them do not appear in the general Index, which has been prepared with the care and efficiency that is her hallmark by Dr. Jean O'Grady.

ACKNOWLEDGMENTS

WE ARE GRATEFUL to all those institutions and persons mentioned in first footnotes who have provided texts and given permission to publish, and to those institutions referred to in Appendix D which supplied much helpful information enabling us to locate letters written to Mill. Unpublished Crown-copyright documents in the India Office Records reproduced/transcribed in this volume appear by permission of the Controller of Her Majesty's Stationery Office.

We are especially grateful to those who have made available and permitted us to publish letters from their own collections: Arnold Heertje, J.R.deJ. Jackson, Isaac Kramnick, Toshio Ohfuchi, Mrs. S. Sokolov-Grant, John Spedding, Paul Streeton, Akira Tada, and Satoshi Yamasaki, and to Mrs. J. Beal for permission to print letters written to James Beal now in the Greater London Record Office.

Scholars who have edited letters first published in the *Mill News Letter* have generously allowed us to make use of their work: Marcia Allentuck; T.P. Foley; Joseph Hamburger; Arnold Heertje; Bruce L. Kinzer; Mary and Lionel Madden; Ged Martin; Anna J. Mill; Eric Nye, who has, as well, been generous in providing informaton about John Sterling and his circle; Jean O'Grady; Margaret Schabas; J.B. Schneewind; Evert Schoorl; and Natalie and Gerald Sirkin. We are especially grateful to colleagues in Japan: Shohken Mawatari and Shigekazu Yamashita, mentioned above, Takutoshi Inouye, Shiro Sugihara, who allowed us to publish letters that first appeared in the *Mill Society Bulletin, Japan*, and Kimiyoshi Yura, editor of that journal. The extent of our debt to Martin and Zawahir Moir has, we hope, been adequately explained above; our gratitude must be repeated here.

Librarians and staff at the John P. Robarts Library of the University of Toronto and the Pratt Library of Victoria College have been continually helpful and courteous, as have the staffs of the British Library, Reference, Newspaper, and India Office Library and Records Divisions, and of the British Library of Political and Economic Science.

Of many others to whom we owe thanks, we would like to mention especially Donald Anderle of the New York Public Library; John Arnold of the State Library of Victoria; the Librarian of the Athenaeum Club; Richard Bingle of the India Office Library and Records; Simon Blundell, Librarian of the Reform Club; Trajano B. de Berrêdo Carneiro of the Maison d'Auguste Comte; Herbert Cahoon of the Pierpont Morgan Library; Bernard Crystal of Columbia University; Vicki Denby of the Houghton Library; G.M. Furlong of University College London; Michael Halls of Trinity College, Cambridge; M. Hayez at the Archives

Départementales de Vaucluse; Cathy Henderson of the Harry Ransom Humanities Research Center; Teruyoshi Higashiohji of Nihon University; Hiroshi Ishida of Fukuyama University; Gwyn Jenkins of the National Library of Wales; Hugh Kennedy and Michael Ostrove of the Osborn Collection; Karen Kearns of the Huntington Library; Donald Lawler of the *Victorians Institute Journal*; Robert McGown of the University of Iowa; J.A. Parker of Manchester College; Sigrid Perry of Northwestern University; Bruce Ralston of the National Library of New Zealand; Angela Raspin of the British Library of Political and Economic Science; Pam Ray of the National Library of Australia; Cynthia Requardt of Johns Hopkins University; Nancy Romero of the University of Illinois; Alice Rossi of the University of Massachusetts; Nicholas Scheetz of Georgetown University; Judith Schiff and Diane Kaplan of Yale; Helen Sherwin of Boston University; R.A.H. Smith of the British Library; Paul Sorrell and Pamela Treanor of the Dunedin Public Library; Stephen Tomlinson of the Bodleian Library; P.R. Webb of the Bishopsgate Foundation; Inge Wojtke of the Prussian State Library; and Marian Zwiercan of the Jagiellonian Library.

We are indebted to Maria Manganelli, who gave us information concerning Ernest Naville; to Clyde Ryals of the Carlyle Letters Project, Duke University, for information about the correspondence between Carlyle and Mill; to R.S. Woof of the University of Newcastle-upon-Tyne for providing letters held by the Wordsworth Trust at Dove Cottage; to Donna Halladay, who helped with the material at Cambridge; and to Gina Feldberg, Peter Hess, Samuel Hollander, and Bruce L. Kinzer for their assistance and support.

Jonathan Cutmore, Michele Green, Elizabeth King, and Jannifer Smith-Rubenzahl, who have worked at the Mill Project at Victoria College, have given valuable assistance. Our thanks go as well to Rea Wilmshurst, the Project's editorial assistant, whose knowledge and skill have resulted in the production of a clear and—on her part—accurate text.

We gratefully acknowledge how much our work has depended upon that of Professors F.A. von Hayek, Francis E. Mineka, and Dwight N. Lindley, who have in the past been responsible for the collection and publication of the bulk of Mill's letters. Our correspondence society has had spousal support for a total of some one hundred years: our editing, to perceptive eyes, will reveal traces of the judgment, tolerance, and love of William Filipiuk, Mabel Laine, and Ann P. Robson, to whom we offer these and other thanks.

ADDITIONAL EARLIER LETTERS
1824–1848

Additional Earlier Letters

8.1. TO GEORGE AND HARRIET GROTE[1]

East India House
1st September, 1824

MY DEAR FRIENDS,

Not knowing which of you to write to, and being thus placed in the situation of the ass, I am wiser than he, and instead of starving I seize both the bundles of hay,[2] and write to you both. Your journal has been received, & read with great interest, but we have been grieved to hear of Mr Grote's indisposition, and surprised to learn that you have had so much rain. Last week was with us one of the finest weeks we have had this summer, and the harvest-work which has been done surpasses all belief. This week is equally fine, and corn will be excessively cheap—especially as I hear the harvest is as far advanced in Scotland as here. —I suppose you will be more interested by hearing all that has passed in the Utilitarian world since your departure, than by anything else that I can say.—In the first place, then, last Monday week my father and I dined with Hume, where we met Anthony Hammond, and on the whole we are very much satisfied with that personage.[3] Without being much of a philosopher, or possessing very clear or definite notions on law and legislation in general, he carries his ideas of reform to a

---

[1]MS in the India Office Library and Records. *Folded and addressed:* George Grote Junr. Esq. / Queen's Hotel / Edinburgh. *Cancelled for:* Buck's Head Inn / Glasgow. Wax seal bears initials JSM. The square brackets in the text indicate conjectural readings made necessary by rips caused by the seal. Published in *MNL*, XX (Summer 1985), 4–7, edited by John M. Robson.

George Grote (1794–1871), banker, M.P. (1822–41), and, later, historian of Greece; Harriet Grote (née Lewin, 1792–1878). The Grotes were central to the Benthamite group.

[2]The donkey, placed equidistant from two bundles of fodder, starves because it cannot decide which to eat. The dilemma, known as *asinus Buridani*, is traditionally attributed to Jean Buridan (ca. 1290–ca. 1358).

[3]Joseph Hume (1777–1855), Radical M.P. for Montrose, best known for his constant attempts at economic reform, close associate of James Mill (1773–1836), whose schoolmate he had been. Anthony Hammond (1758–1838), barrister and advocate of Benthamite legal reforms.

very great extent. He has already consolidated the whole of the Criminal Law, which it is intended to bring into Parlt either as one bill or a series of bills so as to supersede all the present system:[4] he means next to go to work upon the civil law, & consolidate that too: but this consolidation he himself declares to be only preparatory to a complete codification of the whole law, common & statute: on the subject of which he has very rational ideas; and he says it would destroy the whole of the system of pleading as at present constituted, and would leave nothing to the discretion of the judge, of the evils of which he has a very strong impression. Hume expressed on the same occasion some most admirable opinions on the subject of charity, which he declared that he had recently adopted, & tho' they seemed new to Hammond, he came into them tolerably well. — In the next place, William Whitmore has brought his cousin the member to call upon my father at the India House.[5] As I was conversing all the time he staid, with Wm W. in a separate part of the room, I heard very little of what passed between my father & the other Whitmore; but my father says that he fully understands the question of the corn laws, which was the only subject on which they conversed: that he understands not only the general principle, but its practical bearings: & he declares himself fully resolved, if the ministers do not anticipate him, to bring forward a motion & force a discussion every session until he succeeds in carrying the question. As there will be an elaborate article in the Edin. Rev. by M'Culloch to prepare the way before him, it will be of great importance that we should have an article in the Westminster Review which may bear a comparison with it: for this purpose we are anxious to ascertain, first, whether Whitmore *can*, and secondly, whether he *will*, write one.[6] William W. whom we employed to get us a copy of Whitmore's

---

[4]See "Report from the Select Committee on the Criminal Law of England" (2 Apr., 1824), *Parliamentary Papers* [*PP*], 1824, IV, 39–405; the recommendations, based entirely on Hammond's testimony and submissions, led eventually to partial consolidation of the criminal code in 7 & 8 George IV, cc. 27–31 (1827).

[5]William Whitmore, a young Benthamite, of a family that produced several members of parliament, now less well known than William Wolryche Whitmore (1787–1858), his cousin, M.P. for Wolverhampton.

[6]Mill is forecasting the appearance of "Price of Foreign Corn—Abolition of the Corn-Laws," *Edinburgh Review*, XLI (Oct. 1824), 55–78, by James Ramsay McCulloch (1789–1864), the Scottish economist who was, in spite of his strayings from pure orthodoxy, closely associated with the Radicals, for example in the founding of the London Debating Society and of London University. Indeed, in 1828 J.S. Mill contributed a note on rent to McCulloch's edition of Adam Smith's *Wealth of Nations* (in *Essays on Economics and Society*, *CW*, Vols. IV–V [Toronto: University of Toronto Press, 1967], Vol. IV, pp. 161–80). The views of the *Westminster* on the matter were in the event expressed by Mill himself: "The Corn Laws," *Westminster Review*, III (Apr. 1825), 394–420 (in *CW*, Vol. IV, pp. 45–70). Evidently W.W. Whitmore either could not, or would not, write an answer to McCulloch. Mill, however, took the pamphlet mentioned in the next sentence, Whitmore's *A Letter on the Present State of and Future Prospects of Agriculture*, 2nd ed. (London: Hatchard, 1823), as the occasion for his "Corn Laws," in which he argued against

pamphlet, as a sort of test of his capability, wormed out of Prescott[7] our ulterior designs, & has taken them up with the utmost eagerness. —I dined at Wimbledon with Mr Tooke[8] on Friday last, having gone from the India House to his counting house, & thence with him to his carriage at a quarter before five: from which time till near eleven, we were engaged almost without intermission in discussing the exclusion of Irish labourers.[9] In the course of the dispute he was driven, among other things, to deny the principle of population. I could perceive considerable annoyance on his part at the escape of Eyton from the paternal apron string: Two or three times he put him down with considerable harshness, & was continually making indirect hits against the dogmatism, & want of candour, of some of his opponents; by which some, he meant Eyton: who took as well the indirect as the direct reproofs, with the most infidel charity & resignation. I contrived, towards the close of the evening to take a turn with Eyton in the garden, and we had some very profitable conversation: he is eager to do whatever good he can, & to qualify himself for doing more.—The Austins are now domiciled at your *quondam* lodging on Brockham Green: and we regularly walk with Austin on the Sunday when we go down.[10] I am in considerable doubt whether the review of Preuves will ever make its appearance, tho' I am informed by Mrs Austin that he works at it

---

McCulloch's article (without mentioning his name), while praising another of McCulloch's articles (see *CW*, Vol. IV, pp. 51 and 53). Mill also there cites Whitmore's promise to raise the issue in parliament (*ibid.*, pp. 69–70).

[7]William George Prescott (1800–65) became a partner in Prescott, Grote, in 1822, and was an original member of the Utilitarian Society, founded by Mill.

[8]Thomas Tooke (1774–1858), a banker, was one of the best known economic writers of the period, much noticed by Mill. He had reviewed in the *Globe* and the *Morning Chronicle* Tooke's *Thoughts and Details on the High and Low Prices of the Last Thirty Years* (London: Murray, 1823) on its appearance, and had just praised it in an article, "War Expenditure," in the 3rd number of the *Westminster*, II (July 1824), while apologizing for not reviewing it (*CW*, Vol. IV, p. 4n). Tooke's son, William Eyton Tooke (1806–30), known by his middle name, whose views were evidently becoming incompatible with his father's, was one of Mill's closest friends in these years. Tooke's suicide on 27 January, 1830, deeply affected Mill; see *CW*, Vol. XII, p. 19, and Letter 29.1 below to J.B. Say.

[9]The question centred on the increased numbers of Irish migrant labourers who had found quicker and cheaper passage to Britain when regular steamboat services began in 1816, and who were able to obtain work partly because of the reluctance of British workers to migrate for temporary work as they would lose their right to parish poor relief. It was also becoming apparent that the Irish population was growing very rapidly; it almost trebled between 1785 and 1841.

[10]John Austin (1790–1859) and Sarah Austin (1793–1867) were almost second parents to John Mill, who, after his return from France, had studied law under John's tutelage, and had played with their young daughter Lucy in the gardens of the houses in Queen's Square Place, where they were near neighbours. The Mills in these years rented summer accommodation at Dorking, in Surrey, where they spent their weekends and vacations; Brockham Green is about two miles east of Dorking, a trivial distance for the perambulating Mills.

during a portion of every day.[11] I wish he could complete any thing, no matter what: as a given quantity of reputation, *plus* a given number of pounds sterling, would probably supply as great a stimulus, as his mental constitution is capable of receiving. —Charles Austin[12] has been laid up, but is now, I believe, at Norwich, whence he goes to Southampton, & returns not till October. Bingham is absent: Graham not yet returned: Ellis fast bound in his new office, so that the Utilitarian community stagnates.[13] Our society waxes thin, & but for the approaching batch, I should say it verged fast to decay. Patten has withdrawn: Secretan has tendered his resignation; his brother having been appointed manager to the marine department of the Alliance, the conduct of the business falls wholly upon him, & he says it leaves him no time for attendance on the society, nor yet upon our Pol. Ec. Conversations.[14] If he leaves us it is all over with him. *En revanche*, I can give the most favorable bulletin of Harfield & of Edw. Ellis.[15] The former produced at the last meeting of the society an essay on population, which obtained universal, and, considering it as a first attempt, well-deserved applause; in it he kept the promise he had made, of writ-ing sar-cas-ti-cal-ly, and some of the sar-casm was exceedingly good. He complained however that we all laughed at his or-tho-e-py,

---

[11] This is a very early reference to John Austin's almost complete inability to fulfill the great promise everyone agreed he possessed. He never did review Etienne Dumont's redaction of Jeremy Bentham (1748–1832), *Traité des preuves judiciaires*, 2 vols. (Paris: Bossange, 1823).

[12] John Austin's brother Charles (1799–1874) was at this time one of the most outspoken of the young Radicals. He became a very successful barrister, but retired from public life and issues.

[13] Peregrine Bingham (1788–1864), a Benthamite barrister, friend of the Austins, helped edit and wrote extensively for the early numbers of the *Westminster*. George John Graham (1801–88), whose first article in the *Westminster* appeared in July 1825, later was an official assignee of the Bankruptcy Court. William Ellis (1800–81), subsequently known for his educational and economic views, had just moved to the Indemnity Marine Insurance Co. from Lloyds; he had written in the 2nd and 3rd numbers of the *Westminster* (for the latter, see n21 below), and was preparing the one mentioned in n17 below for the 4th number.

[14] Patten might be either George (1801–65), the painter, who studied at the Royal Academy after 1816, or John Wilson-Patten (1802–92), later Baron Winmorleigh, who went up to Magdalen College, Oxford, in 1821. One of the Secretans is probably John James, author of *Epitome of Foreign Stocks, Most Currently Bought and Sold in London* (1824), and other works on commercial and financial topics.

[15] A James Harfield is listed as one of the members of the London Debating Society, but nothing more has been discovered about him. While no trace has been found of an Edward Ellis, it may be that Mill had not yet learned the spelling of the name of Edward Ellice Jr. (1810–80), son of the well-known M.P., who later was secretary to Lord Durham in Russia and Canada, and was known by Mill; though only in his fourteenth year at the time, he may well fit the description in the letter, for Mill and his friends were certainly not given to discouragement of precocity.

(vulgarly called pronunciation): and in truth we had good reason: Doane[16] complimented him upon having written a ighly able, a excellent, a admirable, and in some parts, a ironical essay. Edward Ellis is studying political economy with so much ardour and application, as leaves no fear of his ultimate success in that and in every other branch of useful knowledge which he attempts.—Next, as to our occupations: My father is about to open his battery upon the Quarterly Review: I am still upon Brodie: Ellis is upon the Elements of Pol. Ec.[17] Of the occupations of any one else among our friends, I am in ignorance, except as to Arfield,[18] who is reading I do not know how many books, & writing, or about to write, I do not know how many essays.—A critique on the first number of the W.R. has appeared in the North American Review: They quote largely from the first article, which they applaud greatly, as well as Bingham's two articles on America (tho' they say he knows very little about America—as how can he? or any one here:—& that his stateme[nts] are some of them no longer true, & others never were true).[19] They also m[ake] an ingenious attempt to shew, that the Whigs & Tories are two [aristo]cratic parties, & that the Edinburgh Rev. only supports the aristocracy [of] the Whigs, instead of that of the Tories.[20] But farther this deponent saith no[t.] You have seen, or will see, the attack on the 3d No. & particularly on poor Ellis, in the last Blackwood.[21] I have not seen it yet, but am to see it tomorrow. Malthus, it

---

[16]Richard Doane (1805–48), Bentham's amanuensis, had preceded Mill as a guest of the Samuel Benthams in France, and was connected with Mill in all his early endeavours, including the Mutual Improvement Society that was a forerunner of the Utilitarian Society.

[17]All three articles appeared in the 4th number of the *Westminster*, II (Oct. 1824): James Mill, "Periodical Literature: *Quarterly Review*," 463–503; John Stuart Mill, "Brodie's *History of the British Empire*," 346–402 (in *Essays on England, Ireland, and the Empire, CW*, Vol. VI [Toronto: University of Toronto Press, 1982], pp. 1–58); and William Ellis, "Political Economy," 289–310 (a review of James Mill's *Elements* [London: Baldwin, Cradock, and Joy, 1821; 2nd ed. revised, 1824]).

[18]I.e., Harfield.

[19]"Miscellaneous Notices, No. 11. *Westminster Review*," *North American Review*, n.s. IX (Apr. 1824), 419–26. Particular notice was taken of William Johnson Fox (1786–1864), "Men and Things in 1823," *Westminster Review*, I (Jan. 1824), 1–18; and Peregrine Bingham, "Travels of Duncan, Flint and Faux," and "Periodical Literature: The *Quarterly Review*, No. LVIII—Faux's *Memorable Days in America*," ibid., 101–20, and 250–68.

[20]Mill is being mildly ironic, this idea being in fact the central point in "Periodical Literature: *Edinburgh Review* (Part I)," in the 1st number, 206–49, written by James Mill with considerable help from J.S. Mill (see *Autobiography*, in *Autobiography and Literary Essays, CW*, Vol. I [Toronto: University of Toronto Press, 1981], pp. 93–5), who himself wrote the continuation of the attack in the 2nd number (Apr. 1824), 505–41 (in *CW*, Vol. I, pp. 291–325).

[21]William Maginn (1793–1842), "Letters to Timothy Tickler, Esq. (No. XVII): To Christopher North, Esq., on the last *Westminster Review*," *Blackwood's Edinburgh Magazine*, XVI (Aug. 1824), 222–6, attacking particularly William Ellis, "Charitable Institutions," *Westminster Review*, II (July 1824), 97–121.

seems, has been puffing himself again in the Quarterly—tho' I have not seen the article, it propounds what no other mortal would think of propounding, his *Measure of Value*.[22] Not more certainly is our friend Satan known by his cloven foot, than the Rev. T.R. Malthus by this unfortunate hobby.—If any thing was wanting to ensure the success of the W.R. the badness of the Edin. R. would do it. Only contrast the last Edin. with the last Westmr. That miserable stuff of M'Culloch about primogeniture *must* be answered[23]—& will, I trust, with the grace of my lord the devil, with whose school, I have no doubt, we are already classed by the enlightened Southey,—or, if not now, shall be so classed, as soon as the article makes its appearance on his book of the Church.[24] When that time arrives, I shall expect to see our names, or at any rate, that of the review, introduced into his next dissertation *de omni scibili*,[25] with the addition of a few gentle epithets of disapprobation, as ruffian, miscreant, incendiary, & so forth; or who knows? atheist, perhaps: since, as Ellis says, those who are infidels in tithes, are necessarily infidels in all the other doctrines of religion. The Courier has already expressed some inclination to see "a well-seasoned mess of impiety from Carlile, dished up by the Morning Chronicle."[26] By the way, Black is doing

---

[22]Thomas Robert Malthus (1766–1834), "Political Economy," *Quarterly Review*, XXX (Jan. 1824), 297–334. Though he had not seen this article, Mill had written a year earlier an attack on Malthus's view in reviewing his pamphlet, *The Measure of Value Stated and Applied* (1823), in the *Morning Chronicle*, 5 Sept., 1823, p. 2 (in *Newspaper Writings*, *CW*, Vols. XXII–XXV [Toronto: University of Toronto Press, 1986], Vol. XXII, pp. 51–60).

[23]McCulloch's "Disposal of Property by Will—Entails—French Law of Succession," *Edinburgh Review*, XL (July 1824), 350–75, was answered in one of John Austin's rare articles: "Periodical Literature: *Edinburgh Review*, Number XL, Art. IV—Disposition of Property by Will [and] Primogeniture," *Westminster Review*, II (Oct. 1824), 503–53.

[24]James Mill, in "Southey's *Book of the Church*," *Westminster Review*, III (Jan. 1825), 167–212, made an onslaught on *The Book of the Church*, 2 vols. (London: Murray, 1824), by Robert Southey (1774–1843), the poet, friend of Coleridge and Wordsworth, who, like them, had deserted early radical views for conservative ones. The term, "the Satanic school," had been applied by Southey in the Preface to his *A Vision of Judgement* (London: Longman, *et al.*, 1821) to those "of diseased hearts and depraved imaginations, who, forming a system of opinions to suit their own unhappy course of conduct, have rebelled against the holiest ordinances of human society" (pp. xvii–xxii).

[25]"Knowledgeable about all things one can know." The traditional title of the "900 Theses" of Giovanni Pico della Mirandola (1463–94), often quoted with the tag added by a wit (possibly Voltaire), *et quibusdam aliis* ("and even a few others").

[26]The *Courier and Evening Gazette* (founded 1792), a conservative paper, referred, in a leading article of 28 August, 1824, p. 2, to the Radicalism of the *Morning Chronicle*, which defended the free-thinking Richard Carlile (1790–1843), a target for governmental blasphemous libel charges. The *Chronicle* replied to this attack on 30 August, p. 2, and the *Courier* (an evening paper) responded on the same day, p. 2, quoting from both its account on the 28th and the *Chronicle*'s reply. Mill had himself at the beginning of 1823 written five articles over the signature "Wickliff," protesting against the prosecution of Carlile, his wife, and sister. Three of these were published under the title "Free Discussion" in the

admirable service—particularly with respect to the unpaid magistracy; who, I think, must smart under his lash: he is the greatest enemy they have.[27] Prescott is, as usual, "writing an Essay for the society." Doane is, as far as I know, doing nothing; & Place is doing every thing.[28] With all our wishes for your welfare, & speedy return, I remain &c

J.S. MILL

8.2. TO JOHN BOWRING[1]

[April, 1825]

DEAR SIR

I leave you the article on Pleadings, cut down to a moderate compass—there will be more of it afterwards for another number if you approve of it.[2]—I think it will do much good, & may excite controversy—Grimgribber[3] has never been attacked in a periodical publication with any thing like the same severity—or if at all, only in general terms. This is specific, & the lawyers will understand its drift better.

Yours truly

J.S. MILL

Morning Chronicle of 28 January, 8 and 12 February, 1823 (*CW*, Vol. XXII, pp. 9–12, 12–15, 15–18). The other two, Mill says in his *Autobiography*, contained "things too outspoken for that journal, [and] never appeared at all" (*CW*, Vol. I, pp. 89–91).

[27]John Black (1783–1855), who had begun to take major responsibility for the policies of the *Morning Chronicle* in 1817, was greatly influenced by James Mill, and printed most of the journalism of John Mill in the 1820s. For the latter's mature confirmation of the early judgment, see *Autobiography*, *CW*, Vol. I, pp. 91–3, which includes mention of the attacks on the "unpaid magistracy." Some of these were, in fact, written by Mill himself; e.g., "Blessings of Equal Justice," and "Securities for Good Government," *CW*, Vol. XXII, pp. 43–6 and 62–4.

[28]Francis Place (1771–1854), the "Radical tailor of Charing Cross," organizing force behind the Radicals' agitations and campaigns, who had received much of his political education from James Mill, was active at this time, *inter alia*, in promoting Neo-Malthusianism.

---

[1]MS at the College of Law, Nihon University, Tokyo. *Addressed:* John Bowring Esq. Dated in another hand.

John Bowring (1792–1872), Bentham's disciple, was editor of the *Westminster Review*, 1824–36.

[2]George John Graham's "Law Abuses: Pleadings," appeared in the *Westminster Review*, IV (July 1825), 60–88; he continued the attack in "Law Abuses: Pleading—Practice," *ibid.*, V (July 1826), 39–62.

[3]A term adopted by Bentham from Richard Steele and John Horne Tooke to apply to legal jargon: see, e.g., Bentham, *Rationale of Judicial Evidence*, ed. J.S. Mill, 5 vols. (London: Hunt and Clarke, 1827), Vol. V, p. 344.

8.3. TO JOHN BOWRING[1]

Croydon
Monday evening
[11 June, 1825]

DEAR SIR

I send you the article on the Game Laws,[2] which I hope is not too long—there is more scratching in it than there usually is in my articles and there will be a great deal of small print—If anything must be left out, I think it should be some of the extracts, however of this you will judge for yourself—I also send a little poem which was written by a niece of Mr Mushet of the Mint,[3] and given by him to me for you. All I have to ask is that if it cannot be praised it may not be noticed at all.

Eyton Tooke has finished his review of Lord John Russell[4]—I suppose he will send it to you immediately, if he has not sent it already—

Please to send my proofs to Ellis at the Indemnity Office—He comes to Croydon every day—

I should like to suspend a review of Brown's works and particularly of his *Lectures* upon this *Life* of his which has just appeared, by the Rev. Mr Welch.[5] You have not had any metaphysical articles yet—It will help to give that variety to the work which has been wanting hitherto—I have heard it suggested that you should have some philological articles—Perhaps James Gilchrist[6] (not Borthwick) would write one—I know of no one else who could do it.

Yours very truly
J.S. MILL

John Bowring Esq.

[1] MS in the Cornell University Library. Dated in another hand.
[2] J.S. Mill, "The Game Laws," *Westminster Review*, V (Jan. 1826), 1–22; in *CW*, Vol. VI, pp. 99–120.
[3] Robert Mushet (1782–1828), a senior officer of the Royal Mint, was an original member of the Political Economy Club. The niece was probably Margaret Mushet (1799–1885), who later contributed to periodicals; her poem was not noticed in the *Westminster*.
[4] "Memoirs of the Affairs of Europe," *Westminster Review*, IV (July 1825), 178–83, a review of the first volume of John Russell (1792–1878), *Memoirs of the Affairs of Europe from the Peace of Utrecht*, 2 vols. (London: Murray, 1824–29).
[5] Mill was at this time (see *CW*, Vol. I, p. 71) reading the *Lectures on the Philosophy of the Human Mind*, 4 vols. (Edinburgh: Tait, 1820), by Thomas Brown (1778–1820), Professor of Moral Philosophy at Edinburgh. He did not, however, review David Welsh (1793–1845), *An Account of the Life and Writings of Thomas Brown* (Edinburgh: Tait, 1825).
[6] James Gilchrist (1783–1835), a General Baptist preacher and author of etymological and philological works; Mill distinguishes him from John Borthwick Gilchrist (1759–1841), formerly a surgeon in the East India Company service, then Professor of Hindi at the Company's College, who wrote on Hindi philology. Neither wrote for the *Westminster*.

29.1. TO JEAN BAPTISTE SAY[1]

London
2d March 1830

MY DEAR SIR,

You will, I am sure, readily believe with how much regret & sympathy all your friends here have learned the great affliction which you have recently sustained.[2] None of them can possibly have so much reason to know and appreciate the greatness of your loss as I have, who had so much experience of Madame Say's excellence, and have received so much kindness from her. I beg that you will assure the remainder of your family of the part which I take in their grief. My father also is most anxious to assure you how deeply he sympathizes with you and how greatly he esteemed and respected Madame Say. He would have written to you himself long before this if he had not known that I was about to write.

I have myself suffered a most grievous and unexpected loss, by the death of my poor friend Eyton Tooke, who was well-known to you as one of the most excellent and promising of all his contemporaries, and who would have been a blessing to his country and to his kind.[3] The loss of such a man will be felt in a thousand ways by persons who never knew him nor were aware what things were to be expected from him if he had lived to pursue the career of self-improvement and philanthropic exertion which he had entered upon; and how admirable a moral influence he would have exercised on all with whom he came in contact, by the unrivalled purity and rectitude of his purposes, combined with the largest and most comprehensive liberality and philanthropy. To his immediate friends, and associates in his labour and plans, the loss is irreparable and to me especially.

Poor Mr. Tooke, the father, although he has in some degree recovered from the first shock, is quite incapable of writing to you either on his own loss or on yours, and he has entrusted to me the duty of sending to you the enclosed paragraphs, extracted from the newspapers of the time, respecting the particulars of the fatal event.[4]

I owe you a long debt of gratitude for your kindness in sending me successively the six volumes of your work,[5] which I have read with the greatest pleasure and instruction, and which I think is likely to be read by more persons, and with more

---

[1]MS in the possession of Professor Arnold Heertje, University of Amsterdam. Published in *MNL*, VIII (Fall 1972), 11–13, edited by Heertje and Evert Schoorl.
Jean Baptiste Say (1767–1832), French economist, visited England in 1814 and met James Mill and Bentham. J.S. Mill was his guest in France in 1820 and 1821, at the beginning and end of his year in France.
[2]Say's wife, Julie Gourdel-Deloche, died on 10 January, 1830.
[3]Eyton Tooke committed suicide on 27 January, 1830.
[4]Perhaps those on 29 January in the *Morning Chronicle*, p. 3, and *The Times*, p. 2.
[5]*Cours complet d'économie politique*, 7 vols. (Paris: Rapilly, 1828–29).

advantage, than any other treatise on the subject which is now extant. You will hardly be surprised that I should not quite concur in the whole of your strictures on those whom you call the "économistes politiques abstraits";[6] though I am forced to admit that they have frequently occupied public attention, to the great detriment of the science, with discussions of mere nomenclature and classification, of no consequence except as to the manner of expressing or of teaching the principles of the science; and that they have occasionally generalized too far, by not taking into account a number of the modifying circumstances, which are of importance in the various questions composing the details of the science. I have myself derived several most important corrections of my speculative views from your work, and from the reflections which it suggested. I am happy to find that there is much less in your principles, than I thought there was, which is positively at variance with the rigidly scientific economists of this country. I believe that their principles when duly modified, constitute a deeper and more searching analysis of the phenomena of wealth than yours, but that they are not materially different in their practical result. I should wish to see the science taught in both ways; in one for the public, in the other for students: though I sometimes lament to see that the two sorts of teachers scarcely understand the scope or appreciate the whole merit of each other. But the rising generation of political economists in this country are not only capable of unity, but do actually unite both, and you will find when their speculations come before the public, that they have benefitted as fully by your writings as by those of Ricardo, and partake in nothing of the forms or of the spirit of a sect or school.

I consider myself to be discharging a duty towards my friend Eyton Tooke, who would have been so distinguished in this very department of science, in telling you how highly he thought of your work. In one of the last conversations I had with him, he spoke to me of it with great admiration and expressed himself almost enthusiastically on the fine spirit of general benevolence, and devotion to the cause of social improvement in all its branches, which runs through the work, and which distinguishes your writings in so honorable a manner from too many of our English economists.

Believe me,
Most sincerely yours
J.S. MILL

---

[6]See *Cours*, Vol. I, pp. 125–6, with reference especially to David Ricardo (1772–1823), and J.R. McCulloch.

[*June 1830*] To John Bowring

31.1. TO JOHN BOWRING[1]

Saturday
[19 June, 1830]

MY DEAR SIR

I am canvassing very earnestly for the following candidates for the Atheneum, several of whom you probably intend to vote for, and if you would do as much for the remainder, you would greatly oblige me.

Mr Charles Austin
John Sterling
Coulson
John Fonblanque
Charles Buller M.P.
Charles Romilly
A. Hayward
James Booth
Wm Ogle Carr[2]

I can strongly certify the fitness of all except the last, who is strongly recommended by Mr George Bentham.[3]

Yours very truly
J.S. MILL

---

[1]MS at the College of Law, Nihon University, Tokyo. Dated in another hand; verified from the postmark. *Addressed:* Dr Bowring / No. 5 Milman Place / Bedford Row.

[2]In 1830 the Athenaeum Club, founded in 1824, decided to expand its membership by 200 to pay for its new building (still used). One hundred new members, including Mill, were chosen by a committee (on which his father sat); their nomination was announced on 12 June. The second hundred were to be elected by the full membership. Of those Mill lists, Charles Austin, Charles Buller (1806–48), recently elected M.P. for West Looe, and Charles Romilly (1808–87) were successful at this time. Walter Coulson (1794–1860), a barrister and editor, once amanuensis to Jeremy Bentham, Abraham Hayward (1801–84), Tory barrister, whose relations with Mill were seldom cordial, James Booth (1796–1880), a freethinking Chancery lawyer, and William Ogle Carr (ca. 1802–56), another barrister, were all elected to the Athenaeum in the next five years. Never elected were John Sterling (1806–44), the brilliant Cambridge graduate, then becoming a close friend to Mill, and John Samuel Martin de Grenier Fonblanque (1787–1865), brother of Albany Fonblanque, the editor of the *Examiner*, for which Mill was beginning to write.

[3]George Bentham (1800–84), later a distinguished botanist, son of Jeremy's brother, Brigadier-General Sir Samuel Bentham, was one of the recently elected members. In 1820 he had been Mill's instructor in botany and much else. William Carr was the son of Thomas William Carr (d. 1829) a friend of Sir Samuel; George Bentham had been enamoured of William's sister, Laura.

40.1. TO SARAH AUSTIN[1]

Tuesday
[5 July, 1831]

MY DEAR MÜTTERLEIN

I set off so soon that I cannot *count* upon being able to call upon you before I go, which I should have preferred rather than to write, even without any of the additional temptations that you held out to me in your note. I am going to spend a month on and about the lakes of Cumberland & Westmoreland,[2] & shall probably see a good deal of Wordsworth, who when he was last in town, very kindly asked me to his house[3]—but this invitation I cannot now accept, as I shall have a companion—my friend Grant, whom I am very glad that you have at last seen.[4] His extreme modesty—for it is not exactly bashfulness—never would let him call upon you before.

Another excellent friend of mine, Crawley,[5] who frequently walks home with Mr. Austin from the lecture,[6] would, I am certain, be much pleased by making your acquaintance—though I suppose he was afraid of intruding upon you by coming to the proper side of your door, i.e. the inside. I have taken upon myself to say that you will be glad to see him—& I think I might also have safely promised that you would like him.

I look forward with great pleasure to cultivating a further acquaintance with Mr. Empson under your auspices.[7] I know not to what I can be indebted for so very favorable an opinion as that which you mention, except to your *mütterlich*

---

[1] MS in the Varnhagen von Ense Collection, Jagiellonian Library, Cracow. *Envelope addressed:* Mrs Austin / 26 Park Road / Regent's Park. Published in *Victorians Institute Journal*, V (1987), 138–9, edited by T.H. Pickett, and in *MNL*, XXIII (Winter 1988), 17–18, edited by Joseph Hamburger. Mill set out for the Lake District on Friday, the 8th; so this letter probably dates from the preceding Tuesday.

[2] Mill's journal of this walking tour in Yorkshire and the Lake District (8 July–8 August) is in *Journals and Debating Speeches*, *CW*, Vols. XXVI–XXVII (Toronto: University of Toronto Press, 1988), Vol. XXVII, pp. 501–56.

[3] Mill is probably referring to his breakfasting with William Wordsworth (1770–1850) at Henry Taylor's on 27 February, 1831. He saw Wordsworth, then living at Rydal Mount, briefly on 18 July, and spent 4–7 August at Ambleside in order to visit him and his sister Dorothy.

[4] Horace Grant (1800–59), like Mill, worked as a clerk in the Examiner's department at the India Office.

[5] Francis Edward Crawley (1803–32), a member of the London Debating Society, had accompanied Mill on a walking tour of Berkshire, Buckinghamshire, Oxfordshire, and Surrey in July 1828.

[6] I.e., from John Austin's lectures on jurisprudence at the University of London, which began in January 1831, with only eight students.

[7] William Empson (1791–1852), Professor of Polity and Laws of England at Haileybury College, contributor to and later editor (1847–52) of the *Edinburgh Review*.

kindness, which makes you see every thing about me in far brighter colours than those of reality.

I am very happy to hear that Mr. Austin is better. I hope Lucy is quite recovered from all ailments.[8]

Yours most affectionately
J.S. MILL

49.01. TO WILLIAM CABELL[1]

Examiner's Office
9th May 1832

MY DEAR SIR

The Bengal Political Draft No 237 having passed the Court before the additional matter arrived from India, we did not think it worth while to keep back the Draft, thinking that it would give less trouble to prepare another Draft which might follow the former almost immediately. It might perhaps be expedient, with reference to Mr Murchison's explanations,[2] to make one or two slight alterations in the strictures on his conduct but I think they should be only verbal.

If, however, you should be of a different opinion there are several courses which might be taken.

The entire Draft might be kept back but I can see no advantage in this.

Or the Draft might be passed with the omission of the additional paragraphs which were inserted subsequently to its return from P.C.

Or paras 426, 427 of the letter dated 26th August, with the collection No 194 corresponding to these paras containing Mr Murchison's explanations might be added to the Kedah Collection now at the Board & the Draft might be modified by the Board with reference to those particular paras, the remainder of the newly arrived matter respecting Kedah & Nanning being reserved for a future Despatch.

Or lastly, the Board might modify the Draft with reference to the whole of the recent arrivals; but as this would introduce new matter of considerable interest and

---

[8]Lucie Austin (1821–69), later Lucie Duff Gordon, the Austins' only child.

[1]MS in L/P&S/6/283, pp. 91–[n.p.], India Office Library and Records. See Check List of Mill's Indian Despatches in *CW*, Vol. XXX, App. A, No. 46.

William Cabell (1786–1853) was at this time Senior Clerk in the Secret and Political Department at the Board of Control. In August 1839, his responsibility for the Secret Department was transferred to Thomas Nelson Waterfield, but he continued as Senior Clerk in the Political Department. From September 1835 until his retirement in May 1841, he was also Assistant Secretary to the Board of Control.

[2]Murchison had explained his conduct in connection with his negotiations with the Ex-Rajah of Kedah in a Political letter from Bengal dated 26 August, 1831.

importance, it would, I think, be more convenient that it should be taken in the regular course of correspondence.

When you have decided which of these alternatives to adopt, we will act accordingly.

At any rate we were thinking of making application to the Board, for leave to make public the Secret letter of 2d December 1831.

>Believe me
>Most truly yours
>J.S. MILL

52.1. TO SARAH AUSTIN[1]

>Thursday
>I.H.
>[mid-June 1832?]

DEAR MÜTTERLEIN

I know you will never suspect me of being indifferent to your company, therefore I will not scruple to tell you that I had rather not come on Friday: there will be too many without me, and one only goes to see people in a crowd when one does not care to see them otherwise, or when one does not venture to refuse—at least that is the case with me.

The attendance at the lectures is rather slack, certainly, but it is chiefly from unlucky accidents. Roebuck has been ill.[2]—Crawley, who has the greatest admiration for the lectures & attended regularly last year, has for the last three or four months been dangerously ill of the only serious illness he ever had, & is not even now recovered. Romilly has been overwhelmed with duties insomuch that he is at this moment failing of one very imperative one, his engagement with Cochrane (no blame to him, however).[3] Graham, ever since his appointment as

---

[1] MS in the Varnhagen von Ense Collection, Jagiellonian Library, Cracow. *Addressed:* Mrs. Austin / 26 Park Road / Regent's Park. Published in *Victorians Institute Journal*, V (1987), 138, edited by T.H. Pickett, and in *MNL*, XXIII (Winter 1988), 18–20, edited by Joseph Hamburger. Dated certainly between January and July 1832, during John Austin's third series of lectures on jurisprudence at the University of London, which Mill attended. Francis Crawley (see Letter 40.1 above) had attended the lectures in 1831. The reference to Chadwick's heavy commitment to Bentham's "affairs" suggests that the letter was written after Bentham's death on 6 June, 1832.

[2] John Arthur Roebuck (1801–79), barrister, disciple of Bentham's, and intimate friend of Mill's, M.P. 1832–37, 1841–47, 1849–79.

[3] The reference is probably to Charles Romilly (see Letter 31.1), but could be to one of his brothers, John (1802–74) or Edward (1804–70), both of whom were in the philosophic radical circle. The "engagement" was presumably for an article in the *Foreign Quarterly*

official assignee, has had all his time taken up. Strutt has been always at the House of Commons,[4] Chadwick, latterly, has been engrossed by Mr. Bentham's affairs;[5] & so on.

I think there may be a class of some ten or a dozen next year among persons whom I myself know, or know of.

Your question "what *can* Pelham do here" shews little knowledge of the said Pelham.[6] I should not at all wonder if he became a frequenter of yours. There is much good in Bulwer.

Give my love to Lucy—I trust it is not her birthday[7] which I am refusing to celebrate.

Ihre Sohn
J.S.M.

53.1. TO HENRY COLE[1]

Saturday
[14 July, 1832]

DEAR COLE

I have got the tickets for *Don Juan* on Monday, and "request the pleasure of your company."[2] If I do not see you in the interval, we will meet at the Arcade door a little before seven.

Review, edited by John George Cochrane (1781–1852) from July 1827 through December 1834.
[4]Edward Strutt (1801–80), Baron Belper, 1856, M.P. for Derby 1830–48, 1851–56, was associated with the philosophic radicals in the 1830s.
[5]Edwin Chadwick (1800–90), barrister, close friend of Mill's, was a disciple of Bentham's, and an executor of his will.
[6]The allusion is to Edward George Bulwer, Lord Lytton (1803–73), novelist, editor, politician, member of the London Debating Society, and author of the popular novel *Pelham; or, The Adventures of a Gentleman* (London: Colburn, 1828).
[7]Her birthday was 21 June.

[1]MS not located; typescript McCrimmon. For the dating, see n2.
Henry Cole (1808–82), active in postal reform, member of the London Debating Society, Mill's companion on the tour to the Lake District described in Letter 40.1 above, and on another later that month; see Letter 54.1 below.
[2]*Don Giovanni*, by Wolfgang Amadeus Mozart (1756–91), was produced at the King's Theatre, Haymarket, on 16 July, 1832, the role of Donna Elvira being sung by Henriette Méric-Lilande (1798–1867), and that of Donna Anna by Wilhelmine Schröder-Devrient (1804–50). For Mill's comments on the latter during this season, see *CW*, Vol. I, p. 351, and *CW*, Vol. XXIII, p. 465.

54.1. TO HENRY COLE[1]

Wednesday
[18 July, 1832]

DEAR COLE

I have taken places by the Red River Southampton coach, which leaves the Bolt in Tun at halfpast 8, and the Gloucester Coffee House at nine. Perhaps it might be as well, as we are to meet G. & R. at Lymington to send some additional linen &c. &c. thither in their parcel or box or what not; but of this each must judge for himself, & G. & R. must act as a court of appeal from both tribunals.

Mit Heil und Gluck
J.S. MILL

58.1. TO HENRY COLE[1]

Polvellen—Looe
30 September, [1832]

MY DEAR COLE

I inclose the letter to Paris which I said I would request you to despatch for me. For the postage thereof as far as Dover you will consider yourself as the creditor of,

Yours faithfully
J.S.M.

The Music-buyers of Devonport are by this time aware of the name & reputation of Marinelli.[2]

---

[1]MS not located; typescript McCrimmon. Dated from internal evidence.

Mill and Cole set out the following morning, 19 July, for a walking tour of Hampshire, West Sussex, and the Isle of Wight that lasted until 6 August. The plan to meet G. and R. (probably Grant and Roebuck) seems not to have materialized. Mill's journal is in *CW*, Vol. XXVII, pp. 557–611.

---

[1]MS not located; typescript McCrimmon, who indicates it is addressed on verso: Henry Cole Esq. / 4 Adam Street / Adelphi.

Mill had obviously been visiting the Buller family at Looe before setting out on his tour of Cornwall; for the journal of this tour, see *CW*, Vol. XXVII, pp. 613–37.

[2]Gaetano Marinelli (1754–1820), Italian composer mainly of comic operas, was popular among musical amateurs such as Mill and Cole.

70.1. TO HENRY COLE[1]

India House
Friday
[15 March, 1833]

DEAR COLE

If you are disengaged on Monday evening next, my mother and sisters will hope to have the pleasure of seeing you.[2] You will meet the Fonblanques and two or three other people[3]—come early, by which I mean come soon after seven if you can, or as early as you are able.

76.1. TO WILLIAM CABELL[1]

Examiner's Office
4th June 1833

MY DEAR SIR,

My father has received from Mr Lawford the accompanying note on the power of Govt to detain a civil servant in India against his will.[2] It appears they cannot do it except by application to the Supreme Court; and it is perhaps more than we could be warranted in affirming positively here that they were wrong in not making such an application in Mr Ricketts' case because there is some doubt whether the presumption they could have established against him were such as the Court would have proceeded upon, & because he could probably have quitted India before process could have issued.[3]

As the P.C. is with you, perhaps the requisite alteration in the wording could be most conveniently made at the Board.

Would it not be highly advisable that the Government of India should have the

---

[1] MS not located; typescript McCrimmon. Dated from the entry in Cole's Diary for 18 March, 1833, Victoria and Albert Museum.
[2] Mill's mother, Harriet (née Burrow) (ca. 1782–1854), and his sisters Wilhelmina Forbes (1808–61), Clara Esther (1810–86), Harriet Isabella (1812–97), Jane Stuart (ca. 1816–83), and Mary Elizabeth (1822–1913).
[3] Albany William Fonblanque (1793–1872), his wife (née Keane), and her sister, plus Nassau Senior and his sister (Cole's Diary).

---

[1] MS in L/P&S/6/289, n.p. (before Bengal PC 1153), India Office Library and Records. See *CW*, Vol. XXX, App. A, No. 58.
[2] The note, also dated 4 June, and directed to James Mill by Edward Lawford, solicitor to the Company, follows J.S. Mill's letter to Cabell in L/P&S/6/289.
[3] PC 1153 concerned the dismissal of the Resident at Lucknow, Mordaunt Ricketts, for having taken bribes.

power given it of detaining its servants in India until their accounts with Government are settled? By their covenants they are bound to remain—but it seems that the Govt cannot compel them to do so.

Believe me
yours faithfully
J.S. MILL

82.1. TO HENRY COLE[1]

[2 Aug., 1833?]

DEAR COLE

I am at your service this evening for anything—Fonblanque, Mrs. Kingston,[2] or what not—only it is not the best of all times for Fonblanque.

I shall call here as soon as I have had my dinner somewhere.

J.S. MILL

85.1. TO JÉRÔME ADOLPHE BLANQUI[1]

India House
10th September 1833

MY DEAR SIR

I avail myself of your permission to answer your questions in my own language.

All the chairs of Political Economy which exist in England are of very recent foundation. The professorship at the London University you are probably aware of: the lectures however were so ill attended that for the last session or two none have been delivered.[2] There is also a professorship at the rival institution in

---

[1]MS not located; typescript McCrimmon. Presumably after 15 Mar., 1833, when Cole met Fonblanque at the Mills', apparently for the first time (see Letter 70.1 above), and quite possibly Friday, 2 Aug., 1833. Cole's Diary indicates that Mill called on him in the evening; they went to the Kingstons, but as no one was home, they called on Horace Grant.

[2]In the early 1830s Cole and the Mill family frequently spent musical evenings with the Kingstons, who are otherwise unidentified.

---

[1]MS in the German National Museum, Nuremberg.

Jérôme Adolphe Blanqui (1798–1854), pupil and assistant to Jean Baptiste Say, Professor of Industrial Economy and History from 1825 at the Conservatoire des Arts et Métiers, in 1833 succeeded Say as Professor of Political Economy at the Conservatoire.

[2]J.R. McCulloch was appointed to the Chair of Political Economy in the University of London in July 1827, and held it until 1837; however, he stopped lecturing in 1831 because attendance at his lectures was minimal (sometimes indeed there were no students), and his remuneration was inadequate.

London, called King's College.³ At Oxford a chair was founded a few years ago by and at the expense of an individual, a wealthy banker of London, Mr Henry Drummond. This chair has been filled successively by Mr Senior, and Dr Whately, the present Archbishop of Dublin; and you are doubtless acquainted with the excellent lectures which those distinguished persons have in each successive year, published, pursuantly to one of the provisions of the act of endowment.⁴ What effect the lectures produced upon those who heard them delivered, I know not; but when published they have added greatly to the reputation of their authors and have conduced to the diffusion of a taste for the science.⁵

Mr Pryme, a private individual, what is called in this country a provincial barrister, (now member of parliament for the town of Cambridge) for some years delivered lectures on political economy at that town, on his own private authority, without any connexion with the University: some years however after the establishment of the Oxford Professorship, the University of Cambridge followed the example, by *recognizing* Mr Pryme's lectures and giving him the title of Professor of Political Economy at the University.⁶ Whether any emoluments from the University are annexed to the Professorship, I know not.

I am not aware of any other chairs of Political Economy in England. I am informed that one has recently been established in the University of Dublin through the influence of the Archbishop.⁷ There is no such chair at any of the Scotch universities, but courses of political economy have been occasionally

---

³Nassau William Senior (1790–1864) was appointed to the Chair in King's College London (established 1829), but was appointed a tithe commissioner before the College opened in 1831, and consequently never lectured. He resigned in March 1832, and was succeeded in January 1833 by Richard Jones (1790–1855).

⁴Henry Drummond (1786–1860) established the Oxford Chair in 1825; for the provisions, see *CW*, Vol. XXII, p. 327. Senior, who assumed the Professorship in 1826, published *An Introductory Lecture on Political Economy* (London: Mawman, 1827), *Three Lectures on the Transmission of the Precious Metals* (London: Murray, 1828), *Three Lectures on the Cost of Obtaining Money* (London: Murray, 1830), and *Two Lectures on Population* (London: Murray, 1831). Whately published his *Introductory Lectures on Political Economy* (London: Fellowes, 1831).

⁵Favourable reviews of Senior's lectures appeared, e.g., in the *Westminster Review*, VIII (July 1827), 177–89, and, by Whately, in the *Edinburgh Review*, XLVIII (Sept. 1828), 170–84. Whately's *Lectures* were widely praised; see, e.g., Mill's review, *Examiner*, 12 June, 1831, 373 (in *CW*, Vol. XXII, pp. 327–9), and Thomas Perronet Thompson's in the *Westminster*, XVI (Jan. 1832), 1–22.

⁶George Pryme (1781–1868), M.P. for Cambridge 1832–41, who began to lecture in 1816, was recognized as Professor by the Senate in May 1828 and continued to lecture until 1863, evidently without salary. He published *A Syllabus of a Course of Lectures on the Principles of Political Economy* (Cambridge: printed Smith, 1816), which went through subsequent editions, to which he added *An Introductory Lecture* in 1823.

⁷Whately privately endowed the Chair at Trinity College Dublin in 1832; Mountifort Longfield (1802–84) was the first incumbent, 1832–34.

though rarely delivered by the Professors of Moral Philosophy at Edinburgh.[8] Some years ago (during Lord Liverpool's ministry) a number of distinguished persons at Edinburgh presented a memorial to the King (who is the head of the Scottish universities though not of the English) requesting that he would authorize the establishment of a chair of Political Economy; but their request was *refused*.[9]

The views taken of the science in the lectures delivered from these several chairs, are of course determined by the particular opinions of the Professors; who differ, as in the present state of the science may be expected, on a great number of important points, but the tendency of all their doctrines is in favour of liberty of commerce.

I had nearly forgotten to mention that there is a chair of Political Economy at the College of Haileybury, for the education of the Civil Servants of the East India Company. This chair has for many years been filled by Mr Malthus.[10]

In answer to your question, "quelles doctrines sont aujourdhui en faveur" I hardly know what to say. The subject is so little studied *scientifically* that there can scarcely be said to be any "doctrines of political economy" in favour among any class; but in commercial & financial legislation the Tories are generally for keeping up the old institutions, the Whigs and Radicals generally for the removal of restrictions, whether imposed by monopolies, duties on importation, or indirect taxation involving an inconvenient interference with processes of manufacture.

There are no periodical papers which pay any special attention to political economy. Mr MacCulloch occasionally writes articles in the Edinburgh & Foreign Quarterly Reviews;[11] and Colonel Perronet Thompson, the proprietor of the

---

[8] Some of the lectures on political economy by Dugald Stewart (1753–1828), who held the Chair of Moral Philosophy at Edinburgh 1785–1809, are in Vols. VIII and IX of his *Collected Works*, ed. William Hamilton, 11 vols. (Edinburgh: Constable, 1854–60).

[9] In 1825, during the administration of Robert Banks Jenkinson (1770–1828), Lord Liverpool, McCulloch, with the assistance especially of Macvey Napier (1776–1847), editor of the *Edinburgh Review*, attempted to have a Chair in Political Economy established. Their *Memorial to the Government Concerning a Chair of Political Economy in the University of Edinburgh* (BL Add. MSS 38746, f. 219) was unsuccessful, being opposed strongly by Robert Saunders Dundas (1771–1856), Viscount Melville, Lord Privy Seal of Scotland.

[10] At the end of 1805 Malthus was appointed Professor of History and Political Economy in the newly founded College.

[11] McCulloch's far from occasional contributions to the *Edinburgh Review* began with "Ricardo's *Political Economy*," XXX (June 1818), 59–87; his most recent was "Complaints and Proposals Regarding Taxation," LVII (July 1833), 434–48. He wrote less frequently for the *Foreign Quarterly Review*, his first article being "Wine Trade of France," III (Jan. 1829), 636–49, and his most recent the two-part essay, "Prussian Commercial Policy," IX (May 1832), 455–70, and XI (Apr. 1833), 403–6.

Westminster Review, frequently writes on questions connected with the science:[12] he has taken more pains than most men in the study of it as a science. In Tait's Edinburgh Magazine there are frequently good articles by a scientific political economist.[13]

The University of London has I believe got over its pecuniary difficulties, rather by reducing its expenses than by increasing its number of pupils. But the lectures on the moral & political sciences are so ill attended that several of the professors have ceased to lecture: particularly the professors of Jurisprudence and Political Economy.[14] The lectures best attended are those on English law and the medical sciences,[15] because those kinds of knowledge may be turned into money—which is a consideration nearer to the heart of most English fathers than the desire to make their sons wise or accomplished men.

I should be most happy to communicate any other information in my power, which you may desire to possess on these or other points.

Believe me, My dear Sir
Most sincerely yours
J.S. MILL

I forgot to ask you the other day, whether a successor is yet appointed to our friend M. Say, and to enquire concerning another valued friend of my father's and mine, whom you are doubtless well acquainted with—M. Comte.[16]

---

[12]Thomas Perronet Thompson's first economic article in the *Westmister* was "Absenteeism in Ireland," X (Jan. 1829), 237–43, and his most recent, "Property Tax," XIX (July 1833), 1–9. (For full lists, see *The Wellesley Index to Victorian Periodicals*, Vol. V.)

[13]Mill is preserving the anonymity of John Pringle Nichol (1804–59), astronomer and political economist, who was unsuccessfully recommended in 1833 by James Mill and Nassau Senior for the Chair of Political Economy at the Collège de France vacated by the death of Say. Nichol's first article in *Tait's Edinburgh Magazine* was "Incidence of Tithes," I (May 1832), 224–8; his most recent, "Political Economy for Farmers," III (May 1833), 191–8.

[14]In addition to John Austin, whose lectures in Jurisprudence ceased in June 1833, and McCulloch (see n2 above), Mill is referring to John Hoppus (1789–1875), who was appointed late in 1829 to the Chair in the Logic and Philosophy of the Human Mind. His much criticized lectures, which began in 1830, were very poorly attended.

[15]The highly acclaimed Professor of English Law was Andrew Amos (1791–1860). In medicine, the professors were John Conolly (1794–1866), on the nature and treatment of diseases, David Daniel Davis (1777–1841), on midwifery and the diseases of women and children, and Anthony Todd Thomson (1778–1849), on materia medica and therapeutics.

[16]In November 1833, Pellegrino Luigi Edoardo, Count Rossi (1787–1848), an Italian who had been Professor of Roman History at Geneva before moving to France, was appointed Say's successor at the Collège de France. One of the unsuccessful applicants was François Charles Louis Comte (1782–1837), a liberal political writer, son-in-law of Say, known personally to the Mills for a decade.

96.1. TO FORTUNATO PRANDI[1]

India House
20 January 1834

MY DEAR PRANDI

Would you so far oblige me as to take charge of the accompanying letter & two packets? There is nothing sealed, & you have unlimited license to untie.

Shall you be long absent? & will you not let me see something of you when you return? we never meet.

yours ever
J.S. MILL

96.2. TO WILLIAM CABELL[1]

Examiner's Office
5th Feb. 1834

MY DEAR SIR

We have no clue to trace the project of Mr Elphinstone[2] respecting lapsed Jageers,[3] except that which is afforded by paras 18 & 19 of Political Letter from Bombay of 2d March 1822, which state that a scheme of the kind you mention was once contemplated but afterwards abandoned.

We have vainly attempted by means of this indication to discover any Minute or Dispatch in which the proposition was made.

Believe me
Yours very truly
J.S. MILL

---

[1] MS in the Reed Collection, Dunedin Public Library, New Zealand. Published in *MNL*, XXIII (Winter 1988), 22, edited by Eric W. Nye.
Fortunato Prandi (d. 1868), an Italian political refugee and journalist, was a member of Sarah Austin's circle. He was presumably going to France.

---

[1] MS in L/P&S/6/288, pp. 463–[4], India Office Library and Records. See *CW*, Vol. XXX, App. A, No. 923.
[2] Mountstuart Elphinstone (1779–1859) was Governor of Bombay 1819–27.
[3] A jagir was a right, enjoyed by an official (or a family), to collect revenues from specified villages, or districts, in lieu of salary.

98.1. TO EFFINGHAM WILSON[1]

India House
14th February 1834

My dear Sir

The accompanying MS. on education has been sent to me with a request that I would offer it to you for publication.[2] I hear the highest character of it from a friend of mine whom I think fully competent to judge of the merits of such a work—& I should have liked much to read it before putting it into your hands—but as I have no time just at present, I send the MS.[3] There is in addition to what I now send, a mass of very valuable and erudite notes, which with the present MS. would make a good sized 8vo volume.

The author would be glad of an early answer if possible.

Ever yours
J.S. Mill

E. Wilson Esq.

101.1. TO HORACE HAYMAN WILSON[1]

India House
29th March 1834

Sir,

I have had the honor of receiving and laying before Mr. Loch[2] your letter of the 6th Ultimo; and I am desired to express to you his acknowledgments for the

---

[1] MS in the Osborn Collection, Yale University.
Effingham Wilson (1783–1868), London publisher.
[2] The application was successful: the work by Victor Cousin (1792–1867), translated by Sarah Austin, was published as *Report on the State of Public Instruction in Prussia* (London: Wilson, 1834).
[3] Mill's authority might have been Harriet Taylor (1807–58), later his wife, whose views on education he much valued. Whether or not he had read the manuscript—and it seems unlikely that he had not—he quickly reviewed the published work, "Mrs. Austin's Translation of M. Cousin's Report on the State of Public Instruction in Prussia," *Monthly Repository*, n.s. VIII (July 1834), 502–13 (in *Essays on Equality, Law, and Education*, *CW*, Vol. XXI [Toronto: University of Toronto Press, 1984], pp. 61–79).

---

[1] MS in the India Office Library and Records. Published in *MNL*, IX (Summer 1974), 3–4, edited by Gerald and Natalie Robinson Sirkin.
Horace Hayman Wilson (1786–1860), in the Indian Government in India, Sanskrit scholar.
[2] John Loch (1781–1868), a Director of the East India Company 1821–54, was the Chairman of the Court of Directors at the time.

readiness with which you have consented to afford your valuable aid in the selection of a competent person for the office of Head Master in the Anglo Indian College,[3] and which was no more than he expected from your zeal for the interests of Native Education in general, and of that Institution in particular. I have also to express his obligations to you for your remarks on the nature of the office, and on the qualifications which it requires; and, above all, for your public spirited offer to give preparatory instruction in the native languages to any gentleman whom the Court may nominate to it. Such instruction, and the continued communication with yourself which it would involve, are advantages of the value of which, to any person who may be selected for the duties in question, Mr. Loch is deeply sensible.

Your observations on the expediency of attaching a higher salary to the office than that now appropriated to it from the Education Fund, have been perused by Mr. Loch with every attention. But while he feels the force of your reasons, and the weight due to your opinion, he would not consider himself justified in proposing to the Court the adoption of the measure which you recommend, until trial shall have been made of the possibility of procuring a competent person on the terms originally proposed. He will therefore feel greatly indebted to you if you will endeavour to obtain a person qualified for the office, and willing to undertake it on the present conditions. Should this be found impracticable, it will no doubt be advisable for the Court to take into consideration the expediency of increasing the Salary.

I have the honor to be, Sir
Your most obedient Servant
J.S. MILL

103.1. TO WILLIAM CABELL[1]

Ex. Off.
9 June 1834

MY DEAR SIR

I have the pleasure of returning to you the papers on Mr Masson,[2] to stand as a fourth volume in the Colln in the manner you propose.

---

[3]This College, also known as the Hindu College and as the Vidyalaya, was organized in 1816 by a group of leading Hindus in Calcutta for the purpose of teaching English and Western science to high-caste Hindu boys. The College ran out of funds because of mismanagement, and by 1823 it asked the government for financial assistance. The government was soon providing nearly all the required funds, although the administration remained in the hands of the "native managers."

---

[1]MS in L/P&S/6/290, pp. 517–[20], India Office Library and Records. See *CW*, Vol. XXX, App. A, No. 69.

[2]Charles Masson (identified only as "a traveller in Central Asia") was apparently the pseudonym of James Lewis, an authority on Indian inscriptions.

On the subject of the Board's alteration in the reply to Bengal Pol P.C. 1308,[3] (concerning the Boondela chiefs & jageerdars) as the Chairman[4] has not adopted the passage which you have inserted, I may take this opportunity of mentioning why. No 49 in the classified list annexed to the H. of C. Report,[5] viz the Nana of Calpee, is the chief of Jaloun, he is no longer called Nana of Calpee because Calpee has been ceded to the British Govt. No 52 is probably Kishore Sing of Punnah. The others who are referred to in the Board's insertion (most of whom appear to be of the Chobey family) are entirely insignificant. The Chairman has often seen them when he was in Bundlecund and says they are petty Jageerdars of no sort of consequence, and their engagements are not treaties but are constituted by Sunnuds on our part, & acknowledgments of allegiance on theirs.

You will find that we have made several additions to this PC since it returned to us. We find that it saves much time & trouble to continue the subjects up to the latest advices.

Believe me, Dear Sir
yours faithfully
J.S. MILL

105.1. TO JOHN BOWRING[1]

India House
1st July [1834]

MY DEAR SIR

Would you oblige me by letting me know by 2d post as soon as your second Report is procurable,[2] as my friend Mr Nichol of Montrose has written to me to send him a copy as early as possible.

You have been in communication with Mr Nichol recently & are aware of the

---

[3]The altered paragraphs are in L/P&S/6/290, pp. [510–12].
[4]Henry St. George Tucker (1771–1851) was Chairman of the Court of Directors at this time.
[5]The names of the Boondela chiefs apppear in Appendix No. 29 to the "Minutes of Evidence Taken before the Select Committee on the Affairs of the East India Company," *PP*, 1831–32, XIV, 447.

[1]MS in the possession of Professor Arnold Heertje, University of Amsterdam. Dated by postmark. *Addressed:* Dr Bowring / 1 Queen Square / Westminster.
[2]Bowring was one of two Commissioners who had submitted a "First Report on the Commercial Relations between France and Great Britain," *PP*, 1834, XIX, 1–257; the "Second Report. . . . Silks and Wine," by Bowring, did not appear until the following year, both as a pamphlet (London: Clowes) and in *PP*, 1835, XXXVI, 441–697.

purpose for which he is anxious to see your report as soon as may be,[3] & therefore you will, I know, excuse my troubling you with my present request—

Believe me
Yours ever
J.S. MILL

107.1. TO JOHN ARTHUR ROEBUCK[1]

[2 August, 1834]

... I have not yet seen Falconer[2] not that I have thought of any better person nor so good. But I have been rather dilatory though all this week I have been intending to call & at last have written to him to come to me. Apropos I have seen a composition which I understand to be his, lately, which I did not think showed much editorial talent, a project of a programme for a Finsbury Electoral Committee.[3] The ideas were all good but it was very clumsily drawn up, and was not good English . . . .

108.1. TO HENRY COLE[1]

India House
26th August 1834

DEAR COLE

I am sorry to say that I shall not be able to join you at Chepstowe or anywhere else, as my father has not yet returned, & I do not like during his absence to be away for more than a day or two—& for several other reasons. I should have enjoyed exceedingly the Wye and meeting with you—however it cannot be helped.

---

[3]Nichol presumably wanted the information in the reports as he was preparing "Rae's *New Principles of Political Economy in Refutation of Adam Smith*," *Foreign Quarterly Review*, XV (July 1835), 241–66.

---

[1]MS in the National Archives of Canada, Ottawa. Dated extract in an unclasped notebook of Harriet Roebuck, his wife.
[2]Thomas Falconer (1805–82), a barrister, was brother to Roebuck's wife. The proposal was probably that Falconer become nominal editor of the projected *London Review*; he was chosen, and served rather badly as, in effect, sub-editor under Mill's direction.
[3]Not located.

---

[1]MS in the Reed Collection, Dunedin Public Library, New Zealand. Watermarked 1834. Published in *MNL*, XXIII (Winter 1988), 22–3, edited by Eric W. Nye.

I am very glad that Cornwall has fulfilled your expectations. I think you would have admired Falmouth as much as I did, if I had not praised it so much beforehand—& you had perhaps seen, as I had not, the parts about St. Blazey, and Tregony, & also Fowey harbour.[2]

Grant is still in the vale of Festinniog (or ffestinniog, is it?) but has had, it seems, quantities of rain. We have not had any here, for more than a fortnight, untii the last three days. If you have been as lucky you have had the finest weather possible in the finest places.

Did you see anything of Buller while you were at Looe?

Ever yours truly

J.S. MILL

110.1. TO ADOLPHE NARCISSE THIBAUDEAU[1]

[13 September, 1834]

MON CHER THIBAUDEAU

Vous voyez par la lettre de Wilson, quelles sont les conditions pécuniaires de la correspondance du Globe, et quel en est le genre de correspondance qu'il faut à ces messieurs.[2] Je ne sais si cela vous convient; tout ce que je sais, c'est que vous êtes l'homme en France le plus propre à une correspondance quelconque entre les deux pays, dans un journal quelconque, soit français, soit anglais.

Dans le cas où cela ne vous convînt pas, je voudrais bien que cela pût convenir à Dussard.[3] Je sais combien il serait au-dessous de vous pour une pareille tâche; mais il en a besoin et il vaudrait mieux que les correspondans actuels des journaux anglais.

[2]For Mill's journal of his tour of Western Cornwall in 1832, see *CW*, Vol. XXVII, 612–37.

---

[1]MS in the possession of Professor Akira Tada, Chiba, Japan. Dated from postmark. *Addressed:* Monsieur / M. Adolphe Thibaudeau / au bureau du journal / "Le National de 1834" / Rue du Croissant / No 16 à Paris. Mill's letter is written on pages 3 and 4 of a letter dated 11 Sept., 1834, from John Wilson, a Factory and Poor Law Commissioner, and editor of the *Globe and Traveller*.

Adolphe Narcisse, comte Thibaudeau (1795–1856), one of the editors of the radical Paris paper, *Le National*, who spent some time in England after June 1832.

[2]Wilson was offering three guineas for, at most, two articles per week. He suggested that "minor points of difference between *parties* in *France* . . . not be made too prominent," and that "to censure Louis Philippe & his government as they perhaps deserve would be to play into the hands of the Tories." He recommended that Thibaudeau treat of "the general relations" and "the state of feeling" between the two countries, and "the grand continental divisions of interest in which France & this country are opposed to the absolute military powers."

[3]Hippolyte Dussard (1798–1876), another radical journalist.

Je ne veux plus *bore you* par rapport à la Niobé;[4] j'ai donné cette commission à un voyageur anglais.

Carrel s'occupe à apprendre l'anglais;[5] les Buller l'ont invité à leur faire visite en Cornwall, je l'ai conseillé d'accepter, s'il doit rester encore quelque temps en angleterre. Il n'y a presque personne à Londres qui parle français.

Donnez-moi de vos nouvelles quand vous en aurez le temps et croyez que je suis toujours

votre dévoué
J.S. MILL

125.1. TO WILLIAM CABELL[1]

Exam. Off.
7th March 1835

MY DEAR SIR,

We have discovered an agreement with Scindia respecting the Contingent,[2] posterior to that which you allude to. I send you a copy of it, together with copies of paragraphs which will refer you to subsequent reductions in the strength of the Contingent,[3] by the act of the British Government alone. Should you wish the paragraphs from India to be copied also, I shall have great pleasure in ordering it to be done.

Believe me
yours very truly
J.S. MILL

---

[4] Perhaps Mill was trying to obtain music from the opera, *La Niobé* (first performed 1826), by Giovanni Pacini (1796–1867).

[5] Jean Baptiste Nicolas Armand Carrel (1800–36), the French radical editor whom Mill most admired, was visiting England at this time.

---

[1] MS in L/P&S/6/293, pp. 49–[50] (before India PC 1411), India Office Library and Records. See *CW*, Vol. XXX, App. A, No. 79.

[2] "Engagement between the British Government and the Maharajah Dawlut Rao Sindiah" (22 Apr., 1820), is in L/P&S/6/293, pp. 53–[8].

[3] The paragraphs are *ibid.*, pp. 61–9. The issue was whether the British Government had the right to supply or withold military services at its discretion.

126.1. TO WILLIAM CABELL[1]

Ex. Off.
11th March 1835

MY DEAR SIR,

The grounds, on which in PC 1411, the distinction is made between the British Levy & the remainder of Scindia's Contingent, are solely those which appear in the Collection. Of their sufficiency or otherwise you can judge. I do not distinctly recollect them.

The Ajmere Engagement[2] shall be looked at.

Believe me, My dear Sir
Yours very truly
J.S. MILL

139.1. TO HENRY SCOTT ALVES[1]

E.I. House
4 July 1835

Political Department

Mr J.S. Mill presents compliments to Mr Alves, and by desire of the Chairman & Deputy Chairman,[2] transmits in duplicate Draft of a proposed reply to various paras. of the Political Letters from Bengal, dated the 13 March, 10 July, & 13 November 1834, relative to the North Eastern & Eastern Frontiers.[3]

15 collections, in 1327 pages, accompany the Draft.

H.S. Alves, Esq &c &c &c

---

[1]MS in L/P&S/6/293, pp. 73–[4] (before India PC 1411), India Office Library and Records. See *CW*, Vol. XXX, App. A, No. 79.

[2]Presumably an engagement similar to that referred to in Letter 125.1 above.

---

[1]MS in the possession of Mrs. Barbara McCrimmon.

Henry Scott Alves (d. 1859), at that time Assistant Secretary to the Board of Control.

[2]This formula covers the transmission of Draft Despatches from the Examiner's Office to the Board of Control; the Chairman and Deputy Chairman of the East India Company's Court of Directors were then William Stanley Clarke and James Rivett Carnac (1785–1846).

[3]This despatch, entitled "North Eastern and Eastern Frontier" and dated 25 Sept., 1835, is given as Mill's in his handlist; see *CW*, Vol. XXX, App. A, No. 111.

159.1. TO HORACE HAYMAN WILSON[1]

India House
5th January 1836

MY DEAR SIR

Some months ago, by the desire of the then Chairman,[2] I had the honour of placing myself in communication with you with a view to obtain your valuable aid in procuring a person qualified to superintend the Anglo Indian College & to be the principal teacher in that Institution, and you kindly consented to look out for a fit person. The Managers of the Institution have since withdrawn their application, stating that they have now no doubt of being able to select a competent person in India and I am consequently directed by the Revenue & Judicial Committee to apprise you that any further continuance of your endeavours to procure a person in this country will be unnecessary.

Having thus fulfilled my instructions, permit me in my individual capacity to say how much pleasure I have derived from your letter in this month's Asiatic Journal.[3] The Government of India in their recent conduct have gone directly in the teeth of the instructions they have received from this country—as well as violated the most obvious rules of policy & common prudence.

Believe me, My dear Sir
Very truly yours
J.S. MILL

163.1. TO SARAH AUSTIN[1]

India House
8th Feby 1836

MY DEAR MÜTTERLEIN

Thanks for letting me know when there was an opportunity of writing. How are you? & how "is" Mr Austin? I wish much to know—as for me I am much the same

---

[1]MS in the India Office Library and Records. Published in *Journal of General Education*, XXIV (Jan. 1973), 231, and in *MNL*, IX (Summer 1974), 4, edited by Gerald and Natalie Robinson Sirkin.
[2]John Loch; see Letter 101.1 above.
[3]"Education of the Natives of India," *Asiatic Journal*, n.s. XIX (Jan.–Apr. 1836), 1–16.

---

[1]MS in the Varnhagen von Ense Collection, Jagiellonian Library, Cracow. Published in *Victorians Institute Journal*, V (1987), 139–40, edited by T.H. Pickett (where it is followed by a letter dated 21 June, by James Mill to Sarah Austin), and in *MNL*, XXIII (Winter 1988), 20–1, edited by Joseph Hamburger.
The Austins were staying at Boulogne, as John Austin's work in London, both the Inner

as when I last wrote neither better nor worse—& I do not find that I get better—however the medical men think it is a very trifling ailment.[2] While it lasts, however, it cripples me for many things. My father also is *in statu quo* or nearly so—& will not get rid of the remains of his complaint till the warm weather.[3] My brother James goes to Deal tonight to join his ship in the Downs.[4] News of any other sort I have none as to anybody in whom you take interest. Nor is there anything *doing* by anybody—except indeed in India—where Cameron is going on very satisfactorily & there is a prospect of his being able to do some good.[5] I send you a copy of the review.[6] Now that Von Raumer is done (which by the bye I have asked Buller to review) could not you do something for it?[7]

You have heard I suppose from Bickersteth all the circumstances attending his appointment[8]—which is worth all other things put together that the Whigs have done—though they ought to have done it long before.

Henry Taylor is printing a little book on *Statesmanship* in which I have no doubt there will be good things, & I should think some weak ones.[9]

I hardly ever go out now—so you will not wonder that I have so little to tell.

Yours affectionately

J.S. MILL

Temple lectures and his connection with the Criminal Law Commission, had terminated. John Austin at this time was a victim of depression and other ailments, and Sarah Austin recently had experienced a nervous breakdown.

[2]Mill was suffering from exhaustion and general debility, and he soon had other symptoms—weakened lungs, a deranged stomach, and a nervous twitching of the right eye.

[3]James Mill became seriously ill, probably with tuberculosis, in August 1835, and died 23 June, 1836.

[4]James Bentham Mill (1814–62) was on his way to India, where he joined the East India Company's civil service.

[5]Charles Hay Cameron (1795–1880), a lawyer and one of Bentham's disciples, was on the law commission which was part of the Supreme Council of India. He worked with T.B. Macaulay in preparing the penal code for India.

[6]Sarah Austin's article, "D'Israeli's *Vindication of the English Constitution*," had appeared in *London Review*, II (Jan. 1836), 533–52.

[7]Sarah Austin translated the first two volumes of *England in 1835*, 3 vols. (London: Murray, 1836), by Frederick Ludwig Georg von Raumer (1781–1873). Charles Buller did not review Raumer, at least not in the *London Review*, nor did Sarah contribute.

[8]Henry Bickersteth (1783–1851) became Baron Langdale in 1836, when he was appointed Master of the Rolls. A friend of Bentham's, he promoted law reform.

[9]Henry Taylor (1800–86), poet, Colonial Office official, author of *The Statesman* (London: Longman, *et al.*, 1836), which Mill with George Grote reviewed in the *London and Westminster Review*, V & XXVII (Apr. 1837), 1–32 (in *Essays on Politics and Society*, *CW*, Vols. XVIII–XIX (Toronto: University of Toronto Press, 1977), Vol. XIX, pp. 617–47.

177.01. TO J.B. ALEXANDRE PAULIN[1]

Paris
samedi
[6 August, 1836]

MON CHER MONSIEUR PAULIN

En passant par Paris trop vîte pour aller voir mes amis, je vous écris à la hâte un petit mot de réponse à votre lettre. L'Histoire Parlementaire aura bientôt un article dans le London Review, article fait par un de mes amis qui a beaucoup étudié la Révolution française et qui fait très grand cas de cet ouvrage.[2] L'espace seul a manqué à l'Examiner pour en rendre compte il y a déjà longtemps. J'ai pris des démarches pour qu'il soit parlé dans quelques journaux anglais de votre traduction de l'excellent ouvrage de Ritter, et je ferai de mon mieux pour les autres ouvrages, notamment pour celui de M. Fauriel.[3]

Comme la revue n'a pas d'abonnés en france il serait inutile qu'elle persiste à faire les frais d'une agence parisienne. Si donc vous voulez bien écrire à M. Falconer en vous servant de mon nom et l'indiquer ce qui nous reste à payer, nous terminerons à la fin du mois courant l'arrangement que nous avons fait ensemble il y a quelque temps.

Quel funeste evenement, mon cher M. Paulin, que la mort de Carrel—la france perd en lui le plus grand de ses hommes politiques et la cause populaire son plus noble défenseur.[4] J'ai peu joui de l'avantage immense de son intimité—malgré

---

[1]MS in the German National Museum, Nuremberg. *Addressed:* "Monsieur / Monsieur Paulin / libraire / Rue de Seine". Dated from postmark.
J.B. Alexandre Paulin (1796–1859), publisher and bookseller, was agent for the *London and Westminster Review* in France.

[2]In "Parliamentary History of the French Revolution," *London and Westminster Review*, V & XXVII (Apr. 1837), 233–47, Thomas Carlyle (1795–1881), then an intimate friend of Mill and Harriet Taylor, reviewed the published volumes of Philippe Joseph Benjamin Buchez and Prosper Charles Roux, eds., *L'histoire parlementaire de la révolution française*, which was being published in Paris by Paulin. (It was completed, in 40 vols., in 1838.)

[3]The early volumes, dealing with Africa, of Karl Ritter, *Die Erdkunde im Verhältnis zur Natur und zur Geschichte des Menschen oder allgemeine vergleichende Geographie*, 19 vols. in 21, 2nd ed. (Berlin: Reimer, 1822–59), were issued in Paris by Paulin in 1835–36 as *Géographie générale comparée, ou Etude de la terre dans ses rapports avec la nature et avec l'histoire de l'homme*, 3 vols. trans. E. Buret. Paulin also published in 1836 the four volumes of *Histoire de la Gaule méridionale sous la domination des conquérants germains*, by Claude Charles Fauriel (1772–1844), historian and philologist. The notices Mill refers to have not been located.

[4]Carrel, whom Mill had met first in 1833, died on 24 July, 1836, from wounds suffered in a duel with Emile de Girardin. For Mill's tribute, see "Armand Carrel," *London and Westminster Review*, VI & XXVIII (Oct. 1837), 66–111 (in *Essays on French History and Historians*, *CW*, Vol. XX [Toronto: University of Toronto Press, 1985], pp. 167–215.

cela j'ai senti sa perte comme celle d'un père.⁵

tout à vous
J.S. MILL

201.2. TO HENRY COLE¹

India House
Thursday
[April 1837?]

MY DEAR COLE—Under the circumstances you mention I should wish to have the longer passage omitted entirely. The shorter one may stand as it is, except that instead of "indispensable to insure confidence abroad" I would rather say "the most effectual means of insuring" etc.²

Yours
J.S. MILL

212.1. TO WILLIAM CABELL¹

Examiner's Office
5th August 1837

MY DEAR SIR

In the PC herewith forwarded on the subject of Baroda affairs, you will find that orders are given for the removal of Mr Williams from the Office of the Commissioner & Resident.² Similar Orders were inserted by the Board in the P.C. recently returned on the subject of Myhee Caunta—but the Chairman did not think that so good an occasion as the present one & consequently the P.C. has been laid before the Committee recently as it originally stood. It seems more just & less embarrassing in its consequences to remove Mr Williams for general unfitness as

---

⁵James Mill had died on 23 June, 1836.

---

¹MS not located; typescript McCrimmon.
²The reference would appear to be to an economic article in the *Guide*, a newspaper edited by Cole that began publication on 22 April, 1837, to which Mill contributed; see *CW*, Vol. XXIV, pp. 793–4.

---

¹MS in L/P&S/6/302, n.p. (after Bombay PC 1934), India Office Library and Records. See *CW*, Vol. XXX, App. A, No. 946.
²James Williams of the Bombay Civil Service was Commissioner in Gujerat and Resident at Baroda. His death precluded his dismissal for general incompetence.

proved by the general state of affairs at the Court to which he is accredited, than for specific instances of misconduct of which his superiors (the Bombay Government of the time) must share the blame & which the home authorities when they first animadverted on them, did not deem worthy of so serious a punishment, for you will observe that the misconduct of Mr Williams in regard to the Myhee Caunta was as fully known to the Court when they sent out their last dispatch on that subject as it is now.

The Board have also inserted in the PC on the Myhee Caunta, an order for the removal of Mr Erskine from Kattywar.[3] This seems very severe treatment for an error of judgment which in *him* was comparatively venial. He had never since he was in India been under any proper superintendance; his superior was Mr Williams, who, as well as the Government to whom they naturally looked for instructions, for years countenanced & approved all he did. If this does not render an error of judgment excusable, would it not at least be hard to ruin the entire prospects of a young man for errors committed under such circumstances.

I trouble you with this to explain the reason why the alterations have not been adopted.

Believe me
ever truly yours
J.S. MILL

220.01. TO WILLIAM CABELL[1]

Ex. Off.
8 November 1837

MY DEAR SIR

With reference to Political Draft No 487, in which the Board have inserted a paragraph they inserted before in the PC, relating to the inexpediency of including a multiplicity of subjects in the same letter—the Court I dare say will not make any remonstrance—but the reason why the paragraph was struck out, was, that the substance of it was embodied in an additional paragraph to a previous P.C. & thereby reached India earlier than it would have done if left in the P.C. in which the Board originally inserted it. With reference to the subject generally it seems to me very important that any instructions given to the Govt of India to matters in their separate letters, they should be warned at the same time not to discontinue the

---

[3] James Erskine was the Political Agent at Kathiawar.

[1] MS in L/P&S/6/305, pp. 339–[44], India Office Library and Records. See *CW*, Vol. XXX, App. A, No. 159.

practice of sending quarterly General letters embracing all subjects not already reported on separately. The necessity of this appears from the conduct of the Bombay Government which ever since it has written none but separate letters has made a practice of having a great part of its proceedings unreported for years together & obliging us occasionally to take up subjects from the Consultations alone. The natural tendency of the system of separate letters seems to be to leaving subjects unnoticed until either some grave event happens, or a considerable quantity of matters has accumulated or the attention of Govt or the Court is drawn to the fact that there has been no report for a long time & the only check to this tendency seems to be making obligatory on somebody to look through a whole quarter's or half year's proceedings & report everything of any moment.

If you should agree in these views you will no doubt use your influence with the Board in support of them. As it is, we are writing as often & as vigorously to Bombay to demand General letters, as to Bengal to do what looks very like demanding their discontinuance or at least might admit of that interpretation.

Believe me, My dear Sir
Most truly yours
J.S. MILL

227.01. TO JOHN ROBERTSON[1]

I.H.
Wednesday
[December 1837]

DEAR ROBERTSON

I send you a letter from Col. Napier for your consideration. If you think what he proposes will do, I am quite willing to acquiesce.[2]

I left at Reynell,[3] the whole of "Caricatures" except the one page herewith enclosed, which I have omitted because (while it makes no gap) I cannot at present see what is the merit you ascribe to Gilray's idea or in what you consider it to

---

[1] MS in the Prussian State Library, Berlin.
John Robertson (ca. 1811–75), nominal editor (in fact, sub-editor) of the *London and Westminster Review* from early 1837 until 1840.

[2] It is probable that Colonel William Francis Patrick Napier (1785–1860), historian of and participant in the Peninsular War, proposed that he contribute the article that was published as "The Duke of Wellington," *London and Westminster Review*, VI & XXVIII (Jan. 1838), 367–436. (Mill appended an editorial note indicating that the views were those of the author, not of the review; see *CW*, Vol. I, p. 604.)

[3] Charles Wetherby Reynell (1798–1892), printer of the *London and Westminster*.

resemble & surpass Hogarth's.[4] Of course reinsertion in the proof is practicable if desirable.

I send Adams' article: he has done all we desired & inserted a splendid joke about Anthracite in p. 31.[5] It will do very well now, only I am not certain about pp. 4 to 7. If you think they do not come in well, put them in somewhere as a note, or omit part of them or the whole, just as you like.

I would come to you tonight—but must work at Palmyra[6]—I will come as soon as I can.

faithfully yours
J.S. MILL

228.1. TO WILLIAM CABELL[1]

Ex. Off.
21 Dec 1837

MY DEAR SIR

The paragraphs respecting Col. Alves[2] were omitted in the Draft to which you allude, because the Committee considered that the only reason for releasing the other Madras officers from the retrenchment,[3] was its being retrospective & that if an officer had been retrenched without hardship of a refund, and in obedience to

---

[4]As published, John Robertson's "Caricatures," *London and Westminster Review*, VI & XXVIII (Jan. 1838), 261–93, contains only slight reference to James Gillray (1757–1815) and William Hogarth (1697–1764) on pp. 279–80; evidently what Mill omitted stayed out. See also Mill to Robertson, *CW*, Vol. XII, pp. 362–3, presumably earlier.

[5]William Bridges Adams ("Junius Redivivus") (1797–1872), "Dr. Arnott, *On Warming and Ventilation*," *ibid.*, 345–67. The joke reads thus: "A proprietor who wished much to render his mines available to the public, applied to a scientific gentleman ... for a certificate of [anthracite's] durability. He obtained it, to the effect that the certifier verily believed that it would be the last thing destroyed on the day of judgment. About the same period a barn, in which a quantity of the coal was stored up, caught fire, and the part not destroyed was covered by the coal." (P. 365.)

[6]I.e., Mill's "Ware's Letters from Palmyra," *ibid.*, pp. 436–70 (in *CW*, Vol. I, pp. 431–61).

---

[1]MS in L/P&S/6/304, n.p. (before India Draft 600), India Office Library and Records. See *CW*, Vol. XXX, App. A, No. 170.

[2]Lieutenant-Colonel Nathaniel Alves of the Madras Establishment was at this time Political Agent at Rajputana.

[3]Military officers holding civil positions, such as political agent, in which no military duties were involved, had been forbidden to receive their military pay in addition to their civil allowances. This regulation had not been enforced for some years, and then retrenchment, or recovery of monies paid, had been instituted, causing some hardship and much dissatisfaction among the officers affected.

the regulations of the service he had no claim to the restoration of the money. If the money were repaid to Col. Alves, the Committee thought that the Bengal officers would ask for it & on the whole it appeared to them that if Col. Alves thought himself aggrieved he would memorialize the Govt or the Court & the question might then be decided with a knowledge of the sentiments of the Govt.

These, as far as I could collect from the discussions in Committee, were the reasons which led to striking out the paragraph respecting Col. Alves.

Believe me, My dear Sir
most truly yours
J.S. MILL

229.02. TO WILLIAM CABELL[1]

Ex. Off.
6 Jany 1838

MY DEAR SIR

From a PC herewith forwarded on the Affairs of Oude, you will perceive that the death of the King of that country[2] has not, in the opinion of the Chairs,[3] obviated the necessity of taking into consideration the great principles of general policy laid down in the Resolutions of Govt which contemplated the removal of that prince from the throne.

It was to these general principles only, that any allusion was intended in the Hyderabad P.C. & the Chairman, with reference to the nature of the paragraphs now submitted, does not see any necessity for the remodelling of the concluding part of the Hyderabad paragraphs. If the President[4] after reading the Oude P.C. should continue of his former opinion I should be much obliged to you if you would suggest to me the sort of modification which would best meet the President's views. In the mean time the Hyderabad paragraphs will be kept in abeyance.

Believe me
Ever truly yours
J.S. MILL

---

[1]MS in L/P&S/6/307, pp. 387–9, India Office Library and Records. See *CW*, Vol. XXX, App. A, No. 172.
[2]Nasir-ud-Din Haidar (d. 1837).
[3]James Rivett Carnac was Chairman, and James Law Lushington (1779–1859) Deputy Chairman of the Court of Directors at this time.
[4]John Cam Hobhouse (1786–1869) was President of the Board of Control from April 1835 to September 1841.

233.1. TO WILLIAM CABELL[1]

India House
3d Feby 1838

MY DEAR SIR

With reference to your note of the 31st ulto, I have caused search to be made for any documents respecting the amount of crime in the Guicowar's territory,[2] but none can be found, nor do I well understand how any such can exist. The great amount of crime in our own territories the authors of which find refuge in the Guicowar's, will appear from the Collection to the P.C. in the affairs of the Guicowar, herewith sent.

I am also directed by the Chairman[3] to call your attention to the observations respecting Mr Williams,[4] (to a similar effect with those inserted by the Board in Draft 50) which are contained in the present P.C. 2095 & which were reserved for it instead of being put into Draft 50, because when the original P.C. was divided & the portions of it which related to the general government separated from those which touched upon special points, the remarks on Mr Williams' conduct seemed to belong rather to the former division. This is still the view entertained by the Chairs, & they are on that account, desirous that the insertion in Draft 50 may be withdrawn, for which an application will probably be made in the regular form.

Believe me
ever truly yours
J.S. MILL

237.1. TO HENRY COLE[1]

Kensington
Tuesday evg.
[March 1838?]

DEAR COLE

I am obliged to send this article back to you; I never had so unmanageable a one in my life.[2] Not only is it often quite impossible for me to make out what you mean,

---

[1]MS in L/P&S/6/305, pp. 575–7, India Office Library and Records. See *CW*, Vol. XXX, App. A, No. 955.
[2]I.e., in the territory of Sayaji Rao, Gaikwar of Baroda, who ruled 1819–47.
[3]For the Chairs see Letter 229.02 above.
[4]See Letter 212.1 above.

---

[1]MS not located; typescript McCrimmon.
[2]Almost certainly a draft of Cole's "Uniform Penny Postage," which remained somewhat disorganized when published in the *London and Westminster Review*, VII & XXIX (Apr. 1838), 225–64.

but there is not one sentence in the whole article in its proper place. I wish you would rewrite it or rearrange it, on the principle of proving only one thing at a time & not jumping from one point to another & back again several times in a page. The article is utterly unmanageable by me—it can only be disentangled by the hand that entangled it—but the material is all excellent.

Ever yours
J.S. MILL

You must lose no time if it is to be in this number.

237.2. TO WILLIAM CABELL[1]

India House
1 March 1838

MY DEAR SIR

With reference to your note of yesterday's date which has just been handed to me by Mr Peacock;[2] I have to state that Draft No 70, respecting the family of Wittul Rao[3] formed (with a slight exception) a part of P.C. 2002 on the affairs of Baroda which was returned by the Board (so far as that portion of it was concerned) unaltered.

Believe me my dear Sir
ever truly yours
J.S. MILL

239.2. TO WILLIAM CABELL[1]

India House
26th March 1838

MY DEAR SIR

With reference to the alteration in PC 2072 (Affairs of Kattywar) just returned; I

---

[1] MS in L/P&S/6/307, p. 313, India Office Library and Records. See *CW*, Vol. XXX, App. A, No. 953.

[2] Thomas Love Peacock (1775–1866) had succeeded James Mill as Chief Examiner of India Correspondence in 1836.

[3] Wittul Row Dewanjee, dismissed as minister of the Gaikwar of Baroda in 1827, had subsequently been employed by the British Government to administer a sequestered district, and large allowances had been granted to him and his family. On his death, the legality of these payments was called into question, and his nephew and adopted son, Christna Rao, was making a strong claim for their continuance.

---

[1] MS in L/P&S/6/309, pp. 449–51, India Office Library and Records. See *CW*, Vol. XXX, App. A, No. 954.

do not clearly understand in what manner the Joonaghur chief is to continue his responsibility for the Babrias, when he is specifically interdicted from interfering with them. It strikes me that a clearer statement of the Board's intentions would be desirable[2] & would facilitate the passing of the Draft through the Court.

Ever yours truly
J.S. MILL

239.3. TO WILLIAM CABELL[1]

Ex. Off.
18 April 1838

MY DEAR SIR

With reference to Mr Gordon's letter of this day's date respecting Colonel Gowan,[2] & the desirableness of requiring from the Indian Govt their reasons for the appointment you may perhaps not be aware what those reasons may very naturally be presumed to be, viz. that Col. Gowan is a connexion by marriage of Mr Ross in whose gift as Lieutenant Governor of Agra[3] the appointment was.

Believe me
Ever truly yours
J.S. MILL

---

[2]Cabell's reply of 28 March follows Mill's letter in L/P&S/6/309, pp. 453–[6], and provides a better statement: "My Dear Sir/ The alteration in PC 2072 is, as you justly remark in yr letter of the 26th Instant, rather obscurely worded: Its intention, I have ascertained would be more clearly expressed if it were to run thus — '& tho' it might be very desirable, as you state, to induce this Chief to continue responsibility for the good conduct of the Babriawur Villages, we are not aware how this could be allowed, as you have no right to enforce any such obligation now that you have deprived him of sovereign Power over these Villages.'"

[1]MS in L/P&S/6/308, pp. 25–[6], India Office Library and Records. See *CW*, Vol. XXX, App. A, No. 183.

[2]Robert Gordon (1791–1847), M.P. for Windsor, was Joint Secretary to the Board of Control from 1835. He had written about the apparently much earlier appointment of George Edward Gowan (d. 1865), of the Bengal artillery, to the position of Commissioner in Kumaun.

[3]Alexander Ross (b. 1777) was Member of the Supreme Council of India from October 1833, and Lieutenant-Governor of Agra December 1835 to June 1836.

241.1. TO WILLIAM CABELL[1]

Ex. Off.
8 June 1838

Private

MY DEAR SIR

Can you give me any idea whether P.C. 2133, sent to the Board on the 19th March, is likely to be soon returned? It reviews the proceedings of the Agra Lieutenant-Governor[2] from April to June 1836, & as several subsequent Agra P.C.s have been returned, which being full of references to P.C. 2133 are kept waiting by it, I would venture to suggest that in case any point or points should require prolonged consideration or are likely to give rise to correspondence, the paras relating to them might perhaps be detached & made into a separate P.C. & the rest proceeded with. I wish the same course had been adopted in this office respecting Draft 3, one point of which (that relating to the tomb of the Persian ambassador)[3] is still under discussion between the Board and the Court, during which time all the other parts of the Draft (some of which have been referred to in subsequent dispatches being signed & sent off) are detained in this country.

Believe me, My dear Sir
Yours most truly
J.S. MILL

248.2. TO JAMES STEPHEN[1]

India House
3d November 1838

MY DEAR SIR

The enclosed paper has been given to me by some of my Italian friends in this

---

[1]MS in L/P&S/6/305, pp. 173–5, India Office Library and Records. See *CW*, Vol. XXX, App. A, No. 149.
[2]See Letter 239.3 above.
[3]Hajee Khuleel Khan, Ambassador to Bombay from Persia, had been killed by a random shot during an altercation between his attendants and some Sepoys in 1802. Since he was deemed to have been under British protection at the time, the Government had offered, as a gesture of compensation, an annual sum of money for purposes of charity, and devotion at his tomb at Mujiff, in Persia. Arrears were now being claimed by his son.

---

[1]MS at the Public Record Office.
James Stephen (1789–1859), Under-Secretary for Colonial Affairs from 1836.

country, who knew of no better means of forwarding it to its destination.[2] It appears to be intended as a sort of Memorial to the Colonial Department & is, as you will see, signed by the party in whose name it is made out & who is a Sicilian refugee at Malta—but it has been very long on its way hither, & the friends of the party are in complete ignorance whether his case has been decided or not. I know nothing whatever personally of the man, but I am informed, that his removal from Malta would be ruinous to his circumstances, & that his conduct while there has never incurred the slightest censure from the authorities.

With many apologies for adopting this mode of communication which I do from not knowing the proper one,

believe me
yours faithfully
J.S. MILL

249.1. TO ROBERT GORDON[1]

Examiner's Office
24 Novr 1838

Mr Mill presents his compliments to Mr Gordon,[2] & although unable to refer him at once to any authority, he believes Mr Gordon will find that the provision in question of the Canon Law (which it need not be observed is founded on the Roman Catholic religion) was the occasion of the famous *Nolumus leges Angliae mutari*.[3] The barons, in that instance, were resisting the attempt to introduce into English law the *legitimatio per subsequens matrimonium* of the Canon Law.

---

[2]With the letter is a "Statement of Facts" of the case, dated at Malta, 23 August, 1838, signed by Diego Arangio, a merchant, the political refugee in question, who had fled to Malta in 1837, where he was refused asylum. Accepted by a French possession in Africa, he subsequently obtained a passport, and returned to Malta to reestablish his business. The British authorities there, under pressure from the Neapolitan Consul, had then tried to expell him. Mill's "Italian friends" included Giuseppe Mazzini (1805–72) and Angelo Usiglio (1803–75), both of whom were in exile in England.

---

[1]MS in L/P&S/6/314, n.p. (before India PC 2278), India Office Library and Records. See *CW*, Vol. XXX, App. A, No. 216.

[2]Mill was responding to Robert Gordon's note of 23 Nov., 1838, which immediately precedes this letter in L/P&S/6/314, asking legal assistance with the case of the legitimacy of the children of Francis Steddy, Deputy Post Master at Ryepur, who had died intestate. As Steddy and his wife, who were both Roman Catholics, had married after the birth of their children, an opinion had been expressed that "according to the Roman Catholic religion, children born of parents previous to their marriage become legitimate on such subsequent marriage."

[3]See 20 Henry III, Statutes of Merton, c. 9 (1235).

Wherever the municipal laws of the nations of Europe are of Roman origin, Mr Mill believes that this rule will be found to prevail — & he would instance Scotland & France.

253.1. TO JOHN AITKEN CARLYLE[1]

Rome
18th March 1839

MY DEAR SIR

I received your two letters both together today, not from any negligence of mine in asking for them, but from the carelessness of the Post office people in telling me there was nothing for me. Many thanks for the trouble you have taken. The packet containing the first part of the report[2] is not worth paying $12\frac{1}{2}$ piastres for, or one piastre, as I have already seen the whole document here in a newspaper, & can have as many copies of it as I like in England, where alone they can be of any use, therefore pray do not trouble yourself any further about the packet. I will give the 17 carlini[3] to Sterling or to somebody else who may be going to Naples, as there appears to be some fear that Dr Calvert's[4] health may prevent Sterling from going there — he will at any rate not stay more than ten days, as he will set out if at all about the 1st of April & return about the 15th with a brother of his who is bringing home a sick wife from Corfu.[5] Your messages shall be given to him. I believe he knows Severn — Wolff[6] I have not heard him speak about.

The two other parts of the Report reached me duly. I am really concerned that you have had so much more trouble about a matter of such small consequence, than I expected, or than I should ever have dreamed of imposing upon you.

---

[1]MS at the National Library of Scotland. *Addressed:* Dr Carlyle / Poste Restante / a Napoli. *Postmark:* Naples, 27 March.
John Aitken Carlyle (1801–79), younger brother of Thomas Carlyle, was visiting the Continent at this time as travelling physician to the Duke of Buccleuch.

[2]The reference is to "Report on the Affairs of British North America, from the Earl of Durham," *PP*, 1839, XVII, 1–690. In the previous year, Mill had written three articles in defence of Durham's policies: see *CW*, Vol. VI, pp. 405–64.

[3]Unit of Italian currency.

[4]John Mitchinson Calvert (1801–42) had become a friend of John Sterling when both were wintering in Madeira for their health in the previous year.

[5]Anthony Coningham Sterling (1805–71), brother of John, Captain in the 23rd Foot, and his wife Charlotte (d. 1863) apparently met John on the outskirts of Rome on 4 April (see Carlyle's *Life of Sterling* [London: Chapman and Hall, 1851], pp. 236–7). Anthony and Charlotte visited Dr. Carlyle in Naples in April, but John Sterling's plans were altered by the death of his infant son in England on 30 March.

[6]Joseph Severn (1793–1879), artist and friend of John Keats, who was still living in Rome at this time, and, presumably, Joseph Wolff (1795–1862), missionary and orientalist.

One of the letters which you forwarded tells me what you probably have heard from your brother direct, that the whole edition of his History is sold, except a few copies.[7] He was well & in spirits.

I have attended to your advice about riding, but have not found it possible to ride so much or so often as I intended, on account of a pain in my side which invariably comes on after I have ridden a very short time. I do not find myself at all better, or getting better, & have renounced the hope of any considerable benefit from this journey or climate. I still adhere to my macaroni diet which I find as pleasant & as least as wholesome as any other.

Pray command my services to the utmost for anything you may wish done here or in the way to England. I have for sundry reasons given up all thought of Sicily.

Excuse this trumpery affair of a letter which I write only to thank you for your kindness & believe me

ever yours truly
J.S. MILL

259.1. TO HORACE GRANT[1]

[1 July, 1839?]

DEAR GRANT

I am here—so please send me my papers by bearer.

yours
J.S. MILL

260.1. TO EDWARD SCOTT[1]

India House
30th July 1839

MY DEAR SIR

Your very kind letter increases my mistification at what has happened.

---

[7] Thomas Carlyle, *The French Revolution: A History*, 3 vols. (London: Fraser, 1837).

---

[1] MS in the Hollander Collection, University of Illinois, Urbana-Champaign. Dated on the assumption that Mill had returned to India House after a lengthy absence, during which Grant looked after his papers; see letter of 18 Oct., 1839, *CW*, Vol. XVII, p. 1990. The first of July was the Monday following Mill's return from the Continent.

---

[1] MS in the National Library of Wales, Aberystwyth. *Addressed:* Edward Scott, Esq., Bodtalog, Machynnlleth, N. Wales. Published in *National Library of Wales Journal*, XXIV (1986), 354–5, edited by Mary and Lionel Madden.

Edward Scott (1752/3–1842), a friend of Thomas Love Peacock, through whom he met James and J.S. Mill, was interested in Welsh culture.

I was aware that you valued the book highly as a gift from a friend, & as not easy to be replaced; but I was quite unaware that it was (or that as a Prospectus of an unpublished work it was likely to be) in such request or of such value in the market, as could make it an object with any one to become possessed of it by dishonest means.[2]

I have no clue whatever to trace it by, but if you would have the kindness to give me the exact title, I will set my bookseller to look out for it. I fear there is little chance of success since whoever got possession of it most probably desired to keep it rather than to sell it — or if to sell it, intended to sell it immediately, having some customer in view.

yours ever truly

J.S. MILL

With regard to the Saumaise papers your directions shall be attended to. Perhaps if you have time you would write a letter to the Trustees of the Museum for me to send with the papers — which would increase their value both to the institution & to posterity.[3]

265.1. TO JOHN MITCHELL KEMBLE[1]

India House
10th October 1839

MY DEAR SIR

Perhaps a former slight acquaintance with you, which I always look back to with pleasure, may be a sufficient excuse for my troubling you with this note on a subject in which you also are interested though not so directly as myself. I have been for some time engaged in carrying on a review, from which various reasons now conspire to make me desirous of disconnecting myself. Though its circulation is steady, it is not sufficient to cover the expenses; & the deficit would be still greater unless I were to continue devoting an amount of my own time & exertion to the review which is not convenient to a person who has other pursuits, & is not justified by any amount of good likely to be produced in the existing state of the public mind by a person of my particular cast of opinions & general mental qualifications, at least through the channel of a periodical work. Now your review

---

[2]The work has not been identified.
[3]In 1789 Scott married Louisa Mary (née Anwyl), widow of comte Louis de Saumaise of the Burgundy family. The family papers presumably came to Scott on her death in 1812. The collection was given to the British Museum in 1839; it includes BL Add. MSS, 11,644–54, and Add. Charters 4608, 4615–4717.

---

[1]MS at Wasada University, Tokyo.
John Mitchell Kemble (1807–57), philologist and historian, edited the *British and Foreign Review* 1836–44. For the sequel to this letter, see *CW*, Vol. XIII, p. 410.

has the same difficulties to struggle against, & if there are any two reviews which more particularly stand in each other's way it is the British & Foreign & the London & Westminster. The proprietor of the British & Foreign[2] has shewn an honorable perseverance in carrying on a review which cannot hitherto have been prosperous as a mere pecuniary speculation, in which quality I should be very glad to imitate him if I had his resources & his consequent means of obtaining the best help.

Now therefore what I should wish to know is, whether it is probable that he would be willing to become a purchaser of the L. & W. & I prefer asking your opinion on the matter in this way, because if you think that he certainly or almost certainly would not, I should proceed no farther in the business. I am aware of no one to whom the acquisition of the review would be so advantageous, no one else indeed to whom in a pecuniary sense there would be much likelihood of its being at all advantageous, unless possibly to some bookseller as an instrument of puffing & to such I should not chuse to be the means of consigning it. Some one might perhaps be found who would undertake it from higher motives & whose circumstances would enable him to be indifferent to the very moderate pecuniary loss at present incurred. But I should very willingly see it united to your review, since the only individualizing character which it has possessed in all its *avatars* & which therefore it ought not to part with, & live, is that of an organ of radicalism, & the article on the State of the Nation, in your last number but one, rather surpasses in point of radicalism, than falls short of, my limits.[3]

Believe me, My dear Sir
Yours most truly
J.S. MILL

268.1. TO HENRY COLE[1]

I.H.
Tuesday
[12 November, 1839?]

DEAR COLE

I have seen Robertson once since he saw you.[2] We separated with a half

---

[2]Thomas Wentworth Beaumont (1792–1848), formerly M.P. for Northumberland, from 1835–44 owned the *British and Foreign Review*, which supported liberal principles with special reference to foreign countries.

[3]"State of the Nation," *British and Foreign Review*, IX (July, 1839), 273–319, was written by Kemble, with Beaumont's assistance.

---

[1]MS in the William R. Perkins Library, Duke University.

[2]According to Cole's diary, he and Robertson first conferred on Thursday, 7 November, 1839, and not again until 20 February, 1840. See Introduction, pp. xii–xiv above.

intention of calling on you when he comes again to town this week. He seemed to me to be neither *for* nor *against* the plan, but to await my decision. Now my decision, if I consider myself only, will be, whatever becomes of the review, to withdraw myself from it. I have not yet received any answer from Beaumont, but I cannot be much longer without it: if I do not come to terms with him, I will make up my mind once for all. I should like best, in that case, that your schemes should proceed, with some other person than myself as the proprietor.

ever yours
J.S. MILL

268.2. TO NASSAU WILLIAM SENIOR[1]

18 K.[ensington] S.[quare]
Thursday
[before 5 Dec., 1839]

MY DEAR SENIOR

As I see a question of mine stands first for the P.E. Club I think it right to let you know beforehand that I shall not be there this time. I hope to be at the February meeting, & the subsequent ones to the end of the season.

Perhaps Merivale, or you, who stand next, will bring on your questions.[2]

ever yours
J.S. MILL

N.W. Senior Esq.

---

[1] MS in the National Library of Wales, Aberystwyth.

[2] Senior was on the supervising committee of the Political Economy Club from 1835–1849, and so would be concerned about the schedule. In the event, the question of Herman Merivale (1806–74), the Drummond Professor of Political Economy at Oxford, was discussed on 5 December, 1839: "What general principles should be adopted relatively to the employment of Paupers, Soldiers, and Prisoners in productive labour?" Mill's question came forward on 6 February, 1840: "What would be the effect produced upon Wages, if the rich should adopt the practice of expending a large portion of their income on menial servants and retainers, and a smaller portion in the purchase of Commodities?" Senior's question was discussed on 5 March: "What is the connection between the price of Provisions and the Price of Labour?"

270.01. TO THOMAS CARLYLE[1]

I.H.
Monday
[January 1840]

MY DEAR CARLYLE

Let us have Milnes' article at all events to see & judge of, since it is written. I dare say it will suit the review very well.[2]

I have read "Chartism" with renewed pleasure but only found out *one* new passage.[3]

ever faithfully yours
J.S. MILL

270.03. TO WILLIAM CABELL[1]

Ex. Off.
29th Jany 1840

MY DEAR SIR

According to your request I send the Secret Letter of 7th November with its enclosures, as a supplement to the Joudpore Collection. I do not think that the information contained in these papers, is likely to occasion any alteration in the PC though it may require the addition of a sentence or two, chiefly respecting the restoration of the Joudpore share of Sambur.[2]

ever truly yours
J.S. MILL

---

[1] MS at Trinity College, Cambridge. Dated on internal evidence.
[2] "American Philosophy: Emerson's Works," by Richard Monckton Milnes, Baron Houghton (1809–85), appeared in the *London and Westminster Review*, XXXIII (Mar. 1840), 345–72.
[3] Carlyle's *Chartism* (London: Fraser, 1840), actually appeared in December, 1839. Mill had read it in manuscript just before publication; see *CW*, Vol. XIII, p. 414.

---

[1] MS in L/P&S/6/318, n.p. (before India Draft 135) India Office Library and Records. See *CW*, Vol. XXX, App. A, No. 243.
[2] Further comments by Cabell on the cession of this territory are contained in his Draft 135, which follows Mill's letter in L/P&S/6/318.

270.4. TO AN UNIDENTIFIED CORRESPONDENT[1]

[February 1840?]

... sum you mention—the more especially as circumstances at present render me unable to make any arrangements with respect to any number of the review but the forthcoming one. I hope I may rely upon having, for the present number, ... prefer

Yours truly
J.S. MILL

271.1. TO WILLIAM CABELL[1]

Ex. Off.
14 Feb. 1840

MY DEAR SIR

The additional matter in para 7 of Draft 61 was inserted in the Political Committee on the proposition of a Director & I presume he cannot have adverted to the passages in the Collection, to which you have now been so obliging as to refer me. (If I had remembered their existence I would have pointed them out to him.) His object was to discourage the Government from embarrassing themselves with the domestic disputes of stipendiaries.

Ever truly yours
J.S. MILL

277.1. TO HENRY COLE[1]

20 minutes before 6
[27 February, 1840?]

DEAR COLE

Pray come or send your answer to the printer's,[2] where I shall be for some time.

---

[1]MS fragment in the Pforzheimer Collection, New York Public Library. Dated on internal evidence.

---

[1]MS in L/P&S/6/317, n.p. (before India Draft 61), India Office Library and Records. See *CW*, Vol. XXX, App. A, No. 228.

---

[1]MS not located; typescript McCrimmon. For the dating, see the Introduction, p. xiv above.
[2]Charles Wetherby Reynell; see Letter 227.1 above.

If you do not, I shall return here. I am pressing because there must be an announcement in the present number which must be printed tonight.³

I have had an offer from the other quarter I alluded to in my note⁴ — & if you are willing to carry it on our agreement must be conditional on the very probable event of my refusing that.

Ever yours
J.S. MILL

277.2. TO HENRY COLE¹

Friday
[6 March, 1840]

DEAR COLE

The responsibility thus devolving wholly on me I must take till Monday to consider. But I will be prepared to give you an answer positively on that day.²

Ever yours
J.S. MILL

---

³The announcement appeared in the June number of Vol. XXXIV, on the verso of the Table of Contents: "The present number of this Review appears under a new Proprietorship and Editorship, but without any changes in the principles, nor, it is hoped, in most of the contributors, among whom the present proprietors had long been numbered. . . . / No one connected with the proprietorship or editorship of the London Review being concerned in the present management, the word 'London,' which had been annexed as part of the title on the junction of the London and Westminster Reviews in 1836 will henceforth be dropped, and the Review will appear under its original title of the Westminster Review. / The only new features intended to be introduced into the management are exemplified on the present occasion by the graphic illustrations appended to the article which heads the number, and the miscellaneous notices which conclude it."

⁴The "note" is Letter 277, *CW*, Vol. XIII, pp. 421–2; the source of the other offer, which was not accepted, is unknown.

---

¹MS not located; typescript McCrimmon. For the dating, see Introduction, p. xv above.
²I.e., concerning the transfer of the *London and Westminster* to Cole and William Edward Hickson (1803–70), educational and municipal reformer.

281.1. TO WILLIAM CABELL[1]

Ex. Off.
April 14 1840

Private

MY DEAR SIR

On my return here[2] your note of the 19th ulto respecting P.C. 2674 was shewn to me.

The reasons for keeping the paragraphs respecting the Institution Fee in the Political Department are, *first*, that the former correspondence on the subject has been in that Department. *Secondly* that the question to be at present decided is a *Mysore* question exclusively & it was not the intention of the Chairs[3] that the decision should be considered as prejudging in any degree the question respecting the abolition of the Institution Fee in our own territories—which would in some measure at least apparently be the case if these paragraphs were sent to India in the Legislative or Judicial Departments.

For my own part, believing that an Institution Fee is everywhere objectionable & that the arguments in Cameron's admirable report[4] are conclusive everywhere I should be happy to see the abolition made general but the Court, at present, are certainly not prepared for such a measure.

ever truly yours
J.S. MILL

284.1. TO JOHN MITCHINSON CALVERT[1]

India House
25th April 1840

MY DEAR CALVERT

I have hitherto kept in view the physiological maxim inculcated in the

---

[1]MS in L/P&S/6/319, n.p. (before India PC 2674), India Office Library and Records. See *CW*, Vol. XXX, App. A, No. 250.

[2]Mill had been with his mother and sisters in Falmouth, attending his younger brother Henry; see Letter 284.1 below.

[3]Richard Jenkins (1785–1853) was Chairman, and William Butterworth Bayley (1782–1860) Deputy Chairman of the Court of Directors at this time.

[4]For Cameron, see Letter 163.1 above. He had been responsible for the "Report . . . of His Majesty's Commissioners of Inquiry, upon the Judicial Establishments and Procedure in Ceylon" (31 Jan., 1832), *PP*, 1831–32, XXXII, 119–52.

---

[1]MS at the Wordsworth Trust, Dove Cottage, Grasmere. *Addressed:* Dr Calvert / Falmouth. *Postmark:* 25 April, 1840.
Calvert, whom Mill had met in Rome the previous year (see Letter 253.1 above), was

conclusion of your note to me, & I should probably have allowed myself a few more days of gestation if I had not wished to ask your opinion as to a certain matter. I had arranged with the undertaker, McDowell,[2] that the grave should be built up to a certain height above the ground: that being done, an iron railing round it would have been unnecessary & expensive.[3] On the very morning of the funeral McDowell informed me that the rector would not allow the grave to be built up as high as we had intended—& when I saw it, I found the gravestone quite on a level with the surface of the earth. Had I known this previously I would have had an upright, not a flat gravestone: but the mischief being done, I wrote to McDowell to express my wish to erect an iron railing round the grave, to which he replies that the rector objects to that too, & he recommends my writing to Mr Coope himself.[4]— Now it is on this that I wish to ask your advice, viz. as this Coope seems a queer customer, whether there is any use in applying to him at all & if so, what is the best mode of doing so—whether directly by letter, or in any more circuitous mode: & whether any of my friends at Falmouth would be likely to mend the matter by interesting themselves in it.

We are again all assembled here, & all tolerably well. I have written once to Sterling since I arrived,[5] but have not heard from him, as indeed I did not expect. I have a "pretty considerable" quantity of business on my hands here at present & my head is rather confused, which must account for my writing so trumpery a letter—

ever yours truly
J.S. MILL

I hear good accounts of Cunningham's performance from the Foxes as well as from you.[6] There is no hurry about sending it. I have remitted the ten guineas for him to Mr Robert Fox, as I had forgotten C.'s christian name & feared the bankers might not know to whom to pay it. Bullmore is paid.[7]

---

staying in Falmouth for ill-health early in 1840, and there met the Fox family and the Mills. In March, Mill had joined his mother and sisters Clara and Harriet, who were attending his second youngest brother Henry (1820–40) in his last illness. The Foxes, with whom the Mills also became very friendly, were Robert Were (1789–1877), his wife Maria (née Barclay) (1786–1858), and their children, Anna Maria (1816–97), Robert Barclay (1817–55), and Caroline (1819–71), for whom Mill prepared a "Calendar of Odours" of flowers (in *CW*, Vol. XXXI, p. 257).

[2] Probably William McDowell (b. 1794), who practised in Falmouth as a cabinet-maker, upholsterer, and auctioneer.

[3] Henry had died of tuberculosis on 4 April, at the age of nineteen.

[4] William John Coope (1809–70), rector of Falmouth 1838–70.

[5] Mill's letter to Sterling of 22 April, is in *CW*, Vol. XIII, pp. 428–9. Sterling had met Calvert in Madeira in 1837.

[6] Henry Francis Cunningham (dates unknown, but active in Falmouth artistic circles 1837–43), made portraits of John and Henry Mill.

[7] Probably Frederick Charles Bullmore (1801–96), the surgeon who had attended Henry Mill.

285.1. TO JOHN MITCHINSON CALVERT[1]

India House
1st May 1840

MY DEAR CALVERT

First, let me thank you for taking so much trouble about the affair with Coope.[2] We have finally determined that the thing had better remain as it is; although McDowell is much to blame for having told me positively that the matter could be arranged as we at first ordered it; but for which assurance, I should have chosen one of the numerous other spots in the burial ground the choice of which he offered me & in respect to some of which the objection derived from the necessity of passing over the place to get beyond it would not have had existence. But it is too late to remedy this now. A headstone would be absurd unless for the purpose of an inscription; & an inscription twice over would be almost equally so.

Sterling is here, as you know, & I have seen as much of him as his engagements allowed. We do not think he is so well as when he was at Falmouth, but there seems no decided change for the worse. He still coughs more than one likes to see. I dined along with him on Tuesday, with the Sterling Club,[3] where I saw for the first time your friends Samuel and Robert Wilberforce,[4] — with whom, especially the latter, Sterling had a controversy touching the purposes of Christianity, the essential Christianship of whosoever acknowledges in Christ the *model-man*, & the bad effect upon most minds of dwelling more upon any set of *means* than upon the *end*, viz. individual holiness, very beautiful to hear, & very edifying to the rest of us, & to me particularly valuable as helping me to a clearer knowledge of what is in such minds as those of the Wilberforces on such subjects. This discussion went off into one as to whether philosophy tended—or should tend to make men believe *more*, or *less*, W. maintaining the former & S. the latter view; the Wilberforces both contending that philosophy enables one to give credit not only to all the Bible miracles but to a considerable scantling of the legends of saints & even of the Pagan prodigies besides.

You said in one of your letters to me, that Sterling's departure & mine had closed your philosophical season. I might almost say that the loss of Sterling & you had suspended mine, for till now when I have him again for a few days I have

---

[1]MS at the Wordsworth Trust, Dove Cottage, Grasmere. *Addressed:* Dr Calvert / Falmouth. *Postmark:* May 1840.
[2]See Letter 284.1, above.
[3]The Club, made up of Sterling's friends, was founded in 1838 after his return from Madeira; it met monthly for dinner and discussion. A list of forty-one members is given in Carlyle's *Life of Sterling* (London: Chapman and Hall, 1851), p. 208.
[4]Samuel Wilberforce (1805–73) was then rector of Brixton, Isle of Wight, and later prominent as Bishop of Oxford. His brother Robert (1802–57) was rector of East Farleigh, Kent, and then (in 1840) of Burton Agnes, Yorkshire; he later converted to Roman Catholicism. Neither is listed in the original membership of the Sterling Club.

thought but little on any of the topics on which we used to converse. I have indeed written no small number of pages on subjects of great importance viz. the "affairs of the Guicowar" and the "disputes between the Rao of Cutch and certain Wagur chiefs"[5]—with one considerable advantage over the more speculative topics which I have sometimes written about, that I can foresee much more exactly the effects with which my lucubrations will be attended. It would be vastly more agreeable if in writing on Bentham or Coleridge to a host of review readers[6] one could adopt the "Do this" style, with a prospect of being obeyed. (At this crisis I have made a great blot lower down the page, which I hope you will impute to the liveliness of my feelings.) My evenings have been employed in the tedious task of revising old review articles for republication[7]—taking the sharpness, or rather tartness, out of some of them, & alas! sacrificing some splendid passages because I find they are ignorant nonsense! but what goes to my heart most of all is, spoiling the music of some of my most rhythmical periods by the painful necessity of substituting one foot of truth for two of error or exaggeration: while the feelings which inspired the sentences being clean gone, any attempt to re-modulate them would only give rise to choice specimens of lumbering affectation. But as Swift would say, "as the old saying is, an ounce of sense is better than a pound of sound."[8]

A propos of review articles, if it comes in your way do read Stephen's review (in the last Edinburgh) of the writings of Isaac Taylor of Ongar, author of the "Natural History of Enthusiasm."[9] It is in great part made up of two *verae historiae*, viz. first a supposed Biography of the author, written twenty years hence, & next a supposed Autobiography *by* him, relating the particulars of his posthumous existence, & how he gets on in the sun, which it appears is to be the scene of our

---

[5]Two of Mill's Despatches from the Examiner's Office of the East India Company: "Affairs of the Guicowar" (2 July, 1840), partly printed in *PP*, 1852–53, LXIX, 259; and "Dispute between the Rao of Cutch and Certain Wagur Chiefs" (8 July, 1840); listed as Nos. 979 and 980 in *CW*, Vol. XXX, App. A.

[6]An allusion to Mill's well-known articles, "Bentham" and "Coleridge," in the *London and Westminster Review*, respectively VII & XXIX (Aug. 1838), 467–506 (in *Essays on Ethics, Religion, and Society*, *CW*, Vol. X [Toronto: University of Toronto Press, 1969], pp. 75–115), and XXXIII (Mar. 1840), 257–302 (in *CW*, Vol. X, pp. 117–63).

[7]On 6 April, 1842, Mill proposed to John William Parker a collection of his articles; nothing came of it, however, until 1859, when Parker brought out *Dissertations and Discussions* in two volumes. (A third was added in 1867, and a fourth, posthumously, in 1875.) For his later description of the revisions, see the "Preface" to *Dissertations and Discussions*, *CW*, Vol. X, pp. 493–4.

[8]Not located.

[9]James Stephen, "Works of the Author of the *Natural History of Enthusiasm*," *Edinburgh Review*, LXXI (Apr. 1840), 220–63, is ostensibly a review of *Physical Theory of Another Life. By the Author of "Natural History of Enthusiasm."* The invented title is ascribed to Isaac Taylor (1759–1829), engraver and later non-Conformist pastor of Ongar, author of practical as well as uplifting works for the young.

next stage of existence. Our souls no doubt continue to gravitate, while the centrifugal force perishes with our material integuments.

Sterling tells me you have been seen to eat "a potatoe"—if that is the cause of your not being in force, those are right who say that potatoes are poison, as is natural to the plants of the genus Solanum, natural family Solanaceae &c. &c.[10] I presume you add to your potatoe what Carlyle speaks of as "an unknown condiment named Point."[11] If you go to Penzance pray go to Lemorna Cove, the Logan stone, the Land's End, & St Just & pray do *not* go to Kynance, for I do not want to be the only person who has not been there. It will be very pleasant to see you in town.

ever yours truly
J.S. MILL

287.1. TO WILLIAM CABELL[1]

Ex. Off.
21 May 1840

Private
MY DEAR SIR

In the Political PC 2695 which either has been or will immediately be sent to you from the Court in the official form, you will find two material variations from the paragraphs which were originally sent to you. One is on the subject of the proposed reform of the Jyepore Army by the substitution for the greater part of it of a force under British officers:[2] this the Court are disposed to encourage provided it can be done without an abuse of our superior power; & on the whole I may say the Court are much more favourable than they had been until recently to Lord Auckland's view on the subject of bringing the armies of the native states under our control as

---

[10]As the *Encyclopedia Britannica*, 11th ed. explains, when potatoes lie above ground, "they become green and have an acrid taste, which renders them unpalatable to human beings, and as poisonous qualities are produced similar to those of many *Solanaceae* [e.g., henbane, deadly nightshade] they are unwholesome."

[11]*Sartor Resartus*, 2nd ed. (Boston: Munroe, 1837), p. 285 (Bk. III, Chap. x). The allusion is to Diogenes Teufelsdröckh's account of the sect of Drudges (as compared to the Dandies), who live on "Potatoes-and-Point." Teufelsdröckh pretends not to know the meaning of "Point," which derives from the poor "pointing" with their potato towards bacon, cheese, or other inaccessible extras, and then eating the potato ungarnished.

---

[1]MS in L/P&S/6/319, n.p. (before India Draft 286), India Office Library and Records. See *CW*, Vol. XXX, App. A, No. 251.

[2]The variations appear on pp. [496–500] of PC 2695, in L/P&S/6/319.

opportunities offer,[3] provided we avoid what would have been the effect of the proposed Oude Treaty viz. to make a prince pay a second time for what he had paid the full value for already.

The second alteration is in the paragraph respecting a misstatement by Moosherraf Begum of Joura affecting the character of Major Borthwick.[4] I enclose Copy of a Memorandum by Sir H. Willock,[5] concurred in by Mr Edmonstone, which will explain to you the reason of the alteration or rather omission in this instance.

yours ever truly
J.S. MILL

287.2. TO HENRY COLE[1]

[before 26 May 1840?]

DEAR COLE

I have read all the notices, & if certain corrections are made which I have suggested I think none of them will be any discredit to the review. Whether they will be of any use to it is a matter on which I retain my original opinion.[2]

J.S.M.

---

[3]The opinion of the Governor-General, George Eden (1784–1849), Earl of Auckland, is given *ibid.*, pp. 529–[30].

[4]The Begum had apparently accused Major W. Borthwick, Political Agent for Mehidpur, of misappropriating funds paid to the Government.

[5]A copy of the Memorandum from Henry Willock (1788/89–1858) follows Mill's letter, *ibid*. Both he and Neil Benjamin Edmonstone (1765–1841) were Directors of the Company.

---

[1]MS not located; typescript McCrimmon. Dated by Cole's participation in the editing of the *Westminster*, from which he withdrew after the June number, published on 26 May (Cole's diary).

[2]Mill had not favoured the introduction of the section headed "Critical and Miscellaneous Notices," though he contributed three notices to the September number; see *Essays on Philosophy and the Classics*, *CW*, Vol. XI (Toronto: University of Toronto Press, 1978), pp. 239–43; Vol. I, pp. 517–21; and Vol. XVIII, pp. 149–52.

289.1. TO THOMAS CARLYLE[1]

I.H.
Friday
[29 May, 1840]

MY DEAR CARLYLE

Can you & Mrs Carlyle[2] come to Kensington on Wednesday? not to dinner if you would rather not, but as early in the evening as you can. Barclay Fox & his father & mother & sisters will probably come at some time or other in the evening but I hope you will come whether they do or not.

ever faithfully
J.S. MILL

290.1. TO WILLIAM CABELL[1]

Ex. Office
12 June 1840

MY DEAR SIR

I am requested by Mr Edmonstone to send you a second memorandum on the Rohilla jageer of Rampore,[2] which he has prepared in conformity to the desire expressed in your note to Mr Melvill[3] of the 27th ulto. He also desires me to say that it would have been prepared sooner, but that other business claimed his prior attention.

Ever yours, etc
(signed) J.S. MILL

---

[1]MS in the Varnhagen von Ense Collection, Jagiellonian Library, Cracow. *Addressed:* Thomas Carlyle Esq. / 5 Cheyne Row / Chelsea.
Dated from Caroline Fox, *Memories of Old Friends*, 2nd ed., 2 vols. (London: Smith, Elder, 1882), Vol. I, pp. 203–4, where she describes an evening with the Carlyles at the Mills' Kensington home on Wednesday, 3 June, 1840.
[2]Jane Baillie Carlyle (née Welsh) (1801–66).

---

[1]MS copy in L/P&S/6/318, n.p. (before India Draft 165), India Office Library and Records. See *CW*, Vol. XXX, App. A, No. 239.
[2]"Memorandum on the Distinctive Character of the Rampore Jageer and on the Equity and Policy of Resuming or Continuing It after the Decease of the Present Head of the Rohillas, the Nawab Ahmed Alli Khaun," dated 10 June, 1840, and signed by Edmonstone, follows Mill's letter in L/P&S/6/318, n.p.
[3]James Cosmo Melvill (1792–1861) held the most senior position in the Home Establishment as Secretary of the Company.

290.2. TO WILLIAM CABELL[1]

Ex. Off.
13 June 1840

MY DEAR SIR

I have just discovered to my great mortification that by some gross & untraceable blunder in this office, the Guicowar PC which was borrowed in consequence of the last arrivals was sent to the Board again verbatim the same as before, instead of a greatly altered PC which I prepared & which the Chairs[2] sanctioned. Nothing can now be done but to send at once the altered paragraphs to you, which ought to have been sent a month ago, & I apologize for the needless trouble occasioned to you by one of the absurdest pieces of official negligence I have ever known of.

Yours ever truly
J.S. MILL

290.3. TO ROBERT WERE FOX[1]

I.H.
Monday
[about 14 June, 1840?]

MY DEAR SIR

Nichol bids me "tell Mr Fox that he will do me a great service by taking the construction of that instrument entirely into his own hands & making it what he thinks it ought to be. I do not at all care for a few pounds."[2]

Calvert is staying near Sevenoaks with his convalescent sister,[3] & bids me tell you that his absence there prevents his calling upon you.

ever yours truly
J.S. MILL

---

[1] MS in L/P&S/6/319, n.p. (after Bombay PC 2726), India Office Library and Records. See *CW*, Vol. XXX, App. A, No. 979.
[2] Jenkins and Bayley (see Letter 281.1 above) served for two consecutive years.

---

[1] MS in the possession of Professor Arnold Heertje, University of Amsterdam.
[2] The letter from John Pringle Nichol has not been located. During 1840, Nichol was commissioning new equipment for the Glasgow observatory. The matter had evidently been discussed during the Foxs' recent visit to London. Cf. *CW*, Vol. XIII, p. 436. Robert Were Fox was an inventor of scientific instruments.
[3] Mary Stanger (1804–90), John Calvert's younger sister.

293.1. TO AN UNIDENTIFIED CORRESPONDENT[1]

India House
Thursday
[after July 1840?]

MY DEAR SIR—Mr Hickson will be very happy to receive your article, & it will reach him if addressed W.E. Hickson Esq. care of Mr Lunford, East Temple Chambers, Whitefriars Street.[2]

very faithfully yours
J.S. MILL

294.1. TO WILLIAM CABELL[1]

Ex. Off.
2d Septr 1840

MY DEAR SIR

The Rampore papers will be taken into consideration immediately. The Governor General[2] takes Mr Edmonstone's view as to the expediency of continuing the Jageer in the Rohilla family[3] but has adopted, apparently without much examination, a different opinion from Mr Edmonstone as to the eventual rights of the Oude State.

Ever truly yours
J.S. MILL

294.2. TO WILLIAM CABELL[1]

Ex. Off.
2d Septr 1840

MY DEAR SIR

The reference has been made to the Company's Counsel and the Queen's

---

[1]MS at the Ueno Library, Kyoto City, Japan. Dated from Henry Cole's withdrawal from his association with Hickson in the *London and Westminster* during July (Cole's diary).
[2]Not further identified.

---

[1]MS in L/P&S/6/318, n.p. (before India Draft 165), India Office Library and Records. See *CW*, Vol. XXX, App. A, No. 239.
[2]See Letter 287.1 above.
[3]See Letter 290.1 above.

---

[1]MS in L/P&S/6/320, n.p. (before India Draft 624, by Cabell, which comments on this letter), India Office Library and Records. See *CW*, Vol. XXX, App. A, No. 260.

Advocate General,² but as yet we have not received their answer. It was not supposed that the paragraph would be affected by it & any additional instructions can be sent hereafter if required.

While I am writing I will say one word respecting the Board's addition to paragraph 64 of PC 2810, respecting the Bhonsla's villages in the Nizam's country.³ It strikes me that the plan suggested by the Board would never answer. *We* could manage the villages of a native prince & pay over the revenues to him, because he can trust us—besides he *must*. But they never trust one another, & there is no instance among them I believe of a joint property in which the agents of both sharers do not exercise a right of joint management. It must end therefore in our managing the villages for both governments; which neither would like.

Would it not be better to refer to the Govt of India as a general question, the possibility of negotiating an arrangement by which the double Revenue agency might be avoided?

ever truly yours
J.S. MILL

296.1. TO WILLIAM CABELL[1]

Ex. Off.
29th Septr 1840

MY DEAR SIR

With reference to the India Political P.C. 2810, & to the paragraphs in it which relate to the Bhonsla's Deshmooky rights in the Nizam's territory;[2] in addition to the remarks which I took the liberty of privately communicating to you on the subject of the proposed commutation of those rights, it may be added that no such commutation could possibly satisfy the Nagpore Raja.[3] It is not the money, but the tenure, as an ancient family possession, that he is solicitous about; & no money grant would compensate for the cession of a privilege venerated for its antiquity.

There is another alteration made by the Board in the same P.C. which appears founded on a misapprehension; I allude to the subject of the Title offered by Shah

---

²Sergeant Spankie was Standing Counsel to the East India Company, and George Grey (1799–1882) was Judge Advocate General at this time.

³Paragraph 64, relating to villages within the territory of Nasir-ud-Daula, Nizam of Hyderabad (ruled 1829–57), in which the chief of "the Bhoonslah family" had hereditary rights to revenue, and the Board's addition to it, are in L/P&S/6/320, pp. 395–[8a].

---

[1]MS in L/P&S/6/320, n.p. (before India Draft 624 and Letter 294.2 above), India Office Library and Records. See *CW*, Vol. XXX, App. A, No. 260.

[2]See Letter 294.2 above.

[3]Raghuji III (1818–53).

Shooja to Sir C. Wade[4] which it would seem the Board conceive to be of the nature of those honours which can only be accepted by express permission of the Sovereign. This applies to *Orders*, Decorations etc but not to *Titles*, which have been very often conferred upon Company's Servants without any other mention than that of their own Government at Calcutta. The King of Delhi[5] used to create, almost as a matter of course, the officer who was the organ of communication with him, a something ool Moolk or ood Dowla etc etc.

ever yours truly
J.S. MILL

308.1. TO WILLIAM CABELL[1]

Ex. Off.
14 Jany 1841

MY DEAR SIR

With reference to your note dated this day[2] respecting para 8 of PC 2954; I had not overlooked the opinion of Mr Sutherland[3] which you mention; but it appeared to me that the reasons originally given for transferring the Kunkraj Zillah to the charge of the Agent at Pahlunpore,[4] were strong, & the only valid reason against it seemed to be that mentioned by Capt Lang[5] in p. 34 of the Colln, which is of a temporary nature and depending upon the fact the Pahlunpore Agent is at present virtual manager of the Pahlunpore country.

Believe me, my dear Sir
Very truly yours
J.S. MILL

---

[4]The first Afghan War, in 1839, had resulted from Lord Auckland's attempt to restore to power Shah Shuja (1780–1842), the exiled King of Afghanistan. Lieutenant-Colonel Claude Martine Wade (1794–1861) had had singular success in forcing the Khyber Pass and capturing Kabul.

[5]Mill is presumably thinking of Akbar II, who was titular ruler of the district 1806–37.

[1]MS in L/P&S/6/322, n.p. (before Bombay PC 2954), India Office Library and Records. See *CW*, Vol. XXX, App. A, No. 988.

[2]Cabell's letter immediately precedes Mill's in L/P&S/6/322.

[3]James Sutherland, Political Agent in Gujerat.

[4]The matter of the transfer of the zillah, or district, is raised in paragraph 8, pp. 169–[70], *ibid*.

[5]James Strachan Lang, Political Agent in the Mahi Kantha.

321.1. TO HENRY COLE[1]

I.H.
Friday
[11 June, 1841]

DEAR COLE

I hope you will come to the Kensington Anti Corn Law meeting at the King's Arms on Tuesday evening at half past five.[2]

yours ever
J.S. MILL

322.1. TO RICHARD BENTLEY[1]

India House
8th July 1841

Mr Mill presents his compliments to Mr Bentley and has the pleasure of inclosing a letter which he has just received from Professor Nichol on the subject of the proposition which he made some time ago through Mr Mill respecting the copyright of his astronomical & other writings.[2]

---

[1] MS in the University of Iowa Library, Iowa City.
[2] At the meeting, on Tuesday, 15 June, a petition for free trade written by Mill was approved. For the petition, which was printed in the *Morning Chronicle* on 17 June, p. 6, see *CW*, Vol. V, pp. 761–3, and Vol. XXIV, pp. 803–6. Mill "had a great share in getting up the public meeting" (*CW*, Vol. XIII, p. 478), which was described in the *Spectator*, 19 June, p. 580.

---

[1] MS in the William R. Perkins Library, Duke University.
Richard Bentley (1794–1871), publisher.
[2] Nothing is known of Mill's earlier approach on this matter, and the effort seems to have been fruitless.

339.1. TO THOMAS N. WATERFIELD[1]

Ex. Off.
16th Jan 1842

MY DEAR SIR

I answer your questions respecting Draft 356 under considerable disadvantages from not having the Collection to refer to. But I think I can answer them tolerably correctly.

The reason why I draw a distinction between the Myhee Caunta division & the other ceded possessions is that Capt. Carnac then Rest at Baroda who negotiated the treaty[2] says expressly in his letter of 16th August 1817[3] "The cession does not include any part of the dues from the Myhee Caunta division including Pahlunpore & Ballasmore which remain with the Guicowar under his accession to the late Treaty with H.H. the Paishwa."[4] The Ghans Dana from the M.C. division must therefore be deemed to have been distinctly & purposely withheld from us. It appears however that under the Partition Treaty between the Guicowar & the Peshwa the G. never had really any right to this Ghans Dana & therefore his not waiving a claim which was never well grounded, did not constitute any reason for our paying him the exactions in question. Still, we have paid them & are therefore estopped from disputing the right.

But in regard to the other ceded possessions the G. did not himself claim to have any right to Ghans Dana subsequently to the Treaty, & if he had any clearly alienated it in our favour by the Treaty. If therefore we had ever paid Ghans Dana (which we did not) it would be no disputable point but a manifest oversight & would not therefore, I conceive, have been binding upon us after we found out that he had expressly renounced the claim.

ever yours
J.S. MILL

---

[1] MS in L/P&S/6/328, n.p. (before Bombay Draft 356), India Office Library and Records. See *CW*, Vol. XXX, App. A, No. 1015.
Thomas Nelson Waterfield (1799–1862), Cabell's successor as Senior Clerk in the Secret and Political Department.

[2] "Treaty with the Peishwah, Dated 13th June, 1817," *PP*, 1818, XI, 346–50, concluded an agreement among Baji Rao II (1775–1851?), Peshwa of the Marathas, Arnand Rao, Gaikwar of Baroda (ruled 1800–1819), and the East India Company.

[3] A copy of James Rivett Carnac's letter immediately follows Mill's in L/P&S/6/328; the following quotation is on p. 41.

[4] "Treaty between the East India Company and the Peshwa, Concluded at Bassein, the 31st December, 1802," *PP*, 1803–04, XII, 90–3.

342.1. TO AN UNIDENTIFIED CORRESPONDENT[1]

I.H.
Wedy
[23 Feb., 1842?]

I find scarcely anybody is going tomorrow whom you would probably care to see, except Peacock & Dr Royle.[2]

As you were doubtful before, this will probably decide you, & it therefore decides me—in the negative.

J.S.M.

If you have not engaged your name to any visitor for the Pol. Ec. club next Thursday will you give it to Charles Buller & me for Monckton Milnes?

352.1. TO JOHN WILLIAM PARKER[1]

India House
13th April 1842

MY DEAR SIR

On further consideration of the suggestion I threw out in my last note to you, on the subject of gratis copies of the book on Logic, I do not think it would be quite fair to you in the shape in which it first occurred to me.[2] What I am now inclined to propose is that whatever copies I wish to give away may be debited to me at trade price, & in the event of there being any profit, that the half profit which you so liberally offer may be set against those copies, & if there be a balance against me I shall be happy to pay it. If there should fortunately be a balance on the other side of the account I have no desire to receive it, but am perfectly ready without any such

---

[1]MS in the Houghton Library, Harvard University. Dated tentatively by the postscript. Richard Monckton Milnes, known to Mill from about 1840, attended the meeting of the Political Economy Club (of which he never became a member) on 3 March, 1842, when Mill, but not Buller, attended.

[2]For Peacock, see Letter 237.2, above. John Forbes Royle (1799–1858), surgeon and naturalist, who shared Mill's botanical interests, was in charge of East India Company correspondence relating to vegetable production.

---

[1]MS in the William R. Perkins Library, Duke University.
John William Parker (1792–1870), printer and publisher, who had agreed to bring out Mill's *A System of Logic, Ratiocinative and Inductive* (published February 1843); *CW*, Vols. VII–VIII (Toronto: University of Toronto Press, 1973). Parker remained Mill's publisher until the business was transferred to Longman in 1864.

[2]In his earlier letter to Parker (*CW*, Vol. XIII, p. 514), Mill mentioned "some 25 or 30 copies."

condition to engage that if there be another edition you shall have the refusal of it on the terms you propose.

ever yours
J.S. MILL

What time will suit you best for beginning to print?

372.1. TO JOHN WILLIAM PARKER[1]

India House
26th Septr 1842

MY DEAR SIR,

The page[2] will I think do very well, except that there is not quite margin enough for the quantity of letterpress, but that I suppose will be amended.

I have returned the proof to your office, corrected, & shall be able to go on steadily.

I have been requested by two gentlemen to have the sheets sent to them: the one wishes to translate the book into French,[3] the other is under engagement to review it in the *Edinburgh Review*.[4] As they are both living abroad I can only send to them as opportunities occur & as I also wish to have the sheets for myself as they are struck off, I shall be much obliged if you will direct three sets to be sent to me regularly.

very truly yours
J.S. MILL

---

[1]MS at Kokugakuin University, Tokyo.

[2]I.e., the layout of the pages for Mill's *System of Logic*.

[3]Sheets were sent to Armand Marrast (1801–52), who had edited *La Tribune* and *Le National*, but whom Mill correctly thought would not complete the work (see *CW*, Vol. XIII, pp. 587 and 632). No French version appeared until 1886, when the 6th ed. was translated by Louis Peisse.

[4]John Austin, then living in Prussia, had proposed to review the *System of Logic* in the *Edinburgh Review* (see *CW*, Vol. XIII, pp. 527–8); he failed to do so, and no review ever appeared in the *Edinburgh*.

374.1. TO JOHN MITCHELL KEMBLE[1]

India House
12th October, 1842

MY DEAR SIR

If you are still of the same mind in regard to Mr Potter's article on Socrates, would you be kind enough to leave it at the publisher's for him?[2]

very truly yours

J.S. MILL

386.1. TO THOMAS CARLYLE[1]

[February 1843]

I send what I can, viz. Bentham, my father, Brougham, & four others, which you can send if you think Varnhagen will care for them, viz. Ram Mohun Roy, Sir Alex. Burnes, Lords Lansdowne & Palmerston.[2]

Yours ever

J.S. MILL

---

[1] MS in the possession of Professor Toshio Ohfuchi, Nihon University, Tokyo.

[2] Apparently Kemble had indicated unwillingness to publish the article, which Mill had forwarded to him (see *CW*, Vol. XIII, p. 515), by John Phillips Potter (1793–1861). He changed his mind, however, and "The Philosophy of Socrates" appeared in the *British and Foreign Review*, XIV (Feb. 1843), 289–333. The publisher was Richard Taylor (1781–1858).

---

[1] MS in the Varnhagen von Ense Collection, Jagiellonian Library, Cracow. Dated by the librarian.

[2] Mill is replying to Carlyle's request for autographs, on behalf of Karl August Varnhagen von Ense (1785–1858), Prussian diplomat and biographer. The autographs are, in addition to those identified above, of Henry Peter Brougham (1778–1868), judge and prolific writer; Ram Mohun Roy (1774–1833), Indian reformer, who became known to the Bentham circle while on visits to England; Alexander Burnes (1805–41), a political officer in India who travelled extensively, and was killed in an Afghan uprising; Henry Petty-Fitzmaurice (1780–1863), Marquis of Lansdowne, prominent Whig statesman; and Henry John Temple (1784–1865), Viscount Palmerston, an even more prominent Whig politician.

415.1. TO WILLIAM EMPSON[1]

[December 1843]

Sir—When I requested the Editor of the Ed. Review to insert a contradiction of the assertions in the article on Bentham in the October number, I did not ground my request on relationship, nor did I use the terms father & "son"—the word father, where it occurs in the letter, was inserted by Mr Napier[2]—I was actuated solely by a sense of justice, & your polite acknowledgment of regret for any pain you have caused me in no degree alters my opinion of the merits of the article in question.

I am Sir your obt Servt

J.S. MILL

420.1. TO THOMAS N. WATERFIELD[1]

Ex. Off.
29 Jany 1844

MY DEAR SIR

With reference to Mr Stark's letter to me on the subject of PC 4194[2] (respecting the proposed Pension Fund for the Nizam's local officers) it seems to me there is a misapprehension respecting the nature of the proposition which is *now* before the Court.

There will not, in the present plan, be any annual subscriptions from the

---

[1]MS in the Hill Memorial Library, Louisiana State University, Baton Rouge. Headed in Mill's hand: "Copy of my letter to Empson in answer to his disclaimer of intention to offend—December 1843."

William Empson (1791–1852), later editor of the *Edinburgh Review* 1847–52, author of "Jeremy Bentham," *Edinburgh Review*, LXXVIII (Oct. 1843), 460–516, which provoked Mill's "Letter to the Editor of the *Edinburgh Review* on James Mill," *ibid.*, LXXIX (Jan. 1844), 267–71 (in *CW*, Vol. I, pp. 533–8).

[2]Macvey Napier (1776–1847) was then editor of the *Edinburgh Review*; Mill wrote to him on 14 October, 1843, asking that a reply to Empson's article be printed (*CW*, Vol. XIII, pp. 598–9). At the end of the first paragraph of Mill's article, as printed, appeared: "I mean the late Mr. James Mill, my father." "Son" does not appear in the article, but does in the accompanying editorial note; see *CW*, Vol. I, p. 536.

---

[1]MS in L/P&S/6/334, n.p. (before India PC 4194), India Office Library and Records. See *CW*, Vol. XXX, App. A, No. 374.

[2]A copy of the letter from Hugh Stark, Assistant Secretary and Senior Clerk in the Revenue Department, immediately precedes Mill's in L/P&S/6/334.

officers, no more than there are to the Civil Annuity Fund in Bengal,[3] which is the model that has been followed in the proposed arrangements. The fund will be formed by the Nizam's annual contribution & its interest, together with the payment which each officer will make on accepting the annuity viz one half its computed value.

In reality the plan is simply one by which the Nizam's Govt would grant pensions to the local officers, not gratuitously but on payment of one half their value[4] computed at 9 per cent interest which is a very low rate compared with that which the Nizam's Govt habitually pays:[5] & even at that rate it could only cost the Nizam (according to the McGriffith Davies calculations) a few hundred rupees a year over & above the 12000 RS which his Govt has already expressed willingness to pay.[6]

I apprehend that there would be in the nature of the case an implied guarantee on the part of the British Govt to the intent, that if the Nizam *promised* this boon to the officers he would not afterwards break his promise without a breach of faith with us. But the engagement would be so little onerous that there would be small temptation to break it.[7]

very truly yours

J.S. MILL

427.1. TO THE FINANCE AND HOME COMMITTEE[1]

Examiner's Office
India House
9th April 1844

I certify that the education of George Grote Mill[2] has been under my exclusive

---

[3] Above the line, in pencil, is "A," keyed to a note at the foot of the page, in another hand: "This is, I imagine, a mistake—five per cent is deducted from all salaries on account of the Fund."

[4] In the same hand, interlined in pencil: "then—the other half is given gratuitously—".

[5] Similar interlineation: "because its credit is so bad that people will not lend to it at a lower rate."

[6] Similar interlineation: "rather, which Chundoo Loll, at that time, was willing to promise—".

[7] Similar interlineation over the last sentence: "that is—we should make him pay —consequently we give our guarantee—but these officers cannot be allowed to have the advantage of both Hydrabad interest & British security."

---

[1] MS in L/F/2/82, No. 31 of April 1844, India Office Library and Records.

[2] George Grote Mill (ca. 1825–53), Mill's youngest brother, who served in the Home Establishment of the East India Company from 1844–48, when he moved to Madeira, on account of ill health.

superintendance during the last seven years, with the exception of short intervals: that his conduct & character have always been excellent & that his acquirements considerably surpass the average of well educated youths.

J.S. MILL

438.1. TO JOHN MITCHELL KEMBLE[1]

India House
22d Aug. 1844

MY DEAR MR KEMBLE

I accept very thankfully the additional time which you give me.[2]

Masson is I think a young man of great promise & even the faults of his stile are not of a discouraging kind—but he is not yet out of his apprenticeship. If you return his article I will offer to *edite* it for him & make it if possible admissible.[3]

I have some, but a very slight knowledge of Thommerel,[4] but I do not know where he is to be found at present. Four years ago his address at Paris was 34 Rue des Postes.

Very truly yours
J.S. MILL

J.M. Kemble Esq

447.1. TO JOHN AUSTIN[1]

Extract B

I.H.
30th Decr. 1844

MY DEAR AUSTIN

I have been hoping for some time to hear from you finally about the pecuniary

---

[1]MS in the Reed Collection, Dunedin Public Library, New Zealand. Published in *MNL*, XXIII (Winter 1988), 23, edited by Eric W. Nye.
[2]Mill had offered to Kemble the article that eventually appeared as "Duveyrier's Political Views of French Affairs," not in the *British and Foreign Review* but in the *Edinburgh Review*, LXXXII (Apr. 1846), 435–74 (in *CW*, Vol. XX, pp. 295–316); see *CW*, Vol. XIII, pp. 627 and 632–3.
[3]Mill had earlier written to Kemble to introduce David Masson (1822–1907), a Scot who became a prominent man of letters. No article by him appeared in the *British and Foreign Review*, though he proposed one on Wallace; see *CW*, Vol. XIII, p. 628.
[4]J.P. Thommerel published in the 1830s and 1840s on English prose and poetry.

---

[1]MS in the Yale University Library consists of a single page, containing two extracts in an unknown hand, headed respectively, as here, "Extract B" and "A" (see Letter 447.2 below), with a page of accounts verso.

matter & get it finally settled, & I have thought it might be facilitated by my sending you a statement of the various receipts & disbursements in case the principle you adopt for fixing the Interest should require them. [See other side]² (The rest of the letter regards some of the items & does not require to be copied.)

Very truly yours

J.S. MILL

Receipts		Payments	
22 July '36	3791. 6. 7	22 July 36	100. 0. 0
23	605.16.11		198. 0. 8
27	47. 2. 6	23	31.10. 0
18 Nov.	47. 5. 0		7.12.10½
7 Dec.	95. 2. 9		14.14. 4½
10	4. 0. 0		8. 3.10
12	. 2. 0	24	54. 9. 6
22	324. 6. 6	24	31. 6. 0
24	9. 9. 0	27	11.12.11
10 Jany '37	47. 2. 6	28	1. 7. 9
5 Feby	312. 9. 6	18 Nov.	17.11. 8
27 Jun	9.10. 0	19	1.13. 4
10 Jun	2.19. 4	26	6.16. 5
19	3.19. 0	1 Dec.	41.14. 0
25 May '38	95. 5. 0	3 Jny 37	1. 9. 0
1 Aug.	47. 2. 6	21	35.14. 0
18 Dr.	94.12. 0	2 Mar.	4. 4. 2
5 July '39	16.16. 0	27	9.
13	94. 5. 0	10 June	39.14. 4
22 Nov.	94.12. 0	29 July	21. 0. 0
20 Jny '40	47. 2. 6	8 Aug.	13.10. 0
23 Apʳ	16. 7. 3	19	15. 0. 0
30 Apʳ	5. 0. 0	7 Nov.	41.16. 0
8 Aug.	47. 2. 6	14 Dec.	81.15. 2
3 July '41	47. 2. 6	12 Jny '38	80. 5. 6
26 July	47. 2. 6	18 June	2. 0. 4
10 July '42	47. 2. 6	17 Oct.	7.15. 0
18 July	47.15. 1	19 Dec.	14. 0. 0
20 July '43	45.15. 1	5 July '39	5. 5. 1
17 July '44	45.15. 1	19 Oct.	7.16. 0
21 Aug.	94.12. 0	9 Jny '40	1. 1. 6
21 Nov.	13.10. 0	5 May	1.10. 0
Still to be rec'd	89. 7. 7	22 June	2.10. 6
	£6382.13. 9		

---

²This square-bracketed note by the copyist refers to the accounts.

Payments [cont'd]

4 July	1. 4. 6
3 Feby '41	20. 4. 9
9 June	34. 6. 6
10 Jny '42	10.14. 0
3 Feby	10.10. 0
19 Feby '42	10.16. 0
1 Mar.	10.10. 0
21 Mar.	10.10. 0
22 Apl.	10.10. 0
20 Aug.	10.10. 0
20 June	10.10. 0
21	1. 1. 6
5 Sept.	1. 5. 4
10 Feby '43	6. 0. 0
17 Mar.	3. 0. 0
2 June	4. 6. 0
30 Oct.	2.13. 0
6 Feby '44	2. 0. 0
9 June	2. 0. 0
13 Sept.	2. 0. 0
	1069. 0. 0

447.2. TO JOHN AUSTIN[1]

A

India House
Tuesday*

MY DEAR AUSTIN

After my interview with you I have never felt much doubt as to what Kindersley's[2] opinion would be; but I should like to know why the Interest is fixed at 4 per Cent, a rate which certainly cd not have been obtained in the 3 per cents, since it implies their price to be 75. When as you are aware they have been during the whole period varying only from about 90 to 100, their present price.

It is necessary also to determine how the Interest is to be calculated. Is it to be made up to the end of each year & added to the principal, i.e. is compound Interest to be given? or, is Interest to be charged upon each item from the date of its receipt? Is a balance in hand to be allowed &c. &c.

Yours ever
J.S. MILL

[1] See Letter 447.1, n1.
Copyist's note: There is no other date; but the note was clearly written subsequently to Kindersley's opinion.
[2] Richard Torin Kindersley (1792–1879), a barrister, K.C. 1835, active in Chancery.

455.1. TO [JOHN HAMILTON THOM?][1]

India House
1st March 1845

MY DEAR SIR

An elderly lady[2] from whom I once submitted to you some manuscripts for publication, which did not suit you, having heard of your new Magazine has asked me to offer to you the inclosed papers for it.[3] I have not read them but I know her to be a meritorious person & very much in want of anything, however small, which she might be able to earn by her pen.

Very truly yours
J.S. MILL

468.1. TO AN UNIDENTIFIED CORRESPONDENT[1]

India House
Tuesday
26th Augt [1845]

MY DEAR SIR

Having just returned to town I have found your note — written I know not how long ago, as there is no date or postmark. Will you be kind enough to inform me whether the letter you ask me to write will still be useful.

Very truly yours
J.S. MILL

---

[1] MS in the Bodleian Library.
John Hamilton Thom (1808–94) had founded, with James Martineau and John James Tayler, the *Prospective Review* in February 1845. He had previously edited the *Christian Teacher*, and while that seems an unlikely place for Mill to submit manuscripts, Thom was known to Mill through Joseph Blanco White.
[2] Not identified.
[3] If the identification of Thom is correct, and if any of the "papers" were accepted, the most likely article is "The White Lady and Undine," *Prospective Review*, I (May 1845), 275–82.

---

[1] MS in the Pierpont Morgan Library, watermarked 1844. Since 26 August was a Tuesday in 1845, that is the likely year.

[Oct. 1845] To Henry Reeve

473.1. TO HENRY REEVE[1]

India House
Wedy
[after 24 Oct., 1845]

MY DEAR REEVE

I have quite given up dining out, but I hope to see both you & Beaumont[2] at the India House.

I am afraid the letter which will be written to the Govt of India about Capt. Taylor will be virtually this—"do as you please, on your own responsibility. We praised Capt Taylor but we did not mean you to keep him unless you like."[3] However as his removal is suspended, I do not think there is much danger of its taking effect.

Yours ever truly
J.S. MILL

508.2. TO [JAMES?] HUTCHINSON[1]

73 Eccleston Square
June 26 1847

Mr Mill presents his compliments to Mr Hutchinson, & begs to mention that he is much obliged by his interesting work having been transmitted to him, but that Mr Mill's department being *wholly unconnected with* the subject, Mr Mill did not

---

[1]MS in the Pierpont Morgan Library. Dated by a letter from Beaumont to Alexis de Tocqueville of the same date.

Henry Reeve (1813–95), nephew of Sarah Austin, was from 1837 an official of the Judicial Committee of the Privy Council.

[2]Gustave Auguste de Beaumont de la Bonninière (1802–66), writer on social and political topics, was visiting London for a week or two.

[3]Philip Meadows Taylor (1808–76), a cousin of Reeve's, in the military service of the East India Company, had been Resident in Shorapore after pacifying it in 1841. An unsuccessful attempt was made in 1845 to replace him as Resident by a member of the Company's civil service. See two earlier letters to Reeve on this matter, *CW*, Vol. XIII, pp. 680–1.

---

[1]MS, in Harriet Taylor's hand, in the possession of Professor Arnold Heertje, University of Amsterdam.

James Hutchinson, a surgeon, may be the person addressed; he was author of *A Report of the Medical Management of the Native Jails throughout the Territories Subject to the Governments of Fort William and Agra* (Calcutta, 1835), which was republished in 1845 as *Observations on the General and Medical Management of Indian Jails*.

immediately direct his attention to Mr Hutchinson's communication for which he begs that he will have the goodness to excuse him.

513.1. TO JOHN WILLIAM PARKER[1]

India House
15 Nov. 1847

DEAR SIR—Not having received any answer to my note of the 27th of last month, I suppose it must have miscarried. If you have received it, I must request an immediate answer to it.

Yours truly
J.S. MILL

530.1. TO THOMAS STORY SPEDDING[1]

India House
31st August 1848

DEAR SIR

I beg to acknowledge the receipt of your pamphlet on the Poor Laws, & of the very flattering letter which accompanied it.[2] I am much gratified that you should have found in my Political Economy, or in my other writings, anything which appeared to you to deserve being so spoken of.

Your pamphlet, and particularly the concluding letter of the series, contains much in which I heartily concur, & which I think likely to be very useful.[3] Of all contained in it, the thing which seems to me especially valuable is the strong recognition of the very early & very low state of advancement in which civilized society now is, compared with what may one day be realized, & may already be reasonably aimed at. It is probable that a greater amount of alteration in existing opinions & institutions, than you contemplate, would be included in my idea of

---

[1] MS in the Houghton Library, Harvard University.
On 27 October, 1847, Mill had written to Parker concerning the contractual arrangements for his *Principles of Political Economy*; see *CW*, Vol. XIII, pp. 723–4. Another letter to Parker, in *CW*, Vol. XVII, p. 2006, with the conjectural date of November 1847, is evidently the first of this series, and should probably be dated 25 October.

---

[1] MS in the possession of Mr. John Spedding, Mirehouse, Keswick.
Thomas Story Spedding (1800–70), lawyer, author of *Letters on the Poor-Laws* (London: printed Odell, 1847).
[2] The letter has not been located.
[3] Letter VIII, "The Prospects of Society," *Letters on the Poor-Laws*, pp. 51–81.

this possible & desirable improvement; but I am happy to find that we completely agree in thinking that neither individuals nor classes can expect permanently to retain any power or influence except by taking a lead in promoting this great object.

On the more especial subject of the pamphlet, I sympathize entirely in the feelings which make you desire that the conditions of relief should be made less onerous to those who wish to maintain themselves, but cannot, than to those who can, but will not.[4] But in regard to the ablebodied I can see at present no means of sifting the one class from the other, except by making the conditions such that no one will accept relief who can possibly do without it. I suspect that the present poor law is the best possible, *as* a mere poor law; that any nearer approach to abstract justice is not to be had in a poor law, & must wait for a revision of social arrangements more fundamental than poor laws. I think it likely that society will ultimately take the increase of the human race under a more direct controul than is consistent with present ideas; in which case an unlimited "droit au travail"[5] for all who are born, as well as many other things, would not be the chimeras which they seem to be in the present state of opinion & feeling.

I am, Dear Sir
Yours faithfully
J.S. MILL

530.2. TO EDWIN CHADWICK[1]

India House
Thursday
[September 1848?]

MY DEAR CHADWICK

I delayed sending you the notice you asked for because I rather fancied

---

[4]See, e.g., *ibid.*, p. 34.
[5]Established by the short-lived Provisional Government in Paris after the Revolution of 1848; see *Le Moniteur Universel*, 26 Feb., 1848, p. 503.

---

[1]MS at University College London.
The paper is watermarked 1848, the year when Chadwick was seeking an appointment for Alexander Bain (1818–1903), Mill's chief Scottish disciple, to the Metropolitan Sanitary Commission. In the absence of other information it may be hypothesized that the reference is to Mill's "Bain's On the Application of Science to Human Health and Well-being," *Examiner*, 2 Sept. 1848, p. 565 (in *CW*, Vol. XXV, pp. 1118–20), a laudatory review of Bain's *On the Application of Science to Human Health and Well-being* (London and Glasgow: Griffin, 1848). Chadwick believed that Bain's work would help establish his credentials for the position—which he did not receive (Bain, *Autobiography* [London: Longmans, Green, 1904], p. 197n).

(erroneously as it now appears) that its anonymousness might be inconsistent with the intentions you had in asking for it.

ever yours
J.S. MILL

ADDITIONAL LATER LETTERS
1849–1873

Additional Later Letters

16A. TO HUGH STARK[1]

East India House
13 June 1849

Mr Mill presents his compliments to Mr Stark & by desire of the Chairman & Deputy Chairman[2] transmits in P.C. a draft in duplicate of a Report by the Political & Military Committee respecting the case of Mr Alexander Maclean.[3] 1 collection containing 49 pages accompanies the Draft.

16B. TO THOMAS N. WATERFIELD[1]

[?22 June 1849]

In Maclean's Case, the Chairman thinks that the course which the Court have taken, *is* a middle course—in as much as Mr Maclean's position in being compelled to resign, and retire with disgrace, although not a rich but a ruined man, is very different from that of a servant retiring on an independence at his own choice. The annuity, if he gets it, will, I fancy, benefit nobody but his creditors. No other middle course seemed possible, except to dismiss him, and give him a pension from the Court—which could not have been charged on the Annuity Fund, and this was deemed objectionable.

---

[1]MS copy in L/P&S/6/359, n.p. (before Madras PC 6649), India Office Library and Records. See *CW*, Vol. XXX, App. A, No. 869, and Letter 16B below.
For Stark, see Letter 420.1 above.
[2]Archibald Galloway (ca. 1780–1850) and John Shepherd (d. 1859) were Chairman and Deputy Chairman of the Court of Directors at this time.
[3]Maclean, of the Madras Board of Revenue, had been charged with being improperly implicated in loans to the Nawab of the Carnatic.

---

[1]MS copy in L/P&S/6/359, n.p. (before Madras PC 6649), India Office Library and Records. See *CW*, Vol. XXX, App. A, No. 869, and Letter 16A above. Dated prior to the Board's meeting, on Maclean's case.

23A. TO JOHN WILLIAM PARKER[1]

India House
21st Jany 1850

DEAR SIR—I regarded your insertion of an attack on an article which had appeared in Fraser,[2] as a favour done to me rather than as the opposite, & I think it quite unfair that I should be paid for it—I therefore return the cheque with thanks & am

yours truly
J.S. MILL

78A. TO JOHN WILLIAM PARKER[1]

India House
May 4. [1852]

DEAR SIR

I was not aware that you wished for a letter today & have not had time to write one, but I will send a few lines tomorrow.[2] I am

yours truly
J.S. MILL

87A. TO JOHN CHAPMAN[1]

East India House
Nov. 8. 1852

DEAR SIR

The beginning of the session[2] seems so little likely to afford materials or an

---

[1] MS in the Pierpont Morgan Library.
[2] Parker, the proprietor and publisher of *Fraser's Magazine* 1847–60, had inserted Mill's "The Negro Question" in *Fraser's*, XLI (Jan. 1850), 25–31 (in *CW*, Vol. XXI, pp. 85–95), in reply to Thomas Carlyle's "Occasional Discourse on the Negro Question," *ibid.*, XL (Dec. 1849), 670–9.

---

[1] MS in the Reed Collection, Dunedin Public Library, New Zealand. Paper watermarked 1851. Published in *MNL*, XXIII (Winter 1988), 23–4, edited by Eric W. Nye.
[2] The reference is almost certainly to Mill's letter of 8 May, 1852, printed in *The Opinions of Certain Authors on the Bookselling Question* (London: Parker, [1852]), p. 47 (in *CW*, Vol. XXV, p. 1189).

---

[1] MS in the Reed Collection, Dunedin Public Library, New Zealand. Published in *MNL*, XXIII (Winter 1988), 24, edited by Eric W. Nye.
John Chapman (1822–94), physician, author, and publisher, became proprietor and editor of the *Westminster Review* in 1851.
[2] I.e., of the parliamentary session, on 4 November.

occasion for writing on general politics before the time when anything intended for your next number must go to press, that I have given up for the present all thought of the article I spoke to you about.[3] I write as soon as possible after making up my mind, that there may be no chance of putting you to any inconvenience.

          I am Dear Sir
            yours truly
            J.S. MILL

136A. TO FREDERICK J. FURNIVALL[1]

         East India House
            Monday
        [27 February, 1854]

DEAR SIR

I am much obliged to you for the lists of Cooperative Associations. What amount of foundation is there for the statements in Lechevalier's pamphlet, which tend to throw doubt on the indication which the number of Associations appears to give, of a corresponding amount of progress in the Cooperative cause?[2]

Do you possess any information respecting the French associations of later date than that in Feugueray's book?[3] I have none at all recent, & it would take a considerable time to obtain any which I could rely on.

          I am yrs very truly,
            J.S. MILL

---

[3]Mill did not write any further articles for the *Westminster* until January 1862.

---

[1]MS in the Huntington Library, San Marino, California. *Addressed:* F.J. Furnival Esq. / 11 New Square / Lincoln's Inn. Dated from postmark.

Frederick James Furnivall (1825–1910), scholar and editor, an active Christian Socialist, had asked Mill's permission to reprint "On the Probable Futurity of the Labouring Classes" (Bk. IV, Chap. vii of the *Principles of Political Economy*; *CW*, Vols. II–III [Toronto: University of Toronto Press, 1965], Vol. III, pp. 758–96) for distribution among the working classes to encourage their interest in the cooperative movement. Mill agreed to the proposal, but wished first to "make some little additions to the chapter, tending to increase its usefulness," Furnivall apparently helping with lists of existing associations. The chapter was, in fact, never reprinted; see *CW*, Vol. XV, pp. 157, 159, 162, 624, and esp. 166.

[2]André Louis Jules Lechevalier-Saint-André, *Five Years in the Land of Refuge: A Letter on the Prospects of Co-operative Associations in England* (London: Richardson, 1854), esp. pp. 44–9 and the Appendix, pp. 93–6. Mill did not cite the pamphlet in later editions of the *Principles*.

[3]Henri Robert Feugueray (1813–54), one of the editors of the *Revue Nationale*, author of *L'association ouvrière, industrielle et agricole* (Paris: Havard, 1851).

136B. TO JEAN GUSTAVE COURCELLE-SENEUIL[1]

India House
27 Févr 1854

MONSIEUR—Votre lettre du 26 Octobre et votre Traité des opérations de banque[2] me sont parvenus à mon retour d'Italie, près de trois mois après leur envoi. Veuillez n'attribuer qu'à cet absence le retard que j'ai mis à témoigner mes remerciements à un écrivain que j'avais appris à connaître et à estimer par ses nombreux articles dans le journal La République, et qui a fait beaucoup d'honneur à mon Traité d'Ec. Pol. en s'occupant de le traduire.[3]

C'est bien aujourdhui le temps de lire et de penser pendant qu'il n'est plus possible d'agir; et puisque le pays dont l'Europe attend des leçons d'amélioration sociale se trouve momentanément frappé d'impuissance pratique, il est à désirer que les bons esprits s'y occupent comme vous de perfectionner les théories. Je trouve dans votre livre des vues très éclairées sur le crédit. Vous en signalez bien sa véritable importance, tandis que vous réduisez à une juste mesure les notions vagues et exagérées sur sa puissance créatrice qui ont été la partie la plus faible de plusieurs systèmes socialistes. Vous établissez ensuite contrairement aux idées reçues la supériorité d'un régime de liberté. Il y a bien quelques questions sur lesquelles je ne suis pas d'accord avec vous, mais connaissant mon Ec. Pol. vous n'avez pas besoin que je vous les indique du reste. Ce caractère en quelque sorte professionel de votre ouvrage devant lui donner de nombreux lecteurs parmi les hommes d'affaires, il me semble très propre à former une opinion publique éclairée sur une classe d'intérêts très débattus aujourdhui et jusqu'ici peu compris.

Agréez Monsr l'expression de ma plus haute considération amicale.

---

[1]MS draft in Mill-Taylor Collection, British Library of Political and Economic Science, with Courcelle-Seneuil's letter of 26 October, 1853.
Jean Gustave Courcelle-Seneuil (1813–92), authority on banking, Professor of Political Economy, Santiago, Chile, from 1852, who had worked in Paris as a radical journalist on *La République*, *Le National*, and other newspapers.
[2]*Traité théorique et pratique des opérations de banque* (Paris: Guillaumin, 1853).
[3]With Hippolyte Dussard, Courcelle-Seneuil translated Mill's *Principles* as *Principes d'économie politique*, 2 vols. (Paris: Guillaumin, 1854).

137A. TO EDWIN CHADWICK[1]

I.H.
Monday
[Feb.–Mar. 1854?]

MY DEAR CHADWICK

I know that some years ago in consequence of Mr Finlaison's calculations & other considerations which were so fully set forth in your article on Life Annuities[2] the Govt made some alterations in their system on that subject. Can you inform me where I can obtain the most recent account of their regulations & of the terms on which annuities are now granted on lives?

Very truly yours
J.S. MILL

258A. TO THE FINANCE AND HOME COMMITTEE[1]

Examiner's Office
5 April 1856

HONORABLE SIRS,

The number of the Officers employed in conducting the correspondence in this Office having by the Court's resolution of the 28th ult been increased by one, and there being at present no room in which the additional Officer can be accommodated, I respectfully request the sanction of your Honorable Committee to some arrangement by which an additional room may be provided.

I take this opportunity of bringing to the notice of your Honorable Committee the inconvenience occasioned by the want of a waiting room or other vacant room in the office. It frequently happens that permission is granted by the Chairman to gentlemen in the Honorable Company's Service or others, to consult the official records either for public or private purposes, and there is at present no place in

---

[1] MS at University College London. Dated to 1854 when, considering retirement because of ill-health, Mill and his wife were concerned about annuities; see letter of 28 February, 1854, *CW*, Vol. XIV, p. 170.

[2] The calculations of John Finlaison (1783–1860), statistician and Government actuary, responsible for many studies of actuarial problems, were outlined in Chadwick's "Life Assurances," *Westminster Review*, IX (Apr. 1828), 384–421. Full details are in *PP*, 1825, IV, 321–497; 1826–27, III, 869–1003; and 1829, III, 247–355.

---

[1] MS in clerk's hand, signed by Mill, in L/F/2/192, No. 57 of April 1856, India Office Library and Records.

which they can make use of such permission except the compound of the Clerks in the Office.

> I have the honor to be, Honorable Sirs
> Your most faithful and obedient Servant
> J.S. MILL

258B. TO THE FINANCE AND HOME COMMITTEE[1]

> Examiner's Office
> 6 May 1856

HONORABLE SIRS,

One of the two extra offices not having been included in the general order for painting the rooms and Offices of this Department passed by your Honorable Committee on the 29th of August last, and the present being a convenient opportunity for putting that Office into the same condition with the other offices, I have requested the Clerk of Works to prepare an Estimate for that purpose, and I respectfully recommend that it may receive the sanction of your Honorable Committee.

> I have the honor to be, Honorable Sirs
> Your most faithful and obedient Servant
> J.S. MILL
> Examiner

258C. TO THE FINANCE AND HOME COMMITTEE[1]

> Examiner's Office
> 24th May 1856

HONORABLE SIRS,

I beg most respectfully to lay before you a letter which has been addressed to me by the Registrar of the Book Office[2] reporting the death, on the 19th instant, of John Howell, one of the messengers in that Department, and to state that I consider it necessary that the vacancy should be filled up.

---

[1] MS in clerk's hand, signed by Mill, in L/F/2/193, No. 12 of May 1856, India Office Library and Records.

---

[1] MS in clerk's hand, signed by Mill, in L/F/2/193, No. 129 of May 1856, India Office Library and Records.
[2] Christopher Waud.

I have the honor to be, with the highest respect, Honorable Sirs
Your most faithful and obedient humble servant
J.S. MILL

258D. TO THE FINANCE AND HOME COMMITTEE[1]

Examiner's Office
2nd June 1856

HONORABLE SIRS,

I most respectfully have to represent that the new room ordered by the Honorable Committee for Mr Kaye[2] is now completed, and to solicit that provision of the necessary furniture may be sanctioned.

I have the honor to be, Honorable Sirs,
Your most faithful and obedient servant
J.S. MILL

258E. TO THE FINANCE AND HOME COMMITTEE[1]

Examiner's Office
2d June 1856

HONORABLE SIRS,

I most respectfully solicit your attention to the accompanying letter which has been addressed to me by Mr Waud the Registrar, respecting the completion of the basement floor of the House for the reception of the Honorable Company's records under his charge, and asking the sanction of the Committee in his suggestions connected with the removal and final arrangement of the books.

I have the honor to be, Honorable Sirs,
Your most faithful and obedient servant
J.S. MILL

---

[1] MS in clerk's hand, signed by Mill, in L/F/2/194, No. 41 of June 1856, India Office Library and Records.
[2] John William Kaye (1814–76) had previously served in India, and was joining the Home Establishment at this time as Assistant Examiner in the Political Department.

---

[1] MS in clerk's hand, signed by Mill, in L/F/2/194, No. 42 of June 1856, India Office Library and Records.

258F. TO THE FINANCE AND HOME COMMITTEE[1]

Examiner's Office
2d June 1856

HONORABLE SIRS,

I most respectfully beg leave to lay before you a letter addressed to Mr Waud by A. Howell requesting that the salary of his late father,[2] who died on the 19th Instant may be continued to the widow for the current quarter.

I have the honor to be, Honorable Sirs,
Your most faithful and obedient Servant
J.S. MILL

258G. TO THE FINANCE AND HOME COMMITTEE[1]

Examiner's Office
10th June 1856

HONORABLE SIRS,

In obedience to the instructions given in the Minute of your Honorable Committee dated the 4th instant, I have the honor to report that the following parties have been selected to assist in moving and arranging the portion of the Records, intended to be deposited in the basement floor viz

Writer: Mr Wharton Rundall,[2] who has been employed before.

Labourers: Wm Hare,
I. White,
Thos Baker,
Philip Slater,
Francis Brown,   ⎫
Charles Chedzoy,   ⎬ Warehouse pensioners
John Young,   ⎭
George Mitchell, pensioner messenger
Edd Rock, Assistt fire-lighter
Thos McKennie . . . do . . .

I have the honor to be, Honorable Sirs,
Your most faithful & obedient Servant
J.S. MILL

---

[1] MS in clerk's hand, signed by Mill, in L/F/2/194, No. 43 of June 1856, India Office Library and Records.
[2] See Letter 258C above.

---

[1] MS in clerk's hand, signed by Mill, in L/F/2/194, No. 94 of June 1856, India Office Library and Records.
[2] Wharton Rundall appears to be one of the temporary writers referred to in Letters 262D, 283A, 293A, and 306A below.

258H. TO THE FINANCE AND HOME COMMITTEE[1]

Examiner's Office
16th June 1856

HONORABLE SIRS,

In obedience to the orders of your Honorable Committee of the 26th March 1845, requiring a report of the cases of such of the Extra Clerks and Writers as are employed either on duties formerly discharged by established clerks or on duties distinct from copying, I have the honor respectfully to state that since the last report made by the Examiner on the subject, dated the 9th June 1845, Mr Charles Bell and Mr Frederick Charles Danvers have been employed in the manner above specified, the former in the Judicial Department since the year 1847; and the latter in the Public and Public Works Departments since the year 1853;[2] and I respectfully request that the employment of Messrs Bell and Danvers as now reported, may be sanctioned by the Honorable Committee.

I have the honor to be, Honorable Sirs,
Your most faithful and obedient Servant
J.S. MILL

260A. TO THE SECRETARY TO THE BOARD OF CONTROL[1]

East India House,
9th September 1856

Secret.
SIR,

I have laid before the Secret Committee of the Court of Directors[2] Mr Danby Seymour's letter of the 20th ultimo,[3] with its enclosure from the Under Secretary of State for the Foreign Department,[4] communicating the modified proposal of the

---

[1] MS in clerk's hand, signed by Mill, in L/F/2/194, No. 210 of June 1856, India Office Library and Records.

[2] Charles Bell and Frederick Charles Danvers (1833–1906), were employed as writers in their respective departments. Danvers, an author on engineering subjects, later became Registrar and Superintendent of Records in the India Office.

---

[1] MS copy in L/P&S/3/1, pp. [440–2], India Office Library and Records. See also Letters 263B, 266A, 283B, and 309A below.

The joint Secretaries to the Board of Control at this time were Henry Danby Seymour (1820–77), M.P. for Poole, and George Russell Clerk (1800–89).

[2] The Secret Committee was composed of the Chairman and Deputy Chairman, at that time William Henry Sykes (1790–1872) and Ross Donnelly Mangles (1801–77), and one senior Director.

[3] A copy of Seymour's letter to Mill is *ibid.*, p. 433.

[4] Henry Thomas Petty-Fitzmaurice (1816–66), Earl of Shelburne, had been Under-Secretary of State since July.

French Government, of which Captain Pigeard is the bearer,[5] with respect to exchanges of territory in India; and desiring to be informed of the opinion of the Secret Committee on that proposal.

The arrangement which was understood to have been accepted by the French Government in 1855[6] provided for the cession of all the French possessions in India except Pondicherry, as well as of such part of the territory attached to that settlement as lies outside a certain proposed boundary; Her Majesty making over to France all British territory lying within that boundary, and the nation which should be a gainer in revenue by the double transfer making to the other a pecuniary compensation calculated at twenty years purchase.

The French Government now disavows the assent which it was supposed to have been given to this arrangement, and desires to limit its cessions to the Pondicherry villages outside the proposed boundary, together with the settlements of Chandernagore and Yanoon, and the French Establishments at Calicut and Masulipatam; retaining the valuable possessions of Maké and Karical, and the factories at Surat, Patna, Cossimbazar, Dacca, Balasore and Jugdea. And these more limited transfers the French Government proposes that Her Majesty should receive as a full equivalent for the cession of the British territory within the proposed Pondicherry boundary, no pecuniary compensation being made payable as in the former Draft from the gaining to the losing nation.

As a reason for omitting this last stipulation, it is affirmed by Captain Pigeard that the possessions which the French Government proposes to cede would be worth more to the British Government than the amount of the revenue which those possessions at present yield to France. While the Secret Committee admit that to a certain, though a moderate extent, this estimate may be well founded, they must observe that the French Government also would derive from the acquisition of villages inconveniently intermixed with its territory a benefit far exceeding the mere revenues of those villages: and it appears from Lord Cowley's letter to Lord J. Russell dated 31st January 1852,[7] that the French Colonial Minister at that time[8] even expressed his willingness "to accept less than he gives, because he shall receive a compensation in the suppression of the expenses of the French outlying establishments."

The Committee consider the question of an interchange of Indian possessions to be one which is more important to French than to British interests. Nevertheless,

[5]Jean Charles Edouard Pigeard (b. 1818), "délégué du Gouvernement Français"; his letter to Lord Shelburne of 14 August, 1856, and the draft Convention are *ibid.*, pp. [436–40].

[6]The account of an earlier attempt to arrange an exchange of British and French territory is contained in the copy of a letter from Lord Shelburne to George Clerk of 16 August, 1856, *ibid.*, pp. [434–6].

[7]The letter from Henry Richard Charles Wellesley, Earl Cowley (1804–84), British Ambassador to Paris, to the then Prime Minister Lord John Russell has not been located.

[8]Mill is presumably referring to Louis Félix Etienne, marquis de Turgot (1796–1866), Minister of Foreign Affairs at that time.

and although the French Government withdraws the most valuable part of the cessions originally contemplated, the opinion of the Committee is in favor of accepting those which are now offered, if the French Government will consent to receive in exchange territories of equivalent pecuniary value in the neighbourhood of Pondicherry; but the Committee are decidedly adverse to purchasing those transfers by cessions of greater value, because they do not consider the acquisition as of sufficient political importance to be worth any sacrifice of revenue; and also because by making over to France all the territory which she desires for the consolidation of her Pondicherry possessions and the rectification of her boundary, the British Government would lose the power of hereafter offering an equivalent likely to be accepted for the cessions, formerly contemplated, but now withheld.

I am, Sir,
Your obedient servant,
(Signed) J.S. MILL.

260B. TO THE FINANCE AND HOME COMMITTEE[1]

Examiner's Office
9th September 1856

HONORABLE SIRS,

I have the honor to lay before you a letter from Mr Waud, the Registrar, enclosing a Petition to your Honorable Committee from the four Messengers attached to the Registrar's Department (Henry Thomas Drew, James Tarrant, John Lee Turner, and Edwin Norris) praying to be granted a gratuity to remunerate them for the extra-work imposed on them by the recent re-arrangement of a considerable portion of the Company's Records, together with the expenses they have incurred. Mr Waud bears testimony to the severe labour entailed on the Petitioners, to the extra-time during which they have been employed, to the extra expenses entailed on them, to the strenuous exertions made by each man to assist in carrying out the arrangement, and recommends the prayer of the Petitioners to favorable consideration.

I beg leave respectfully to support the recommendations of Mr Waud, and humbly submit that the indulgences solicited may be granted to the Petitioners.

I have the honor to be, Honorable Sirs,
Your most faithful and obedient Servant
J.S. MILL

---

[1] MS in clerk's hand, signed by Mill, in L/F/2/197, No. 58 of Sept. 1856, India Office Library and Records.

260C. TO THE FINANCE AND HOME COMMITTEE[1]

Examiner's Office
16th September 1856

HONORABLE SIRS,

I most respectfully lay before you a Memorandum prepared by Mr Prideaux[2] in obedience to the Chairman's[3] commands, in which he submits his opinion of the merits and services of Mr Wm Peters, a writer in this office, and recommends his case for favorable consideration.

And in consequence of the representations made to me of the zeal, intelligence and ability with which Mr Peters has discharged his official duties, I beg leave to express my concurrence in the views of Mr Prideaux.

I have the honor to be, Honorable Sirs,
Your most faithful and obedient Servant
J.S. MILL

262A. TO THEODOR GOMPERZ[1]

Blackheath
Sept. 30 [1856]

DEAR SIR

Will you write and fix a day when you will come down to Blackheath and dine and stay the night, when we shall have an opportunity of talking over the subject of the Logic.[2] If you will call on me at the India House (Examiner's Office) before four o'clock we can go down by the railway together.

I wrote to you at Vienna only last Saturday in reply to your letter,[3] which I found on my return to England after an absence of two months.[4]

---

[1] MS in clerk's hand, signed by Mill, in L/F/2/197, No. 104 of Sept. 1856, India Office Library and Records.
[2] Francis William Prideaux (d. 1871), Assistant Examiner in the Revenue and Separate Revenue Department.
[3] See Letter 260A, n2 above.

---

[1] MS at Kokugakuin University, Tokyo. "30/9/56/" written on MS in another hand, perhaps that of Theodor Gomperz or his son Heinrich. See Introduction, pp. xvi–xviii above.
Theodor Gomperz (1832–1912), Austrian philosopher and philologist, a great admirer of Mill, later supervised and contributed extensively to the German edition of many of Mill's writings: *Gesammelte Werke*, 12 vols. (Leipzig: Fues, 1869–80).
[2] Gomperz's translation of the *System of Logic*, based on the 3rd edition (1851), and incorporating the changes in subsequent editions, finally appeared as *System der deductiven und inductiven Logik*, Vols. II–IV of *Gesammelte Werke* (1872–73).
[3] Not located.
[4] Mill and his wife, with her son Algernon and daughter Helen, spent July and August in Switzerland.

Are you acquainted with Dr. Arnold Ruge, who is now living at Brighton?[5]

I am Dear Sir
yrs truly,
J.S. MILL

262B. TO THEODOR GOMPERZ[1]

Blackheath Park
Wednesday
[1 Oct., 1856]

DEAR SIR

I shall be disengaged tomorrow, at any time you like to come and shall be very glad to see you. There are trains, hourly, which stop at the Blackheath station.

If tomorrow should not suit you, Friday, or any other day (except Saturday afternoon) will be equally convenient to us.

I am Dear Sir
yours very truly
J.S. MILL

262C. TO THEODOR GOMPERZ[1]

East India House
Oct. 3 [1856]

DEAR SIR

If equally convenient to you, will you allow me to fix Monday instead of tomorrow?

I have desired Messrs Parker to send to you in Finsbury Square the new edition of the Logic which contains some additions likely to interest you.[2] I had ordered it to be sent to Vienna, but was fortunately in time to stop it.

I am Dr Sir
very sincerely yrs
J.S. MILL

[5]Arnold Ruge (1802–80), German writer on politics and philosophy, had emigrated to England following the collapse of the revolution of 1848. Gomperz had been staying in Brighton with his three sisters, before going up to London.

---

[1]MS at Kokugakuin University, Tokyo. "Herbst 56" in another hand on MS. Dated by Letter 262C below.

---

[1]MS at Kokugakuin University, Tokyo.
[2]The fourth, which had appeared at the beginning of August; see *Examiner*, 2 Aug., 1856, p. 495.

262D. TO THE FINANCE AND HOME COMMITTEE[1]

Examiner's Office
20th October 1856

HONORABLE SIRS,

I beg most respectfully to represent to you that the great pressure of business in this office has brought about an accumulation of work which, in spite of every exertion, cannot be got through without some increase to the present strength of the Extra Department. Under these circumstances I submit to you the propriety of authorizing the employment, as a temporary measure, of two extra writers in this office for a period of six months;[2] in order to form a judgment at the expiration of that time, whether any and what permanent addition to the number of Writers may be required.

I have the honor to be, Honorable Sirs
Your most faithful and obedient Servant
J.S. MILL

262E. TO THOMAS N. WATERFIELD[1]

East India House
24th October 1856

Secret.
SIR,

I have had the honor to receive and lay before the Secret Committee your letter dated the 22nd instant,[2] enclosing copies of letters from Captains Ring and Green offering to proceed on service to Herat,[3] and I am desired by the Secret Committee to state in reply that three officers having already received orders to proceed to Herat, the Committee do not think it at present advisable to add to the number.

I am, Sir,
Your most obedient Servant
J.S. MILL

---

[1]MS in clerk's hand, signed by Mill, in L/F/2/198, No. 174 of Oct. 1856, India Office Library and Records.
[2]The two writers were probably Wharton Rundall and W.I. Upton; see Letters 258G above, and 283A, 293A and 306A below.

---

[1]MS in clerk's hand, signed by Mill, in L/P&S/3/50, p. 249, India Office Library and Records.
[2]A copy of Waterfield's draft letter is *ibid.*, pp. 233–[4].
[3]Captains W.I. Ring, of Her Majesty's 87th Foot, and M.S. Green, of the 16th Regiment of Bombay Native Infantry, had volunteered to take part in a mission to the fortress city that was central to a dispute with Persia. War was declared on 1 November. See also Letters 262F, 270B, 270C, 270E, 286E and 321A below.

Oct. 1856   *To Thomas N. Waterfield*   93

262F. TO THOMAS N. WATERFIELD[1]

East India House,
October 28th 1856

Secret.

SIR,

I have had the honor to receive and lay before the Secret Committee your letter dated the 10th instant,[2] transmitting for any observations which the Committee might desire to make, a copy of a letter in which the Secretary of State for Foreign Affairs[3] expresses the opinion of Her Majesty's Government that it might be advisable to take possession of Mohummerah for the purpose of increasing the pressure upon Persia.[4]

Since receiving your letter the Secret Committee have endeavored to procure the best information within their reach bearing on the question therein adverted to. The information which they have been enabled to obtain is comprised in the following documents, copies of which I have the honor to annex.

A Memorandum by Lieutenant Colonel Hennell, formerly Resident in the Persian Gulf.[5]

A Chart of the Korun river prepared from actual Survey by Lieutenant W.B. Selby of the Indian Navy,[6] and transmitted to this country by the Bombay Government as an inclosure in their letter to the Secret Committee dated 10th June (No. 45) 1845.

A Memorandum by Sir W.F. Williams of Kars, Bart.[7] who as Commissioner for the settlement of the boundary between Turkey and Persia, resided for a considerable time at Mohummerah and in its vicinity.

Having thus put the Board and through them Her Majesty's Government in possession of all the information they themselves possess, the Committee refrain from expressing any opinion on the course which it may be most expedient to adopt.

As connected with Lieutenant Colonel Hennell's Memorandum I am directed to transmit two copies of a Sketch made by that Officer from Memory, of the country

---

[1]MS copy in L/P&S/3/1, pp. 445–[6], India Office Library and Records.
[2]A copy of Waterfield's letter is *ibid.*, p. [444].
[3]George William Frederick Villiers (1800–70), 4th Earl of Clarendon, had been Secretary of State for Foreign Affairs since February 1853.
[4]These views are expressed in a copy of a letter, dated 10 Oct., 1856, from Edmund Hammond (1802–90), permanent Under-Secretary of State for Foreign Affairs, *ibid.*, pp. [444]-5.
[5]Samuel Hennell had been the British Resident in the Persian Gulf in 1852.
[6]W.B. Selby is listed as being a Commander in the Navy from August 1856.
[7]William Fenwick Williams (1800–83) had been knighted for holding Kars against the Russians from June to November 1855.

adjoining Bushire on the South side.

I am, Sir,
Your obedient Servant,
(Signed) J.S. MILL

263B. TO THE SECRETARY TO THE INDIA BOARD[1]

East India House,
18th November 1856

Secret.
SIR,

In reply to Sir George Clerk's letter of the 14th instant,[2] requesting the opinion of the Secret Committee on a modified proposal of territorial exchanges with the French Government,[3] I am directed by the Secret Committee to state that they are not in possession of information enabling them to judge to what extent the financial result of the territorial arrangement in question would differ from that of the arrangements formerly contemplated. As far however as the Committee possess the means of forming an opinion, they are disposed to think that the unreserved relinquishment of all the French possessions in India with the exception of Pondicherry and its districts, would be an object worth purchasing by the cession to France of the additional territory near Pondicherry, included within the widest of the boundary lines marked in the Map; which according to the desire of the Board is returned herewith.

I am, Sir,
Your obedient Servant,
(Signed) J.S. MILL

266A. TO THOMAS N. WATERFIELD[1]

East India House,
November 26th 1856

Secret.
SIR,

I have laid before the Secret Committee your letter of the 21st instant[2]

---

[1]MS copy in L/P&S/3/1, pp. [448]-9, India Office Library and Records.
[2]A copy of Clerk's letter is *ibid.*, pp. 447–[8].
[3]See also Letters 260A above, and 266A, 283B, and 309A below.

---

[1]MS copy in L/P&S/3/1, pp. [450]-1, India Office Library and Records.
[2]A copy of Waterfield's letter is *ibid.*, pp. 449–[50].

requesting to be informed whether the Committee would object to a proposal considered likely to be made by the French Government, that the value of the addition to be made to the district round Pondicherry shall be one eighth or one sixth of the value of the addition which would have been made to that district under the Convention formerly proposed to France.[3]

I am directed by the Committee to observe in reply that the annual revenue of the British Villages which would have been ceded to France by the Convention formerly proposed was (as pointed out in their letter of 27th June 1855)[4] Rupees 1,30,485.9.3 but that the Committee were not then, and are not now acquainted with the value of the French Villages which, by the same Convention would have been ceded to Great Britain. Unless that value be such as to be a considerable set off against the large amount of revenue which it was proposed to cede, the Committee are disposed to think that the addition of one sixth, or even of one eighth, to the cession, would render very doubtful the expediency, in a financial point of view, of the exchange.

The Committee moreover are disinclined to extend any farther the area laid down in the last proposal of the French Agent, as shewn in the Map.

I am, Sir,
Your obedient Servant,
(Signed) J.S. MILL

269A. TO THE FINANCE AND HOME COMMITTEE[1]

Examiner's Office
24th December 1856

HONORABLE SIRS,

I beg to submit to the favorable consideration of your Honorable Committee a Medical Certificate and a letter from Mr Morgan, the father of Mr H. Morgan, a Writer in this Office, applying for further leave of absence in consequence of continued indisposition.

I have the honor to be, Honorable Sirs
Your most faithful and obedient Servant
J.S. MILL

---

[3]See Letters 260A and 263B above.
[4]The letter, sent to R. Vernon Smith, M.P., signed by Elliot Macnaughten, Chairman 1855–56, W.H. Sykes, Deputy Chairman, and Charles Mills, the senior Director, is in L/P&S/3/1, pp. 409–[10].

[1]MS in clerk's hand, signed by Mill, in L/F/2/200, No. 153 of Dec. 1856, India Office Library and Records.

269B. TO THE FINANCE AND HOME COMMITTEE[1]

Examiner's Office
13 January 1857

HONORABLE SIRS,

Your Honorable Committee is aware that systematic arrangements are now in force under all or most of the Indian Governments for the destruction of useless records. I venture to suggest that a similar arrangement is highly desirable with regard to that portion of the records of this office which consists of Duplicate Collections.

The transmission of Collections from India commenced in 1831, and they have always been transmitted in duplicate: one copy of each Collection, after their subjects have been disposed of by Despatches to India, remaining with the Board of Commissioners. The duplicate Collections are very serviceable until the arrival of the Books of Consultations, which are often considerably in arrear. They are also useful, though in a less degree, for some time longer, by saving the trouble of searching the Indexes, or the delay of borrowing the original Collections from the Board. But after a certain lapse of time, references to them become infrequent, and while their rapidly increasing mass is an encumbrance to the office, they answer no useful purpose except occasionally to save the delay and expense of transcription when papers of old date are required for the Honorable Court of Proprietors, or called for by the Houses of Parliament.

I beg therefore to propose that measures be taken for the destruction, (with the exception to be presently stated) of all duplicate Collections bearing an earlier date than that of the 1st January 1852; and that hereafter, at the end of each year one year's duplicate Collections be disposed of in a similar manner so that only those of the five years last expired may at any time remain.

The only exception which it seems necessary to make from this destruction, is in the case of papers which may appear likely to be required at some future period by Parliament or the Proprietors: and I recommmend accordingly that the Chief Clerk in each of the several Departments of this Office be directed to take such general cognizance of the Collections previously to their destruction as may enable him under instructions from the Examiner to select for preservation such of them as may seem worth retaining for that use.

I have the honor to be, Honorable Sirs,
Your most faithful and obedient Servant
J.S. MILL

---

[1]MS in clerk's hand, signed by Mill, in L/F/2/201, No. 159 of Jan. 1857, India Office Library and Records.

269C. TO THE FINANCE AND HOME COMMITTEE[1]

Examiner's Office
13th January 1857

HONORABLE SIRS,

In the early part of the present year, the Court was pleased to add one to the number of the Assistants to the Examiner,[2] in consequence of a necessity created chiefly by the extraordinary growth of the business devolving upon the Assistant in charge of the Public Department.

Since that time the Department has been divided into two branches, one of which retains the original name, and the other is the Public Works Department[3] each being under the charge of a separate Assistant. No addition however was at that time made to the number of Clerks in the office, nor was any separation effected between the Clerks attached to the two branches: and the business of both continues to be carried on by the same Clerks who formed the Establishment of the Department before it was divided.

I beg to represent to your Honorable Committee that the business which had outgrown the powers of a single Assistant Examiner, equally exceeds those of the number of Clerks which was sufficient under circumstances entirely different from the present; and that in consequence, notwithstanding the great efficiency of the gentlemen who conduct the correspondence of the two Departments, the business of both still remains considerably in arrears.

I therefore respectfully submit for consideration that such provision be made for the increased business devolving on the Clerks in the Departments, as your Honorable Committee may deem advisable. The subjoined statement exhibits the present distribution of Clerks among the several Departments of the office.

I have the honor to be, Honorable Sirs
Your most faithful and obedient Servant
J.S. MILL

---

[1]MS in clerk's hand, signed by Mill, in L/F/2/201, No. 190 of Jan. 1857, India Office Library and Records.
[2]Edmund D. Bourdillon had been appointed Assistant Examiner in charge of the Public Department.
[3]Mill's great friend and long-time associate in the East India Company, William Thomas Thornton (1813–80), had been appointed Assistant Examiner in charge of this new branch.

270A. TO THOMAS N. WATERFIELD[1]

East India House,
26th January 1857

Immediate
SIR,

Having laid before the Secret Committee your letter of this day's date,[2] I have received their instructions to acquaint you in reply for communication to the Commissioners for the Affairs of India, that the Secret Committee are of opinion that the Government of Madras will be able to place one Regiment of Native Infantry at the disposal of Her Majesty's Government for immediate service at Hong Kong,[3] on receiving an emergent requisition to that effect. In the event of this requisition being sent the Committee would suggest that the Government of Madras may be apprised that the Regiment will be brought back to Madras as soon as the necessity for their employment on Foreign Service has ceased.

The Secret Committee understand that the whole of the expenses attending this re-inforcement will be borne by Her Majesty's Government.

I have the honor to be, &c,

(Signed) J.S. MILL

T.N. Waterfield Esqre.
&ca &ca &ca

270B. TO THOMAS N. WATERFIELD[1]

East India House,
26th January 1857

Secret
SIR,

I have had the honor to receive and lay before the Secret Committee your letter dated the 22nd instant, enclosing a letter from Mr Hammond dated the 21st instant, on the subject of the postal communications with the Persian Gulf during the present War with Persia;[2] and I am desired to state in reply that the Committee

---

[1] MS copy in L/P&S/3/1, p. 475, India Office Library and Records.
[2] A copy of Waterfield's letter is *ibid.*, p. [474].
[3] Waterfield reported a request to that effect received from the Secretary of State, the Earl of Clarendon.

---

[1] MS copy in L/P&S/3/1, p. 475, India Office Library and Records.
[2] A copy of Hammond's letter to George Clerk is *ibid.*, pp. [460]-1, followed by copies of two memoranda on postal communications, pp. [462–8], and 469–71.

concur with Lord Clarendon in opinion that, the best postal communication for Government purposes will be from Bagdad viâ Constantinople, and that Lieutenant General Sir James Outram[3] will therefore be apprised of the arrangement and instructed to send to Her Majesty's Ambassador[4] a short summary of any important intelligence, which could be put into cypher at the Embassy and so forwarded by telegraph, while on the other hand any similar communication which it might be wished to send from England to overtake the dispatches, could be sent from the India Board to the Foreign Office, where it would be put into cypher and addressed to Her Majesty's Ambassador, who would then forward it by the Tatar proceeding with the dispatches.

I am also desired to suggest that Captain Kemball[5] should be instructed to forward by Tatar to Constantinople all despatches from Lieutenant General Sir James Outram on receipt.

I am, Sir,
Your most obedient Servant,
(Signed) J.S. M<small>ILL</small>

270C. TO THOMAS N. WATERFIELD[1]

East India House
January 28th, 1857

Mr. Mill presents his compliments to Mr. Waterfield, and transmits to him a copy of Mr. Andrew's "Memorandum on the establishment of Postal Communications between England and the Persian Gulf," dated January the 23rd 1857,[2] received from Sir Jas Melvill K.C.B.[3] on the 24th instant.

---

[3] James Outram (1803–63) was the commander of the army in the war against Persia. At that moment he was proceeding to Bushar, where he was successful in an engagement on 9 February.

[4] Stratford Canning (1786–1880), Viscount Stratford de Redcliffe, was Ambassador to Turkey at this time.

[5] Arnold Burrows Kemball (b. 1820) was Political Agent and Consul General at Baghdad.

---

[1] MS copy in L/P&S/3/51, p. [284], India Office Library and Records.

[2] The original of the "Memorandum on the Establishment of Postal Communications between England and the Persian Gulf viâ the Euphrates, or by Bagdad and Beyrout," signed by F.P. Andrew (the second memorandum mentioned in Letter 270B n2 above) is *ibid.*, pp. 285–[8].

[3] See Letter 290.1 above.

270D. TO THOMAS N. WATERFIELD[1]

East India House,
30th January 1857

Secret
SIR,

I am instructed by the Secret Committee to acknowledge your letter of the 27th instant,[2] transmitting for any observations which the Committee may wish to make, a copy of a letter from the Under Secretary of State for the Colonies,[3] requesting that a Vessel of the Indian Navy may be sent to the Kooria Mooria Islands for the purpose of protecting the persons to whom the Queen has granted permission to take Guano from these islands.[4]

I am directed by the Committee to suggest in reply that the contents of Brigadier Coghlan's letter of the 19th of December last, No. 23, be communicated to Mr. Labouchere.[5]

The Board is aware from that letter that in the opinion of the Officer most likely to be well informed on the subject, the cession of these Islands to Her Majesty by the Imaum of Muscat is a nullity,[6] as they were not his to dispose of. At all events, the beneficial enjoyment of them, and of the Guano produced in them, has resided from time immemorial in the Arabs of the Coast; whose rights whether acknowledged or not, it would, the Committee submit, be neither politic nor just to overrule by force, while Brigadier Coghlan appears to anticipate little difficulty in obtaining an amicable cession of them.

I am directed to request attention to the injurious consequences which the Brigadier predicts from any renewal of the attempt to take forcible possession of these islands, and in conclusion I am desired to observe, that the same causes which, in Mr Labouchere's opinion, make it inconvenient to employ one of Her Majesty's Ships of War on the proposed service, are applicable in an equal degree to the Indian Navy, and there is every reason to believe that in consequence of the

---

[1] MS copy in L/P&S/3/1, pp. [478–80], India Office Library and Records.

[2] A copy of Waterfield's letter is *ibid.*, pp. [476]-7.

[3] A copy of the enclosed letter, dated 24 Jan., 1857, from Herman Merivale, permanent Under-Secretary of State for the Colonies, is *ibid.*, pp. 477–[8].

[4] The guano was apparently being exploited by a Captain Ord and Messrs Hindson and Hayes, his partners.

[5] The letter from William M. Coghlan (1803–85), Acting Political Resident and Commandant at Aden from December 1854, to Henry Labouchere (1798–1869), Secretary of State for the Colonies, has not been located.

[6] Said ibn Sultan (of Oman), Imaum of Muscat (ruled 1804–56), had relinquished the islands by "Deed of Cession of the Kuria Muria Islands, . . . Signed at Muscat, 14 June, 1854," in *Consolidated Treaty Series*, ed. Clive Parry, *et al.*, 231 vols. (Dobbs Ferry, N.Y.: Oceana Publications, 1969–86), Vol. 112, pp. 39–40.

Persian Expedition it would be impracticable for the Bombay Government to detach a Vessel for the purpose desired by Mr. Labouchere.

I am, Sir,
Your most obedient Servant,
(Signed) J.S. MILL

270E. TO THE SECRETARY TO THE INDIA BOARD[1]

East India House,
31st January 1857

Secret.
SIR,

I am commanded by the Secret Committee to acknowledge the receipt of Mr Waterfield's letter of the 22nd instant,[2] forwarding for their consideration, copies of certain documents on the subject of the stipulations to be made with the Shah of Persia at the cessation of the present hostilities.[3]

The only remarks which it appears necessary for the Committee to make refer to the second Article of the proposed Commercial Treaty.[4] It is suggested by Sir Justin Sheil that there may be "in India various commodities which are classed as contraband and the importation of which is prohibited; such, perhaps, as Opium."[5] I am directed to state that there are no prohibitions of the description referred to in the Customs laws of British India, and that it does not therefore seem requisite, on that account, to modify the language of the Article in question, in the manner proposed in the letter from the Committee of Privy Council for Trade, dated the 22nd instant.

The Secret Committee concur in the view taken by the Lords of the Committee for Trade in respect to the omission from the same Article of the word "European," as applied to the "most favored nation,"—if such omission would, as stated by Sir Justin Sheil, have the effect of admitting goods imported into Persia by British Merchants at the lower rate of 4 per cent, at which goods imported by Turkish traders are admitted under Treaty; but the Committee are not aware why Turkey is less to be regarded as a European power than Russia, both countries, although

---

[1] MS in clerk's hand, signed by Mill, in L/P&S/3/51, pp. 373–[4], India Office Library and Records.
[2] Not located.
[3] A peace was concluded in March with the Shah, Nasr-Ed-Din (1829–96).
[4] "Draft of a Proposed Commercial Treaty between Her Majesty the Queen of Great Britain and Ireland, and the Shah of Persia," L/P&S/3/51, pp. 155–61, esp. 156.
[5] Justin Sheil (1803–71) had been Ambassador to Persia 1844–54, serving, in retirement, as consultant to the Government. His observations, here quoted, are printed in the left-hand columns of the draft treaty.

possessing large territories in Asia, having their respective seats of Government in Europe.[6]

I am, Sir,\
Your most obedient servant,\
J.S. MILL

283A. TO THE FINANCE AND HOME COMMITTEE[1]

Examiner's Office\
22nd April 1857

HONORABLE SIRS,

In October last year your Honorable Committee were pleased to authorize the employment of two extra writers in this office for a period of six months.

That period will expire this day;—but as the business of the extra office still continues without material diminution, I respectfully submit the propriety of retaining the services of the same two writers, Messrs Rundall & Upton,[2]—for a further period of six months,—their conduct during the past period having been unexceptionable.

I have the honor to be, Honorable Sirs,\
your most faithful & obedient Servant\
J.S. MILL

283B. TO GEORGE RUSSELL CLERK[1]

East India House,\
May 11th 1857

Secret.

SIR,

I have had the honor of receiving and laying before the Secret Committee[2] your

---

[6] A note in the margin of the MS, in another hand, reads: "Surely Turkey is to be regarded as rather Asiatic than European—and Russia as rather European than Asiatic."

---

[1] MS in clerk's hand, signed by Mill, in L/F/2/204, No. 161 of Apr. 1857, India Office Library and Records.

[2] See Letters 258G, 262D above, and 293A, 306A below.

---

[1] MS copy in L/P&S/3/1, pp. [482]-3, India Office Library and Records. See also Letters 260A, 263B, 266A above, and 309A below.

[2] At the annual elections in April, R.D. Mangles had become Chairman, and Frederick Currie (1799–1875) Deputy Chairman for the following year.

letter of the 2nd instant,[3] enclosing a paper by Captain Pigeard[4] conveying what the Board consider the ultimatum of the French Government as to the contemplated exchange of British and French possessions, and requesting the opinion of the Committee on the expediency of accepting the proposition as therein stated.

The present proposal differs from the one which immediately preceded it, in relinquishing a triangular piece of land, (of the extent or value of which the Committee have no information) which in the former proposal formed part of the territory to be ceded by the British Government.

The Committee observe that in M. Pigeard's paper, the cessions to be made by France are stated to be Chandernagore, Yanoon and Maha, with the factories of Masulipatam and Calicut, while M. Pigeard also states that the French Establishments in India would be reduced to two, (viz Pondicherry and Karical). M. Pigeard appears to overlook the possession by France of several other factories, at Surat, Patna, Cossimbaza, Dacca, Balasore and Jugdea, and possibly elsewhere. The Committee have always regarded the relinquishment by France of all such outlying possessions as a sine qua non of the proposed exchange.

Assuming that these factories are to be included in the cession, and that the French possessions in India will really be limited to Pondicherry and Karical, the Committee are of opinion that the proposal made by M. Pigeard might be accepted provided that on a reference to the Government of India no objection should be made to it by that authority.

The enclosures in your letter are herewith returned.

                          I am, Sir,
                     Your obedient servant,
                      (Signed) J.S. MILL

283C. TO THOMAS N. WATERFIELD[1]

May 13th 1857

Secret.
SIR,

I am directed by the Secret Committee to request, that you will be pleased to obtain the consent of the Right Honorable the Commissioners for the Affairs of India to the employment, in the Secret Department, of Mr John Henry Willock and

---

[3] A copy of Clerk's letter is *ibid.*, p. [480].
[4] A copy of Pigeard's "Memorandum," dated 29 Apr., 1857, is *ibid.*, pp. 481–[2].

---

[1] MS in clerk's hand, signed by Mill, in L/P&S/3/54, p. 409, India Office Library and Records.

Mr Thomas Alexander Riddell, Clerks in the Examiner's Office, on their taking the prescribed Oath.

I am, Sir,\
Your obedient servant,\
J.S. MILL

T.N. Waterfield Esqre

283D. TO GEORGE RUSSELL CLERK[1]

East India House,\
9th June 1857

Secret
SIR,

I am instructed by the Secret Committee to acknowledge the receipt of your letter dated the 29th ultimo[2] requesting the opinion of the Secret Committee on the suggestion by Lieutenant Burton, in a letter addressed by him to the Geographical Society for the establishment of a British Agency at Berbera.[3]

I am directed to observe that this suggestion had already been made, in a more legitimate manner, by Lieutenant Burton, in his report on Berbera addressed to the Political Agent at Aden[4] on the 22nd February 1855, and was examined by the Governor of Bombay[5] in a Minute dated the 19th March following. Lord Elphinstone for reasons which appear conclusive to the Committee, considered every mode of accomplishing the object proposed by Lieutenant Burton, inadmissible, except one which he described as equivalent to "taking possession of the place"; and it is hardly necessary to say that the Committee would consider any attempt to establish a political, and as its necessary accompaniment, a Military Station, on the African Coast, as in the highest degree objectionable.

I am commanded to add, that the Articles of Peace and Friendship concluded with the Somalis in November 1856, and quoted in your letter,[6] oppose an additional obstacle to the entertainment of the proposal. For inasmuch as those

---

[1]MS in clerk's hand, signed by Mill, in L/P&S/3/54, pp. 473–[4], and copy in L/P&S/3/1, pp. 485–[6], India Office Library and Records.

[2]A copy of Clerk's letter is in L/P&S/3/1, pp. 483–[4].

[3]Richard Francis Burton (1821–90), best known for his later attempt to find the headwaters of the Nile, while on leave from the Bombay army had explored the interior of Somaliland, November 1854 to January 1855. His letter of 15 December, 1856, to the Royal Geographical Society, not published at the time, is in Isabel Burton, *The Life of Captain Sir Richard F. Burton*, 2 vols. (London: Chapman and Hall, 1893), Vol. II, App. F, pp. 560–4.

[4]See Letter 270D, n5 above.

[5]John, Baron Elphinstone (1807–60) was Governor of Bombay 1853–59.

[6]L/P&S/3/1, p. [484].

Articles stipulate that we shall have the power to send an Agent to reside at Berbera during the fair, for the purpose of seeing that the provisions of the Agreement are observed, they by necessary implication preclude us from maintaining an Agent there at any other period, or for any other purpose.

The Committee, I am directed to add, entirely agree in the observation of the Board respecting the impropriety of Lieutenant Burton's conduct in addressing to the Geographical Society criticisms on the political measures of the Government of India.

I am, Sir,
Your most obedient servant,
(Signed) J.S. MILL

286A. TO THE FINANCE AND HOME COMMITTEE[1]

Examiner's Office
20th July 1857

HONORABLE SIRS,

I most respectfully request that your Honorable Committee will be pleased to grant the temporary assistance of a labourer during the usual leave of absence granted the Messengers attached to this Department.

I have the honor to be, Honorable Sirs
Your most faithful and obedient Servant
J.S. MILL

286B. TO THE FINANCE AND HOME COMMITTEE[1]

Examiner's Office
11 August 1857

HONORABLE SIRS,

I have the honor to report the following circumstances which have occurred in connection with John Whatmough a Messenger under the Assistant Registrar in the Book Office[2] attached to this Department.

---

[1] MS in clerk's hand, signed by Mill, in L/F/2/207, No. 175 of July 1857, India Office Library and Records.

---

[1] MS in clerk's hand, signed by Mill, in L/F/2/208, No. 90 of Aug. 1857, India Office Library and Records. The letter immediately preceding (No. 89), from H.S. Lawford, the Company's solicitor, mentions his report on the case, of 5 August, which is probably what Mill is quoting. Whatmough was charged with having stolen thirty-six pounds of paper.

[2] Aaron Atkins.

About six months since Whatmough, who was carrying a bundle, was stopped by a Detective Officer at 6 o'Clock on a Sunday morning; and the bundle being examined, was found to contain "old books torn up." In consequence, however, of the explanation Whatmough gave, the Officer allowed him to "pass on."

On Saturday the 1st of August, Whatmough was again met by the same Detective who had met him on the former occasion. He had, on this occasion, in his possession "a parcel wrapped up in brown paper." Having asserted that the paper was given to him by Mr Atkins, he was confronted with that gentleman who denied the statement. He was thereon taken before the sitting Magistrate at Guildhall, examined, and remanded.[3] On a subsequent occasion he was again brought up, and, on the re-hearing of the charge against him, he was committed for trial at the ensuing Sessions and is now awaiting his trial.

I have the honor to be, Honorable Sirs
Your most faithful and obedient Servant
J.S. MILL

286C. TO THE FINANCE AND HOME COMMITTEE[1]

Examiner's Office
11th August 1857

HONORABLE SIRS,

With reference to the Order of the Honorable Court dated the 18th of February 1857 for the destruction of old and useless duplicate Collections,[2] I now lay before your Honorable Committee a report from the Chief Clerk in this Department shewing that effect has been given to the Court's instructions.

I have the honor to be, Honorable Sirs
Your most faithful and obedient Servant
J.S. MILL

---

[3]No account of Whatmough's case has been located.

[1]MS in clerk's hand, signed by Mill, in L/F/2/208, No. 91 of Aug. 1857, India Office Library and Records.
[2]See Letter 269B above.

286D. TO THE FINANCE AND HOME COMMITTEE[1]

Examiner's Office
11th August 1857

HONORABLE SIRS,

In laying before your Honorable Committee a letter from Mr Atkins, Assistant Registrar under this Office, representing the necessity of whitewashing the rooms occupied by his Department, and of effecting some minor improvements I have the honor to state that from personal inspection I can confirm Mr Atkins' representations, and I beg to recommend that his proposals be carried into effect.

I have the honor to be, Honorable Sirs
Your most faithful and obedient Servant
J.S. MILL

286E. TO GEORGE RUSSELL CLERK[1]

East India House,
20th August 1857

Secret.
SIR,

In reply to your letter dated the 19th instant, I am directed by the Secret Committee to state that they have no objection to the adoption of Mr Murray's[2] proposal for conferring an honorary step of rank on Major Taylor and Lieutenants Clerk and Hardy[3] while employed on a Mission to Herat.[4] I am, Sir,

Your most obedient servant,
(Signed) J.S. MILL

Sir George Clerk
&ca &ca &ca

---

[1] MS in clerk's hand, signed by Mill, in L/F/2/208, No. 92 of Aug. 1857, India Office Library and Records.

---

[1] MS copy in L/P&S/3/1, p. 489, India Office Library and Records.
[2] Charles Augustus Murray (1806–95), Ambassador at the Court of Persia 1854–59.
[3] Possibly Major R.S. Taylor (1826–86), Lieutenants Godfrey Clerk (b. 1835), and John Braithwaite Hardy, the two latter from the Bombay military establishment.
[4] The mission was to ensure that the terms of the treaty, recently concluded with the Shah, would be properly carried out.

292. TO THEODOR GOMPERZ[1]

Blackheath
Oct. 5. 1857

DEAR SIR

On receiving your letter of the 30th September I made enquiry as to the conditions of eligibility to the medical service of the East India Company, and I regret to say that no foreigner can be admitted into it unless he is first naturalized. I confess I do not see why this restriction should exist in the medical service. In the civil and military services there are obvious reasons for it. The restriction does not exist in the educational service, and several of your countrymen (among others a son of the great Liebig)[2] are Professors in the Government Colleges in India. If an appointment of that kind would suit your friend's[3] qualifications and wishes, he might perhaps succeed in obtaining one, as the education department is in a state of rapid growth, and good teachers of science are continually wanted.

Accept our condolences on the loss of your father.[4] We hope your sister,[5] who was ill when we last saw you, is now better. I am much interested in what you say of your literary undertakings, and should be glad to hear more about the philological articles you mention.[6] Do they contain the speculation you told me of, connecting Protagoras with the authorship of one of the Hippocratic treatises?[7] *a*I have nearly finished an Essay "on Liberty" which I hope to publish next winter.[8] As the Liberty it treats of is moral and intellectual rather than political, it is not so much needed in Germany as it is here.*a*

---

[1] MS at Kokugakuin University, Tokyo. Two sentences only of this letter are in *CW*, Vol. XV, p. 539.
[2] Georg (1827–1903), son of the German chemist, Justus von Liebig (1803–73), who contributed to all branches of the science, but is specially known for his development of chemical fertilizers.
[3] Not identified.
[4] Philipp Gomperz (1782–1857).
[5] Josephine von Wertheimstein (née Gomperz) (1820–94).
[6] Presumably "Zu Euripides," and (forthcoming) "Zu den griechischen Tragikern," *Rheinisches Museum*, XI (1857), 470–1, and XII (1858), 477–9.
[7] Part of the collection of 87 treatises, many spurious, connected with the Greek physician Hippocrates (ca. 460–380 B.C.), on medicine and related subjects, found at Herculaneum, had been deposited in the Bodleian Library, where Gomperz would later study them. He attributed the pseudo-Hippocratic treatise, "On the Art," to the sophist Protagoras (ca. 490–420 B.C.). See *Die Apologie der Heilkunst*, in *Sitzungsberichte der Philosophisch-historischen Classe der Kaiserlichen Akademie der Wissenschaft*, Vol. 120 (Vienna, 1890), and his *Griechische Denker*, trans. as *Greek Thinkers*, 4 vols. (London: Murray, 1901–12), Vol. I, pp. 466–70.
[8] It did not appear until February, 1859 (London: Parker), after his wife's death.

a-a[*in* CW]

If you visit England in spring we shall be happy to see you, and to renew our interesting conversations.

I am Dear Sir
Very truly yours
J.S. MILL

293A. TO THE FINANCE AND HOME COMMITTEE[1]

Examiner's Office
14th October 1857

HONORABLE SIRS,

In April last your Honorable Committee were pleased to authorize the re-employment of two extra writers in this Office for a period of six months.

That period will expire on the 22d instant: but as the business of the extra Office still requires their assistance, I respectfully submit to you the expediency of retaining the Services of the same two writers, Messrs Rundall & Upton,[2] for a further period of six months,—their conduct during the past period having been unexceptionable.

I have the honor to be, Honorable Sirs
Your most faithful and obedient Servant
J.S. MILL

293B. TO THE FINANCE AND HOME COMMITTEE[1]

Examiner's Office
21st October 1857

HONORABLE SIRS,

It being necessary for the discharge of the duties of the Public and Ecclesiastical Departments that a Writer should be appointed to assist the Established Clerk in the Office duties of those Departments, in place of Mr. Alexander Ward now retired from the Service, I beg respectfully to request that Mr. John Downton may be

---

[1]MS in clerk's hand, signed by Mill, in L/F/2/210, No. 82 of Oct. 1857, India Office Library and Records.
[2]See Letters 258G, 262D, 283A above, and 306A below.

---

[1]MS in clerk's hand, signed by Mill, in L/F/2/210, No. 203 of Oct. 1857, India Office Library and Records.

relieved from the copying duties hitherto performed by him and appointed to the duties hitherto discharged by Mr. Ward, on the allowances usual in such cases.

    I have the honor to be, Honorable Sirs
        Your most faithful and obedient Servant
            J.S. MILL

299A. TO THE FINANCE AND HOME COMMITTEE[1]

        Examiner's Office
        Jan. 25, 1858

HONORABLE SIRS,

I beg to submit for the favourable consideration of your Honorable Committee, a letter which has been addressed to me by Mr Hawkins,[2] one of the Assistant Examiners, enclosing an application from Mr Charles Bell,[3] one of the Writers in this Office who perform the duties of Established Clerks, to be either placed on the Establishment on his present allowances, or to have his allowances consolidated, as has been done in several cases of a nature similar to his own.

The letter appended to the application will prove to your Honorable Committee, what I can also state from my personal knowledge, that Mr Hill,[4] under whom Mr Bell served for nine years, considered his services to be highly valuable, and his qualification to be of a superior order; and I join with Mr Hawkins in regarding Mr Bell as well worthy of any mark of consideration which may be bestowed on him by the Honorable Court.

    I have the honor to be, Honorable Sirs
        Your most faithful and obedient Servant
            J.S. MILL

---

[1] MS in clerk's hand, except for date and signature, in L/F/2/214, No. 91 of Feb. 1858, India Office Library and Records.

[2] John Abraham Francis Hawkins was Assistant Examiner in the Judicial and Legislative Department.

[3] See Letter 258H above.

[4] David Hill (1786–1866) had retired as Assistant Examiner in March 1856.

299B. TO THOMAS N. WATERFIELD[1]

East India House,
February 10th, 1858

Secret.
SIR,

I am directed by the Secret Committee to request, that you will be pleased to obtain the consent of the Right Honorable the Commissioners for the Affairs of India to the employment, in the Secret Department, of Mr John Stewart Oliphant, a Clerk in the Secretary's Office, and of Mr Frank Mangles, a Clerk, and Mr Richard Upton, a Writer, in the Examiner's Office, on their taking the prescribed oath.

I am, Sir,
Your most obedient servant,
J.S. MILL

T.N. Waterfield Esqre

306A. TO THE FINANCE AND HOME COMMITTEE[1]

Examiner's Office
April 1858

HONORABLE SIRS,

In October last your Honorable Committee were pleased to authorize the reemployment of two extra writers in this office, for a period of six months.

In December last, one of the two extra writers, Mr. W.I. Upton,[2] was appointed a permanent Writer in another Office, — and for some time, one temporary writer only was employed. Mr. Richard Upton, one of the regular Writers, having been subsequently removed from the body of the office to the Secret department, a second temporary writer was again urgently required, and Mr. W.C. Fidler was engaged for the unexpired term already sanctioned. That period will expire on the 22nd instant, and as the business of the office still requires their assistance, I respectfully submit to you the expediency of retaining their Services for such further period as may be required.

I have the honor to be, Honorable Sirs,
Your most faithful and obedient Servant
J.S. MILL

---

[1] MS in clerk's hand, signed by Mill, in L/P&S/3/60, p. 145, India Office Library and Records.

---

[1] MS in clerk's hand, signed by Mill, in L/F/2/216, No. 164 of Apr. 1858, India Office Library and Records.
[2] See Letters 262D, 283A, and 293A above.

309A. TO THE SECRETARY TO THE INDIA BOARD[1]

East India House,
23rd April 1858

Secret.
SIR,

I have laid before the Secret Committee of the East India Company[2] Sir George Clerk's letter of the 20th instant,[3] inviting the observations of the Committee on the letter from the Government of India dated the 8th ultimo,[4] respecting the proposed exchange of territory in India between the British and French Governments: and I am directed to state in reply that the Committee entirely concur in the opinions expressed by the Government of India, and in their recommendation that the proposed Convention should be concluded, with the slight modification suggested in paragraph 2 of the letter from the Government of India, and the verbal correction indicated in para 3. I am, Sir,

Your obedient Servant,
(Signed) J.S. MILL

309B. TO THE FINANCE AND HOME COMMITTEE[1]

[ca. 22 June, 1858]

HONORABLE SIRS,

I beg to lay before your Honorable Committee the accompanying Petition which has been placed in my hands by the Messengers in the Book Office.

I have the honor to be, Honrble Sirs
your most obedient servant
J.S. MILL

---

[1] MS copy in L/P&S/3/1, pp. [490]-1, India Office Library and Records.
[2] At the April elections, Frederick Currie had become Chairman, and William Joseph Eastwick (1808–89) Deputy Chairman of the Company.
[3] A copy of Clerk's letter is in L/P&S/3/1, p. [490].
[4] Not located.

---

[1] MS in L/F/2/218, No. 164 of June 1858, India Office Library and Records.

321A. TO THOMAS N. WATERFIELD[1]

East India House,
3rd August 1858

Secret.
SIR,

I have received and laid before the Secret Committee your letter dated the 28th ultimô forwarding for any remarks the Committee might desire to make, a letter from Her Majesty's Minister at the Court of Persia[2] respecting the composition and the allowances of the Commission about to proceed to Herat, and I am directed to state in reply that the Committee have no objection to make to any of the arrangements recommended by Sir James Outram.[3]

I am, Sir,
Your most obedient Servant,
(Signed) J.S. MILL

T.N. Waterfield Esqre

323A. TO THE FINANCE AND HOME COMMITTEE[1]

Examiner's Office
East India House
24th August 1858

HONORABLE SIRS,

I have the honor to submit, for the favorable consideration of your Honrble Committee, a Memorandum placed in my hands by Mr Prideaux, Assistant Examiner of India Correspondence, bringing to notice the Services rendered, in addition to those required from him in the discharge of his ordinary Official Duty, by Mr William Peters, an Established Clerk in the Revenue Department of this Office. Under an Order of the House of Commons, he has been, for a considerable time, employed in selecting from a vast mass of correspondence, documents illustrative of the measures taken by the East India Company for increasing the

---

[1] MS copy in L/P&S/3/1, p. [488], India Office Library and Records.
[2] See Letter 286E above. The letter referred to has not been located.
[3] Outram had been appointed the military member of the Governor-General's Council in April of 1858.

---

[1] MS in clerk's hand, signed by Mill, in L/F/2/220, No. 171 of Aug. 1858, India Office Library and Records.

quantity or improving the quality, of the supply of Cotton from India,[2] for the use of manufacturers in this Country.

In order that the Return to the requisition of the House of Commons should be made as extensively useful as possible, to those who were likely to consult it, Mr Peters has devoted much time and labour to the arrangement, under distinct heads, of the matters treated of in the papers; so as to render them easy of reference;—and he has, moreover, carefully corrected the proof sheets, during their passage through the Press.

I desire to add that I concur in Mr Prideaux's testimony in favor of Mr Peters.

I have the honor to be, Honorable Sirs,
With the greatest respect,
Your faithful and obedient Servant
J.S. MILL
Examiner of India Correspondence

323B. TO THE FINANCE AND HOME COMMITTEE[1]

[ca. 24 Aug. 1858]

HONORABLE SIRS

I beg to lay before your Honorable Committee an application from Mr Atkins, Deputy Registrar in the Book Office, to be allowed to retain the services of William Spence, an Assistant Messenger in his Department, who has been called on to take the duties of Messenger, but whose knowledge of his present duties renders him more useful in his existing position than in that to which he would be transferred. I therefore submit the request of Mr Atkins to the favorable consideration of your Honorable Committee.

I have the honor to be, Honorable Sirs
your most obedient Servant
J.S. MILL

---

[2]"Return to an Order of the Honourable House of Commons Dated 24 August 1857; for, a Selection of Papers Showing the Measures Taken since 1847 to Promote the Cultivation of Cotton in India," *PP*, 1857 (II), XXXI.

[1]MS in L/F/2/220, No. 178 of Aug. 1858, India Office Library and Records.

324. TO THEODOR GOMPERZ[1]

East India House
Aug. 30. 1858

DEAR SIR

*a b*have received your letter of the 21st,[2] and*b* have been interested by the information as to your papers in the Rhenish Museum.[3] I was disappointed however at your not saying anything of your historical work on Greek philosophy,[4] which I expect will be very valuable, not only by throwing new light on historical points, of which there are always a great number to be cleared up by any competent enquirer, but also by exhibiting the speculations of the ancients from the point of view of the experience philosophy, a thing hardly yet attempted, and least of all in your country.

I have no objection to your annexing to the Logic any part of the controversy with Whewell[5] which you think likely to be useful. There are not many defences extant of the ethics of utility, and I have sometimes thought of reprinting this and other papers I have written on the same as well as on other subjects.*a*[6]

We were glad to hear of the improvement in your sister's health.[7] With regard to my own, which you kindly enquire about, there is nothing alarming in it, but I require a long recruiting, not so much from work, as from the confinement of an office, which has made it advisable for me to decline the position offered me in the new government of India.[8] I am Dr Sir

yrs very truly
J.S. MILL

---

[1]MS at Kokugakuin University, Tokyo. The first two paragraphs are in *CW*, Vol. XV, pp. 569–70.
[2]Not located.
[3]See Letter 292 above.
[4]Eventually published as *Griechische Denker. Eine Geschichte der antiken Philosophie*, 3 vols. (Leipzig: Veit, [1893]-1909).
[5]I.e., Mill's "Whewell on Moral Philosophy," *Westminster Review*, LVIII (Oct. 1852), 349–85; in *CW*, Vol. X, pp. 165–201. Gomperz did not include it in *Gesammelte Werke*.
[6]In 1859 he included "Whewell on Moral Philosophy" in *Dissertations and Discussions*, Vol. II, pp. 450–509.
[7]Cf. Letter 292 above.
[8]When the Crown took over the full government of India, and the East India Company was dissolved, Mill was offered a seat on the new Council by Edward Henry Stanley (1826–93), Lord Stanley, the Secretary of State for India.

a-a[*in* CW]
b-b[*not in* CW]

336A. TO JACOB WALEY[1]

Blackheath Park
Nov. 29. 1858

SIR

Having been absent, I only received your note two days ago. I am at present little capable, and little disposed, to apply my mind to such subjects. But I owe you an acknowledgment, as your note shews that you have entered intelligently into a train of reasoning which it is impossible to make anything of without a real capacity for these enquiries, and a real application of mind to them. It is always a satisfaction to a writer on any scientific subject to find such readers. As to the particular point on which we differ,[2] it makes, as you justly remark, no difference in the result, as the conditions of the international demand finally decide the terms of international exchange, whatever may be the effect of the improvement in the first instance. But I still think I was right, as the result of an improvement in any article brought to a given market must surely be, in the beginning, to cheapen it relatively to *all* articles previously sold in that market. I am Sir

Yrs faithfully
J.S. MILL

376A. TO WILLIAM STEBBING[1]

Blackheath Park
March 26. 1859

DEAR SIR

Your note has only just reached me. If my doing so can be of any use to you, I cannot possibly have any objection to state, that from such consideration as I had time to give to your Analysis of my Logic,[2] it appeared to me not merely well, but

---

[1]MS in the Anglo-Jewish Archive, Mocatta Library, University College London. Published in *MNL*, XXI (Winter 1986), 2–3, edited by J.M. Robson.

Jacob Waley (1818–73), Conveyancer to the Court of Chancery, philanthropist, Professor of Political Economy at University College London.

[2]Waley's letter has not been located, but the reference is surely to "Effect of improvements in production on international values," Bk. III, Chap. xviii, Sect. 5 (added in the 3rd ed., 1852, and not thereafter modified) of Mill's *Principles*; in *CW*, Vol. III, pp. 604–7.

---

[1]MS in the Harry Ransom Humanities Research Center, Unversity of Texas at Austin. *Addressed:* William Stebbing Esq. / Rolls Chambers / 89 Chancery Lane.

William Stebbing (1832–1926), journalist and editor.

[2]*An Analysis of Mr. Mill's System of Logic* (London: Longman, *et al.*, 1864).

extraordinarily well done. I was surprised to find so much of the meaning so well packed into so few words. I am

yrs very faithfully
J.S. MILL

381. TO THEODOR GOMPERZ[1]

Blackheath Park
March 31. 1859

DEAR SIR

About the 1st of February a copy of the little book[2] was sent to the friend mentioned by you,[3] but I unluckily omitted writing to let you know. Perhaps you will kindly inform me by letter addressed à Saint Véran près Avignon, Vaucluse, France, whether it has reached you. If not, another copy shall be sent, in any way you direct.

*a*The book has had much more success, and has made a greater impression, than I had the smallest expectation of.

We[4] shall be at Avignon for some time,*a* and shall probably remain abroad at least a year. *b*I hope to hear from you sometimes at that place, as I am very desirous to know how your various literary projects go on.*b* I am

yours very sincerely
J.S. MILL

388A. TO JOHN WILLIAM PARKER[1]

Saint Véran, near Avignon
April 26, 1859

DEAR SIR

The subject of the diminution of the value of gold is not one on which I feel disposed to write, as it requires a minute investigation of details with which I am

---

[1]MS at Kokugakuin University, Tokyo. Part published in *CW*, Vol. XV, p. 613.
[2]*On Liberty*.
[3]Not identified.
[4]The plural pronoun now includes his step-daughter, Helen Taylor (1831–1907), his companion during the remaining years of his life.

a-a[*in* CW]
b-b[*in* CW]

---

[1]MS at Kwansai Daigaku, Suita, Japan. Published in *Mill Society Bulletin Japan* [*MSBJ*], I, no. 6 (1985), 19–23, edited by Shigekazu Yamashita.

not at present well acquainted, and I have not access here to the sources of information. The best paper I have seen on the subject was in the Journal of the Statistical Society of Dublin, and was written by Mr Cairnes, the Whately Professor of Pol. Economy at Dublin University.[2] Perhaps he might be induced to write again on the subject for Fraser.[3]

I thank you for the inclosures you sent which I was well pleased to see, though none of them proved very important or interesting.

If you should think there is sufficient demand for the pamphlet to warrant a second edition, I should like the part of the article in *Fraser* which relates to Hare's book, subjoined by way of Appendix.[4] I should not like simply to reprint the pamphlet as I wrote it before I had seen Hare's book; while it would be troublesome to recast it as completely as would be necessary to incorporate Hare's ideas. If you should at any time be disposed to adopt this plan, I will send you a few words of preface.

Your correspondent Mr Smythe's[5] *original* suggestion is as old as the hills.

yrs very truly
J.S. MILL

392. TO THEODOR GOMPERZ[1]

Saint Véran, près Avignon
May 16. 1859

DEAR SIR

I am now at the above address and shall be here for some time to come; and as the war between France and Austria[2] makes it uncertain whether any letters will be forwarded, the only sure way I have of corresponding with you is through my

---

[2]John Elliot Cairnes (1823–75), a disciple and close friend of Mill's, "The Laws, According to Which a Depreciation of the Precious Metals Consequent upon an Increase of Supply Takes Place, Considered in Connection with the Recent Gold Discoveries," *Journal of the Dublin Statistical Society*, Pt. XIII (Jan. 1859), 236–69.

[3]Cairnes did so: see his two-part article, "Essay towards an Experimental Solution of the Gold Question," *Fraser's Magazine*, LX (Sept. 1859), 267–78, and LXI (Jan. 1860), 38–53.

[4]In the 2nd ed. of *Thoughts on Parliamentary Reform* (London: Parker, 1859; 1st ed. also 1859), the highly laudatory part of "Recent Writers on Reform," *Fraser's Magazine*, LIX (Apr. 1859), 489–508, dealing with *A Treatise on the Election of Representatives Parliamentary and Municipal* (London: Longman, et al., 1859), by Thomas Hare (1806–91) was added; see *CW*, Vol. XIX, pp. 358–70.

[5]Not identified.

---

[1]MS at Kokugakuin University, Tokyo. Part published in *CW*, Vol. XV, p. 621.

[2]From April to July, France and Austria were at war over the place of Piedmont in a unified Italy.

publishers, Messrs J.W. Parker and Son, 445 West Strand, to whom please address any letter you may favour me with. ^{a}I am rather anxious to hear from you, not knowing whether you have received the sheets of the little book, and in case you have, whether you still have any idea of translating it. I should much prefer you to any other translator who is likely to offer, but I have always thought it probable that you might have good reasons against undertaking it, and that some other part of Germany might be more suitable for bringing the book[3] before the German public. In addition to an offer which was made through Messrs Parker, I have lately received one under the signature of Eduard John, Justizrath, at Marienwerder^a in Prussia,[4] ^{b}who^b writes like a competent person, and ^{c}has sent me a portion of a translation actually executed; but as it is in the German Manuscript character, which I do not read fluently, I am not at present able to judge of its merits.^{c} Do you know anything of this gentleman, and would you advise me, in case the undertaking should not suit yourself, to close with his offer?

^{d}I could write much about politics, but think it more prudent to wait for some better opportunity; though I certainly do not side with France in this miserable war, which I condemn as strongly as any Austrian can.^{d}

I am Dear Sir
very truly yours
J.S. MILL

398. TO THEODOR GOMPERZ[1]

Saint Véran, near Avignon
June 11. 1859

DEAR SIR

^{a}I sincerely condole with you on the unhappy events which have caused you so much pain and disturbance of mind. The delay in answering my letter has occasioned no inconvenience, and since you are willing to translate the little book,[2] or rather have by this time actually done so, I desire nothing better than to

---

[3]Gomperz translated *On Liberty* as *Über die Freiheit*, which later appeared in *Gesammelte Werke*, Vol. I (1869), pp. 1–123.
[4]Richard Eduard John (1827–89), German jurist, author of *Einiges über das Unterrichts-Gesetz* (1861).

$^{a-a}$[*in* CW]
$^{b-b}$[*in* CW]
$^{c-c}$[*in* CW]
$^{d-d}$[*in* CW]

---

[1]MS at Kokugakuin University, Tokyo. Most included in *CW*, Vol. XV, p. 625.
[2]*On Liberty*; see Letter 392.

$^{a-a}$[*in* CW]

leave it in your hands, and certainly should not think of giving the preference to any other translator. I have no objection to the omission of any part or the whole of the note to which you refer, nor of the sentence ^{b}in^b page 9,³ though in the latter case I have not been able to discover what there is which renders it more unsuitable for publication than all the rest of the chapter. Perhaps^a you think ^{c}some words in it may be understood as a declaration against Kingly government, but nothing of the sort was intended, nor did it occur to me that any one ^{d}would^d think so. The only opinion expressed or implied is in favour of free political institutions, and even that is but incidental. But I do not think the retention of the sentence of any importance.^{c}

When you next do me the favour to write, it would interest me to hear something of your other literary projects. I am Dear Sir

Yours very truly
J.S. MILL

408A. TO HENRI BORDÈRE¹

Saint Véran, Avignon
le 14 août 1859

MON CHER MONSIEUR BORDÈRE

Je vous remercie beaucoup de votre aimable lettre. L'échantillon du Myosotis n'était pas, en effet, suffisant pour reconnaître l'espèce, à moins qu'elle ne vous fût déjà très bien connue. Maintenant j'envoie un meilleur échantillon et je serai bien aise si, par un hasard heureux, je puis vous offrir une plante que vous ne possédiez pas. Cela ne pourrait être que si vous n'avez jamais herborisé à Panticose,² car je trouvai la plante dans le village même, à côté de la route.

L'ami à qui je compte m'adresser pour le catalogue des plantes britanniques ne

---

³The sentence in question reads: "And so long as mankind were content to combat one enemy by another, and to be ruled by a master, on condition of being guaranteed more or less efficaciously against his tyranny, they did not carry their aspirations beyond this point" (*CW*, Vol. XVIII, p. 218).

$^{b\text{-}b}$CW on
$^{c\text{-}c}$[*in* CW]
$^{d\text{-}d}$CW could

---

¹MS in the Prussian State Library, Berlin.
Henri Bordère (1825–59), botanist of the Hautes Pyrénées, whom Mill presumably met on his trip to the area in July 1859. Bordère's letter has not been located.
²A village in the Spanish Pyrenees close to the French border.

sera à Londres que dans quinze jours.³ Je lui écrirai sans délai pour le prier de vous l'expédier.

votre dévoué
J.S. Mill

430A. TO SAMUEL LUCAS[1]

Saint Véran, Avignon
Dec. 24. 1859

Dear Sir

If your letter of November 28 had reached me before, instead of long after, that of December 2, I could have done nothing better than to have referred you to Mr Kaye as the fittest person to write such a biographical sketch of Mr Elphinstone as you required.[2]

I was glad to hear that you have a share in the editorship of "Once a Week." It is a good literary connexion, and may lead to other things. With regard however to your proposal on the subject of writing for it, I have so many calls on my time, and I have so much in hand which tasks to the utmost all my capacity of writing, that I cannot hold out any prospect of my being able to do what you suggest.

I am Dear Sir
yours faithfully
J.S. Mill

---

[3] The most likely friend is one of his companions on botanical field trips, Alexander Irvine (1793–1873), compiler of the *Illustrated Handbook of the British Plants* (London: Nelson, 1858), and also editor of the *Phytologist*, for which Mill wrote.

---

[1] MS in the University of Iowa Library.
Samuel Lucas (1818–68), editor of *Once a Week* 1859–65, and brother of Frederick Lucas, another of Mill's correspondents.

[2] For Kaye, see Letter 258D above. He had continued in the India Office after the transfer of the Company's Charter to the Crown in 1858. In the interval Mill mentions, he had supplied for Lucas an obituary, "Mountstuart Elphinstone. In Memoriam," *Once a Week*, I (10 Dec., 1859), 502–4. Elphinstone (1779–1859), whose successful career in India was capped by his Governorship of the Bombay Presidency 1819–27, was regarded, on his return to England, as a major authority on India.

443A. TO HERBERT SPENCER[1]

Blackheath
Feb. 11. 1860

DEAR SIR

I have not the smallest objection to your making the use you propose of my name, or indeed any other use.[2] I considered my consent to that as included in becoming a subscriber. The names in your note are very good ones & I hope you will have many more of the same high character.

yours very truly
J.S. MILL

460A. TO FRANÇOIS AUGUSTE MARIE MIGNET[1]

Amélie les Bains
Pyrénées Orientales
le 17 mai 1860

MONSIEUR

Je viens de recevoir votre lettre du 28 avril, dans laquelle vous m'avertissez que l'Académie des Sciences Morales et Politiques de l'Institut m'a nommé un de ces correspondants pour la section d'Economie Politique en remplacement de mon excellent ami M. Tooke.[2]

Veuillez, Monsieur, servir d'interprète auprès de l'Académie, à mes sentiments de respectueuse reconnaissance. De tous les honneurs qui pourraient m'arriver, il n'y en a pas un auquel je pourrais être plus sensible qu'à celui qui m'associe au plus illustre de tous les corps savants. Ce sera pour moi un nouveau motif d'essayer de me montrer de plus en plus digne de cette distinction, en continuant de travailler consciencieusement aux sciences dont l'Académie s'occupe, et qui aujourdhui

---

[1] MS in the University of London Library.
Herbert Spencer (1820–1903), philosopher, social scientist, and psychologist.
[2] Spencer was collecting a list of influential subscribers to his projected *System of Philosophy* to be issued in quarterly instalments at 2/6, so that he could go to the public for more support in a circular, which was issued in the next month. He finally obtained between 300 and 400 subscribers, but the scheme was unfulfilled; the first part of the proposed work, *First Principles* (London: Williams and Norgate, 1862) was sold in the normal fashion.

---

[1] MS at the Archives de l'Institut de France, Paris.
François Auguste Marie Mignet (1796–1884), journalist and historian, Permanent Secretary of the Académie des Sciences Morales et Politiques of the Institut de France 1837–84, and Director of the Foreign Office Archives until 1848. See also Letters 487A and 600A below.
[2] I.e., Thomas Tooke; see Letter 8.1 above.

importent encore plus que les sciences physiques à l'amélioration et même au bien-être matériel de l'humanité.

Permettez-moi enfin, Monsieur, de profiter de cette occasion pour vous témoigner, à vous personnellement, la haute estime que je professe depuis longtemps pour vos écrits et pour votre caractère.[3]

J. STUART MILL

487A. TO FRANÇOIS AUGUSTE MARIE MIGNET[1]

Blackheath Park, Kent
le 8 avril, 1861

MONSIEUR

Je suis au moment de publier un Traité du Gouvernement Représentatif,[2] dont un exemplaire vous sera promptement expédié, avec prière de le soumettre à l'Académie.

Je n'ose croire que l'ensemble des opinions exposées dans cet ouvrage obtiendra l'assentiment général de l'Académie. Mais j'espère qu'elle m'accordera sa sympathie, que je suis beaucoup plus sûr de mériter; et quel que puisse être son jugement sur l'ouvrage, j'ose dire qu'elle y trouvera un désir vrai d'envisager les questions de tous les côtés, sans parti pris de part ou d'autre.

J'ai l'honneur d'être, Monsieur, avec les sentiments les plus distingués,

votre dévoué serviteur
J. STUART MILL

487B. TO THEODOR GOMPERZ[1]

Saint Véran, Avignon
April 18, 1861

DEAR SIR

I am sorry to say I have mislaid the address you gave me, and I am afraid this

---

[3]One of Mill's earliest writings on history was his "Mignet's French Revolution," *Westminster Review*, V (Apr. 1826), 385–98; in *CW*, Vol. XX, pp. 1–14.

---

[1]MS in the possession of Professor Satoshi Yamasaki, Kagawa University. *Addressed:* Monsieur le Sécrétaire Perpetuel de l'Académie des Sciences Morales et Politiques. See also Letters 460A above and 600A below.

[2]*Considerations on Representative Government* (London: Parker, 1861); in *CW*, Vol. XIX, pp. 371–577.

---

[1]MS at Kokugakuin University, Tokyo.

note may not reach you. If you receive it, will you kindly let me know how to address you in future, and in particular how to send you a copy of a volume I have just published on Representative Government.[2]

I was much surprised a short time ago to learn from a review which was sent to me, that a translation of the "Liberty" has been published in Germany.[3] I know nothing of the translator, who neither had, nor asked for, any authority from me.

In the uncertainty whether what I write will reach you, I say no more at present.

I am Dear Sir

Very truly yours
J.S. MILL

I propose remaining here till the beginning of June.

492A. TO NASSAU W. SENIOR[1]

Avignon
May 24. 1861

DEAR SENIOR

As far as I have power over the paper by Tocqueville in the London and Westminster (if I have any such power) I most willingly consent to its being made use of in the manner you propose.[2] I believe however it will be found that the article, though in itself of very great interest, is superseded by the volume "L'ancien régime et la révolution,"[3] of which it may be said to be, as far as it goes, the first draft.

If we could but have your volumes of Tocqueville's conversations! Some time or other, doubtless, they will be published.[4]

I am very desirous to read your book on Education, which I suppose is the separate report Chadwick told me of, and I am glad it has the dimensions of a book.[5] Please send it, not here, but to Blackheath Park, as I expect to be there early

---

[2]The first edition of *Considerations on Representative Government* was published by Parker in April.
[3]*Über die Freiheit*, trans. F. Pickford (Frankfurt: Sauerländer, 1860).

---

[1]MS in the National Library of Wales, Aberystwyth.
[2]When editor of the *London and Westminster Review*, Mill had solicited from Alexis Henri Charles Maurice Clérel, comte de Tocqueville (1805–59), social analyst, historian, and politician, one article, "Political and Social Condition of France," for Vol. III & XXV (Apr. 1836), 137–69. It is not known what use Senior wished to make of the article.
[3]Tocqueville, *L'ancien régime et la révolution* (Paris: Lévy, 1856).
[4]They eventually were, by Senior's daughter, as *Correspondence and Conversations of Alexis de Tocqueville with Nassau William Senior from 1834–1859*, ed. M.C.M. Simpson, 2 vols. (London: King, 1872).
[5]Senior, who was a member of the Royal Commission on Popular Education 1858–61,

in June. My full address here is Saint-Véran, près Avignon, Vaucluse, but your letter came duly, though directed simply Avignon, France.

I am Dear Senior
very truly yours
J.S. MILL

494A. TO THEODOR GOMPERZ[1]

Blackheath Park
Kent
July 3, 1861

DEAR SIR

About three months ago I published a volume on Representative Government of which one of the first copies would have been sent to you, had I not unfortunately forgotten and mislaid your address.[2] I wrote to you from Avignon a note directed only to Herr Theodor Gomperz, in Wien, on the bare chance that it might reach you, but I suppose it did not. On returning from the South I have for the first time been able to make a regular search for the address you gave me, and have fortunately found it. I have therefore directed my publisher to send you a copy without delay.

I was vexed to find, from a German Review which was sent to me, that a translation has been made into German, I know not by whom, of the little volume on Liberty.[3] Had my consent been asked, I should not have given it, unless I had heard from you that you had abandoned the intention you at one time had of translating the book. But as I made no reservation of the right of translation, my consent was not necessary. Indeed I do not even know that England has any convention on the subject with the German States.

I should much like to hear from you respecting yourself, and your literary and other doings and projects. I am Dear Sir

yours very truly
J.S. MILL

---

decided to publish his views, not adopted by the Commission, in *Suggestions on Popular Education* (London: Murray, 1861).

[1] MS at Kokugakuin University, Tokyo.
[2] See Letter 487B.
[3] See Letter 487B.

503A. TO ANDRÉ COCHUT[1]

Blackheath Park, Kent
le 8 août 1861

MONSIEUR

Quand j'eus l'honneur de vous voir à la réunion de la Société d'Economie Politique,[2] vous avez eu la bonté de m'offrir des renseignements sur l'état actuel des associations ouvrières. Je tiens beaucoup à être bien informé sur ce sujet, d'autant plus que je m'occupe actuellement de la révision de mon traité d'Economie Politique pour une édition nouvelle;[3] et comme nul autre en France n'est plus compétent, je crois même que nul n'est aussi compétent que vous en cette matière, ce serait une véritable obligation que je vous aurais si vous vouliez bien me donner les renseignemens en question, ou m'indiquer le moyen de me les procurer.

Ne sachant pas votre adresse, je vous écris par l'intermédiaire de M. Guillaumin.[4]

Veuillez agréer, Monsieur, l'expression de mes sentiments les plus distingués.

J.S. MILL

527A. TO CATHERINE HELEN SPENCE[1]

Saint Véran, Avignon
Jan. 12. 1862

DEAR MADAM

I received your letter at this place, but the pamphlet you did me the favour to send has not been forwarded, and I do not expect to see it until I return to England.[2]

---

[1] MS in the Fonds Cochut, Archives Nationales, Paris.
André Cochut (1812–90), a collaborator on the *Revue des Deux Mondes* 1837–69, writer on economic and political affairs, including workers' associations.
[2] Probably at the meeting held on 11 April, 1861, when a question of Mill's was discussed: "What is the value of Moral Education to Economical Improvement; and conversely, what are the bearings of Economical Prosperity on Moral Excellence?"
[3] The 5th ed., 1862.
[4] Gilbert Urbain Guillaumin (1801–64), co-founder of the *Journal des Economistes* in 1842, was the publisher of the French translation of the 3rd ed. of Mill's *Principles*.

---

[1] MS in the Mitchell Library, State Library of New South Wales. *Addressed:* Miss Spence / Stepney / near Adelaide / South Australia.
Catherine Helen Spence (1825–1910), Australian novelist and leading advocate of women's rights.
[2] Inspired by Mill's account of Hare's scheme in his "Recent Writers on Reform," Spence wrote *A Plea for Pure Democracy: Mr. Hare's Reform Bill Applied to South Australia* (Adelaide: Rigby, 1861). It was being forwarded through Henry Parkes (1815–96), an Australian statesman who corresponded with Mill.

I therefore suggest your making other arrangements for sending the pamphlets to Mr Helps and Mr Buckle;³ neither can I, in general, undertake to forward papers. I have read your letters in the Adelaide newspaper,⁴ and found them a very clear and useful statement of Mr Hare's plan and its merits. You will be glad to hear, if you have not already heard it from himself, that Mr Hare thinks very favourably of your pamphlet. It is much to be desired that the attempt to bring the plan before your House of Assembly, should be repeated.⁵ The question is sure to be advanced by discussion. It is decidedly making progress in many other parts of the world besides England and Australia.

I was not aware that, as you say, the association with my name is likely to bring discredit on the plan in South Australia, and I am sorry to hear that you think so: if it is so, however, you do judiciously to avoid it. I suppose I am to understand the sentence in your letter which includes giving the suffrage to women in the category of "absurdities" as ironical.

                                          I am Dear Madam
                                          yours very faithfully
                                                       J.S. MILL

527B. TO CAROLINE WELLS DALL¹

                                          Saint Véran, Avignon
                                                  Vaucluse, France
                                                        Jan. 15. 1862

DEAR MADAM

I had the honour of receiving at this place, your letter of November 1st: but as the book you were kind enough to send,² does not seem to have found its way to my

---

³Arthur Helps (1813–75), reforming author, Clerk of the Privy Council from 1860, and Henry Thomas Buckle (1821–62), historian of civilization.
⁴Letters to the editor, entitled "Representation of Minorities," signed C.H.S., in the *South Australian Gazette and Colonial Register* for 31 Aug. and 9 Sept., 1861, both p. 3.
⁵The plan was introduced as part of 14 & 15 Victoria, 1861, No. 20, to the South Australian parliament in ineffectual speeches on 3 May and 1 August, 1861, by Lavington Glyde (1823–90), an English-born accountant and parliamentarian. He vainly raised the issue again in 1871 and 1872. After a period when her reforming energies were directed to other projects, Spence returned to proportional representation in the 1890s, and from 1902 to 1910 a bill embodying her version of the plan was introduced annually in the South Australian parliament.

¹MS at the Massachusetts Historical Society.
Caroline Wells Dall (née Healey) (1822–1912), advocate of equal opportunity in education and economic life.
²Dall, *Woman's Rights under the Law: In Three Lectures Delivered in Boston, January, 1861* (Boston: Walker, Wise, 1861). Mill is mentioned on pp. 92–4, and Harriet Taylor Mill's "Enfranchisement of Women" on p. 108.

publishers, Messrs Parker, along with the letter, I am as yet ignorant even of its subject. But I cannot doubt that one who expresses so strong an interest in the memory of her whom I have lost, is a participator in her and my opinions, at least on the one point which, with us both, was and is the most fundamental of all. You ask for information respecting her. About two years ago, in reprinting from the Westminster Review her article headed "Enfranchisement of Women," to be included with some of my own writings in a collection entitled "Dissertations and Discussions," I prefixed a few paragraphs, containing what I felt prompted to say, and as much as I thought suitable to be said, to those who were personally strangers to her.[3] Only those who knew her can appreciate how vain it would be to attempt to convey in words an impression of a character so rich and various as hers. It is the object of my life to express in my writings as much as I can render of the thoughts and sentiments which she inspired.

I am Madam
very faithfully yours
J.S. MILL

529A. TO GILBERT URBAIN GUILLAUMIN[1]

Saint Véran, Avignon
le 22 janvier 1862

MON CHER MONSIEUR

J'apprends de M. Dupont-White que sa traduction va paraître très prochainement.[2] Outre l'exemplaire que je vous ai prié d'envoyer, pour mon compte, à M. Auguste Picard[3] je vous prie de vouloir bien en envoyer un autre à M. le capitaine d'artillerie Célestin de Blignières,[4] Rue de Madame, 40.

Je vous ai expédié, il y a quelques semaines, par mandat de poste, avec le prix de plusieurs livres, le montant de mon abonnement au Journal des Economistes pour

---

[3]"Enfranchisement of Women," *Westminster Review*, LX (July 1851), 289–311, was reprinted in *Dissertations and Discussions*, 2 vols. (London: Parker, 1859), Vol. II, pp. 411–49; in *CW*, Vol. XXI, pp. 393–415. For the prefatory paragraphs, see *Dissertations and Discussions*, Vol. II, pp. 411–12; in *CW*, Vol. XXI, pp. 393–4.

---

[1]MS in the possession of Professor Arnold Heertje, University of Amsterdam. For Guillaumin, see Letter 503A above.
[2]Charles Brook Dupont-White (1807–78), French economist, translated Mill's *Representative Government* as *Le gouvernement représentatif* (Paris: Guillaumin, 1862).
[3]A writer on economic and agricultural subjects, and friend of Mill's in Avignon.
[4]Célestin le Barbier de Blignières (1822–1905), positivist philosopher. Mill wrote to him on the same day, thanking him for his *Exposition abrégée et populaire de la philosophie et de la religion positives* (Paris: Chamerot, 1857), and promising him a copy of the translation of *Representative Government*; see *CW*, Vol. XV, pp. 768–70.

l'année suivante. Le numéro du 15 janvier ne m'est pourtant pas encore parvenu. Je pars le 29 janvier pour voyager en Grèce, mais comptant revenir ici avant de passer en Angleterre, je vous engage à envoyer toujours le Journal à Saint-Véran comme auparavant.

Ma fille se recommande aux souvenirs amicaux de Mademoiselle Guillaumin,[5] et je vous prie, mon cher Monsieur, d'agréer mes salutations amicales.

J.S. MILL

M. Littré a écrit pour le Journal des Débats des articles sur mon livre et sur les livres de M. Dupont-White.[6] Oserai-je vous prier, lorsqu'ils auront paru, de m'envoyer les numéros qui les contiennent? Adressés Poste Restante à Athènes, ils me trouveraient jusqu'au milieu ou à la fin de mai. Je vous en rembourserai à la première occasion.

J.S.M.

529B. TO JOHN WILLIAM PARKER[1]

Saint Véran, Avignon
Jan. 25. 1862

DEAR SIR

Many thanks for the cheque, and for your attention to my wishes about the separate copies.[2] We shall not be able to leave till the 30th, so that I can have a day's more proofs.[3] Anything posted on Tuesday will reach me before I start. And anything sent so as to be delivered here by the 12th (to make sure of which, it would have to be posted not later than the 9th if a letter, or the 8th if anything printed) will reach Athens by a private hand, as soon as I shall myself. I should therefore like the February Fraser to be sent here in the usual manner. The separate copies may remain with you for the present, as I may perhaps think of some more

---

[5] Guillaumin's daughter, who continued his publishing business after his death; see Letter 1699A below.

[6] The anticipated articles by Maximilien Paul Emile Littré (1801–81), lexicographer, scholar, and positivist philosopher, seem not to have been published in *Le Journal des Débats*. Mill's review of Dupont-White's *L'individu et l'état*, 2nd ed. (Paris: Guillaumin, 1858), and *La centralisation* (Paris: Guillaumin, 1860) appeared as "Centralisation," *Edinburgh Review*, CXV (Apr. 1862), 323–58; in *CW*, XIX, 579–613.

---

[1] MS in the Houghton Library, Harvard University.

[2] I.e., offprints of Mill's "The Contest in America," *Fraser's Magazine*, LXV (Feb. 1862), 258–68 (in *CW*, Vol. XXI, pp. 125–42); the list of recipients has not survived. A copy of the offprint is in Mill's library, Somerville College, Oxford.

[3] He and Helen Taylor (1831–1907), his step-daughter, companion, and collaborator after her mother's death, were setting out for a trip through Greece.

persons to whom I should wish copies sent. Newspapers from Australia, and the Séances et Travaux de l'Académie,⁴ may wait for the present.

After the 9th, please direct Poste Restante, Athens, till further notice. Any letters with "to be forwarded" written on them, I should wish sent there. Any others may be sent here, to wait for my return. If there is a book post to Athens, I should be obliged by your sending the March and April numbers of Fraser by it: if not, please send them here as usual.

I inclose the list of persons whom I wish to receive copies of the new editions of the Logic and Political Economy;⁵ all expenses of carriage to be at my charge. Please remember to have "from the author" written in all of them. I am, Dear Sir

yrs very truly

J.S. MILL

538A. TO CHARLES EDWARD TREVELYAN[1]

Athens
June 11. 1862

MY DEAR SIR CHARLES

Professor Villari, of the University of Pisa, a very valued friend of mine,[2] is in England on a mission from the Italian Government to collect information useful to Italy on the subject of public education. He is particularly interested in the question of competitive examination, which has been mooted in Italy also, with a practical object. The manner in which you have laboured in that cause,[3] and the inestimable obligations which it owes to you, have emboldened me to think that an opportunity of serving it further might be agreeable to you, and that I might venture to give Mr Villari an introduction to you. You will find him a highly favourable specimen of a country in which all liberal Englishmen now feel so deep an interest; and there are,

---

⁴*Séances et Travaux de l'Académie des Sciences Morales et Politiques* was issued in Paris from the office of the *Moniteur*, beginning in 1842.

⁵The 5th ed. of the *Logic* appeared in March; the 5th ed. of the *Principles* in April. No list of recipients has survived.

---

¹MS at the College of Law, Nihon University, Tokyo. *Addressed:* Sir Charles Trevelyan K.C.B. &c.

Charles Edward Trevelyan (1807–86), who had been a civil servant in India 1826–38, became Assistant Secretary to the Treasury in 1840, and in that capacity administered relief in Ireland during the famine. He returned to India as Governor of Madras in 1858, but was recalled in 1860.

²Pasquale Villari (1826–1917), Italian historian and statesman, known to Mill since 1854, was appointed Professor of History at Pisa in 1859.

³Trevelyan was mainly responsible for the controversial "Report on the Organisation of the Permanent Civil Service," *PP*, 1854, XXVII, 1–31, which advocated that competitive examinations replace patronage.

I should think, few persons whose opinions on Italian affairs are better worth having, as well as on many other subjects. Among other writings of merit, Mr Villari is the author of an interesting and valuable life of Savonarola.[4]

I am my dear Sir Charles

very truly yours
J.S. MILL

538B. TO THEODOR GOMPERZ[1]

Athens
June 12. 1862

DEAR SIR

My daughter and I have been travelling in Greece and purpose to take Pesth and Vienna in our way back. I should be very sorry to be in your neighbourhood without seeing you, and you would much oblige me if you would write a line to me, directed Poste Restante Constantinople (where we shall be in a month from this time, and perhaps sooner) to tell me whether you expect to be in Vienna, or where else, during the month of August. Hoping for the pleasure of seeing and conversing with you at that time, I am Dear Sir

yours very truly
J.S. MILL

554. TO THEODOR GOMPERZ[1]

Saint Véran, Avignon
Sept. 17. 1862

DEAR SIR

*a*We have now been more than a fortnight in this quiet harbour, after our *b*long*b* journey, and are fully enjoying its peacefulness. We did not see so much of the Alps as we expected after leaving Ischl*a*: the ascent of the Schaffberg the next day was very pleasant, but the rain which set in on that very evening kept us three days within doors at Salzburg, and then only intermitted long enough to enable us to see

---

[4]*La storia di Girolamo Savonarola e de' suoi tempi*, 2 vols. (Florence: Le Monnier, 1859–61).

---

[1]MS at Kokugakuin University, Tokyo.

---

[1]MS at Kokugakuin University, Tokyo. Most published in *CW*, Vol. XV, pp. 795–6.

a-a[*in* CW]
b-b[*not in* CW]

Berchtesgaden and the Königsee, which came up to our highest expectations. By the time we reached Gastein, the rain had come again, and the place being quite full, we did not remain. Had we done so, we could not have made a single excursion, so rainy did the weather become, and we had no more fine weather, except one day at Innsbrück. What is more, we have found rainy weather here also, which usually does not set in till the latter half of October. ^cI am doing little at present but reading up the French and English reviews. But since I arrived I have written and sent off an article on the American question (à propos of Mr Cairnes' book) which will be in the Westminster Review next month.² A very interesting series of notes on America and on the war have been published this summer in an English periodical (Macmillan's Magazine) and are, I see, lately reprinted as a volume, under the title of "Six Months in the Federal States": the author is a Mr Dicey, who had within the last two years published a book on Rome and Italy.³ He writes very judiciously, as well as with right feeling, on the whole subject, and what he says respecting the people of the North, being evidently a faithful transcript of what he has seen and heard, ought to have some influence. The Times, as might be expected, is as bad as ever, and even more undisguised in the expression of its bad wishes. It let out, however, a curious admission the other day—that whatever might be in other respects the issue of this war, it must lead to the destruction of Slavery.⁴ This will be true if the North succeeds; but if the South should be successful, I expect the very reverse. In Europe things appear to be going on well, as far at least as mental progress is concerned. This is very visible in the higher order of writers in France; among whom I invariably remark that what is bad in thought or sentiment is found chiefly in the publicists who had made themselves known before 1848, and that the ^dgeneral tone^d of those who have risen into notice since that time is both higher in morality, and more philosophic in ^e intellect. The Garibaldi affair is very painful, but it has ended as little mischievously as perhaps it could have done.⁵ It has at least given Louis Napoleon no pretext for intervention,

---

²"The Slave Power," *Westminster Review*, n.s. XXII (Oct. 1862), 489–510 (in *CW*, Vol. XXI, pp. 143–64), reviewing John Elliot Cairnes's *The Slave Power: Its Character, Career, and Probable Designs* (London: Parker, Son, and Bourne, 1862).

³The series, by Edward James Stephen Dicey (1832–1911), author and journalist, ran from April to September 1862, in *Macmillan's*, V, 453–62, and VI, 16–29, 138–53, 177–91, 284–97, 408–20. The reprint, *Six Months in the United States*, 2 vols. (London and Cambridge: Macmillan), did not in fact appear until 1863. Dicey had earlier published *Rome in 1860* (London: Macmillan, 1861).

⁴The cause of the North was faring badly at this point, and *The Times* was predicting eventual victory for the South. Mill was perhaps referring to the comments on Lincoln's attitude towards slavery in "The Civil War in America," *The Times*, 8 Sept., 1862, p. 9.

⁵Giuseppe Garibaldi (1807–82), the Italian patriot, had initiated an effort to take Rome, but at Aspromonte, on 27 August, he was wounded and captured by government forces. He was soon liberated, however, under an amnesty.

^{c-c}[*in* CW]
^{d-d}CW   generation
^eCW   the

and less excuse than ever for keeping his troops in Rome;[6] while Garibaldi, it is to be hoped, is still reserved for better times. If it also destroys Rattazzi,[7] that will be another benefit arising from it.*c*

I have found Dr Schiel's letter;[8] it is dated Frankfurt. Let me hear from you now and then. —*f*With our compliments to your sister I am

yours very *g*truly*g*

J.S. MILL

P.S. I had written the preceding before I received yours.*f* We have, as you see, arrived safely, and *h*I should have written before, had I thought you would have felt any such anxiety as you mention on our account.[9] It will always be a pleasure to me to hear from you: let me know what you are doing and thinking, and how the political affairs of your country are proceeding. I can assure you that however little expression I may habitually give to such a feeling you are one of the few persons whose friendship I value, and whom I would gladly see asserting an influence on the current of public affairs.*h*

J.S.M.

564. TO THEODOR GOMPERZ[1]

Blackheath Park, Kent
Dec. 14. 1862

DEAR SIR

*a*I am here, and in good health, and*a* I will not wait for the further letter which you promise, before saying how glad I shall be to see you in January, and thanking you

---

[6]Napoleon III (1808–73), Emperor of the French, was maintaining a garrison in the Vatican area, in support of the Pope as a sovereign prince against Victor Emmanuel, the King of Italy, who had been recently recognized by the great powers; see "The Roman Question," *The Times*, 27 Sept., 1862, p. 9.

[7]Urbano Rattazzi (1808–73), had been Prime Minister of Italy since March; he was driven from office in December, because of the popular reaction against the government's treatment of Garibaldi at Aspromonte.

[8]No letter has been located from J. von Schiel, who had translated the inductive part of Mill's *Logic* as *Die inductive Logik* in 1849, and the full work as *System der deductiven und inductiven Logik*, 2 vols., in 1862–63 (both Braunschweig: Vieweg).

[9]Gomperz had alluded, too indirectly for Mill's comprehension, to his growing feelings for Helen Taylor. See Letter 644 below.

f-f[*in* CW]
*g-g*CW sincerely
h-h[*in* CW]

[1]MS at Kokugakuin University, Tokyo. Most of the letter, without the questionnaire sent by Gomperz, published in *CW*, Vol. XV, p. 809. The questionnaire follows, with the questions given in italics.

a-a[*not in* CW]

as well for the kind and friendly feelings shewn in your letter as for the very interesting information contained in it. I am particularly glad of what you have been doing on the subject of the Principle of Contradiction, as I have commenced writing something[2] to which a full understanding of that subject is indispensable, and I do not feel that I have yet thoroughly mastered it. Your account of Austrian politics is very valuable, and I thank you for the American news, which, as you anticipated, was entirely unknown to me. The paper giving an account of my article in Fraser reached me duly.[3] I am much gratified that you thought the article worth so full an abstract even for Germany, though I am almost ashamed of the very flattering terms in which you spoke of it and of me.

I am very glad that you are so far advanced with the Logic, and I return your paper of questions duly filled up. I am much interested also with your Herculanean speculations. *b*En attendant your further letter I am, Dear Sir

yours very truly
J.S. MILL*b*

Dez. 62

1. *Will you kindly allow me to apply to you even now for such information and advice, as I am unable to get from any other quarter and also to signify this fact, the assistance given me by you both on the title-page by calling the translation executed: Mit Genehmigung und unter Mitwirkung,*[4] *of the Author, and in the preface, where this cooperation is to be more strictly defined and limited to what it really is?*

Certainly.

2. *The fallacies of* Simple Inspection[5] *have always been a stumbling block to me, not the thing but the name you have chosen to designate them. I had translated the words by "Trugschlüsse der einfachen* Wahrnehmung,*" but this word, the equivalent of* Perception *has too special a meaning to be used in so wide a sense. Would it falsify or distort your meaning to call them "Trugschlüsse des unmittelbaren Bewusstseins," that is "Fallacies of Consciousness"? If being the distinctive property of this tribe of fallacies is to be—wrong—inferences which are mistaken for self-evident or intuitive truths, this designation might perhaps fit them?*

The description seems a good one, and in any case you are the best judge.

---

[2]*An Examination of Sir William Hamilton's Philosophy* (London: Longmans, *et al.*, 1865); *CW*, Vol. IX.
[3]"The Contest in America." Gomperz's abstract has not been located.
[4]The phrase duly appeared on the title page of Vol. II of *Gesammelte Werke*.
[5]See *System of Logic*, *CW*, Vol. VIII, pp. 746–72 (Bk. V, Chap. iii).

b-b[*not in* CW]

3. *You will probably not object to my omitting the note at the foot of I, p. 36 and for other reasons the foot-notes I p. 108–9 and I p. 343–4?*[6] *I confess, I ask such questions as these chiefly in order that I may be able to declare, without untruth, that no note has been omitted without your express permission. In the text nothing has been omitted, except untransleatable passages, viz. those which refer to peculiarities of the English language or of single terms and their acceptations.*

All these suppressions are very proper.

4. *I p. 4, l. 15 fr. bel. "sanctioned by high authorities"*[7] *refers to the term, not to "an extension of the term"?*

To "an extension of the term."

5. *I p. 308, l. 17 fr. bel. "an assertion involved in the meaning of terms"*[8] = concerned *with the meaning &c, not* = *implied in the meaning &c? In other words I am not quite sure whether that expression is an equivalent of "an identical proposition" or of "a mode of defining" &c which follows.*

A definition is, in my sense of the terms, an "identical proposition." But it is of no consequence which of the phrases is used as either will fit my idea.

571A. TO EDWIN CHADWICK[1]

Blackheath
Tuesday
[1863?]

DEAR CHADWICK

The statistics you refer me to would be of great use to me. How are the "Miscellaneous Statistics of the United Kingdom for 1862" to be got?[2] Are they on sale anywhere,

yrs in haste
J.S. MILL

---

[6]The reference is to three footnotes added in the 5th ed. of 1862; *ibid.*, Vol. VII, pp. 34–5 (Bk. I, Chap. ii, Sect. 5), p. 98 (Bk. I, Chap. v, Sect. 4), and pp. 308–9 (Bk. III, Chap. iii, Sect. 1), respectively.

[7]*Ibid.*, p. 6 (Introduction, Sect. 3); Gomperz gives the line number, counting "from below."

[8]*Ibid.*, p. 277 (Bk. II, Chap. vii, Sect. 5).

---

[1]MS at University College London.
[2]As a blue book from the Queen's Printers, Eyre and Spottiswoode; in *PP*, 1862, LX, 443–783.

571B. TO AN UNIDENTIFIED CORRESPONDENT[1]

[1863–64?]

La prospérité et le bonheur de la Grèce seront assurés du jour que son peuple saura imposer à ses hommes politiques l'obligation de s'occuper des intérêts matériaux et moraux de la nation.

J. STUART MILL

589A. TO THEODOR GOMPERZ[1]

Blackheath
Feb. 20. 1863

DEAR SIR

I think it is as well to send you at once an introduction to Mr Grote, which can be presented whenever it happens to be convenient. If he should not be at his town residence when you call, you could leave the note with your card and address, when he would probably write to let you know when he would be disengaged. I am, Dear Sir

ever yours truly
J.S. MILL

589B. TO THE EDITOR OF THE SPECTATOR[1]

Blackheath Park
Feb. 20. 1863

Mr J.S. Mill presents his compliments to the Editor of the Spectator, and

---

[1] MS in the possession of Professor Isaac Kramnick, Cornell University.
This statement in support of constitutional government in Greece may have been solicited from Mill following the revolution in 1862 (cf. the hope expressed in Helen Taylor's article "Greece," *Penny Newsman*, 22 Mar., 1863, p. 1, that the result would be "the establishment of a good and popular government"); or it may date from the end of 1864, when the recently installed King of the Hellenes, George I, was forced to accept an ultra-democratic constitution, drawn up by the National Assembly.

---

[1] MS at Kokugakuin University, Tokyo. See Introduction, p. xxi above.

---

[1] MS at not located. Copy in the British Library.
Meredith White Townsend (1831–1911) and Richard Holt Hutton (1826–97) had been co-proprietors and joint editors of the *Spectator* since June 1861.

encloses for any use which the Editor may be able to make of it, some valuable remarks on Austrian politics, extracted from a letter which he lately received from a very able, highly cultivated, and high principled Austrian.[2]

Mr Mill cannot omit the opportunity of expressing the very high estimation, both moral and intellectual, in which he holds the Spectator, under its present management.[3]

594A. TO JAMES EDWIN THOROLD ROGERS[1]

Blackheath Park
Feb. 25. 1863

DEAR SIR

Many thanks for your kind invitation, but I am quite unable to spare time for the visit you propose.[2]

The extension of the middle class examinations to both sexes would indeed be an important improvement.[3]

The system of farming which you mention[4] differs from the metayer system in its characteristic feature, the division of the produce. That the landlord should provide the stock and implements is a matter of necessity in a state of things in which the tenant cannot; unless, as in Ireland, both parties are willing to dispense with anything which can be called stock or implements at all. In this point of view, the beginning and ending of the system you mention must be among the landmarks in the progress of society in England.

I am Dear Sir
very truly yours
J.S. MILL

[2]Mill is undoubtedly referring to Theodor Gomperz; the information may be that mentioned in Letter 564 above.

[3]The editors, like Mill, were running counter to prevailing public opinion by supporting the cause of the North in the American Civil War.

---

[1]MS in the Bodleian Library.

James Edwin Thorold Rogers (1823–90), first Tooke Professor of Statistics at University College London from 1859, and Drummond Professor of Political Economy at Oxford from 1862.

[2]The nature of the invitation—presumbly to Oxford—is unknown, Rogers' letter not being extant.

[3]Rogers was an advocate of opening to girls the matriculation examinations at grammar schools. Oxford refused, but Cambridge agreed to a trial, conducted in the London local examinations in December 1863, and then opened the examinations to girls in 1864. Oxford followed in 1870.

[4]Rogers was working on his great *History of Agriculture and Prices in England*, 7 vols. (Oxford: Clarendon Press, 1866–1902).

595A. TO JOHN WILLIAM PARKER[1]

Blackheath
March 4. [1863]

DEAR SIR

I yesterday sent you a list of persons to whom I wish to have copies sent, in my name, of the Utilitarianism,[2] and I now write to request that you will also send to Max Kyllmann Esq. Manchester[3] twelve copies of the second edition of "Thoughts on Parliamentary Reform."

I am Dear Sir
yrs very truly
J.S. MILL

595B. TO MOUNTSTUART ELPHINSTONE GRANT DUFF[1]

Blackheath
March 4, 1863

DEAR SIR

I am glad that the editorship of the National Review is in what you consider competent hands[2] though want of time and the greater urgency of other claims have obliged me to decline Mr Pearson's proposal.

I do not like to ask my friends to come to this distance for the very little time I can spare to them, but if you should happen to be coming into this neighbourhood I should at any time be happy to see you.

I am Dear Sir
very truly yours
J.S. MILL

---

[1]MS in the Georgetown University Library. Dated from internal evidence.
[2]Published in book form by Parker in 1863; first published in parts in *Fraser's Magazine*, LXIV (Oct., Nov., Dec. 1861), 391–406, 525–34, and 658–73 (in *CW*, Vol. X, pp. 203–59). The list has not survived.
[3]Max Kyllman (1832–67), German-born anti-slavery activist and promoter of the co-operative movement.

---

[1]MS not located. Copy in the British Library.
Mountstuart Elphinstone Grant Duff (1829–1906), statesman and author, at this time M.P. for Elgin Burghs.
[2]Grant Duff had apparently recommended his friend, Charles Henry Pearson (1830–94), Professor of Modern History at King's College, London, for the editorship of the *National Review*, a Unitarian journal, the previous year. Pearson retained the post from June 1862 to July 1863. See also Letter 595C below.

595C. TO CHARLES HENRY PEARSON[1]

Blackheath Park
March 5. 1863

DEAR SIR

I think very favourably of the National Review, and consider it and its writers as an important element in the mental progress of this country; but I have so many other calls on me and so little time at my disposal to meet them, that it is quite impossible for me to undertake the article you propose, or to come under any new literary engagement whatever.

Periodical writing of any kind is with me only an exception.

I am Dear Sir
yrs very truly
J.S. MILL

C.H. Pearson Esq.

600A. TO FRANÇOIS AUGUSTE MARIE MIGNET[1]

Blackheath Park, Kent
le 21 mars 1863

MONSIEUR

J'ai chargé mon éditeur de vous adresser par la poste un petit volume sur la morale de l'utilité,[2] dont je vous prie de vouloir bien faire hommage en mon nom à l'Académie des Sciences Morales et Politiques de l'Institut.

Je sais, Monsieur, que les opinions énoncées dans cet opuscule ont peu ou point d'approbateurs dans l'Académie, et que le seul genre de succès qu'il me soit permis d'espérer pour lui auprès de cet illustre corps, est celui d'être regardé comme ayant une certaine valeur en qualité de simple discussion. Mais je sais aussi que les membres de l'Académie sont trop éclairés pour ne pas reconnaître que la discussion consciencieuse et réfléchie des grandes questions de l'humanité fait toujours jaillir quelque lumière.

Agréez, Monsieur, l'expression de ma haute et sincère estime, et de ma considération la plus respectueuse.

J.S. MILL

---

[1] MS in the Bodleian Library. See Letter 595B above.

---

[1] MS at the College of Law, Nihon University, Tokyo. The letter is addressed to Mignet as the Permanent Secretary of the French Académie des Sciences Morales et Politiques. See also Letters 460A and 487A above.

[2] I.e., *Utilitarianism*.

603A. TO THEODOR GOMPERZ[1]

Blackheath
Wednesday
[25 Mar., 1863]

DEAR SIR

Mr Fawcett,[2] who is going to the meeting tomorrow,[3] undertakes to get an admission for you; so if you will come here and take your dinner with us we will go together afterwards to the meeting, calling on Mr Fawcett by the way.

If anything should prevent you from coming here, Mr Fawcett's address is 16 Spring Gardens Charing Cross and if you will go there at half past seven I will meet you there. But I hope to see you here.

yours very truly
J.S. MILL

617. TO THEODOR GOMPERZ[1]

Blackheath
Thursday *evg*
[11 June, 1863]

DEAR SIR

M. Louis Blanc[2] *being unable to come tomorrow*, has fixed to dine with us on Sunday (at five). We shall therefore hope to see you and Mr Wessel[3] on Sunday *instead of tomorrow*.

very truly yours
J.S. MILL

---

[1] MS at Kokugakuin University, Tokyo. Dated from the reference to the meeting and Gomperz's presence in London.

[2] Henry Fawcett (1833–84), Professor of Political Economy at Cambridge, friend and disciple of Mill.

[3] Presumably the meeting on 26 March, 1863, of Trade Unionists in support of the North in the U.S. Civil War. John Bright presided, and Mill was on the platform. Reported in *The Times*, 27 Mar., p. 12. (Cf. *CW*, Vol. XV, p. 851.)

---

[1] MS at Kokugakuin University, Tokyo. Mostly published in *CW*, Vol. XV, p. 862. Dated from a letter from Gomperz to his sister of 15 June, 1863, in which the invitation is mentioned.

[2] Jean Joseph Louis Blanc (1811–82), socialist politician and historian, had been in exile in England since the French Revolution of 1848, in which he had played a leading role.

[3] Eduard Wessel (1822–79), a journalist and teacher, had joined Gomperz in England. He later contributed translations of *Considerations on Representative Government* and *Dissertations and Discussions* to *Gesammelte Werke*, Vols. VIII and X–XI, respectively.

a-a[not in CW]
b-b[not in CW]
c-c[not in CW]

617A. TO JAMES EDWIN THOROLD ROGERS[1]

Blackheath Park
June 14. 1863

DEAR SIR

You have done very rightly and judiciously, and I am glad to be spared the crowd and turmoil of the present occasion. I should be a little ashamed, too, as well as surprised, at being thought sufficiently orthodox when Kingsley is not.[2]

I think with you that both American and French affairs look more hopeful. The French elections must startle the wise journalists and others who have been affirming for years that the French like and demand despotism, though they knew all the while that the French had no means (except a general election) of publicly shewing dislike to it.[3]

In America the pertinacity of the Free States gives me great confidence in their ultimate success, and I have always thought that this war and all its circumstances were very likely to elevate the national character, as well as to stir up thought in the more cultivated minds, in a way that there seemed little hope of before. I am Dear Sir

very truly yours
J.S. MILL

637A. TO THOMAS BAYLEY POTTER[1]

Blackheath
Aug. 24. 1863

DEAR SIR

Allow me to thank you for the present of game which you have been kind enough to send.

All the recent American news is most cheering, and there now seems little ground of fear for the future. I wish I could see signs of a corresponding improvement in English opinion on the subject. It is still the working classes and

---

[1] MS in the Bodleian Library.
[2] On 16–17 June the Prince of Wales with the Princess visited Oxford so that he could be awarded a D.C.L. Charles Kingsley withdrew his name from the list of candidates because Pusey, on theological grounds, threatened to cry "*non-placet*" at the ceremony. It seems possible that there had been some attempt to propose Mill for the honour.
[3] In the elections that began on 31 May not a single Government candidate had been elected in the Paris region; see "French Elections," *Examiner*, 6 June, 1863, p. 354.

---

[1] MS in the Osborn Collection, Yale University.
Thomas Bayley Potter (1817–98), a Manchester businessman, founder in 1861 of the Union and Emancipation Society.

the greater as well as better part of the literary class, against all other classes, with comparatively few noble individual exceptions. The Union and Emancipation Society counts a great number of these among its promoters, and it has done excellent service by its interesting and important publications.[2] If the Society wants, or whenever it does want, a renewal of subscriptions, I beg you to let me know, and I will again send my mite. I am, Dear Sir

very truly yours
J.S. MILL

T.B. Potter Esq.

639. TO JOSEPHINE VON WERTHEIMSTEIN[1]

Blackheath Park, Kent
le 25 août. 1863

MADAME

a"Pardonnez-moi de n'avoir fait jusqu'ici aucune réponse directe à la lettre que vous avez bien voulu m'écrire.[2] Je croyais mieux remplir votre désir en écrivant à celui qui est, à juste titre, l'objet de notre commune sollicitude. J'écrivis sans délai, mais comme depuis lors je n'ai pas eu de ses nouvelles, je n'ose presque pas lui écrire de nouveau sans avoir préalablement demandé à vous ou à M. Wessel dans quel état d'esprit il se trouve maintenant. En même temps je remplis le devoir de vous assurer directement à quel point nous partageons votre peine et votre inquiétude. Vous vous êtes servie, Madame, dans votre lettre d'expressions de reconnaissance très au-delà de mon droit. Je serais trop heureux de pouvoir les mériter, mais jusqu'ici je ne vois presque rien que j'aie fait pour lui. S'il y a quelque chose que j'aurais pu faire, c'eût été peut-être de lui donner, par des preuves d'estime, la confiance qui lui manquait en lui-même. Ces preuves d'estime, il les a eues, non seulement de moi mais de M. Grote, et je le crois sincèrement, de tous ceux qui l'ont connu ici. Cela n'a servi *b*de*b* rien quant à présent, mais il faut croire que cela ne sera pas perdu dans l'avenir. J'ai reconnu *c*dans*c* lui, dès le commencement, une haute capacité intellectuelle: cette

---

[2]Including, in 1863, *The Speech by William Edward Forster on the Slaveholders' Rebellion; and Professor Goldwin Smith's Letter on the Morality of the Emancipation Proclamation*, and Goldwin Smith, *War Ships for the Southern Confederacy*.

---

[1]MS at Kokugakuin University, Tokyo. Most published in *CW*, Vol. XV, pp. 878–9. See Letter 292 above.
[2]The letter from Gomperz's sister has not been located. Mill had made her acquaintance the previous summer.
a-a[*in* CW]
*b-b*CW à
*c-c*CW en

impression est allée toujours en s'accroissant, tandis qu'une connaissance plus intime y a ajouté une véritable estime morale. Ce n'est que plus tard que j'ai reconnu chez lui cette extrême sensibilité aux impressions pénibles, qui le rend en même temps très susceptible de souffrance et peu accessible aux consolations. En lui écrivant je m'efforce toujours *ᵈ*de*ᵈ* le décider à en chercher dans les hauts travaux intellectuels dont il est si capable, et dans la carrière utile et honorable qu'il peut remplir dans le monde de l'intelligence comme dans celui des intérêts sociaux. Si j'ai quelque pouvoir sur son esprit, je ne me lasserai pas de l'exercer dans ce sens: et, ses autres amis aidant, nous finirons peutêtre par réussir.*ᵃ*

Je dois à M. Wessel des remerciments dont je vous prie, Madame, d'être l'interprète auprès de lui. *ᵉ*S'il est encore avec vous je lui aurai une véritable obligation toutes les fois qu'il voudra bien nous donner des nouvelles de son ami.*ᵉ* Nous partons incessamment pour Avignon, où nous resterons jusqu'au commencement de l'année prochaine.

Veuillez, Madame, agréer l'hommage de mes sentiments les plus distingués.

J.S. MILL

644. TO THEODOR GOMPERZ[1]

Saint Véran, Avignon
Sept. 17. 1863

DEAR SIR

*ᵃ*Let me begin by saying how much I rejoice to hear that you are better both in health and in spirits, and are vigorously at work, with a result satisfactory even to yourself, which is always the most difficult thing to a good writer.

Let me next thank you, which I do *ᵇ*very*ᵇ* sincerely, for telling me frankly what you have *ᶜ*on*ᶜ* your mind against me. The only way to clear up misunderstandings is to speak plainly about them, and some of the impressions which seem to have been made upon you are such as if you had not told them to me, I certainly should never have guessed. I feel as strongly as you do the ludicrousness of your having to ask me what I have seen to make me entertain I know not what mean opinion of you, and I wonder that what you feel to be so ridiculous, you should nevertheless have thought to be probable. I may in my turn ask you, what you have seen in me

*ᵈ⁻ᵈ*CW à
ᵉ⁻ᵉ[*in* CW]

---

[1]MS at Kokugakuin University, Tokyo. Most published in *CW*, Vol. XV, pp. 882–3.

ᵃ⁻ᵃ[*in* CW]
ᵇ⁻ᵇ[*not in* CW]
*ᶜ⁻ᶜ*CW in

which made it likely that, absolutely without cause, I should have formed an unfavourable opinion of one for whom I have professed, and continue to profess, so much esteem and regard? As to the idea that any intimate friend of mine, or any person deriving information from me, has spread any reports or communicated any impressions disadvantageous to you, I am sure, since you say it, that you yourself fully believe it, but I tell you with the same frankness you have used to me, that I disbelieve it totally.

Surely, too, I may well be surprised that you should think anything of a bad joke about Vienna, which I have not the smallest recollection of making, but which, I am quite sure, had not the slightest reference to you? I can only have meant, that the next time we went to Vienna there would perhaps be something new to be seen there.

My letter from Avignon[2] was quite another thing, and knowing as I now do the state of your feelings, I can well understand your being pained by it. But you must recollect that I did not *d*then know*d* what I know now,[3] and it never entered into my head that your object in coming was to say anything particular, which you thought you had not had an opportunity of saying before. I thought that you simply desired to see the place and to see us, and in so doing I neither thought you obtrusive, nor imagined that you expected anything but what your knowledge of our friendship for you perfectly entitled you to expect. But knowing that my time was much occupied, I feared you might be disappointed; and it seemed right to let you know that I could not give you so full and free an invitation to come whenever it might be convenient to you, as I had done in England; and to tell you so before you had undertaken so long a journey under what might have been a mistaken impression that I had more leisure for seeing friends here than in England. I thought I was using a freedom which I could not have taken with a mere acquaintance, but which I *e*was*e* even bound to use with a friend.*a*

To speak now of a pleasanter subject; your publisher[4] has no need to take any steps for obtaining authority to publish a translation of the Utilitarianism. I am the sole owner of the copy right, and neither I nor my publisher has made any reservation of the right of translating that or any other of my works. But as you wish for a declaration that you have my concurrence and sanction for translating it, I give you such a declaration with much pleasure. As you have not told me in what language it should be written, I write it in English, but will repeat it in French if

---

[2]*CW*, Vol. XV, pp. 854–5 (23 Apr., 1863).
[3]That Gomperz wanted to marry Helen Taylor.
[4]Not identified.

*d-d*CW   know then
*e-e*CW   am

desired. I expect both pleasure and benefit from the essay of your own which you intend prefixing to it.[5]

With our kind regards to your sister and to Mr. Wessel, I am, Dear Sir

yours very sincerely

J.S. MILL

671A. TO JOHN PLUMMER[1]

Saint Véran, Avignon
Jan. 24 1864

DEAR SIR,

I thank you for your two letters, and their various inclosures, by which I have been much interested. I hope that your connection with the Sydney Morning Herald[2] will continue as satisfactorily as it has begun. I have read all your articles in the Penny Newsman[3] some of which I liked very much and I have little doubt that I shall like your Essay on Colonies; but I will, as you desire, criticize it freely.[4] I do not, any more than you, agree entirely with Mr Goldwin Smith.[5] I think that a

---

[5]"Mr Theodor Gomperz has my full approbation and sanction for publishing a translation of my book entitled 'Utilitarianism' / J.S. Mill / Avignon / September 17. 1863." This sentence, signature, and date are on a separate sheet. The translation was in fact done later by Adolph Wahrmund (1827–1913), and, corrected and revised by Gomperz, appeared as *Das Nützlichkeits-princip*, in *Gesammelte Werke*, Vol. I (1869), pp. 125–200.

---

[1]MS in the National Library of Australia, Canberra. Published in *MNL*, IX (Summer 1974), 7–8, edited by Ged Martin.
John Plummer (1831–1914), a self-educated factory worker who became a journalist, became acquainted with Mill in 1859, and later emigrated to Australia.
[2]Plummer was London correspondent of the *Sydney Morning Herald*, the leading newspaper in New South Wales.
[3]A newspaper published by Edwin Chadwick and addressed to a working-class readership.
[4]Plummer had won first prize of £30 in a national mechanics' essay competition organized by the Rev. J.P. Gell of Notting Hill, London. His views are summed up in the title of his essay: *Our Colonies: An Essay on the Advantages Accruing to the British Nation, from Its Possession of the Colonies, Considered Economically, Politically and Morally* (London, Kettering, and Sydney, 1864). On 6 March, 1864, Mill wrote to Plummer: "I like your Essay on the Colonies very much, though I do not go the length of all you say respecting their advantages" (*CW*, Vol. XV, p. 923).
[5]Goldwin Smith (1823–1910) published a series of letters in the *Daily News* in 1862–63 advocating independence for the colonies. These were revised in an attempt to add consistency to their arguments, and published as *The Empire* (Oxford and London: Henry and Parker, 1863). On 8 November, 1864, Mill wrote to J.E. Cairnes, "I do not at all agree with Goldwin Smith in thinking the severance actually desirable" (*CW*, Vol. XV, p. 965).

sort of modified federation between a mother country and colonies may be usefully maintained as long as neither party desires to separate.

Do not send anything more to this address at present, as we return to England in a fortnight.[6] I need hardly say that we shall be glad to see you at Blackheath when you are in town and it is convenient to you to come.

With our kind remembrances to Mrs Plummer, I am,

very sincerely yours

J.S. MILL

671B. TO THE GARDENERS' CHRONICLE AND AGRICULTURAL GAZETTE[1]

Saint Véran, Avignon
Jan. 26, 1864

I have just seen in a newspaper a piece of intelligence which I earnestly hope is not true, but which is stated so circumstantially that I fear there must be some foundation for it.[2] The statement is, that the Royal Horticultural Society intends offering three prizes for the three best herbaria of every county in England, and three additional prizes, for the best of these best. If this most inconsiderate resolution has really been taken, I am sure it must have been in the absence of those members of the Council who have any real sympathy with British Botany. If it be carried into effect, the present year 1864 will be marked in our botanical annals as the date of the extinction of nearly all the rare species in our already so scanty flora. If the extirpation of these rarities had been the direct object of the Society, they could have done nothing more effectual than by inviting, not simply three botanists in every county, but all the dabblers in plant collecting, a race whose selfish rapacity certainly needs no additional stimulation, and all of whom may think they have a chance of one of these prizes, and holding out to them a positive inducement to hunt out all the rare plants in every part of the country and to carry off all they find, or destroy what they do not carry off, in order that not only they may themselves possess the plants, but that their competitors may not. Already our rare

---

[6]Mill and Helen Taylor were at Blackheath again on 17 February, 1864 (*CW*, Vol. XV, p. 920).

---

[1]Published as a letter to the editor in the *Gardeners' Chronicle and Agricultural Gazette*, 13 Feb., 1864, p. 150 (and then in an obituary notice, *ibid.*, 17 May, 1873, p. 679); in *MNL*, X (Winter 1975), 2–3, edited by Anna J. Mill.

John Lindley (1799–1865), botanist and horticulturist, was one of the founders of the *Gardeners' Chronicle* in 1841 and principal editor until his death.

[2]Perhaps "Royal Horticultural Society," *The Times*, 22 Jan., 1864, p. 5.

plants are becoming scarcer every year. You are, no doubt, aware how rapidly, for example, the rare Kentish Orchids are disappearing. The Royal Horticultural Society is proposing to treat rare plants as King Alfred treated wolves,[3] and this under the profession of encouraging local botany—as if local botany could be encouraged by destroying that on which it feeds, or as if anyone were likely to begin studying the science in hopes of collecting a good local flora in a single summer. All local botanists will be thrown into consternation by this project, and, if it is not yet too late, I am sure they would all join in entreating you to use your good influence towards stopping so destructive a scheme.[4]

J.S.M.

683A. TO GEORGE GROTE[1]

Blackheath
March 25. 1864

MY DEAR GROTE

I inclose a copy of M. Barrère's printed testimonials.[2] They will shew you how successful he is considered to have been as a teacher; which must tend greatly to make his judgment a good one as to the questions which test acquirements.

He is one of the very few French teachers in England who are teachers by profession and not from accidental circumstances; and the Society of French Teachers in London has shewn its opinion of him by putting him first on the list of its Vice Presidents, M. Cassal, your late Examiner, being President.[3]

With our kind regards to Mrs Grote—I am yrs ever truly,

J.S. MILL

---

[3] It was not Alfred (849–901 A.D.), but Edgar (944–75 A.D.), who extirpated the wolves. See Mill's usual source for such stories, David Hume, *The History of England*, 8 vols. (London: Cadell, Rivington, *et al.*, 1823), Vol. I, p. 126.
[4] See Letter 689A below.

---

[1] MS in the Pierpont Morgan Library.
[2] Probably Pierre Barrère, a teacher of French, author of *Les écrivains français* (1863), who was applying to University College London, of which Grote was Vice-Chancellor, as an Examiner. For further efforts by Mill on his behalf, see Letter 973A below, to William Smith, and *CW*, Vol. XV, p. 1184, to Thomas Henry Huxley.
[3] Hugues Charles Stanislas Cassal (1818–85), exiled from France in 1852, was Professor of French at University College London 1860–85, as well as sometime Examiner.

689A. TO MAXWELL TYLDEN MASTERS[1]

Blackheath Park, Kent
April 7. 1864

Mr J.S. Mill presents his compliments to Mr Masters and if Mr Masters is disposed to join in the accompanying representation to the Council of the Horticultural Society,[2] and has not already signed another copy, requests the favour of his signing and returning it either to the undermentioned address or to Professor Babington, Cambridge.[3]

Many of the most distinguished botanists have already either given or promised their signature.

690A. TO JAMES FITZJAMES STEPHEN[1]

B[lackheath] P[ark]
April 12, 1864

DEAR SIR—You have put to me a question which it is very difficult, or rather impossible, to answer satisfactorily. There is no one living of whom I would venture to affirm beforehand that he might be expected to write such a treatise on the fundamental problems of religion & morals that it would be good for him to give up a profession he likes & change his plans of life rather than not write it. I should expect confidently that if you threw your whole mind into writing such a book, or indeed any other book which you are at all likely to write, it would, at the least, contain a great deal that would be valuable. But it deserves consideration whether even the best book that could be written in our day, on morals & religion

---

[1]MS at the College of Law, Nihon University, Tokyo.
Maxwell Tylden Masters (1833–1907), physician and botanist, lecturer at St. George's Hospital from 1855.
[2]Mill was instrumental in the protest against the Society's offering prizes for herbaria; see Letter 671B above, and for the resultant memorial, *Royal Horticultural Society Proceedings*, IV, 91–4.
[3]The name of Charles Cardale Babington (1808–95), Professor of Botany at Cambridge, heads the signatures to the memorial.

---

[1]MS draft in the University Library, Cambridge. Published in *MNL*, XXII (Winter 1987), 3, edited by Jean O'Grady. In answer to Stephen's letter of 9 April, and replied to by Stephen on 14 April (also at Cambridge).
James Fitzjames Stephen (1829–94), author and later judge, whose "The Study of History," *Cornhill Magazine*, III (June 1861), 666–80, and IV (July 1861), 25–41, was praised by Mill in the 5th ed. of his *Logic* (1862), *CW*, Vol. VIII, pp. 941–2.

generally, would do more good than may be done by the continual illustration & discussion of the leading points of those subjects, in connection with particular speculative or practical questions. For such discussion you have a decided talent, & it would afford the materials of many books as well as periodical writings. However this may be, the question is one which no one but yourself can decide. It is my creed that any one who can do anything, of an intellectual kind, well, is usually a better judge than other people what he can do best, & what it is of most use for him to attempt.

We leave for Avignon before next Sunday, but after our return I shall be happy to have any discussions you may desire with you.

700. TO THEODOR GOMPERZ[1]

Blackheath Park
June 26. 1864

DEAR SIR

I have delayed writing, in hopes that I should, long before this, have heard from you of your intended publication;[2] but *a*I have now been so long without news of any kind from you, that I much wish to know how you are in health, and how you are going on in all respects.[3] You would be very much mistaken if you thought that I feel less interested in you, or less desirous to hear from you, than before the painful circumstances which were the subject of our latest correspondence. If these circumstances make any difference, it is the contrary way. And, besides my interest in you, I feel a strong interest in what you do. I believe you to be capable, as few are, of doing important things both in philosophy and in erudition—the former of a kind specially required at the present time, and perhaps even more so in Germany than elsewhere: and I am anxious that such a capacity should be turned, as much as possible, to the benefit of the world.

I have little to tell *b* which regards us. Our life has been going on in the usual manner. I have been working hard at my book on Hamilton,[4] and it is now well

---

[1] MS at Kokugakuin University, Tokyo. Most published in *CW*, Vol. XV, pp. 944–5.

[2] Gomperz's *Philodemi Epicurei de ira liber* (Leipzig and London: Teubner, 1864); see Mill's letter of 22 August, *CW*, Vol. XV, p. 953.

[3] For Mill's earlier expressions of concern, see Letters 618 and 633, *CW*, Vol. XV, pp. 862–3, 873–5, and Letters 639 and 644 above.

[4] *An Examination of Sir William Hamilton's Philosophy and of the Principal Philosophical Questions Discussed in His Writings* (London: Longmans, *et al.*, 1865); *CW*, Vol. IX (Toronto: University of Toronto Press, 1979).

a-a[*in* CW]
*b*CW   you

advanced towards completion. You are one of the most competent judges of such a book, and one of those whose approbation of it I most desire.

I lately saw M. Littré[5] at Paris, and in conversing with him on the state of German philosophy, I mentioned your name. I was glad to find that he is in correspondence with you, and to the extent of his opportunities, appreciates you justly.[a]

I am Dear Sir
ever sincerely yours
J.S. MILL

713A. TO [WILLIAM DOUGAL CHRISTIE][1]

Blackheath
Aug. 11, 1864

DEAR SIR

I thank you for the volume on Brazil.[2] I am far too deeply interested in the slavery question not to have attended to what is going on respecting it in Brazil as far as I had the means. I have read all the letters signed C (not doubting that they were yours)[3] as well as all those of your antagonist,[4] and the comparison has strengthened the impression I already had that you are entirely in the right. But there is a strong party in England now who will always give slaveholders their good word in spite of all evidence. It is no wonder you have against you those who are again trying to induce England to renounce the attempt to check the African slave trade.[5] But the Daily News ought not to join with them, and, I am convinced, would not, if better informed.

---

[5]Emile Littré had translated of the works of Hippocrates, *Oeuvres complètes* (Greek and French), 12 vols. (Paris: Baillière, 1839–61).

---

[1]MS at Osaka University of Commerce, Japan. Published in *MSBJ*, I, no. 6 (1985), 3, edited by Takutoshi Inouyé.

William Dougal Christie (1816–74), barrister, M.P. for Weymouth 1841–47, in the Foreign Service 1851–63, was minister to Brazil from 1859 until 1863, when diplomatic relations were broken off.

[2]Christie, *The Brazil Correspondence in the Case of the "Prince of Wales" and the Officers of the "Forte," Reprinted from Papers Laid before Parliament* (London: Ridgway, 1863). For the originals, see *PP*, 1863, LXXIII, 121–302.

[3]Christie, *Notes on Brazilian Questions* (London and Cambridge: Macmillan, 1865), republished from the *Daily News*, 2 July to 5 Oct., 1864, where the matter appeared as letters, signed "C."

[4]William Henry Clark, one-time Registrar of the Great Northern Railway, and a member of the Reform Club, who wrote to the *Daily News* as "A Friend to both Countries."

[5]See, e.g., Leader on foreign policy, *The Times*, 14 July, 1864, p. 8.

You are very usefully doing what you can to inform it better. I am
very truly yours
J.S. MILL

720A. TO MESSRS. PRESCOTT, GROTE & CO.[1]

Avignon
Sept. 29. 1864

DEAR SIRS

Be pleased to receive my quarterly payment from the India Office due today, and oblige
yours very truly,
J.S. MILL

Messrs Prescott, Grote & Co

758A. TO JOHN RUSSELL[1]

Blackheath
Feb. 24. 1865

DEAR LORD AMBERLEY

I send you the letter from my friend Mr Kyllmann[2] which I mentioned to you the other day. Since the receipt of it, I have received another, which I also enclose, because I think it alters the aspect of matters considerably and I doubt altogether whether Mr Kyllmann's plans will be carried out for some time to come. But they are for the future: and I think you will be interested in seeing that there is a considerable following for them among the younger leaders of the working men.

As you will see that I was asked to take an active part in the intended movement, it may be well to say that I have refused to join in demanding the suffrage for all men, to the exclusion of women, and required also a writing and cyphering qualification, and Hare's system.[3] I am, Dear Lord Amberley
very truly yours
J.S. MILL

[1]MS formerly in the possession of Mr. David H. Lewisohn, London.
Prescott, Grote & Co., London banking firm.

[1]MS in the Russell Archive, McMaster University.
John Russell (1842–76), Viscount Amberley, son of Lord John Russell, a radical Whig and disciple of Mill's, whom he had met the previous year.
[2]See Letter 595A above.
[3]See Letter 388A above.

806. TO THEODOR GOMPERZ[1]

Saint Véran, Avignon
April 30. 1865

DEAR SIR

^aI have delayed thanking you for the first number of your Herculanean series,[2] in hopes that I should have been able to say something about the work itself. I have, however, been so busy, that I have not yet had time to do more than read your Preface and Introduction and merely glance at the Greek text. What you say of it, however, proves it to be, at the very least, a highly important and novel contribution to the history of Greek thought; and I look forward with great pleasure to making a real study of it at some not distant time.

But, interesting as such labours are, you are capable of things much more valuable than such mere editorial work. I cannot wish that you should leave unfinished what you have so well begun, but I shall be glad when the time comes to which you seemed to be looking forward in your last letter, now some months ago.^a In the same letter you promised me a longer one, which I hope will not be much longer delayed; though, by my own delay in writing to you, I have almost lost the right to say so.

^bI hope, before this, you have received the book on Hamilton, and also the first of two articles which I have written on Comte's philosophy. The second article is in print, and I expect to be able to send it to you before it is published in England.[3] I shall be well content if you are half as well pleased with these, as you are sure to be with Mr Grote's book on Plato.[4] This is nearly all printed, and I have read most of it; and both in point of learning and of thought it comes up to my highest expectations. It cannot, I think, fail to produce a great effect in Germany, where the thoroughness of his knowledge of the subject will be much better appreciated than by an unlearned public, which can only take it on trust.^b

With our kind remembrances to your sister and to Mr Wessel, believe me ever

yours most truly

J.S. MILL

---

[1]MS at Kokugakuin University, Tokyo. Most published in *CW*, Vol. XVI, p. 1040.
[2]Theodor Gomperz, *Herkulanische Studien. Erstes Heft: Philodem über Induktionsschlüsse, nach der Oxforder und Neapolitaner Abschrift* (Leipzig: Teubner, 1865).
[3]"The Positive Philosophy of Auguste Comte," and "The Later Speculations of Auguste Comte," *Westminster and Foreign Quarterly Review*, LXXXIII (Apr. 1865), 339–405, and LXXXIV (July 1865), 1–42, republished as *Auguste Comte and Positivism* (London: Trübner, 1865); in *CW*, Vol. X, pp. 261–368.
[4]George Grote, *Plato and the Other Companions of Sokrates* (London: Murray, 1865).

^{a-a}[*in* CW]
^{b-b}[*in* CW]

819A. TO WILLIAM STANLEY JEVONS[1]

Avignon
May 15. 1865

DEAR SIR

I did receive, and thought that I had acknowledged, the copy you were kind enough to send of your work on Logic.[2] I read it attentively, and the only knowledge I have of Prof. Boole's system is derived from it.[3] My impression was, that there is great ingenuity and power of consecutive thought, both in the system itself, and in your modification of it. But you are quite right in supposing that I do not see, in the result attained, any value commensurate with the mental effort. I look upon it as I do upon Mr De Morgan's elaborate system of numerically definite propositions and syllogisms: as a remarkable feat of mental gymnastics, capable of being very useful in the way of a scholastic exercise, but of no considerable utility for any other purpose.[4]

I did not make any mention of Mr Boole in my book on Hamilton, the book being quite long enough as it was. But if you, or any other of Mr Boole's admirers,[5] should make the book an occasion for raising any discussion on the point, I shall be very well pleased.

I am Dear Sir
yours very faithfully
J.S. MILL

---

[1]MS in The John Rylands University Library of Manchester. Published *MNL*, XVIII (Summer 1983), 25, edited by Margaret Schabas.
William Stanley Jevons (1835–82) was at this time Lecturer in Logic and Political Science at Owens College, Manchester. See also Letter 940A below.

[2]*Pure Logic; or, The Logic of Quality Apart from Quantity, with Remarks on Boole's System and the Relation of Logic to Mathematics* (London: Stanford, 1864).

[3]Jevons devoted Chaps. xiv and xv to discussion and modification of the application of mathematics to logic by George Boole (1815–64), late Professor of Mathematics at Queen's College, Cork, especially in his *An Investigation of the Laws of Thought, on Which Are Founded the Mathematical Theories of Logic and Probabilities* (London: Walton and Maberley, 1854).

[4]Augustus De Morgan (1806–70), Professor of Mathematics at University College London 1828–31 and 1836–66, was a friend and correspondent of Mill. De Morgan's most important work in this area was *Formal Logic; or, The Calculus of Inference, Necessary and Probable* (London: Taylor and Walton, 1847), which Mill criticized, on these same grounds, in his *System of Logic, CW*, Vol. VII, pp. 171n-2n.

[5]Mill may have in mind, in addition to Jevons and De Morgan, John Venn (1834–1923), Lecturer in Moral Science at Gonville and Caius College, Cambridge, since 1862.

833A. TO JAMES FITZJAMES STEPHEN[1]

Mont Doré les Bains
June 18. 1865

DEAR SIR

Of the articles you mention, the only ones I distinctly recollect are those on Newman and Merivale, and of those I well remember that I thought highly.[2] What points there were, if any, on which I differed from you, I could not say from present recollection. But I should suppose that the amount of thought, not of a commonplace kind, which they contain, and their applicability to existing and important controversies, would quite warrant their republication. I will however look at them again. I have most of the numbers of Fraser for the last few years, and could probably turn to all the articles you mention.[3]

I am glad that you have thoughts of standing at the election, and should be much pleased by your success.[4]

I hope to see you at the Club on the 7th,[5] when we may perhaps be able to arrange a walk or a talk before you go on circuit.

yours very truly
J.S. MILL

---

[1] MS in the University Library, Cambridge. Published in *MNL*, XXII (Winter 1987), 4, edited by Jean O'Grady.

[2] Stephen, "Dr. Newman's *Apologia*," *Fraser's Magazine*, LXX (Sept. 1864), 265–303, concerning John Henry Newman (1801–90), the Anglican divine whose conversion to Catholicism in 1845 was a *cause célèbre*; and "Merivale's *Sermons on the Conversion of the Roman Empire*," ibid., LXXI (Mar. 1865), 363–82, concerning Charles Merivale (1808–93), historian and Dean of Ely.

[3] Stephen also contributed to *Fraser's* on religious topics, "Women and Scepticism," LXVIII (Dec. 1863), 679–98; "The Privy Council and the Church of England," LXIX (May 1864), 621–37; "Dr. Pusey and the Court of Appeal," LXX (Nov. 1864), 644–62; and "What Is the Law of the Church of England?" LXXI (Feb. 1865), 225–41. He was contemplating a volume of essays on religious subjects. For a full list of his contributions, see *Wellesley Index to Victorian Periodicals*, Vol. II.

[4] Stephen contested Harwich for the Liberals in 1865, but was notably unsuccessful. This was of course the election in which Mill gained his seat.

[5] I.e., the Political Economy Club, which on that date discussed a question proposed by Mill: "Does the high rate of interest in America and in new Colonies indicate a corresponding high rate of profits? and if so, What are the causes of that high rate?"

839A. TO ALEXANDER BAIN[1]

Blackheath
July 1. 1865

DEAR BAIN

I arrived here yesterday quite unexpectedly, finding it impossible any longer to resist the pressure put upon me by the Westminster Committee to shew myself to my supporters, and to the electors generally.[2] In consequence I find occupation cut out for me for almost every evening up to Friday,[3] and the remainder of my time will not be more than enough for preparation. I might perhaps manage to have a walk with you in the Park on Tuesday afternoon if convenient to you: otherwise I shall be obliged to put off seeing you till Friday, by which time I hope my troubles will be over. We hope you and Mrs Bain[4] will dine with us on Sunday the 9th at six. During the week following I shall be more at leisure, for the election is to be on Tuesday the 11th.

ever yours truly
J.S. MILL

844A. TO [JAMES ALFRED COOPER][1]

Blackheath Park, Kent
July 13. 1865

SIR

I received your letter, and the volume of the British Controversialist long after date, being absent from Avignon at the time, and it was still longer before I had

---

[1]MS in the possession of Professor Toshio Ohfuchi, Nihon University, Tokyo.
[2]On behalf of the Committee working to elect Mill as M.P. for Westminster, its Chairman, Charles Westerton (1813–72), bookseller and librarian, had written to overcome Mill's reluctance to appear before the electors. See Mill's reply of 26 June, 1865, CW, Vol. XVI, pp. 1073–4.
[3]Mill was, in the event, called upon to make four speeches that week (on Tuesday, Wednesday, Thursday, and Saturday) and, more at his leisure, two more on the following Monday before his victory speech after the close of the polls on Tuesday, 12 July. For the speeches, see *Public and Parliamentary Speeches*, CW, Vols. XXVIII–XXIX (Toronto: University of Toronto Press, 1988), Vol. XXVIII, pp. 13–45.
[4]Frances A. Bain (née Wilkinson) (d. 1892).

---

[1]MS at Kwansei Daigaku, Suita, Japan. Published in *MSBJ*, I, no. 6 (1985), 24–6, edited by Shigekazu Yamashita.

James Alfred Cooper (1822–98), founder and editor of the *British Controversialist and Literary Magazine*, which he initiated in 1859. A Birmingham industrialist, he was active in educational reform.

time to examine the notices relating to myself,[2] or to answer your letter. There are in the notices a greater amount of authentic details than I could at all have expected, mixed however with some considerable inaccuracies which I should have been glad to correct, had I not been prevented from doing so in time for the number of the Controversialist which you designated for receiving the correction.

I have hitherto thought that my System of Logic is not of a sufficiently popular character to call for a popular edition.[3] The subject, however, is open to consideration. I am, Sir

very faithfully yours

J.S. MILL

846A. TO WILLIAM LONGMAN[1]

Blackheath
July 15. 1865

DEAR SIR

I thank you for your congratulations and will endeavour to send enough of the Logic[2] to begin printing from at the earliest time possible.

yours very truly

J.S. MILL

862AA. TO JOHN WATKINS[1]

[Blackheath Park]
Aug. 11. 1865

DEAR SIR

My dislike of the majority of the photographs is no disparagement to the

---

[2] Anon. (but probably Cooper), "Modern Logicians: John Stuart Mill," in the numbers for March and April, 1865, pp. 161–73 and 241–56.

[3] Mill continued to resist the proposal; only in 1884, after his death, was a People's Edition of the *System of Logic* published by Longman with Helen Taylor's approval.

---

[1] MS in the Longman Archive, University of Reading. Published in *MNL*, XIII (Summer 1978), 12, edited by Bruce L. Kinzer.

William Longman (1813–77), head of the firm which had taken over Parker's business in 1864.

[2] The 6th ed. appeared in September 1865.

---

[1] MS at the College of Law, Nihon University, Tokyo.

John and Charles Watkins of 34 Parliament St. advertised themselves as "Photographers to the Queen, the Prince of Wales, and the Ex-Royal Family of France."

photographer, as I am much pleased with those I think successful.[2]

I am leaving town very soon,[3] and am so extremely busy that I cannot possibly find time for another sitting during the interval. But is there any hindrance to taking a fresh photograph of the photographs themselves? It is surely often done from engravings.

If it would be any accommodation to you I can dispense with some of the 200 copies. Fifty of each will be quite enough for the present, and I can order others when I want them; going without, in case they are not to be had. You are also welcome to take as many as you like from the cameo.

I will return both the framed portraits, as I do not desire to keep the one in profile, though I quite approve of it.

I thank you for the likeness of Mr Hughes.[4]

                    I am dear Sir
                    yours very faithfully
                    J.S. MILL

John Watkins, Esq.

865A. TO PHEBE LANKESTER[1]

                    Blackheath Park
                    Aug. 14. 1865

DEAR MADAM

I have now the pleasure of inclosing a few photographs,[2] of which I request your acceptance for yourself and any friends who have done me the honour to take interest in the election and to whom you may think fit to offer them.

                    I am Dear Madam
                    very truly yours
                    J.S. MILL

Mrs Lankester

---

[2]After repeated refusals, Mill had agreed to have a photograph taken to give to friends and admirers.

[3]In fact, Mill and Helen Taylor did not leave London for their trip to Germany until after 2 September.

[4]Thomas Hughes (1822–96), author of *Tom Brown's School Days*, who was elected M.P. for Lambeth in 1865, and was frequently allied with Mill in the House of Commons.

---

[1]MS at the College of Law, Nihon University, Tokyo.

Phebe Lankester (née Pope) (d. 1900), author of books on British wild flowers, was the wife of Edwin Lankester, an activist doctor and scientist who had strongly supported Mill in his election campaign.

[2]See Letter 862AA.

872B. TO ARTHUR JOHN WILLIAMS[1]

Prague
Sept. 22. 1865

DEAR SIR

I have only just received your note of the 7th inst. I am very desirous of promoting the abolition of the remaining exclusions of evidence, and will certainly support in Parliament any movement for that purpose.[2] But it is out of my power to attend the approaching meeting of the Social Science Association[3] or to write a paper on the question, nor can I even, at present, think of any person to whom I could advise you to apply.[4] Very few persons except lawyers have turned their attention to the question. I am, Dear Sir

yours very faithfully
J.S. MILL

A.J. Williams, Esq.

895A. TO HENRY WENTWORTH ACLAND[1]

Avignon
Dec. 12. 1865

DEAR SIR

Your letter has been forwarded to me here, but without the Oration[2] and the other works which you have been so kind as to send,[3] and which I shall doubtless

---

[1] MS at the College of Law, Nihon University, Tokyo.
Arthur John Williams (1836–1911), a law student, called to the bar in 1867, a member, like Mill, of the National Association for the Promotion of Social Science (popularly referred to as the Social Science Association).

[2] There was no action then in parliament concerning the abolition of rules for excluding evidence in the courts. Mill's allegiance to the cause dates back to his editing of Jeremy Bentham's *Rationale of Judicial Evidence* (1827); see the Introduction to *CW*, Vol. XXXI, pp. xv–xix.

[3] The meeting was held in Sheffield, 4–12 October, 1865.

[4] In the event, Alfred Waddilove (1806–90), ecclesiastical lawyer and author, spoke on the matter: "Is It Expedient to Remove Any and What of the Remaining Restrictions on the Admissibility of Evidence in Civil and Criminal Cases?" *Transactions of the National Association for the Promotion of Social Science, 1865* (London: Longman, et al., 1866).

---

[1] MS in the Bodleian Library.
Henry Wentworth Acland (1815–1900), Professor of Medicine at Oxford, and Radcliffe Librarian.

[2] *The Harveian Oration* (London: Macmillan, 1865).

[3] Not identified.

find at Blackheath when I return there. I am much obliged to you for them, and will not fail to read them as soon as time permits.

You will have found in Comte a broad enough statement, certainly, of the negative doctrine respecting Final Causes,[4] but very little argument, for he seemed to imagine that the question had been set at rest by others before him.

I am
yours very truly
J.S. MILL

Dr Acland

903A. TO JULES ERNEST NAVILLE[1]

Avignon
le 4 janvier 1866

MONSIEUR

Je vous remercie de bon coeur d'avoir bien voulu m'envoyer votre rapport,[2] que je trouverai sans doute à mon retour en Angleterre pour l'ouverture très prochaine du parlement, et que je lirai avec le plus vif intérêt. Cet intérêt sera vivement partagé par M. Hare l'auteur réel de la grande et féconde idée[3] qui a porté tant de lumières dans mon intelligence comme dans la vôtre. Sans exagération, cette idée a relevé mes espérances et dissipé mes principales craintes pour l'avenir du genre humain.

Je savais déjà, Monsieur, que je n'avais pas l'avantage d'être d'accord avec vous en matière de philosophie. Je n'en mets que plus de prix à l'accord qui existe entre nous sur l'une des plus graves questions de la science politique. Je me flatte d'ailleurs que si nous différons sur quelques-uns des principes les plus généraux, nous tirons souvent peut-être de nos principes différents les mêmes conclusions. Depuis longtemps je pense et je dis que la pratique dépend bien moins de la philosophie première que de la seconde—des *axiomata media* de Bacon:[4] et il

---

[4]The rejection of Final Causes is a basic tenet of the positive philosophy of Auguste Comte (1798–1857), the French philosopher with whom Mill corresponded extensively.

[1]MS in the Bibliothèque Publique et Universitaire de Genève. Published in *Ernest Naville, sa vie et sa pensée*, ed. Hélène Naville, 2 vols. (Geneva: Georg; Paris: Fischbacher, 1913–17), Vol. II, pp. 85–6.

Jules Ernest Naville (1816–1909), Swiss author of philosophical and political works.

[2]*Conseil de l'Association Réformiste. Séance du 21 novembre 1865. Réforme du système électoral* (Geneva: printed Vaney, 1865). This was a report by Naville, President of the Genevan Association, which was founded in 1865.

[3]I.e., of proportional representation, as presented in Thomas Hare's *Treatise on the Election of Representatives*.

[4]For these "middle axioms," see Francis Bacon (1561–1626), *Novum Organum* (1620), in *Works*, ed. James Spedding, *et al.*, 14 vols. (London: Longman, *et al.*, 1857–74), Vol. I, p. 159 (Latin), Vol. IV, p. 50 (English).

m'arrive souvent d'avoir un grand nombre de ceux-ci en commun avec des philosophes qui les acceptent d'intuition tandis que j'y arrive par raisonnement.

Agréez, Monsieur, l'expression de ma haute estime et de mon sincère dévouement.

J.S. MILL

910A. TO THOMAS HAVLIN[1]

Blackheath Park
Jan. 28. 1866

DEAR SIR

I enclose one of the photographs for which you do me the honour to express a wish; and in reply to your other request, [*breaks off*].

I am, Dear Sir

yours faithfully
J.S. MILL

Thomas Havlin Esq.

914A. TO EDWIN ARNOLD[1]

Blackheath Park
Jan. 31. 1866

DEAR SIR

It is a very tempting offer to place the great circulation of the Daily Telegraph at my disposal for so important a purpose as the one you mention. As a mark of confidence in me, it deserves my thankful acknowledgment, and I cannot be supposed to be ill affected to a journal which gave me such able and powerful support at the Westminster election. But it is totally impossible for me to have any personal connexion with a paper which takes the part the Telegraph does on the Jamaica question.[2] Not only every principle I have, but the honour and character of England for generations to come, are at stake in the condign punishment of the

---

[1] MS in the possession of Professor Toshio Ohfuchi, Nihon University, Tokyo.
Thomas Havlin has not been identified.

---

[1] MS in the possession of Professor Arnold Heertje, University of Amsterdam.
Edwin Arnold (1832–1904), then leader writer, and later editor of the *Daily Telegraph*.

[2] The *Daily Telegraph*, with most of the British press, supported Edward John Eyre (1815–1901), Governor of Jamaica, who had crushed the insurrection of 1865 and punished its leaders; see "The Negro Insurrection," and "Governor Eyre," *Daily Telegraph*, 29 and 30 Nov., 1865, both p. 3.

atrocities of which, by their own not confession, but boast, the Jamaica authorities have been guilty; and I cannot, while that question is pending, select as my official organ on another subject, a paper with which, in a matter of such transcendant importance, I am at open war.[3]

I am Dear Sir
very truly yours
J.S. MILL

Edwin Arnold Esq.

914B. TO AN UNIDENTIFIED CORRESPONDENT[1]

Blackheath
Feb. 3. 1866

DEAR SIR

I return the article from the Scotsman[2] which is excellent.

Do you know what are Neate's[3] opinions on the subject? If they are right, he would be a very fit man to make the first move.

I am Dear Sir
yrs very truly
J.S. MILL

---

[3]Eyre's "boast" is in his "Despatch to the Rt. Hon. Edward Cardwell, M.P." (20 Oct., 1865), *PP*, 1866, LI, 158. For Mill's account of the other "authorities," see his speech of 19 July, 1866, "The Disturbances in Jamaica [1]," *CW*, Vol. XXVIII, pp. 93–5. In July Mill would become the Chairman of the Jamaica Committee, dedicated to bringing Eyre to trial.

---

[1]MS in the Pierpont Morgan Library.

[2]Probably the leading article on secular education for Ireland, *Scotsman*, 29 Jan., 1866, p. 2. At this time, Mill, with John Elliot Cairnes the initiator of the effort, was preparing for a struggle in parliament to defend the nondenominational Queen's University in Ireland (a group of three Colleges) from a government scheme that would have crippled it by allowing Catholics to obtain degrees without an attendance requirement. See esp. Mill's letter to Cairnes of 6 January, 1866, *CW*, Vol. XVI, pp. 1133–4, in which he asks about Neate's view of the question. For a full discussion, see Bruce L. Kinzer, "John Stuart Mill and the Irish University Question," *Victorian Studies*, XXXI (Autumn 1987), 59–77.

[3]Charles Neate (1806–79), lawyer and Professor of Political Economy at Oxford, was Liberal M.P. for Oxford 1857 and 1863–68.

914C. TO [RALPH BERNAL?] OSBORNE[1]

Wednesday.
[Feb.–Apr. 1866?]

Mr Mill presents his compliments to Mr Osborne and incloses a gallery order for Monday next, having given his order for every day this week.

920A. TO AN UNIDENTIFIED CORRESPONDENT[1]

Blackheath Park
Feb. 16. 1866

Sir

I have had the honour of receiving your note of yesterday's date, but considering the great pressure of applications for admission for the Speaker's gallery, which on all occasions of interest are much more numerous than can possibly be complied with,[2] I am afraid I cannot undertake to make an application in favour of a gentleman who is neither a personal acquaintance nor a constituent.

I am Sir
yrs very faithfully
J.S. Mill

920B. TO WILLIAM LONGMAN[1]

Blackheath Park
Feb. 18. 1866

Dear Sir

I thank you and Mrs W. Longman for your kind invitation, but I find it

---

[1] MS in the Osborn Collection, Yale University.
Ralph Bernal Osborne (1811–82), liberal M.P. for various constituencies 1841–65, and Secretary to the Admiralty 1852–58, had been defeated in the general election in July 1865. He was elected in a by-election for Nottingham in April 1866. If the letter is indeed to him, it would seem likely that it dates from the first months of the parliamentary session in 1866, when Osborne might have wanted a "gallery order" so that he could follow the debate in the Commons during the brief period when he was not in the House.

---

[1] MS in the Pierpont Morgan Library.
[2] The request may well pertain to the scheduled debate on *habeas corpus* in Ireland, Saturday, 17 February.

---

[1] MS at the College of Law, Nihon University, Tokyo.

absolutely necessary at present to decline all evening engagements.

I am much obliged to you for the promptitude of your answer on the subject of Count Gurowski's work.[2]

[3]I should be glad to have copies of the Political Economy, Liberty, and Representative Government[4] (Library Editions) sent, free of charge, to the "Durham Cooperative Institute" No 6, Claypath, Durham.

          I am Dear Sir
          yours very truly
          J.S. MILL

William Longman Esq.

921A. TO WILLIAM CORRIE[1]

          Blackheath Park
          Feb. 22. 1866

DEAR SIR

I have had the honour of receiving your note inviting me on the part of the Sheriffs of London to dine with them in the House tomorrow (Friday) and I will with much pleasure avail myself of their kind invitation.

          I am Dear Sir
          yours faithfully
          J.S. MILL

William Corrie Esq.

---

[2]Count Adam Gurowski (1805–66), exiled Polish author and agitator, with whom Mill had become acquainted in Paris in the 1830s, emigrated to the United States in 1849. The first two volumes of his *Diary* had been published in America (Boston: Lee and Shepard, 1862; New York: Carleton, 1864). Gurowski had sent Mill a proof copy of Vol. III before its publication (New York: Morrison, 1866). Mill declined either to edit an English edition or to write an introduction to it (see *CW*, Vol. XVI, pp. 1113–14), and no English edition appears to have been published.

[3]This paragraph is cancelled in the MS, possibly by the clerk who filled the order, and noted the transaction with his initials and the date, 21 Feb., 1866.

[4]The most recent editions were, of the *Principles*, the 6th (1865), of *On Liberty*, the 3rd (1864), and of *Representative Government*, the 3rd (1865).

---

[1]MS at the College of Law, Nihon University, Tokyo.
William Corrie (1806–81), barrister and solicitor, was Remembrancer of the City of London from 1864.

933A. TO [JOHN NICOLAUS TRÜBNER][1]

Blackheath Park
April 15. [1866]

DEAR SIR

I have a small packet of books and documents[2] which I am desirous of sending to the Hon. S.S. Cox, Senator now or lately for Ohio, at an address in New York. Would it be convenient to you to forward it? or would you kindly suggest to me the best mode of doing so?

I am Dear Sir
yrs very truly
J.S. MILL

940A. TO THE TRUSTEES OF OWENS COLLEGE[1]

Blackheath Park, Kent
May 4, 1866

Such of Mr. Jevons's writings as I am acquainted with give evidence of decided originality, much knowledge and mental vigour, and an unusual degree of precision of thought and investigation.

His essay on the Gold Question[2] was the first starting point of the important series of discussions which has changed, and, it may now almost be said, settled the opinions of instructed men on the subject.

---

[1]MS in the Prussian State Library, Berlin.
John Nicolaus Trübner (1817–84), publisher, author, and translator, then publisher of the *Westminster Review*, and consequently of Mill's *Auguste Comte and Positivism* (1865), was identified as the probable agent for transmitting books in a letter of this date (*CW*, Vol. XVI, pp. 1158–9) from Mill to Samuel Sullivan Cox (1824–89), tariff reformer, formerly Democratic Congressman from Ohio.

[2]These, as the letter to Cox indicates, concerned the operation of free trade in the U.K., and were supplied by William Newmarch (1820–82), economist and statistician; the only title Mill specifies is Newmarch's "Commercial History and Review of 1865," "Supplement to the *Economist*," XXIV (10 Mar., 1866), 1–64.

---

[1]MS in The John Rylands University Library of Manchester. Published in *Papers and Correspondence of William Stanley Jevons*, ed. R.D. Collison Black, 7 vols. (London: Macmillan, 1972–81), Vol. III, p. 120.

[2]*A Serious Fall in the Value of Gold Ascertained, and Its Social Effects Set Forth* (London: Stanford, 1863).

The merit of his investigation of the "Coal Question" can hardly be rated too highly.³

His "Logic of Quality"⁴ showed extraordinary familiarity with and power over Formal Logic, and if I had a fault to find, it would be that the expenditure of power was greater than any result to be obtained by that mode of employing it would sufficiently remunerate.

Of Mr. Jevons's teaching powers I can say nothing; of these, however, the authorities of Owens College can judge from their own experience. But as regards his knowledge both of Logic and of Political Economy, so far as the whole can be judged from a part, I should form a very high estimate of it.

J. STUART MILL

949A. TO WILLIAM DOUGAL CHRISTIE[1]

Crowcombe, Somerset
May 21. 1866

DEAR SIR

No subject connected with the representation is of greater practical importance than bribery and election expenses, and I hope that a great and united effort will be made by reformers on the subject.² But Gladstone, in introducing the Franchise Bill, was understood to give an express promise to take up this subject when he has done with the other, and he certainly shewed a very strong feeling of its importance.³ It seems to me, therefore, that the time which he indicated for himself, is the best time for us; and it is probable that he will then be willing and desirous to listen to any suggestions on the matter from persons whom he respects.

---

³*The Coal Question: An Enquiry Concerning the Progress of the Nation, and the Probable Exhaustion of Our Coal Mines* (London and Cambridge: Macmillan, 1865). Mill had praised the work on 17 April, 1866, in the House of Commons; see *CW*, Vol. XXVIII, pp. 70–1.
⁴See Letter 819A above.

---

[1]MS at Osaka University of Commerce, Japan. Published in *MSBJ*, I, no. 6 (1985), 4, edited by Takutoshi Inouyé.
²Christie, author of *Electoral Corruption and Its Remedies* and *Suggestions for an Organization for the Restraint of Corruption at Elections* (both published in 1864 by the National Association for the Promotion of Social Science), actively supported Mill's campaign in the Commons for reform of the laws on bribery and corruption; see *CW*, Vol. XXVIII, pp. 9–11, 263–5.
³See William Ewart Gladstone (1809–98), the Liberal leader, "Speech on the Representation of the People Bill" (12 Mar., 1866), *PD*, 3rd ser., Vol. 182, col. 25, in introducing "A Bill to Extend the Right of Voting at Elections of Members of Parliament in England and Wales," 29 Victoria (13 Mar., 1866), *PP*, 1866, V, 87–100.

If the grouping of boroughs has the effect you apprehend, it will still further strengthen our argument. But as far as I am able to foresee, I rather expect from it a contrary effect.

I am sorry you are not member for Cambridge, but I hope you will find another seat after the Reform Bill passes if not before.[4] I am, Dear Sir

yrs very truly

J.S. MILL

W.D. Christie Esq.

949B. TO G. HARVEY[1]

Blackheath Park, Kent
May 21, 1866

DEAR SIR

Although very much occupied I have, with difficulty, found time to read the pamphlet which I am indebted to you for sending me. It has not, however, persuaded me to agree with you; but I cannot possibly undertake to discuss so intricate a subject with you in a letter.

I do not know to what article on Money your letter refers as I have never published any article with that title.

J.S. MILL

G. Harvey Esq.

952A. TO OLIVER WENDELL HOLMES[1]

May 30. [1866]

DEAR SIR

It is unlucky that you are engaged on the days on which I am free. The best proposal I can now make for any day previous to the 8th would be, for you to come to the dinner of the Political Economy Club next Friday, June 1. There will be

---

[4]Christie had been defeated at Cambridge in the general election of 1865, and was again unsuccessful at Greenock in 1868.

---

[1]MS at the College of Law, Nihon University, Tokyo; in Helen Taylor's hand, but signed by Mill.

G. Harvey and the pamphlet he sent Mill have not been identified.

---

[1]MS in the Houghton Library, Harvard University.

Oliver Wendell Holmes Jr. (1841–1935), later Associate Justice of the U.S. Supreme Court, was visiting England.

several persons there whom you may like to see, and I hope to be able to leave the House for a part of the evening to go there.[2] If you will come to the House of Commons soon after ½ past 5, we will go together, or, if I am prevented, my friend Professor Fawcett will be happy to go with you to the Club. Please let me know in the course of Thursday whether you will come. I am, Dear Sir

yrs very truly

J.S. MILL

955A. TO JOSHUA TOULMIN SMITH[1]

June 1. 1866

DEAR SIR

Thank you for your note. I am aware that in this country and in all others whose laws were originally founded on the feudal principle, landed possessions were held subject to, and even as a provision for, public duties, and that the idea of absolute property in land is essentially modern. You, however, as a Constitutional lawyer, know infinitely more on the subject than I do, and I shall be very glad to have the opportunity of consulting you when I again have occasion to touch on the point.

The other fact you mention, that the expenses of elections were once a public charge, is new to me, and will be a most telling point to bring forward when that subject is before Parliament, which it is sure, very shortly, to be.[2] When that time comes, I should be very glad indeed to be able to produce a copy of the writ and read parts of it to the House.

I am with many thanks, Dear Sir

yours very truly

J.S. MILL

Toulmin Smith Esq.

[2]Holmes accompanied Mill and Henry Fawcett to the meeting; for his recollections, see Mark De Wolfe Howe, *Justice Oliver Wendell Holmes*, 2 vols. (Cambridge, Mass.: Harvard University Press, 1957–63), Vol. I, pp. 226–7.

[1]MS in the Lilly Library, Indiana University, Bloomington. Published in *MNL*, XII (Winter, 1977), 2, edited by Marcia Allentuck.

Joshua Toulmin Smith (1816–69), a strong advocate of local government and democratic self-determination.

[2]It is not known what Smith had mentioned; when the issue arose in the Commons, Mill made no reference to the matter.

956A. TO OLIVER WENDELL HOLMES[1]

Blackheath
June 2. 1866

DEAR SIR

I inclose an introduction to Mr Herbert Spencer, and am only sorry that you are not able to meet him at my house.[2]

I hope that we shall dine together at the House of Commons, if not on Tuesday, on some other day before you go.[3]

I am Dear Sir
yours very truly
J.S. MILL

961A. TO JAMES BEAL[1]

Blackheath Park
16 June. 1866

DEAR SIR

Mr Hickson would like before he gives evidence, to see the evidence which has already been given.[2] As he will be one of our most valuable witnesses, and as I have no second copy of the evidence, I should be glad if possible to send him the copy, a portion of which you have. Would you therefore, if not using it, be kind enough to send that portion either to me at the House, or addressed to himself "care of housekeeper, East Temple Chambers, 2 Whitefriars Street"—in the latter case giving me a note of the numbers you have sent, that I may know if I supply him with all the remainder.

We are doing little good in Ayrton's Committee.[3] Vestry clerks and chairmen

---

[1] MS in the Houghton Library, Harvard University.
[2] Holmes did not meet Spencer (see Howe, *Justice Holmes*, Vol. I, p. 226).
[3] On Tuesday, 11 June, Holmes dined in the Members' Room of the Commons with Mill and Alexander Bain (*ibid.*, p. 228).

---

[1] MS in the James Beal Collection at the Greater London Record Office.
James Beal (1829–91), auctioneer and land agent, who had led the movement to elect Mill, was particularly concerned about municipal reform.
[2] Mill was a member of the Select Committee on Metropolitan Local Government, which began to hear evidence on 9 March, 1866. William Edward Hickson (see Letter 277.2 above) appeared before the Committee on 26 July, when he was questioned by Mill. See the Committee's "Second Report," *PP*, 1866, XIII, 569–85. (Mill's part of the questioning is in *CW*, Vol. XXIX, pp. 536–8.) The previous evidence that Hickson wished to see is in the "First Report," *PP*, 1866, XIII, 171–315.
[3] Acton Smee Ayrton (1816–86), barrister, M.P. for Tower Hamlets 1857–74, chaired the Committee on Metropolitan Government.

are coming up one after another to celebrate the admirable working of their own system, and we want people who from their own knowledge can testify to the contrary.

I wish I could have been at the discussion in your Committee[4] on Thursday, but the time (in the middle of a Reform debate with a division possible at any moment) made it impracticable.[5] I have had some talk with Mr. Beggs[6] which I hope to be able to supplement by some talk with you.

I am Dear Sir
yours very truly
J.S. MILL

James Beal Esq.

968A. TO JOSEPH WILLIAM CROMPTON[1]

Blackheath Park
Sunday
[9 July, 1866]

DEAR SIR

On returning home yesterday evening, I heard that you had had the trouble of calling. I shall be engaged all tomorrow forenoon, but if you could come to the House of Commons about five oclock, I have no doubt I should be able to see you. If you cannot do this, perhaps you would be so good as to write.

I am Dear Sir
yrs very truly
J.S. MILL

Rev. Joseph Crompton.

---

[4]Presumably a committee of St. James's Vestry, on which Beal was active.

[5]The Liberal Reform Bill (see Letter 949A above) was before the House from 14 March, with frequent crucial debates. The Bill was finally withdrawn on 20 July, and the Conservatives consequently formed a new administration.

[6]Thomas Beggs (1808–96), an engineer and brass founder, temperance advocate and political reformer, was allied with Beal in Mill's election campaign. He had appeared before the Metropolitan Local Government Committee on 26 April and 10 May; see *PP*, 1866, XIII, 367–73 and 374–8. (Mill's part of the questioning is in *CW*, Vol. XXIX, pp. 471–6.)

[1]MS at the College of Law, Nihon University, Tokyo. Dated from postmark. *Addressed:* Rev. Joseph Crompton / Lauderdale House / Highgate / N.

Joseph William Crompton, sometime minister of the Unitarian Octagon Chapel, Norwich, who had been a classmate of Mill's brother, James, was a trustee for his sister, Jane Ferraboschi.

973A. TO WILLIAM SMITH[1]

Blackheath Park
July 20. 1866

DEAR SIR

Monsieur Barrère, a much esteemed and valued friend of mine, is a candidate for the headship of the International School which is to be founded at Paris, by the Committee of which you are a member.[2] Monsieur Barrère's attainments, his great experience as a teacher both in France and in England, and his general character and disposition, all of which can be most amply vouched for, would render him, I should think, a highly fit person for conducting such a school, and a most likely person to make it succeed. M. Barrère would be happy to give you in a personal interview, all possible information respecting his antecedents, and his qualifications for the post.

I am Dear Sir
very truly yours
J.S. MILL

Dr William Smith.

976A. TO [WILLIAM LONGMAN][1]

Blackheath
25 July. [1866]

DEAR SIR

I duly received your remittance and the accounts—with which I have great reason to be satisfied.

If any thing should occur to me which I wish to say to you before you go, I will either write or call on you.

very truly yrs,
J.S. MILL

---

[1]MS at the College of Law, Nihon University, Tokyo.
Presumably, William Smith (1813–93), lexicographer and classical scholar.
[2]For similar effort by Mill on Barrère's behalf, see Letter 683A above. The International Education Society succeeded in founding a school near Paris, but it lasted only until the outbreak of the Franco-Prussian War; see also *CW*, Vol. XVI, pp. 1087, 1092.

---

[1]MS in the Osborn Collection, Yale University.
It is likely that Mill is acknowledging royalty payments for his works; see his letter of 28 April, 1866, to Longman (*CW*, Vol. XVI, p. 1161). At this time, Mill commonly dated brief notes simply "Blackheath," with month and day.

982A. TO GEORGE JACOB HOLYOAKE[1]

Blackheath Park
Aug. 5. 1866

DEAR SIR

It is quite possible that occasions may at some time or other arise when I might be glad to have the pages of the Working Man open to me for the purpose of addressing things directly to the working classes; but it is impossible for me to make any promise or hold out any prospect of my doing so; for the quantity of work devolving upon me, even independently of Parliament, is already much greater than I can do with complete satisfaction to myself. The work awaiting me for the approaching recess is enough to occupy the whole of my time, and I cannot at present look forward to any period when I shall have leisure for any new engagements.

I am Dear Sir

yrs very truly
J.S. MILL

G.J. Holyoake Esq.

992A. TO WALTER LOWE CLAY[1]

Barcelonette, Basses Alpes
Aug. 30. 1866

DEAR SIR

I am glad that there is to be a discussion at the meeting of the Social Science Association respecting Extradition Treaties, and I think the opinions and feelings which such a discussion is likely to evoke may have a useful influence on the decision of Parliament next year.[2] But it is quite as much out of my power to write a

---

[1]MS at Kwansai Daigaku, Suita, Japan. Published in *MSBJ*, I, no. 6 (1985), 27–9, edited by Shigekazu Yamashita.

George Jacob Holyoake (1817–1906), free-thinking journalist and leader in the development of the co-operative movement, publisher of the *Reasoner*, and editor, during its brief existence, of *The Working Man; a Weekly Record of Social and Industrial Progress*.

---

[1]MS in the William R. Perkins Library, Duke University. *Addressed:* Rev. Walter L. Clay / Social Science Association / 1 Adam Street / Adelphi / London W.C.

Walter Lowe Clay (1833–75), Church of England divine, sometime chaplain of Preston Gaol, and writer on prisons.

[2]When the National Association for the Promotion of Social Science met in Birmingham in October, there was no session devoted to extradition treaties. In parliament, Mill had been successful in limiting to one year the application of 29 & 30 Victoria, c. 121 (10 Aug., 1866), the Act amending the law relating to extradition; later, in 1868, he was an active member of the Select Committee on Extradition (see *CW*, Vol. XXIX, pp. 542–71).

paper on the subject as it is to attend the discussion, having work to do which must be done before the reassembling of Parliament and which will require all the intervening time.[3] I am Dear Sir

yours very faithfully
J.S. MILL

Rev. W.L. Clay.

999A. TO ELIZABETH MALLESON[1]

Avignon
Oct. 2. 1866

DEAR MADAM

I wish every possible success to the Working Women's College; but, independently of my absence from England, it would be quite incompatible with other very pressing occupations for me to attend and take part in the proceedings at the Meeting on the 19th; much more to prepare so important a thing as an inaugural address.[2] Regretting my inability to give a more satisfactory answer, I am, Dear Madam

very truly yours
J.S. MILL

Mrs F. Malleson.

---

[3]The public issue Mill was most involved in was the controversy over ex-Governor Eyre of Jamaica. His pressing authorial work was the 3rd ed. of *An Examination of Sir William Hamilton's Philosophy* (*CW*, Vol. IX) and his *Inaugural Address at St. Andrews* (in *CW*, Vol. XXI, pp. 215–57).

---

[1]MS at Kwanseigakuin University, Nishinomiya, Japan.

Elizabeth Malleson (née Whitehead) (1828–1916), wife of Frank Rodbard Malleson, had founded the Working Women's College two years earlier. For the prospectus, and her inaugural address on the occasion, see the *English Woman's Journal*, XIII (Aug. 1864), 430–2 (in which Mill is mentioned as a subscriber), and *Address at the Opening of the Working Women's College, October 26th, 1864* (London: Kenney, 1868).

[2]Presumably to launch the new academic year.

1017A. TO JOHN MORLEY[1]

Blackheath Park
Kent
Saturday [1867?]

DEAR MR MORLEY

If you are not engaged tomorrow, we shall be very glad to see you. We dine at five, and there is a train from Charing Cross at four. I am,

yours very truly
J.S. MILL

1023A. TO THE REPORTER OF THE *GLASGOW HERALD*[1]

Avignon
Jan. 24. 1867

Mr Mill presents his compliments to the Reporter of the Glasgow Herald, has received his note dated the 19th, and will take care that a printed copy of his Address reaches the Herald on the 1st of February.[2]

1046A. TO JOHN MALCOLM FORBES LUDLOW[1]

Feb. 22. 1867

DEAR SIR

As far as I have any voice in the matter, I think it not only unobjectionable, but

---

[1]MS in the Harry Ransom Humanities Research Center, University of Texas at Austin. John Morley (1838–1923), editor and author, later statesman, met Mill in 1866, and became intimate in subsequent months (see his *Recollections*, 2 vols. [New York: Macmillan, 1917], Vol. I, p. 52), before taking a trip to the U.S.A. in the winter of 1867–68.

---

[1]MS in the Houghton Library, Harvard University.
The reporter is unidentified.
[2]Mill delivered his Rectorial Address at St. Andrews University on 1 February, and it was reported in full in the Scottish and national press before its publication as a book later that month. How he could arrange for a printed text to reach Glasgow on the day of the speech's delivery is not known; the account in the *Herald* (2 Feb., p. 6), while substantial and close to the book version, omits central paragraphs.

---

[1]MS in the University Library, Cambridge.
John Malcolm Forbes Ludlow (1821–1911), lawyer, author, and social reformer.

most desirable, that you should help Mr Scott to put into a proper shape his very enlightened views on the reform of the municipal government of London.[2] I will take an opportunity of speaking to Mr Beal on the subject, but I think there can be little doubt of his assent. I am, Dear Sir

very truly yours
J.S. MILL

J.M. Ludlow Esq.

1046B. TO JOHN MALCOLM FORBES LUDLOW[1]

Feb. 23. [1867]

DEAR SIR

Since I wrote to you, I have seen Mr Beal, and he not only entirely approves of your giving your assistance to Mr Scott, but greatly desires that you would do so. I am, Dear Sir

very truly yours
J.S. MILL

J.M. Ludlow Esq.

1051A. TO ANDREA CRESTADORO[1]

Blackheath Park
March 4. 1867

DEAR SIR

I beg to apologize for having so long delayed to express my thanks to yourself and to the Chairman of the Library for the gift of your excellent Catalogue.[2] I have desired my publishers to send two or three of my books which are not already in the

---

[2]Benjamin Scott (1814–92), Chamberlain of the City of London, was to testify before the Select Committee on Metropolitan Government, of which Mill was a member, on 6 and 28 March, and 1, 11, and 30 April, 1867, as he had in the previous year. For Scott's exchanges with Mill, see *CW*, Vol. XXXI, pp. 390–1, 402–4, and Vol. XXIX, pp. 443–4.

---

[1]MS in the University Library, Cambridge.
For the dating and the references, see Letter 1046A above.

---

[1]MS at the College of Law, Nihon University, Tokyo.
Andrea Crestadoro (1808–79), a bibliographer, had been appointed chief librarian of the Manchester Public Free Libraries.
[2]Crestadoro had prepared an *Index-Catalogue of the Hulme Lending Branch* of the Manchester Public Free Libraries (Manchester, 1867).

Library and of which I request its acceptance.³ There are others which I shall have the pleasure of sending as soon as they are reprinted.⁴ I am, Dear Sir

yours very sincerely

J.S. MILL

Dr Crestadoro
&c &c

1054A. TO GEORGE JOHN GRAHAM¹

Blackheath Park
March 6. 1867

DEAR GRAHAM

I will with the greatest pleasure do what you request.²

With regard to my not going into what is called society, I should not do so even if I had time for it, for as it is neither duty nor pleasure, neither work nor recreation, there is no reason why I should. But seeing you is quite another thing, and would be a real pleasure. Unfortunately the work I am now overladen with, is not like writing a book or an article, but is made up of bits and scraps, and cannot be done in the way you kindly offer, so that I do not see my way to being able to accept your invitation.

I am glad you are going to retire while you have good work in you, and the power of enjoying it. I have always regretted that capacities like yours should have been wholly engrossed by duties which did not require the highest of them.³

I am Dear Graham
ever yours truly
J.S. MILL

---

³The *Index-Catalogue* indicates that the Library already had *On Liberty*, *Principles of Political Economy*, and *Considerations on Representative Government*.

⁴Among "others," Mill was probably planning to send the 2nd eds. of *Dissertations and Discussions* and of the *Inaugural Address* and the 3rd ed. of the *Examination*, all of which appeared in the spring of 1867.

---

¹MS at the College of Law, Nihon University, Tokyo.

²Graham had evidently asked Mill to be surety for a debt; see *CW*, Vol. XVI, pp. 1286 and 1296, and Vol. XVII, p. 1602.

³Graham was retiring as Registrar-General of Births and Deaths, a position he had held since 1838.

1070A. TO HENRY STUDDY THEOBALD[1]

Thursday evg
[28 Mar., 1867]

DEAR SIR

I inclose a note to my old and excellent friend M. d'Eichthal, the best friend I have left at Paris after the many whom death has taken away.[2] He has access to most people that could help you and to most things that would interest you and I am sure of his hearty good will to any friend of mine.

I am Dear Sir
yours very truly
J.S. MILL

1075A. TO JAMES BEAL[1]

Saint Véran, Avignon
April 21. 1867

DEAR SIR

I am sorry that I did not receive your note before leaving England, but as soon as I get back I will send you the minutes of evidence, and there need not be any hurry about returning them.[2] The Committee will meet on Tuesday the 30th to consider the Resolutions and it is probable that they will only report Resolutions instead of making a regular Report.[3] So much the better, as Ayrton[4] is not likely to make the

---

[1]MS at the College of Law, Nihon University, Tokyo.
Henry Studdy Theobald (1847–1934), was then a student at Oxford, and later a lawyer and author. His father, William, an old friend of Mill's, was also an author of legal works, and a member of the Calcutta bar.
[2]The accompanying note, of 28 March, 1867, to Gustave d'Eichthal (1804–86), an early disciple of Saint-Simon, and friend of Mill's from 1828, is in *CW*, Vol. XVI, p. 1261.

---

[1]MS in the James Beal Collection at the Greater London Record Office.
[2]Mill was still in London on 11 April, when he attended a meeting of the Select Committee on Metropolitan Government; he is referring to advance copies of the evidence given to the Committee up to that date. For the evidence, see the Committee's "Third Report," *PP*, 1867, XII, 443–600.
[3]On 30 April the Committee met, Mill present, and debated Resolutions; these were revised in subsequent meetings and the final version was agreed on 6 May, with a short report. See the Committee's "Second Report," *ibid.*, pp. 435–41*.
[4]Acton Smee Ayrton chaired the Committee.

Report we want. I shall be prepared to move for leave to bring in your Bills as soon as they are ready.[5] I am, Dear Sir

yours very truly
J.S. MILL

James Beal Esq.

1076A. TO HENRY WYNDHAM PHILLIPS[1]

Blackheath Park
April 29. 1867

Mr Mill presents his Compliments to the Honorary Secretary of the Artists' General Benevolent Institution, and regrets his inability to accept the invitation with which he has been honoured to attend the Anniversary Festival.[2]

1084A. TO KATHERINE LOUISA RUSSELL[1]

Blackheath Park
May 24 [1867]

DEAR LADY AMBERLEY

Many thanks for your kind invitation. I should really like to look in upon you any evening, but I do not like rushing in just at dinner time and leaving almost before dinner is over. I am afraid the new arrangements in the House for Tuesdays and Fridays will make it more than ever difficult to come to your nine o'clock reception, as that will be the time when the House will resume its sittings and get at once to its principal business.

---

[5] On 13 May Mill moved for leave to introduce "A Bill for the Establishment of Municipal Corporations within the Metropolis," 30 Victoria (21 May, 1867), *PP*, 1867, IV, 447–66, and announced that he would later bring forward "A Bill for the Better Government of the Metropolis," 30 & 31 Victoria (6 Aug., 1867), *ibid.*, 215–56. Both Bills were drafted by Beal, with assistance from Ludlow; see Letter 1112A below. Mill's speeches of 21 May and 7 August, introducing the measures, are in *CW*, Vol. XXVIII, pp. 162–5 and 230–1.

---

[1] MS in the Pennsylvania State University Library.
Henry Wyndham Phillips (1820–68), painter, was Honorary Secretary of the Institution for thirteen years.

[2] The 52nd anniversary was celebrated at the Freemason's Tavern on 18 May with Anthony Trollope in the chair; see *Art-Journal*, XXIX (June 1867), 179.

---

[1] MS at the College of Law, Nihon University, Tokyo.
Katherine Louisa Russell (1842–74), wife of John, Viscount Amberley, was a close friend of Mill and Helen Taylor.

The division was a great triumph, and especially Mr Bright's voting with us.[2] We should have had near 100 votes if all had been present who have told me that they would have voted with us if they had not paired, or been too late. I am, Dear Lady Amberley

very truly yours
J.S. MILL

1103A. TO ALFRED W. BURNETT[1]

Blackheath Park
June 23. 1867

DEAR SIR

In answer to your note, received yesterday evening, I beg to say, that while I am most sensible to the honour of having been thought of to represent so enlightened a body as the University of London, yet as long as the electors of Westminster wish to retain me as their representative, I should not think of leaving them for any other constituency.[2]

I am Dear Sir
yours very sincerely
J.S. MILL

Alfred W. Burnett Esq

1112A. TO JOHN MALCOLM FORBES LUDLOW[1]

Blackheath Park
July 21. 1867

DEAR SIR

Many thanks for your note. I shall give my notice tomorrow for Tuesday week.[2]

---

[2] John Bright (1811–98), M.P. for Birmingham, had voted for Mill's amendment to the Reform Bill (30 & 31 Victoria, c. 102), which would have given votes to women. For the debate, see *PD*, Vol. 187, cols. 817–45; the amendment was lost, 196 to 73. Mill's speech is in *CW*, Vol. XXVIII, pp. 151–62.

---

[1] MS at Osaka University of Commerce, Japan.
Burnett has not been identified.
[2] In August, Sections 24 and 25 of the Reform Bill would give the University of London a representative in the Commons.

---

[1] MS in the University Library, Cambridge.
[2] I.e., to introduce the second of Beal's bills on the municipal reform of London, "A Bill for the Better Government of the Metropolis" (see Letter 1075A above). On "Tuesday week," 30 July, however, the House was "counted out" before Mill could do so, and he had to wait until 7 August.

I was only waiting to be sure that I should have all the necessary materials before that date.

I shall feel obliged to reinsert the clause providing for the election of the Chamberlain &c. by the Common Council of London and not by the Common Hall of the City. I also propose to insert, among the officers so elected, the Common Sergeant.[3]

I am sorry the Draft of the Bill was given (by Mr Beal) to the Star without ampler warning. The article in the Star was well meant,[4] but indiscreet as to the City, and its ascribing your note (notwithstanding the initials) to me, was hardly excusable even by the haste with which leading articles are written. I have been thinking of writing to Chesson to correct the blunder.[5] Do you think that desirable or not?

Adhesions seem to multiply in all quarters. I am Dear Sir

yours very truly
J.S. MILL

J.M. Ludlow Esq.

1118A. TO JOHN MALCOLM FORBES LUDLOW[1]

July 25. 1867

DEAR SIR

I think you are right as to the inexpediency of writing to Chesson.[2]

Mr Beal did not get his copy of the Draft Bill from me. I suppose he must have got it from the Chamberlain.[3] The copy you gave me has not been out of my possession. The one which was sent to the papers was the Draft as altered by the Chamberlain, by the omission of a clause which, as I mentioned to you, I intend to restore.

I have received from Beal a proof of the Memorandum.[4] It is marked "Confidential" and shall not go out of my hands. I am Dear Sir

yours very truly
J.S. MILL

J.M. Ludlow Esq.

[3]See Clause 62, *PP*, 1867, IV, 233.
[4]Unheaded leading article, *Morning Star*, 19 July, 1867, p. 4.
[5]Frederick William Chesson (ca. 1833–88), pamphleteer and activist, was on the editorial staff of the *Morning Star*, a radical daily, normally enthusiastic about Mill's ideas.

[1]MS in the University Library, Cambridge.
[2]See Letter 1112A above for the context of this and the following matters.
[3]Benjamin Scott, Chamberlain of the City of London; see Letter 1046A above.
[4]Not identified.

1122A. TO MOUNTSTUART ELPHINSTONE GRANT DUFF[1]

Blackheath Park
July 31. 1867

DEAR SIR

I have only just heard that you are a member of the constituency of the London University.[2] Some of the electors especially those interested in sanitary and in educational questions, are desirous of proposing Mr Chadwick as a candidate.[3] I have long been very desirous that he should be in Parliament as his great knowledge of many difficult administrative questions and his fertility of practical resource, combined with his great industry and public spirit, would make him useful in a way much wanted, and in which few, if any, are capable of being equally so. I am anxious that you should have an opportunity of considering his claims, if possible before making up your mind to support any of the other candidates. I hope to be allowed to say more on the subject when I meet you at the House. I am Dear Sir

Yours very truly
J.S. MILL

M.E. Grant Duff Esq. M.P.

1127A. TO HENRY SIDGWICK[1]

Aug. 3. 1867

DEAR SIR

The questions mooted in your letter of July 28 are very important, and extremely difficult if not impossible to decide by a general rule, without many allowances for

---

[1]MS in the India Office Library and Records. For Grant Duff, see Letter 595B above.
[2]See Letter 1103A above.
[3]Mill was working hard to promote Chadwick's candidacy; see, e.g., his letters of 25 and 31 July, *CW*, Vol. XVI, pp. 1294–5 and 1296.

---

[1]MS at Trinity College, Cambridge. Published in *MNL*, IX (Summer, 1974), 10, edited by J.B. Schneewind.

Henry Sidgwick (1838–1900), a graduate and fellow of Trinity College Cambridge, classicist and philosopher, was experiencing religious difficulties, especially over the question of subscription to the Thirty-Nine Articles of the Church of England. He wrote to Mill, as a stranger, on 28 July, 1867 (MS at Johns Hopkins), explaining his problems in attempting, on "principles of ethics," to write about the position liberals "ought to take up with regard to the traditional . . . religion of the country." He asked if Mill could devote time to "viva voce" discussion or to reading his "statement" on the subject. The latter presumably was a draft of *The Ethics of Conformity and Subscription* (London: Williams and Norgate, 1870). See Letter 1160A below.

differences of position which point out to different persons different paths of usefulness. As you say, it is absurd to refer each man to his individual conscience since the very question is, what his conscience ought to prescribe. While I sympathize fully in your perplexities, I do not know when I should be able to fix a time for discussing them at length, either viva voce or in writing: but I would endeavour to find time for reading the statement you speak of, and for giving some sort of opinion respecting it. I am, Dear Sir

yours very sincerely
J.S. Mill

Henry Sidgwick Esq.

1128A. TO FRÉDÉRIC PASSY[1]

Blackheath Park
Kent
le 4 août 1867

Veuillez excuser, Monsieur, le retard involontaire de ma réponse à votre trop flatteuse lettre du 17 juillet. Le mouvement d'opinion qui a donné lieu à la formation de la Ligue Internationale de la Paix a toutes mes sympathies.[2] Il appartenait à la France de prendre l'initiative d'un pareil mouvement. J'applaudis de tout mon coeur aux efforts des hommes éminents qui ont fondé la Ligue, et je me félicite de l'honneur qu'ils me font en désirant mon adhésion. Cette adhésion leur est toute acquise, et je vous engage, Monsieur, de vouloir bien inscrire mon nom au nombre des Sociétaires.

Veuillez agréer, Monsieur, l'hommage de ma très haute et très respectueuse considération.

J. Stuart Mill

---

[1]MS at the Archives de l'Ancien Maine et du Département de la Sarthe. Frédéric Passy (1822–1912), French economist and prolific author.
[2]Passy had just founded the Ligue in collaboration with Michel Chevalier (1806–79), early Saint-Simonian and advocate of free trade, Auguste Joseph Alphonse Gratry (1805–72), liberal theologian, and Charles Loyson ("Père Hyacinthe") (1827–1912), also a liberal theologian. The first President was Johann Heinrich (Jean Henri) Dollfus (1800–87), mayor of Mulhouse in Alsace.

1137A. TO EDWIN CARTON BOOTH[1]

House of Commons
Aug. 13. 1867

DEAR SIR

It is scarcely possible for me to appoint any interviews at present with certainty of being able to keep the engagement, but if it is convenient to you to call on me at the House of Commons on Thursday or Friday while the House is sitting, I should be happy to see you. I am, Dear Sir

yours very faithfully
J.S. MILL

E.C. Booth Esq.

1139A. TO THOMAS JOSEPH HASLAM[1]

Blackheath Park
Kent
Aug. 17. 1867

DEAR SIR

Excuse the delay in acknowledging your valuable letter of July 29. Your report, and that of Mr Webb,[2] are not encouraging as to the immediate prospects of the Women's Suffrage movement in Dublin; but though it may not be yet time to organise a Society there, it is all the more desirable to obtain as many adherents as possible from Ireland to the Society of which I have the pleasure of inclosing the papers. Besides the Executive Committee of ladies whose names you will see,[3] the

---

[1] MS in the State Library of Victoria, Australia.
Edwin Carton Booth (ca. 1827–78), an English-born Australian journalist, editor of *Home News for Australia*, then on a tour of the U.K. and the U.S.A.

---

[1] MS in the Library of the Religious Society of Friends in Ireland, Dublin. Published in *MNL*, XX (Summer 1985), 13, edited by T.P. Foley.
Thomas Joseph Haslam (1825–1917), an Irish Quaker, was an advocate of birth control and of repeal of the Contagious Diseases Acts. His wife Anna Maria (née Fisher) (ca. 1830–after 1918) an advocate of women's suffrage, had signed the petition on the subject presented by Mill to the Commons in 1866.
[2] Presumably these were written, not printed, reports by Haslam and Richard Davis Webb (d. 1872), a Dublin printer and Quaker, who was prominent in anti-slavery, temperance, and peace campaigns in Ireland. He joined the Suffrage Society but not the Committee (see Mill's letter to Cairnes, of 1 September, 1867, *CW*, Vol. XVI, p. 1315).
[3] The Executive Committee of the London National Society for Women's Suffrage included at that time Clementia Taylor (1811–1908), wife of Peter Alfred Taylor; Millicent Fawcett (1811–1929), wife of Henry Fawcett; Frances Power Cobbe (1822–1902),

Society consists of a General Committee who are the constituency and subscribe a guinea a year, and of ordinary members subscribing a shilling. If the Society might have the benefit of your name and Mrs Haslam's in either capacity, it would give me very great pleasure.

Several Irish Liberal members of Parliament have already joined the General Committee, among other Messrs Maguire, Blake, O'Beirne, Sir John Gray, and Mr Pollard Urquhart.[4]

I am well acquainted with your pamphlet,[5] which is very good as it is, though I have no doubt that any addition or alteration which you would now make would still further improve it. I regret extremely that the state of your health is such as you mention, and I hope that rest and abstinence from unnecessary nervous and cerebral excitement will in time reestablish it.

I am Dear Sir
yours very sincerely
J.S. MILL

T.J. Haslam Esq.

1152A. TO [JOHN PENTLAND MAHAFFY][1]

Avignon
Oct. 26. 1867

DEAR SIR

Absence from England and accident combined prevented me from receiving your letter of Sept. 7 until two or three days ago, much too late to enable me to be of any use with reference to the appointment of a Professor on the 5th of October.[2]

Had I received your letter in time, I would willingly have given you a statement

---

philanthropist and religious writer; Margaret Lucas (1818–90), wife of Samuel Lucas, the journalist, and sister of John and Jacob Bright; and Katherine Hare, daughter of Thomas Hare.

[4] John Francis Maguire (1815–72), lawyer, author, and politician; John Aloysius Blake (1826–87), politician and author; James Lyster O'Beirne (b. 1820), politician and land reformer; John Gray (1816–75), religious and land reformer, editor and proprietor of *The Freeman's Journal*; and William Pollard-Urquhart (1815–71), politician and author of economic and historical works.

[5] The pamphlet has not been identified, but might be an earlier, unrecorded version of his *The Marriage Problem. By "Oedipus." Printed for Gratuitous Circulation amongst Adult Readers Only* (Dublin: n.p., 1868).

---

[1] MS at Trinity College, Dublin.
John Pentland Mahaffy (1839–1919), classicist, then a Fellow of Trinity College Dublin.

[2] Mahaffy had unsuccessfully applied for the Professorship of Philosophy at Dublin.

in writing that though my view of philosophy is extremely different from yours, you appear to me qualified to state your own with clearness, comprehensiveness, and force, and with candour towards adversaries, and that I think your translation and commentary on Kuno Fischer's book a valuable addition to the literature of philosophy.[3] I am, Dear Sir

yours very sincerely
J.S. MILL

1152B. TO WILLIAM ROSSITER[1]

Avignon
Oct. 27. 1867

DEAR SIR

I should be glad to see a good Working Men's College established, either in South London or anywhere else,[2] but I should not like to connect my name with any particular project of the kind unless I knew and had well considered its plan of teaching and scheme of management, and unless my occupations permitted me to take part in, or at least to keep myself well informed as to the mode in which it was carried on.[3] I am, Dear Sir

yours very faithfully
J.S. MILL

Wm Rossiter Esq.

---

[3] In the introduction to his translation of Ernst Kuno Berthold Fischer (1824–1907), German Hegelian, *A Commentary on Kant's Critique of Pure Reason* (London: Longmans, Green, 1866), Mahaffy had criticized Mill on "the doctrine of Permanent Possibilities, and the subject of Necessary Truths," as Mill indicated in the 3rd ed. of *An Examination of Sir William Hamilton's Philosophy*; see *CW*, Vol. IX, p. civ.

---

[1] MS at Kwanseigakuin University, Nishinomiya, Japan.

William Rossiter (d. 1897), a portmanteau maker who joined the Working Men's College in 1854, was active as a teacher and promoter of education.

[2] In 1868 Rossiter established the South London Working Men's College in Blackfriars Road with Thomas Henry Huxley as Honorary Principal and himself as Secretary.

[3] Mill subscribed to the building fund (*Bee-Hive*, 23 May, 1868, p. 4), but does not seem otherwise to have been active.

1160A. TO HENRY SIDGWICK[1]

Avignon
Nov. 26. 1867

DEAR SIR

Owing to absence from England I did not receive your paper on Tests[2] until long after it was sent, and had to wait much longer before I could give it proper attention. I think it an exceedingly fair and clear statement of many of the considerations and counter considerations which really exist in the minds of conscientious men and influence their personal behaviour in the matter of Tests. And I agree with you in thinking that an ethical theory—a fixed moral principle, or set of principles—respecting the bindingness of the obligation of a test, would be very desirable. But it seems to me that such fixed principles cannot be laid down for the case of Tests by itself; that the question requires to be taken up at an earlier stage, and dealt with as part of the much larger question, What, on the principles of a morality founded on the general good, are the limits to the obligation of veracity? What ought to be the exceptions (for that there ought to be some, however few, exceptions seems to be admitted) to the general duty of truth? This larger question has never yet been treated in a way at once rational and comprehensive, partly because people have been afraid to meddle with it, and partly because mankind have never yet generally admitted that the effect which actions tend to produce on human happiness is what constitutes them right or wrong. I would suggest that you should turn your thoughts to this more comprehensive subject. You possess several, far from common, qualifications for dealing with it: a strong conscientious interest in it, and the power of representing to yourself clearly and distinctly, without prejudice or partiality, the pro's and con's of a moral question. There is therefore good reason to hope that your meditations on the subject would not be unfruitful. Apart from this more general subject of consideration, there would be little use in any remarks that I could make on the special question of Tests; the discussion of which, in the way in which you have treated it, cannot perhaps be carried, with any useful result, much further than you have done. I am Dear Sir
yours very sincerely
J.S. MILL

Henry Sidgwick Esq.

---

[1]MS at Trinity College Library, Cambridge. Published in *MNL*, IX (Summer 1974), 10–11, edited by J.B. Schneewind.
[2]See Letter 1127A above.

1160B. TO [ANTON DOHRN][1]

Avignon
Dec. 1. 1867

DEAR SIR

I have no doubt of the sufficiency of your reasons for postponing the translation of my Address, and had not the smallest notion of complaining of it. With regard to your Preface, you are at full liberty, so far as I am concerned, to put anything you please into it; and criticisms on the German Universities as tried by the standard laid down in the Address, would be very appropriate. The faults of the German Universities are not comparable in badness to those of the English, but that they have many grave faults I am quite prepared to believe, and there can scarcely be a more useful service than to point them out. And just because the German Universities are more learned and more scientific than the English, they are likely to be more imbued with the prejudices of commonplace learned and scientific men, who are generally quite ignorant of everything out of their particular *Fach*, and are almost as insensible to the value of large general ideas as the practical men of common life. I am, Dear Sir

very truly yours
J.S. MILL

1186B. TO MOUNTSTUART ELPHINSTONE GRANT DUFF[1]

Avignon
Feb. 4. 1868

DEAR SIR

I have received the inclosed letter relating to Heligoland,[2] but my hands are so

---

[1]MS in the Prussian State Library, Berlin.
Anton Dohrn (1840–1909), a German zoologist, founder of the Marine Biology Laboratory in Naples, had requested Mill's agreement to his translating the *Inaugural Address* (London: Longmans, *et al.*, 1867). In the event, Dohrn waived his right (see *CW*, Vol. XVI, p. 1391), and Adolf Wahrmund translated the work as *Rectoratsrede, gehalten an der St. Andrews Universität*, in Theodor Gomperz's edition of Mill's writings, *Gesammelte Werke*, Vol. I, pp. 203–63.

---

[1]MS in the India Office Library and Records.
Grant Duff's help may have been solicited in this matter because he was knowledgeable about foreign affairs, and spoke German.

[2]This small island in the North Sea off the mouths of the Elbe and the Weser had been a British possession since 1807. The letter has not been located, but the complaints of the inhabitants were probably related to a proposed change in the constitution, abolishing provisions for elected representatives. See "Return of the Order in Council of the 7th Day of January, 1864, and the 29th Day of February, 1868, as to the Government of Heligoland," *PP*, 1890, XLIX, 503–9.

full that it is impossible for me to enquire into the subject, and ascertain what ground exists for the complaints, which, however, on the shewing of the letter, have a just claim to be heard. It occurs to me that with your extensive knowledge of continental affairs, you may possibly know something about the condition and government of Heligoland, or that you may not be indisposed to look into the matter. It would be a kindness to the Heligoland people if you would do so; for these small dependencies have seldom any one in Parliament who has any connexion with them, or feels at all concerned in their being justly treated.

I am Dear Sir
yours very truly
J.S. MILL

M.E. Grant Duff Esq. M.P.

1188A. TO MOUNTSTUART ELPHINSTONE GRANT DUFF[1]

Blackheath Park
Kent
Feb. 15. 1868

DEAR SIR

I thank you, both for myself and the Heligoland people, for your willingness to look into their case. I have written to them to the effect of your letter, and have given them your address, an[d] I shall be very happy to communicate with you on the subject whenever you think it may be useful. I am, Dear Sir

very truly yours
J.S. MILL

M.E. Grant Duff Esq. M.P.

1189A. TO JULES ERNEST NAVILLE[1]

Blackheath Park, Kent
le 16 février 1868

MONSIEUR

J'ai, en effet, reçu la brochure que vous avez eu la bonté de m'envoyer,[2] et je l'ai lue avec la plus vive satisfaction. Je ne l'ai pas lue dans un esprit de critique, et comme il y a déjà quelque temps de là, je ne saurais dire si j'y ai remarqué, ou non,

---

[1] MS in the India Office Library and Records. See 1186B above.

---

[1] MS in the Bibliothèque Publique et Universitaire de Genève.
[2] Almost certainly Naville, *La question électorale en Europe et en Amérique: Rapport présenté à l'Association Réformiste de Genève* (Geneva: Georg, 1867).

des choses susceptibles de dissentiment, mais je puis assurer que s'il y en a, elles ne sont pas importantes, qu'elles ne touchent à rien d'essentiel dans la question, et ne sont pas de nature à attérir l'admiration que j'éprouve pour la manière dont vous soutenez cette grande et importante lutte.

La formation d'une association à Zurich est très importante. L'adhésion d'un ci-devant vice-roi du Caucase[3] est intéressante comme hommage à la verité des principes que nous soutenons; bien qu'on ne voie guère de quelle manière on pourrait en faire l'application aux institutions de la Russie.

La nouvelle idée fait des progrès ici comme ailleurs, et elle ne manquera pas de profiter des discussions qui seront nécessairement soulevées par l'application imparfaite et bornée qu'on a faite de la représentation des minorités dans la loi de Réforme.[4] *Le principe est si évidemment juste et raisonnable dans tous les systèmes politiques, que pour être accueilli il n'a vraiment besoin que d'être discuté.*

Agréez, Monsieur, l'assurance de ma haute et respectueuse estime et de mes sentiments amicaux.

J.S. MILL

1191A. TO GUSTAV CÖHN[1]

Blackheath Park, Kent
Feb. 22. 1868

DEAR SIR

There is a great want of any means of obtaining a complete view of the progress of the Cooperative System in this country, and I often do not myself know where to go for the latest information. The person that I know of, who has taken the most pains to get together a connected view of the cooperative system both in this country and others, and who, I believe, is in possession of the most general information on the subject, is my friend Mr W.T. Thornton (23 Queen's Gardens, Hyde Park, London)[2] who, I do not doubt, would be willing to communicate with you on any points on which you may desire information. If he is not able to do so, the only other persons that I can think of who might be of use to you in your enquiries are Mr Henry Pitman, editor of the Cooperator, and Mr E.O. Greening,

---

[3]Not identified.
[4]I.e., 30 & 31 Victoria, c. 102 (1867), the Second Reform Act, which made gestures towards minority representation by giving some boroughs three members (the electors voting only for two) and by granting a seat to the University of London.

---

[1]MS in the Niedersächsische Staats-und-Universitäts Bibliothek, Göttingen. *Addressed:* Dr. G. Cöhn, Königle Statistik-Bureau, Berlin.
Gustav Cöhn (1840–1919), a German economist.
[2]William Thomas Thornton (1813–80), economist, long-time friend and colleague of Mill's in the East India Company.

editor of the Industrial Partnership Record.³ I am Dear Sir

> very truly yours
> J.S. MILL

Dr G. Cöhn.

1194A. TO RICHARD DAVIS WEBB¹

> Blackheath Park
> Feb. 24. 1868

DEAR SIR

When I got your former letter on my pamphlet,² I imagined it to refer more particularly to the copy I had directed to be sent to you by the publisher; but from your note just received I am doubtful whether it has been sent to you. Will you kindly inform me whether you received it, that I may make a complaint to Longman if he has omitted to send it.

A copy was also ordered to be sent to Mr Haslam.

I am obliged to you for the report of the Conference.³ The Dublin Corporation, like most other Corporations, seems to require much looking after.

> I am Dear Sir
> very truly yours
> J.S. MILL

R.D. Webb Esq.

1195A. TO R. HENRY TABOUELLE¹

> Blackheath Park
> Kent
> Feb. 26. 1868

MONSIEUR

Je suis très flatté de l'approbation que vous avez bien voulu accorder à ma

---

³Henry Pitman (1826–1909), editor of *The Cooperator*, published in London and Manchester 1860–71, and Edward Owen Greening (1836–1923), editor of the *Industrial Partnership Record* (a monthly) from its founding in 1867 to January 1869.

---

¹MS in the Houghton Library, Harvard University.
See Letter 1139A above.
²Webb's letter has not been located; the pamphlet was *England and Ireland* (London: Longmans, *et al.*, 1868), just published.
³Not identified.

---

¹MS in the John Rylands University Library of Manchester.
R. Henry Tabouelle has not been identified.

brochure sur l'Irlande, et j'accepte avec plaisir votre proposition de la traduire en français.[2] Je n'ai aucune condition à faire, ne désirant en tirer aucun bénéfice pécuniaire. S'il vous plaisait de me faire voir votre traduction avant de la faire imprimer, j'y jeterais volontiers un coup d'oeil.

Agréez, Monsieur, l'expression de ma considération très distinguée.

J.S. MILL

Monsieur R. Henry Tabouelle
   etc. etc.

1195B. TO AN UNIDENTIFIED CORRESPONDENT[1]

Blackheath Park
Feb. 26. 1868

DEAR SIR

I thank you for the notices,[2] but beg you not to take the trouble of sending any more. I had already seen all those you sent. I am

yours faithfully
J.S. MILL

1197A. TO THOMAS HUGHES[1]

Blackheath Park
Kent
Feb. 29. [1868]

DEAR MR HUGHES

The adjournment of the House defeats our scheme of having a Bribery meeting on Monday, but I shall be happy to attend one on any day you can arrange, either before or after the assembling of the House.[2] I am, Dear Mr Hughes

yours very truly
J.S. MILL

---

[2]No such translation of *England and Ireland* seems to have appeared.

---

[1]MS in the Georgetown University Library.
[2]At this date, undoubtedly reviews of *England and Ireland*, such as those on 22 February in the *Examiner*, p. 116, and in the *Spectator*, pp. 216–18.

---

[1]MS at the College of Law, Nihon University, Tokyo.
See Letter 862AA above.
[2]The Earl of Derby resigned as Prime Minister on 25 February, and on the 28th the House adjourned until 5 March, when it reconvened with a new Prime Minister, Benjamin Disraeli

1210. TO JOHN A. ELLIOTT[1]

Blackheath Park
Kent
March 24. 1868

DEAR SIR

[a]If my circumstances permitted me to help all who want aid, or even all authors who want aid; and if I had the pleasure of knowing anything of yourself otherwise than through your writings, the repugnance I feel to the opinions expressed in those writings would very likely be no bar to sympathy and interest in your individual self. But as my own motive for writing has always been the desire to defend and to excite sympathy for that which I hold to be the highest of all causes, that liberty against which the system of Slavery is the deepest outrage, I can never see any attempt to hold up slaveholders to sympathy without deep regret.[a] And I think that even to mention such virtues as they may possess, without accompanying that mention with an expression of abhorrence of their vices, is to deprave the sentiments and confuse the judgment of the public.

Were I in any way peculiarly called upon personally to aid any one engaged in doing this, I should do it, but I should do it with regret. Were there no one else in this country who shares your opinions, I might think myself personally called upon; but while you say that nine tenths of the English public are of your way of thinking, it seems to me that even had I the pleasure of your personal acquaintance, it would be to those nine tenths that you would justly look for sympathy, which such little aid as it could in any case be in my power to give should be reserved for those who have fewer friends. It is not, therefore, from any want of interest in yourself, or want of sympathy with you as a struggling author, but from my deep sense of the moral value of all literary work, that I felt myself obliged to reply as I have done to your letter: and I am Dear Sir

yours very faithfully
J.S. MILL

John A. Elliott Esq

(1804–81). "A Bill for Amending the Laws Relating to Election Petitions, and Providing More Effectually for the Prevention of Corrupt Practices at Elections," 31 Victoria (13 Feb. 1868), *PP*, 1867–68, II, 267–86, came forward for second reading. Mill did not speak on the bill until 26 March (*CW*, Vol. XXVIII, pp. 262–5).

[1]MS in the Pierpont Morgan Library. First two sentences published in *CW*, Vol. XVI, p. 1380.
Probably John Arthur Elliott, whose writings on slavery, to which Mill refers, have not been identified.

[a-a][*in* CW]

1228A. TO MOUNTSTUART ELPHINSTONE GRANT DUFF[1]

Blackheath Park
Kent
April 25, 1868

DEAR MR GRANT DUFF

The deputation from Heligoland has arrived, and is at Kroll's Hotel, America Square. They have probably informed you of their arrival: in any case I have referred them to you. Their names are Payens, Heckens, and Stoldt.[2] I am

very truly yours
J.S. MILL

M.E. Grant Duff Esq. M.P.

1229A. TO WILLIAM DOUGAL CHRISTIE[1]

Blackheath Park
Kent
April 26. 1868

DEAR MR CHRISTIE

I have gone through all the amendments you sent and I like them all.[2] Which of them I shall move, and by whom get others moved, I cannot yet determine.

I have not yet received your paper from the Pall Mall Gazette.[3] Probably the editor[4] means to make use of it.

Serjeant Pulling has sent me clauses (apparently identical with those he published in the Law Magazine) providing for an enquiry into every election before the return of the writ.[5] It would be difficult to make these enter into the plan

---

[1] MS in the India Office Library and Records. See Letters 1186B and 1188A above.
[2] Not further identified.

---

[1] MS at Osaka University of Commerce, Japan. Published in *MSBJ*, I, no. 6 (1985), 5, edited by Takutoshi Inouyé.
[2] In general, Mill followed Christie's guidance in attempting to amend the Bribery Bill; see Letter 1197A above. For a discussion of the campaign and the issues, see Bruce L. Kinzer's Introduction to *CW*, Vol XXVIII, pp. xlvii-l; Mill's own assessment is in *CW*, Vol. I, p. 283.
[3] "Amendment of Election Petitions and Corrupt Practices at Elections Bill," *Pall Mall Gazette*, 24 Apr., 1868, p. 5.
[4] Frederick Greenwood (1830–1909), first editor of the *Pall Mall Gazette* 1865–80, was also co-editor of the *Cornhill Magazine* 1862–68.
[5] Alexander Pulling (1813–95), serjeant-at-law, "The Law of England Relating to Purity of Elections," *Law Magazine and Law Review*, 3rd ser., XXI (1866), 54–68 and 274–82, reprinted in pamphlet form as *Our Parliamentary Elections* (London, 1866).

of the Government Bill, but it may be good to put them on the paper and invite a discussion on them.

I hope Aberdeen will get its second member and return you.[6]

ever yours truly

J.S. MILL

W.D. Christie Esq.

1230A. TO [ROBERT HARRISON][1]

Blackheath Park
Kent
April 28 [1868?]

Mr Mill presents his compliments to the Librarian and begs that Adam Smith's Theory of Moral Sentiments may be sent to him here without delay if it is not out.[2]

1239A. TO WILLIAM ROSSITER[1]

Blackheath Park
Kent
May 19. 1868

DEAR SIR

I should like to be present at Mr Plummer's lecture,[2] but on Monday evening

---

[6]Clause 12 of "A Bill for the Amendment of the Representation of the People in Scotland," 31 Victoria (17 Feb., 1868), *PP*, 1867–68, IV, 579–614, provided the County of Aberdeenshire with two members. The clause became Sect. 9 of 31 & 32 Victoria, c. 48 (13 July, 1868). As noted in n4 of Letter 949A above, Christie unsuccessfully contested Greenock in 1868.

---

[1]MS at Fukuyama University, Japan.

Robert Harrison (1788–1897), Librarian of the London Library, of which Mill was an active member. Dated to 1868 because, though Mill was busy at the time, he was in Blackheath, and was thinking of the edition of his father's *Analysis of the Phenomena of the Human Mind*, which appeared in 1869. There is reference in it to the *Theory of Moral Sentiments* (1759), by Adam Smith (1723–90), the Scottish economist and philosopher; see *CW*, Vol. XXXI, pp. 230–1.

[2]A copy of the 6th ed., 2 vols. (London: Strahan and Cadell, 1790), is in Mill's library, Somerville College, Oxford, but perhaps it was then in Avignon, where Mill had taken many of his books.

---

[1]MS at Kwanseigakuin University, Nishinomiya, Japan.

See Letter 1152B above.

[2]The subject of John Plummer's lecture at the South London Working Men's College has not been identified.

between 8 and 9 the House will probably be in the middle of the proceedings in Committee on the Scotch Reform Bill with divisions constantly impending,³ and it is therefore unlikely that I can attend, and certain that I cannot take the chair. I am most happy to hear of the success of the Institution and particularly of the School.⁴ I am Dear Sir

very truly yours
J.S. MILL

Wm Rossiter Esq.

1246A. TO WILLIAM ROSSITER[1]

May 27. 1868

DEAR SIR

I am happy to hear that Mr Plummer's lecture, which I regret not to have been able to attend, went off so successfully.²

I am much gratified by your wish to be on the Election Committee. I have sent your note to Dr Brewer, who is taking an active part in organising the Committee.³ You are aware that I do not myself take any part in the arrangements.

I send by Book Post a copy of my pamphlet on Ireland,⁴ which I perceive that Messrs Longman have omitted from the books which I desired them to send for the College. I am Dear Sir

yrs very truly
J.S. MILL

W. Rossiter Esq.

---

³See Letter 1229A above.
⁴As well as the evening classes of the College, Rossiter conducted a day school for boys and girls on the premises.

---

¹MS at Kwanseigakuin University, Nishinomiya, Japan.
²See Letter 1239A above.
³William Brewer (d. 1881), physician, chairman of the Metropolitan Asylums Board, who was again active in Mill's support, was himself elected for Colchester in the election of 1868. There is no record of Rossiter's serving on Mill's election committee.
⁴I.e., *England and Ireland*; in *CW*, Vol. VI, pp. 505–32.

1259A. TO WILLIAM DOUGAL CHRISTIE[1]

Blackheath Park
Kent
June 13. 1868

DEAR MR CHRISTIE

Nothing could be more fortunate than that Alderman Lusk has influence at Greenock.[2] One of the subjects which he takes greatest interest in, is the Diplomatic Service, and I had only to tell him of the great use you would be of on that subject, to secure his warm support for your candidature. He knows most of the people of importance at Greenwich on the liberal side, and has promised to give me on Monday a letter to be given by yourself to his brother,[3] which will ensure your being introduced to them. It would, I think, be well if I were to introduce you personally to him, which I can do at almost any time you like to come to the House as he is a very constant attendant.

From your note, I suppose what I had better say to Mr Gladstone is simply to express a hope that no rival candidate will be put up for Greenock.[4]

It is now pretty certain that the Bribery Bill will not be abandoned. Some of the advanced Liberals have been in communication with the Government and have offered a deputation of liberal members to Disraeli if it would help him: and if there is one, I think it will be a very strong one.[5] Nobody whom I have asked has refused to join in it.

I am Dear Mr Christie

yours very truly
J.S. MILL

W.D. Christie Esq.

---

[1] MS at Osaka University of Commerce, Japan. Published in *MSBJ*, I, no. 6 (1985), 5, edited by Takutoshi Inouyé.

[2] Andrew Lusk (1810–1909), a Scot, Lord Mayor of London 1860–61 and 1873–74, Alderman for Aldgate, was a Liberal M.P. for Finsbury 1865–85. For Lusk's assistance to Christie, who was a candidate for Greenock, see Mill's letter to Christie of 16 June, 1868, *CW*, Vol. XVI, pp. 1415–16.

[3] Robert Lusk continued the successful wholesale grocer business in Greenock (not Greenwich) in which Andrew had been engaged before moving to London in 1840.

[4] James Johnston Grieve (1810–91), a Greenock merchant, was elected as a Liberal on 18 November.

[5] No deputation to Disraeli appears to have taken place. For Mill's active part in the debate on the Bill, see *CW*, Vol. XXVIII, pp. 262–328 *passim*.

1260A. TO THOMAS HARE[1]

Blackheath Park
Kent
June 18 [1868]

DEAR MR HARE

I inclose a letter which will interest you, and which can be best answered either by yourself or by the Provisional Committee in course of appointment.

ever yours truly
J.S. MILL

1265AA. TO [PETER ALFRED] TAYLOR[1]

[1 July, 1868]

DEAR MR TAYLOR

I am obliged to go off to Stansfeld who is ill at home, to consult respecting the extradition report which is to be considered in Committee tomorrow.[2] I have not been able to get a pair[3] and must therefore return here before going to the

---

[1]MS formerly in the possession of Mrs. K.E. Roberts, Harrow Weald.
Dated to 1868 by the reference to the Provisional Committee. On 29 February, 1868, Mill attended a conference at the offices of the Reform League, Edmond Beales in the chair, at which it was agreed that, with Hare's assistance, a pamphlet should be prepared, giving a simple explanatory statement of his system of proportional representation. At a subsequent meeting on 13 June, which Mill was not able to attend, a committee was established with the aim of founding an association to collect and disseminate information on ways of improving representative government by reorganizing constituencies. See *The Times*, 2 March, and 15 June, both p. 5.

---

[1]MS not located. Quoted from the catalogue of Elkin Mathews Ltd., [1941]. Dated by reference to the first consideration of the "extradition report" by the Select Committee on 2 July, at which both James Stansfeld (1820–98) and Mill were present.
Peter Alfred Taylor (1819–91), radical M.P. for Leicester 1862–84, was allied with Mill on such major issues as women's suffrage, the Jamaica Committee, and anti-slavery.
[2]For the Committee's report, see *PP*, 1867–68, VII, 129–336; for Mill's involvement, see *CW*, Vol. XXIX, pp. 542–71.
[3]The catalogue reads "pass," but it seems more likely that Mill had failed to get a "pair," and so was obliged to attend the House to vote on the agreement to second reading of "A Bill to Repeal Certain Tests and Alter Certain Statutes Affecting the Constitution of the Universities of Oxford and Cambridge," *PP*, 1867–68, III, 589–92; see *PD*, 3rd ser., Vol. 193, col. 471.

Committee. Will you kindly apologise for me to the Committee[4] and ask them to go on to business without me and I will come as soon as I can.

yrs ever truly
J.S. MILL

1280A. TO AN UNIDENTIFIED CORRESPONDENT[1]

Avignon
Aug. 17. 1868

DEAR SIR

I beg to acknowledge your letter of Aug. 2.[2]

Mr Charles Austin was an early friend of mine[3] but I have for a long time past seen so little of him, that I could not undertake to say what Mr Austin's political opinions now are; nor, since I understand that he is reluctant to come forward as a candidate for Parliament, should I feel entitled to urge him to do so, even if I had more knowledge than I have of his present opinions. I am, Dear Sir

very truly yours
J.S. MILL

1282A. TO HENRY MITCHELL[1]

Avignon
France
Aug. 25. 1868

DEAR SIR

I regret that your letter was not received at my house until after I had left England for the Continent.[2] I wish that my acquaintance with distinguished men of your

---

[4]Probably the Jamaica Committee, of which Mill was Chairman, and Taylor, Treasurer. The Executive was, at this time, preparing an explanation of its course of action in its most recent attempt to bring ex-Governor Eyre to trial. The "Statement," dated 15 July, is in *CW*, Vol. XXI, pp. 429–35.

---

[1]MS in the William R. Perkins Library, Duke University.
[2]Not located.
[3]See Letter 8.1 above.

---

[1]MS in the Pennsylvania State University Library.
Henry Mitchell (1830–1902), the leading hydrographer with the U.S. Coast Survey 1849–88.
[2]On 1 August.

profession were such as to give me greater means than I have of promoting the objects for which you have come to Europe. What little I am able to do is to send you the two inclosed letters of introduction. One is to Mr Tite, M.P., by profession an architect (he built the Royal Exchange) but who is an important member of the Metropolitan Board of Works, and can give you full information about their drainage and other operations.[3] The other is to my particular friend Mr Thornton, the Secretary in the Public Works Department of the India Office, who knows everything that is doing in India in the way of public works, and can place you in communication with the chief authorities on the subject as connected with India, and probably with others. I have written privately to Mr Thornton and I am sure you will find him most desirous to give you every assistance in his power. I am Dear Sir

yours very sincerely

J.S. MILL

Henry Mitchell Esq.

I do not know Mr Tite's private address, but you can find it in the Court Guide or the Post Office Directory.[4]

1295A. TO J.H. HODGES[1]

Avignon
Sept. 27. 1868

DEAR SIR

I beg to acknowledge your communication of the 12th inst. requesting me to become a member of Mr Baxter Langley's Committee with a view to his being returned for Greenwich if a vacancy should be created by Mr Gladstone's being elected for that borough but not requiring the seat.[2]

I warmly applaud Mr Baxter Langley's public spirited conduct in withdrawing in favour of Mr Gladstone; but, while the present election is pending, and I am a

---

[3]William Tite (1798–1873), architect and antiquarian, M.P. for Bath 1855–73, who had served with Mill on the Select Committee on Metropolitan Local Government in 1866 and 1867.

[4]*Post-Office Court Guide* and *The Post-Office London Directory*, both published annually by Kelly.

---

[1]MS in the Pierpont Morgan Library.

Hodges has not been otherwise identified.

[2]Gladstone, the Liberal leader, soon to be Prime Minister, was standing for two seats, in South Lancashire (his former constituency) and Greenwich. It was understood that if elected for the former, where a stiff fight was occurring, he would sit for it, and relinquish the latter. John Baxter Langley, a writer on life insurance and railways, had withdrawn as a Liberal candidate in Greenwich to make Gladstone's election easier. In the event, Gladstone lost in South Lancashire, but was elected for Greenwich.

[Oct. 1868?] To Mary Carpenter 199

member of Mr Gladstone's Committee, I prefer not to join the Committee of any other candidate. I am, Dear Sir

yours very sincerely
J.S. MILL

J.H. Hodges Esq

1305A. TO MARY CARPENTER[1]

[before 17 Oct., 1868]

DEAR MADAM

I am not able to join your deputation,[2] but I thank you for your pamphlet[3] and for your valuable efforts to improve the very defective jail management of India. You will no doubt be listened to [*line torn off in MS*] same respect and attention which you have so justly met with from the local Governments.

I am Dear Madam
yours very truly
J.S. MILL

Miss Carpenter

1322A. TO AN UNIDENTIFIED CORRESPONDENT[1]

Blackheath
Nov. 7. 1868

DEAR SIR

I do not know of any book on the Employment of Women except one of Mrs Jameson's entitled Communion of Labour.[2] The line of argument most relevant to the subject, is the advantage to women of developing their faculties, and to the

---

[1] MS in the Fawcett Library, London.
Mary Carpenter (1807–77), a philanthropist and educational reformer, had gone to India in 1866 to examine the condition of women and of prisons. After communicating with the then Governor-General, John Laird Mair Lawrence (1811–79), on these subjects, she returned to England in mid-1867.
[2] On 17 October there was a deputation of members of the Social Science Association "for the purpose of bringing reforms to the gaols of India," to the Viceroy-elect, Richard Southwell Bourke (1822–72), 6th Earl of Mayo; see *The Times*, 20 Oct., 1868, p. 8.
[3] *Suggestions on Prison Discipline and Female Education in India* (Bristol: Arrowsmith, 1867).

---

[1] MS in the Nottinghamshire Record Office.
[2] Anna Brownell Jameson (1794–1860), a prolific author on various topics, *Communion of Labour: A Second Lecture on the Social Employments of Women* (London: Longman, et al., 1856).

world of getting all that women can do; and the resemblance of the system of restricting particular occupations to one sex, to the old caste and guild systems which restricted them to certain classes and families. One of the American advocates of women's rights has put the case strongly and well by saying that the present system endeavours to do the whole intellectual work of the world with only half its brains.[3] I am

yours very faithfully
J.S. MILL

1326A. TO CAROLINE LINDLEY[1]

Blackheath
Nov. 12. [1868]

DEAR MISS LINDLEY

I thank you most heartily for taking the trouble to procure so much precise information respecting the Birkbeck Schools.[2] I hope to have many occasions for making good use of it.

I heard yesterday from Helen:[3] she is well and in spirits.

Ever, dear Miss Lindley
yours most truly
J.S. MILL

1331A. TO CAROLINE LINDLEY[1]

Blackheath Park
Nov. 19 [1868]

DEAR MISS LINDLEY

Many thanks for your kind present and for your kind enquiries about my cold. I

---

[3]Not identified.

---

[1]MS at Fukuyama University, Japan.
Caroline Lindley, a neighbour of Mill's at Blackheath and a frequent correspondent of Helen Taylor's 1866–82, was active in the establishment of a Birkbeck school at Hethersett, Norfolk, in 1855.
[2]These schools, named for George Birkbeck (1776–1841), founder of the Mechanics' Institutions, were first established in 1848 by Mill's friend, William Ellis. The curriculum emphasized science and utilitarian economics. At one time there were seven schools in London, and others in the provinces.
[3]Mill had returned to London for the election campaign early in November, leaving Helen in Avignon.

---

[1]MS at Fukuyama University, Japan.

am glad to say it is much better, and will probably be gone by tomorrow. I am very thankful for your very friendly invitation, but I have so many things to do just at the last, before going away for a longer time than I expected[2] that I hope you will excuse me if I deny myself the pleasure of passing an evening with you.

Ever, dear Miss Lindley
yours truly
J.S. MILL

1337A. TO GEORGE WASHBURN SMALLEY[1]

Avignon
Nov. 28. 1868

DEAR SIR

Your letter gives me very great pleasure, for it is doubly an honour to receive such expressions of interest and sympathy from one of your country. You have gone through a harder fight than we are likely to face here, and the heroism with which it was fought by the noble minded men of America through all the long years of danger and difficulty, and finally through the sharp crisis of the war, makes the Liberals of all other nations look up to the advanced party in America with respectful admiration. Like yourself I was somewhat surprised and a little hurt at the line the Daily News thought fit to take, but there are reasons to suspect that there may have been personal causes for this, for I thought it my duty to support in one place a candidate who was the rival of a gentleman who, I am given to understand, has influence with the Daily News, and this may have aroused a little unpleasant feeling, which, as I have no reason to suppose it is shared by many persons connected with the paper, we must hope will blow over when the election excitement is past.[2] For my own part, my regret was only at seeing a paper which

---

[2]Having lost the election the previous day, Mill was free to remain abroad longer than anticipated. He left London on the 23rd, and remained in Avignon until the end of February.

---

[1]MS in the Pierpont Morgan Library.
George Washburn Smalley (1833–1916), foreign correspondent of the *New York Tribune*, who had met Mill in Avignon in 1866, lived in London 1867–95. Smalley's reply to this letter is at Johns Hopkins; for Mill's reply to it, see *CW*, Vol. XVII, p. 1541.
[2]Mill's open support for Edwin Chadwick as a Liberal candidate in Kilmarnock greatly offended Edward Pleydell Bouverie (1818–89), a sitting Liberal member, one of the "Adullamites" who had opposed Gladstone's Reform Bill. Bouverie admonished Mill in a letter, and when Mill responded, published the correspondence in the national press (see *The Times*, 16 Oct., p. 10). The *Daily News*, which also printed the correspondence on 16 Oct., published leading articles on the controversy on 21 Oct., p. 4, and 23 Oct., p. 4. These are much more favourable to Mill than his comment implies, the second explicitly blaming Bouverie for publishing the correspondence without Mill's approval. For the full correspondence, see *CW*, Vol. XVI, pp. 1453–4 and 1460–4, and Vol. XXV, p. 1220.

had stood so bravely by the advanced cause in so many great questions, shewing on this occasion less generosity of spirit than the Daily Telegraph, or even perhaps, the Times. I am, Dear Sir

yours very truly
J.S. MILL

G.W. Smalley Esq

1369A. TO JOHN CHAPMAN[1]

Avignon
Dec. 27. 1868

DEAR SIR

I think it of very great importance to free and enlightened thought in politics and philosophy, that the Westminster Review should be maintained in existence, and without any change in its long established character as an organ always open to the thoughts of the most advanced thinkers, and training the minds of the younger men to appreciate new ideas. During the whole term of its existence, now 45 years, it has fulfilled this office. Its disappearance would leave a sad blank in our periodical literature, and would be a severe blow to advanced thought and to the education of future thinkers. With regard to the management of the Review by its present proprietor and editor, knowing as I do the great difficulties it has had to struggle with, and the inferiority, as compared with many other reviews, of the inducements it could hold out to writers, I have been as much surprised as pleased at the high level of merit it has been able to maintain. This could only have been effected by a devotion of time and energy to the purpose, on the part of the editor, which does great honour to his public spirit, and establishes on his part a strong claim to the gratitude of the friends of advanced opinions and independent thoughts, and after the proofs he has given, for a number of years and under great difficulties, of his fitness to conduct such an organ, I hope that he may find such assistance as may enable him still to carry it on, and may afford him an ultimate prospect of some recompense for his sacrifices, other than the consciousness of having made them. I am, Dear Sir

very sincerely yours
J.S. MILL

Dr Chapman

[1]MS in the possession of Professor Paul P. Streeten, Boston University.
This is the statement "in the form of a letter" that Mill refers to in his covering letter to Chapman of 27 December, 1868 (*CW*, Vol. XVI, pp. 1532–3). Mill said that Chapman could "shew" this, but "did not wish it to be published"; see also *ibid.*, p. 1544, to Chapman.

1383A. TO MOUNTSTUART ELPHINSTONE GRANT DUFF[1]

Avignon
Jan. 23. 1869

DEAR MR GRANT DUFF

I hear from the Mauritius sad details of the distress there,[2] with which I do not doubt you are very much better acquainted than I am. Perhaps you may not be as well aware that among a portion at least of the English there, there is a feeling of uneasiness as to the probable action of the local Government in case of disturbances, which seem very probable. The disturbances at Réunion[3] may add to the probabilities of something of the sort at the Mauritius, and the example set by the Government in the one place is not a salutary one for the Government in the other. The inhabitants of the Mauritius are understood to be peculiarly peaceable, and very manageable by gentle means: but there seems to be a sort of apprehension lest the Government should not take as gentle means as might be desired in case any difficulties should arise. When I remember the reiterated warnings which were received at the Colonial Office before the events in Jamaica,[4] and that a hint from home to the Government might have saved such a quantity of suffering, of disgrace, and of embarrassment to everybody concerned, I venture to trouble you with these few lines to say that whether these apprehensions with regard to the Mauritius are well or ill grounded (which I do not know) I know them to be entertained by Englishmen in a respectable and responsible position.

I cannot conclude without expressing the pleasure it gave me to see you appointed to a post where there is so much opportunity of exercising useful influence.[5] I am, Dear Mr Grant Duff

very truly yours
J.S. MILL

M.E. Grant Duff Esq. M.P.

---

[1]MS in the India Office Library and Records.

[2]The British colony of Mauritius had been suffering since December 1866 from a prolonged epidemic of malaria, and there was unrest among the indentured Indian labourers.

[3]In the French colony of Réunion, anti-clerical demonstrations on 2 and 3 December, 1868, were badly handled by the administration, and resulted in a tragic confrontation between government troops and the crowd.

[4]The severe repression of the Morant Bay rebellion of 11 October, 1865, had involved Mill deeply in the Jamaica question. See Letter 914A above and the references there given.

[5]On 8 December, 1868, Grant Duff had been appointed Under-Secretary of State for India.

1397. TO JOSEPHINE BUTLER[1]

March 22. 1869

DEAR MADAM

It would be a very superficial view that could suppose that the permanent improvement of the social, industrial, and economic condition of women can be altogether separated from their claim to political rights. At all times political rights have been the only real security for the permanence of progress in social, industrial, and economical matters: and in the present age, the grant of political rights to any class, or even the demand for their admission to those rights, is the most effectual way of securing better consideration for their interests in all other respects. It does not, however, follow from this that it is equally the duty of every one who desires to improve the condition of women, to engage specially in the task of claiming political rights for them: and therefore, although I could not concur with Dr von Hetzendorf[2] in considering the political enfranchisement of women as of but little consequence (if indeed he does consider it so) the advice he gives appears to me, with one exception, exceedingly judicious. *"I am of opinion that every kind of effort, whether social or political, in favour of women, should be encouraged, so long as it is earnest and genuine; and I am persuaded that those who are in earnest will inevitably be led by experience to see the absolute necessity of political enfranchisement as both the foundation and the safeguard of human worth and happiness."* As regards the details, the earnest minds of each nation are the best judges for that nation. They have but to be in earnest, and to work with all their hearts, and they cannot do wrong. The one point to which I have referred as that on which I differ from Dr von Hetzendorf, is the suggestion to subordinate the whole organisation of the Vereine to one centre. This is the French system, in too many things: England and Germany have progressed by leaving freer play to the varieties of local character and circumstances. What is judicious for Berlin may not be so for Leipzig or Vienna. It is better that the zeal, the earnestness, and the sense of responsibility, of the enlightened persons of each locality, should exhaust itself in doing to the very uttermost all that lies to its own hand to do, and that it should not waste its energy in guiding the hands of others. I am Dear Madam

yours very truly
J.S. MILL

Mrs Butler

[1] MS at St. Andrews University Library. Excerpt published in *CW*, Vol. XVII, p. 1569, dated [March 1869], from A.S.G. Butler, *Portrait of Josephine Butler* (London: Faber, 1954), p. 62.
Josephine Elizabeth Butler (née Grey) (1828–1906), vigorous advocate of women's rights, was best known for her campaign against the Contagious Diseases Acts. She was working at this time on *Women's Work and Women's Culture* (London: Macmillan, 1869).
[2] Not identified.

a-a[*in* CW]

1413. TO THEODOR GOMPERZ[1]

Blackheath Park
March 23. 1869

DEAR MR GOMPERZ

*a*I am not sure whether, when I last wrote to you, I mentioned the work in which I was engaged, of preparing a new edition of my father's "Analysis of the Phenomena of the Human Mind" with notes,[2] bringing up the subject to the latest improvements in psychology. This is now complete, and the notes, to which Mr Grote has contributed, and in which Mr Bain has given, in a condensed form, the most important thoughts of his systematic treatises,[3] form, I think, a very valuable addition to the original work. I hope you have received the copy I directed the publisher to send.*a*

I do not think that my portion of the notes[4] can well be included in the collected German edition, as they would seldom be intelligible if separated from the work to which they belong.

*b*How is the edition *c* proceeding?*b* I have just received an agreeable evidence of the demand for it, in the shape of a proposal from a Dr Bingmann,[5] encouraged, as he says, by two professors of Moral Philosophy in the Universities of Tübingen and Berlin, to translate "Utilitarianism," and after that, the Logic and others of my writings. I have informed Dr. Bingmann of the edition in progress (which he did not seem to have heard of) and have told him that there is no opening for another translator, unless you should be disappointed in some of your arrangements.

When you write to me, which I hope will be soon, I beg you to give me news of your sister, whose sad loss we were so grieved to hear of.[6] I am, Dear Mr. Gomperz

very truly yours
J.S. MILL

---

[1] MS at Kokugakuin University, Tokyo. Part published in *CW*, Vol. XVII, p. 1583. Excerpt in *Theodor Gomperz: Ein Gelehrtenleben*, ed. Robert A. Kann (Vienna: Österreichischen Akademie der Wissenschaften, 1974), p. 44.

[2] James Mill, *Analysis of the Phenomena of the Human Mind* (1829), 2nd ed., ed. John Stuart Mill, with notes by Alexander Bain, Andrew Findlater, and George Grote, 2 vols. (London: Longmans, *et al.*, 1869).

[3] Alexander Bain, *The Senses and the Intellect* (1855), 3rd ed. (London: Longmans, Green, 1868), and *The Emotions and the Will* (1859), 2nd ed. (Longmans, *et al.*, 1865).

[4] They are in *CW*, Vol. XXXI, pp. 93–253; they did not appear in *Gesammelte Werke*.

[5] Not further identified.

[6] Eduard Wessel had apparently told of the death of Gomperz's nephew, Carl Wertheimstein (1847–66), in a letter enclosed with that of Gomperz to Mill of 26 March, 1868 (MS Johns Hopkins); see also *CW*, Vol. XVI, pp. 1356 and 1392.

a-a[*in* CW]
b-b[*in* CW]
*c*CW (of the translation)

1426A. TO CHARLES BRADLAUGH[1]

Avignon
May 7. 1869

DEAR SIR

I am very glad to hear that you will be able to help the petitioning in favour of Women's Suffrage so greatly. I have mentioned the fact to Mrs Peter A. Taylor, Aubrey House, Notting Hill,[2] and I am sure that if you will kindly put yourself in communication with her, she will be very glad of your help in extending the operations of the Women's Suffrage Society in new directions.[3] I am, Dear Sir
yours very truly
J.S. MILL

Charles Bradlaugh Esq.

1431A. TO JAMES FITZJAMES STEPHEN[1]

A[vignon]
May 17, 1869

I am very glad to hear that you intend to answer Lecky on Utilitarianism.[2] It is a subject which finds an active & doughty champion in you. From what I hear it seems that Lecky's ideas on it are both superficial & confused. He has been so useful in popularizing some good ideas that it is a pity he is not only commonplace but even of an antiquated form of commonplace in others; unluckily he is not the only useful & clever man I know in this predicament.

I am not surprised that you do not find time to read the Analysis.[3] I am often

---

[1]MS at the Bishopsgate Foundation, London.
Charles Bradlaugh (1833–91), outspoken advocate of free-thought and political reform, proprietor and editor of the *National Reformer*, in seeking election in 1868 had received support from Mill that had damaged Mill's own campaign.
[2]See Letter 1139A above.
[3]Mill and Helen Taylor had drafted the petition that was circulating through the U.K.; see *CW*, Vol. XVII, pp. 1551–2, 1575–6. Mill thanked Bradlaugh for his aid on 24 May, 1869, *ibid.*, p. 1606.

---

[1]MS draft in the University Library, Cambridge. In answer to Stephen's letter of 24 April, also at Cambridge, thanking Mill for a copy of James Mill's *Analysis*. Published in *MNL*, XXII (Winter 1987), 7, edited by Jean O'Grady.
[2]William Edward Hartpole Lecky (1838–1903), *The History of European Morals from Augustine to Charlemagne*, 2 vols. (London: Longmans, Green, 1869), Chap. i. Stephen does not appear to have pursued his plan to answer Lecky.
[3]See Letter 1413 above.

surprised at the great industry you exhibit but I shd like to see a review of the Analysis by yourself & the book as originally written without the aid of the notes is almost a necessary foundation for efficient thought both in law & politics, for which the doctrine of the Assn of Ideas as there developed is all-important.

I shall be in England early in July & shall be happy to see you if you think you can derive either pleasure or profit from the society of such very decided believers in progress.[4]

1440A. TO JAMES JOHNSTON SHAW[1]

[after May, 1869]

I thank you sincerely for your remarks on my "Examination of Hamilton" and I will not fail, in any further revision of the book, to give them the attention they deserve. The confusion between the two meanings of inconceivable is almost universal, and Hamilton is certainly not free from it.[2] I may, therefore, very possibly have been misled by it in my interpretation of some passages of his writings. But I think my argument against Whewell holds good in either sense.[3]

The concluding paragraph of your letter gives me great pleasure, especially your agreement with my opinions on the great question discussed in my new book.[4] There is, I am convinced, no subject now under discussion on which the improvement of the human race more essentially depends.

---

[4]Stephen's lack of enthusiasm for the notion of progress had been expressed, for instance, in "Christian Optimism," in *Essays by a Barrister* (London: Smith, Elder, 1862), pp. 114–22.

---

[1]Published in Shaw's *Occasional Papers*, ed. Margaret G. Woods (Dublin: Hodges, Figgis, 1910), xii–xiii. In her Introduction, Woods says that Shaw had "a short correspondence with John Stuart Mill" during his first year in Londonderry (1869). In *MNL*, XX (Summer 1985), 15, edited by T.P. Foley. Dated by the reference to Mill's *Examination*, of which the 3rd ed. had appeared in May, and his *Subjection*, first published in the same month.

James Johnston Shaw (1849–1910), then Professor of Metaphysics and Ethics in Magee College, Londonderry.

[2]The discussion of the "inconceivable" is in Chap. vi of *An Examination of Sir William Hamilton's Philosophy*, *CW*, Vol. IX, pp. 66–84. In his revisions for the 4th ed. (1872), Mill makes no reference to Shaw.

[3]See *Examination*, *CW*, Vol. IX, p. 68; *System of Logic*, *CW*, Vol. VII, pp. 238ff, and Vol. VIII, pp. 752ff.

[4]I.e., *The Subjection of Women*.

1447A. TO AN UNIDENTIFIED CORRESPONDENT[1]

Avignon
June 15. 1869

Dear Madam

Your letter has been forwarded to me here, and I beg to thank you for your kind intentions in regard to reviewing my book. What you have seen announced is not a Congress, but a meeting of the London Women's Suffrage Society, at which only members will be present. I am, Dear Madam

yours very faithfully
J.S. Mill

1454A. TO ANTON DOHRN[1]

Blackheath Park
Kent
July 6. 1869

Dear Sir

I regret that there should be so much delay in bringing out the German edition of my entire writings, and I give my full consent to your publishing the translation, as soon as you please; merely reserving the right of the publishers of the complete edition to include it (or another translation) afterwards in their series.[2] I am, Dear Sir

very truly yours
J.S. Mill

Dr Anton Dohrn

---

[1]MS in the possession of Professor Arnold Heertje, University of Amsterdam.

The recipient is presumably either Anne Mozley (1809–91), who reviewed *The Subjection of Women*, the book referred to, in *Blackwood's Magazine*, CVI (Sept. 1869), 309–21, or Margaret Oliphant (1828–97), who reviewed it in the *Edinburgh Review*, CXXX (Oct. 1869), 572–602.

---

[1]MS in the Bibliothèque Publique et Universitaire de Genève.
[2]For the background and result, see Letter 1160B above.

1457A. TO GEORGE CAMPBELL[1]

Blackheath Park
Kent
July 9. 1869

DEAR SIR

I have had the pleasure of receiving your note; and your paper on the Irish land question[2] has been one of the first things I have read after my return here.[3] I need hardly say that I agree with all your principles, and (as far as I can judge) with your details too. Englishmen who know India are the men who can understand and interpret the social ideas and economic relations of Ireland. They are not the slaves of English technicalities, and they know that the English form of property in land is neither a law of the universe nor an immutable principle of morality. The Cobden Club could not have done a more sensible thing than to ask you to give them the benefit of your Indian experience;[4] and I wish they would publish this very instructive paper also. In any case, I trust it will be published.

You seem to think that there is some difference of opinion between us on the subject, but I can see none. You think that my proposal would give more to the landlords than the value of their property: but what I proposed was, that there should be a Commission to adjudicate what the present income and future prospects of the estates was really worth to the landlords, in order to give them that; not a farthing more.[5]

Will you excuse my suggesting the omission of one word (p. 43, last line) the word "woman"?[6] This would be but justice, for women are often most energetic and successful managers of estates in India. I am Dear Sir

very truly yours
J.S. MILL

George Campbell Esq.

---

[1] MS in the India Office Library and Records. Published in *MNL*, XIX (Summer 1984), 3–4, edited by Bruce L. Kinzer.
George Campbell (1824–92), author and Indian administrator.
[2] This paper later formed the first section of *The Irish Land* (London: Trübner; Dublin: Hodges, Foster, 1869).
[3] Mill and Helen Taylor had been in Avignon from April through June.
[4] Campbell's essay, "The Tenure of Land in India," was included in the Cobden Club volume, *Systems of Land Tenure in Various Countries* (London: Macmillan, 1870), pp. 145–227.
[5] See *England and Ireland, CW*, Vol. VI, p. 527.
[6] A perusal of the text suggests that Campbell removed the offending word.

1459A. TO HENRY JOHNSTON[1]

Blackheath Park
Kent
July 16. 1869

DEAR SIR

I am much honoured by the wish of the Directors of the Glasgow Athenaeum to include me in their arrangements for the delivery of Lectures, but I regret that my occupations do not admit of my sparing the time necessary for the preparation of a lecture. I am, Dear Sir

yours very faithfully
J.S. MILL

Henry Johnston Esq

1463A. TO WILLIAM ROSSITER[1]

July 26. 1869

DEAR SIR

I am quite willing that my approbation of Parks for the children of the poor should be made known anywhere;[2] but I would rather not be announced as receiving subscriptions, if for no other reason than that I am often absent from England. I am, Dear Sir

very truly yours
J.S. MILL

Wm Rossiter Esq.

---

[1]MS in the Henry and Jessie Johnston Collection, Dunedin Public Library, New Zealand. Henry Johnston (1842–1919), Scottish writer, of the Kailyard school.

---

[1]MS at Kwanseigakuin University, Nishinomiya, Japan.
[2]Nothing is known of this enthusiasm, though it is compatible with Mill's views generally.

1466A. TO WILLIAM FRASER RAE[1]

Aug 7. [1869]

DEAR MR RAE

Can you come down and dine with us on Sunday Aug. 15 at five o'clock?

yours very truly
J.S. MILL

W.F. Rae Esq

1471A. TO HENRY VILLARD[1]

Aug. 17. 1869

DEAR SIR

This letter will be given to you by my friend Mr W.F. Rae,[2] who, as warmly interested in the political and social questions of our time, and a frequent and valuable writer respecting them,[3] on the side of advanced opinions, has many great points of common interest with you. Mr Rae goes to America for the double purpose of acquiring information respecting the practical working of your Patent Laws, in order to help towards improving ours, and of adding to his general knowledge of America; and any aid that can be given him for either object will not fail to be useful to the public. I am, Dear Sir

very truly yours
J.S. MILL

Henry Villard Esq.

---

[1]MS at Osaka University of Commerce, Japan.
William Fraser Rae (1835–1905), barrister and journalist, contributor to the *Daily News*, who had been editor of *The Reader*, was going to the U.S.A., and Mill hoped to see him before his departure. See Mill's letter to Rae of 19 July, 1869, in *CW*, Vol. XVII, p. 1624, and Letter 1471A below.

---

[1]MS in the Houghton Library, Harvard University.
Henry Villard (1835–1900), a journalist who had been a European correspondent 1865–68, was the Secretary of the American Social Science Association.
[2]One of the letters of introduction promised by Mill in his letter to Rae of 19 July, 1869 (*CW*, Vol. XVII, p. 1624).
[3]For example, the series in the *Westminster Review*, "Reform and Reformers," and "The Hopes and Fears of Reformers," n.s. XXXI (Jan. and Apr. 1867), 171–90 and 472–502, and "The Future of Reform," n.s. XXXII (July 1867), 161–88.

1474A. TO MARY CARPENTER[1]

^aAvignon
Sept. 5. 1869

DEAR MISS CARPENTER

You are welcome to make any use you like of my letter to you,[2] but I do not feel that what the Duke said,[3] which I repeated to you in my letter to the best of my memory verbally, was sufficiently explicit to amount, to my mind, to a promise, and therefore I should not like to write to the Chief on such an assumption. I agree with you most cordially as to the welcome that the Chief and the Ranee[4] ought to receive here, and will lose no opportunity of using any influence I have to secure it. If the Duke of Argyll was more explicit to you than to me, or if what he said to me appears to you explicit I am very happy to hear it, and think you cannot do better than convey it to the Chief. But as the Chief can scarcely so well judge of the exact meaning of the terms used as we can, the responsibility of the precise interpretation to be put upon the Duke's words rests with^a ^bus: and I own that to me they do not seem quite as decisive as might be desirable, seeing how important it is that the Chief and the Ranee should not come over here under a mistaken impression.

If it is your wish, and you are quite sure that it would be the wish of the Chief and the Ranee, I will write to the Duke, and ask him whether what he has said may be reported to them as a promise.

My daughter begs to be kindly remembered, and I am, Dear Miss Carpenter

very truly yours
J.S. MILL^b

---

[1] First part of MS at Manchester College, Oxford; second part at the College of Law, Nihon University, Tokyo.

[2] Not located.

[3] It is not known when Mill spoke to George Douglas Campbell (1823–1900), 8th Duke of Argyll, Secretary of State for India from December 1868.

[4] Not identified.

^{a-a}[*Manchester College MS*]
^{b-b}[*Nihon University MS*]

1476A. TO EDWARD WILLIAMS BYRON NICHOLSON[1]

Avignon
Sept. 9. 1869

DEAR SIR

In answer to your letter of Aug. 28 I beg to say that I should be happy to become an annual subscriber to the projected Magazine.[2] I am

yours very faithfully
J.S. MILL

E.B. Nicholson Esq.

1492A. TO HENRY VILLARD[1]

Avignon
Oct. 23. 1869

DEAR SIR

You are aware of the favour with which the majority of the popular party in Great Britain regard the vote by ballot at parliamentary elections, as a means of restraining bribery and intimidation and the increased interest which this question has assumed through the recent extension of the suffrage.[2] The writer of the inclosed letter[3] and some of his friends are anxious to obtain information that can be depended on, respecting the practical working of vote by ballot in the countries in which it exists by law. Their own opinion, like mine, is unfavourable to it; but their desire is to find the truth, whatever it may be; and the vague impressions current in Europe give no real knowledge of the ballot in America even as it exists by law, much less of the mode in which it is actually conducted, and the advantages and disadvantages which are found in practice to attend it. You would oblige me very much, and would do some public service, if you could kindly

---

[1]MS in the Bodleian Library.
Edward Williams Byron Nicholson (1849–1912), a recent graduate in classics from Oxford, later Librarian of the Bodleian.
[2]Not identified.

---

[1]MS in the Houghton Library, Harvard University.
[2]I.e., by 30 & 31 Victoria, c. 102 (1867), the Second Reform Act.
[3]Identified in Mill's letter on the same subject and of the same date to Theodor Gomperz (*CW*, Vol. XVII, p. 1655), as David McBurnie Watson (d. 1902), of Hawick. Watson's letter has not been located.

supply my correspondent with any of the information which he desires, or refer him to any sources from which he could procure it. I am Dear Sir

yours very truly

J.S. MILL

Henry Villard Esq.

1508A. TO GEORGE CAMPBELL[1]

Avignon
Dec. 31. 1869

DEAR SIR

I am late in thanking you for the gift of your volume on Ireland,[2] because it came to me a short time ago in a parcel from England, and owing to the pressure of other occupations I have only just finished reading it. I wish it was in the hands of everybody who will have any voice in the decision of the Irish Land question, for I have read nothing that comes near it in the fullness and clearness of the knowledge it communicates of the real "situation" in Ireland. There is nothing like Indian experience for enabling men to understand Ireland. Those writers in the newspapers who have some understanding of the Irish question are those who, like one of the editors of the Spectator,[3] know something of India. My own official knowledge of Indian matters has greatly helped me to put the right interpretation on Irish phenomena. I wonder how long it will take the English people to find out, that the Indian service is their best, or rather their only, good school for administrators; and to make the use they might make of that service for difficult work in other parts of the empire. Lord Metcalfe and Sir J.P. Grant[4] are already cases in point.

I am not so clear about the details of your proposed measure, though I agree fully in its principles, and think it quite reasonable that lands which are at present administered on the English system, the landlord making the improvements, and no tenant right or claim to compensation for loss of occupancy being ever

---

[1]MS in the India Office Library and Records. Published in *MNL*, XIX (Summer 1984), 4–5, edited by Bruce L. Kinzer.

[2]*The Irish Land*; see Letter 1457A above.

[3]Meredith White Townsend, co-editor of the *Spectator*, was also editor of *The Annals of Indian Administration* (Serampore: Murray, 1856).

[4]Charles Theophilus Metcalfe (1785–1846) had been Provisional Governor-General between William Bentinck's departure and Lord Auckland's arrival (20 March, 1835, to 4 March, 1836). In July of 1839 he was appointed Governor of Jamaica and in January of 1843 he accepted the Governor-Generalship of Canada. John Peter Grant (1807–93), a Member of Governor-General Canning's Council when the Mutiny broke out, succeeded the notorious Eyre as Governor of Jamaica in 1866.

recognised—where, in fact, the coproprietorship of the tenant never existed, or has been extinguished—should remain as they are, on the footing of contract only.[5] But I have great doubts of the possibility of meeting the justice of each separate case by the award of a Commission,[6] even with the aid of the general instructions laid down in your letter of Nov. 29.[7] I should fear that a decision as to what had or had not been the "ordinary practice of any district, locality, or estate"[8] would continually fail to give satisfaction; first, on account of the difficulty of settling what amounts to "ordinary practice", and next, because a very large proportion of the discontent of the tenantry is on the part of those who have not yet succeeded in establishing any custom in their favour; and these, if your plan is adopted, will find themselves cut off from hope. I am not shaken in my belief that the land difficulty is a knot which cannot be untied, and will have to be cut. — By the way, your principal objection to the plan I proposed rests on a mistake.[9] I proposed giving the landlords more than their present net rent, but not more than the present selling value of their estates, since that includes allowance for prospective increase as well as for present income.[10] I never dreamed of giving them a larger compensation than the amount of consols equivalent to that selling value. No wonder you disapprove of the proposal, when you think it would enable landlords to obtain from the State double the present value of their property.

I am Dear Sir
very truly yours
J.S. MILL

George Campbell Esq.

1521A. TO GEORGE CAMPBELL[1]

Avignon
Jan. 24. 1870

DEAR SIR

It gives me great pleasure to find that, after due explanations, your opinion and mine differ so little, indeed, as far as I perceive, not at all. I have no doubt that your plan would work to the ends you intend by it, if the Commission were an entirely

---

[5]For the details of Campbell's plan, see *The Irish Land*, pp. 85–93 and 166–90.
[6]Campbell's proposal for a commission is *ibid.*, p. 184.
[7]See "The Irish Land Question," *Daily News*, 30 Nov., 1869, p. 5.
[8]"The Irish Land Question," p. 5.
[9]For Campbell's criticism of Mill's plan, see *The Irish Land*, pp. 77–9.
[10]*England and Ireland, CW*, Vol. VI, p. 527.

---

[1]MS in India Office Library and Records. Published in *MNL*, XIX (Summer 1984), 6, edited by Bruce L. Kinzer.

unprejudiced one. But all the probabilities are that it will be a Landlords' Commission. All Englishmen of the higher ranks who have not learnt better things in Ireland or India, have their prepossessions strongly on the side of landlordism. The best that is to be hoped is that the Commission would represent liberal landlordism: but you know how little that amounts to, Lord Dufferin is considered a liberal landlord.[2]

It will give me pleasure to talk over these matters with you, and Indian matters too, after my return to England, which will be in March. I have not forgotten the kind offer you made when I was in the House of Commons, to furnish me with information, an offer of which, coming from you, I was well able to appreciate the value: and though I am no longer in the House, I can still make profitable use of facts that I can rely on, whether about India or Ireland. I am[3]

1521B. TO JOHN MALCOLM FORBES LUDLOW[1]

Avignon
Jan. 24. 1870

DEAR SIR

Your letter[2] was forwarded to me from England. I received it the day before yesterday, and should have answered it before, but I have been incapacitated from work by a very bad cold.

I think you not only perfectly fit for the office of Registrar of Friendly Societies but probably superior to any one likely to be a candidate.[3] The office is one for which your knowledge of the working classes and of their Associations is a valuable preparation. And as to practical ability, no one who goes carefully through the Municipal Bills would think that the man who drew them can be deficient in it.[4] In all the conversations and discussions I had with you respecting those Bills, the part you took was that of a careful, cautious, foreseeing practical mind. If my saying as much in a letter for the purpose could be of any use to you, I should be most happy to do it. But I greatly doubt not only its being of any use, but

---

[2]Frederick Temple Hamilton-Temple Blackwood (1826–1902), 1st Marquis of Dufferin and Ava, Governor-General of Canada 1872–78, Ambassador to Russia 1879 and to Turkey 1881, Governor-General of India 1884–88. Dufferin had no use for Mill's proposals in *England and Ireland*, which he strongly criticized in his pamphlet *Mr. Mill's Plan for the Pacification of Ireland Examined* (London: Murray, 1868).
[3]The end of the letter is cut off, presumably for the autograph.

---

[1]MS in the University Library, Cambridge.
[2]Not located.
[3]Ludlow was appointed as Secretary to the Royal Commission on Friendly and Benefit Societies, serving 1870–74.
[4]For the bills, see Letter 1075A above.

its not being positively detrimental to you. I must in frankness admit that I fully agree in your impression that Mr Lowe probably looks upon you as a sentimentalist.[5] I do not doubt it. But I think you are under a mistake if you do not think he looks upon me as a sentimentalist of quite as deep a dye; if indeed he thinks there can be anything to choose between different degrees of such imbecility. I am afraid that a testimonial from me to your practicality would be to him a testimonial from a blind man in favour of a man with one eye. Nor would it be much better if I gave testimony to your powers as a metaphysician or political economist. None of these are matters on which Mr Lowe would think me capable of aiding his judgment. I only know one man whose testimony in your favour would have much weight with Mr Lowe, and that man is Mr Lowe. Although I doubt whether there exists the man whose judgment would have any intellectual weight with Mr Lowe, it is just possible that some practical influence might be exerted by influential members of the electoral body of the London University, or by his superiors in the Cabinet. I think Mr Lowe would give an office to a competent man if he could find one; but seeing that it is a thousand chances to one that he thinks none of the candidates fit, such trifles as parliamentary or electoral or cabinet influence might decide him where he thinks there is very little to choose. I am, Dear Mr Ludlow

yours very truly
J.S. MILL

J.M. Ludlow Esq.

1522A. TO FRANK HARRISON HILL[1]

Avignon
Jan. 27. 1870

DEAR MR HILL

I saw the article in the *Daily News* on the case of Policeman Smith, and felt very much obliged to you for getting the subject noticed.[2] I understand that the Home

---

[5]Robert Lowe (1811–92), M.P. at that time for London University, and Chancellor of the Exchequer, was a thoroughly orthodox economist, firmly opposed to the radical wing of the Liberal Party.

---

[1]MS at Kokugakuin University, Tokyo.
Frank Harrison Hill (1830–1910), editor of the *Daily News* 1869–86.
[2]Mill had earlier written to Hill about the case, having read "The Police Courts. Thames," *Daily News*, 25 Dec., 1869, p. 2; see *CW*, Vol. XXV, pp. 1221–2. A leading article on the case of Constable William Smith had appeared in *Daily News*, 18 Jan., 1870, pp. 4–5. Smith was dismissed from the force and given a month's hard labour for using what the magistrate, Ralph Augustus Benson (1828–86), deemed excessive force in protecting a woman abused by her husband; see *The Times*, 25 Dec., 1869, p. 9.

Office is inquiring into the case. If the result be favourable, the article in the *Daily News* and other notices in the press will have greatly contributed to it. In any case, a considerable degree of public approbation has been deservedly directed against the magistrate and his dictum.

I am glad that, while you still continue to write for the *Daily News*, there is at the same time a prospect of your being relieved from the mere drudgery of the occupation, and obtaining leisure for other pursuits.

Your account of Cairnes is cheering, and accords with others which we have received.[3] He himself never takes a sanguine view of his condition, but there is ample proof how much of his health and strength he must have recovered, in his ability not only to deliver his lectures, but to write such an article as that in the *Fortnightly*, which, independently of its merits in point of thought, seems to me quite a model of philosophic stile and expository talent.[4]

I have read, I believe, all Rae's letters,[5] for the *Daily News* generally reaches us at some time or other; but ever since the pretence began of not examining foreign newspapers,[6] we do not get them till after ridiculous delays, and not unfrequently a later newspaper before an earlier. The exact reason I do not know, but it is certain that an announcement that a thing will not be done is generally, in France, followed by its being done more than before; as an announcement that it will be done is, in like manner, followed by neglect to do it. I do not know how much depends on the higher authorities, and how much on the subordinates; for in every system of arbitrary government the chiefs find it necessary or convenient to give the underlings their full share of the arbitrary power, and indeed cannot well enforce on them, duties to the public which they themselves habitually violate. One has only to live in a country arbitrarily governed (as France has been under all its governments) to know how utterly mistaken is the idea that a despotic government is a vigorous one.

We are much pleased that you like my daughter's article.[7] With our kind remembrances to Mrs Hill,[8] I am, Dear Mr Hill

Yours very truly

J.S. MILL

F.H. Hill Esq

---

[3]Cairnes suffered from arthritis, which never was relieved. He settled in Blackheath in the spring of 1870, but his health continued to deteriorate, though he lived until 1875.

[4]"Political Economy and Land," *Fortnightly Review*, n.s. VII (Jan. 1870), 41–63.

[5]Collected and published as *Westward by Rail: The New Route to the East* (New York: Appleton, 1870).

[6]*The Times*, 10 Jan., 1870, p. 5, reported, on the basis of the *Moniteur* of 8 Jan., that "henceforth all foreign journals will be admitted into France without restrictions."

[7]Helen Taylor, "A Few Words on Mr. Trollope's Defence of Fox-Hunting," *Fortnightly Review*, n.s. VII (Jan. 1870), 63–8.

[8]Jane Dalzell Hill (née Finlay) (d. 1904), a contributor to the *Saturday Review*, where she reviewed Mill's *Subjection of Women*, XXVII (19 June, 1869), 811–13.

1547A. TO JAMES EDWIN THOROLD ROGERS[1]

Blackheath Park
Kent
April 15. 1870

DEAR MR ROGERS

I thank you very much for the present of your Adam Smith.[2] I have read the Preface, but have not yet made myself acquainted with your notes, which, though they do not occupy much space, seem to go over a good deal of ground. I rather think that I differ from you on some important points; but the old generalisations of political economy are now found to require so much modification, that our opinions may possibly draw nearer together when duly compared.

Thanks for your invitation to visit Oxford. There is no place which at present interests me more, or which seems to be undergoing a more salutary transformation. But I have seen only just enough of it in the body, to have been much impressed by its beauty and imposingness. I certainly did not write any of my books there, nor did I ever take up my abode in Oxford for more than a day or two at a time. I am, Dear Mr Rogers

yours very truly
J.S. MILL

1562A. TO M. MALTMAN BARRY[1]

A[vignon]
June 3. 1870

DEAR SIR—In reply to your communication of May 18 I beg to say that my occupations do not admit of my undertaking to examine & give an opinion & advice respecting manuscripts intended for publication.[2]

---

[1]MS in the Bodleian Library.
[2]Rogers' edition of *An Inquiry into the Nature and Causes of the Wealth of Nations*, 2 vols. (Oxford: Clarendon Press, 1869).

---

[1]MS draft at the Palais du Roure, Avignon. In reply to Barry's letter of 18 May, also at Avignon. Published in *MNL*, XV (Summer 1980), 3, edited by Marion Filipiuk.

M. Maltman Barry (1842–1909), though a Conservative political agent and correspondent of the Conservative *Standard*, was active in the affairs of the International Working Men's Association.

[2]Barry had asked Mill to give his opinion on "a very short letter on Religious Education for the young," and suggest a publisher.

1583A. TO THE GENERAL COUNCIL OF THE INTERNATIONAL WORKING MEN'S ASSOCIATION[1]

[after 23 July, 1870]

"highly pleased with the address.[2] There was not one word in it that ought not to be there; it could not have been done with fewer words."

1587A. TO WILLIAM TRANT[1]

Blackheath Park
July 27. 1870

DEAR SIR

I have received your letter of July 16,[2] and I sympathise in the opposition to an impost which the legislature has plainly declared its purpose of abolishing:[3] but it is impossible for me to contribute pecuniarily to every public object in which I sympathise, and I would recommend that application should be made to some of those who took the lead in the popular movement against Church Rates. I am Dear Sir

yours very faithfully
J.S. MILL

Wm Trant Esq.

---

[1] Printed in *The General Council of the First International (1870–1871): Minutes* (Moscow: Progress, 1967), p. 38. Meeting of 2 August, 1870.

[2] A short address by Karl Marx (1818–83) on the Franco-Prussian War, at a meeting in London of the General Council of the International Working Men's Association: "Working Men and the War" (23 July, 1870), *Pall Mall Gazette*, 28 July, 1870, p. 3; printed in Karl Marx and Frederick Engels, *Collected Works* (New York: International, 1975–), Vol. XXII, pp. 3–7.

---

[1] MS in the Houghton Library, Harvard University.
William Trant was associated with working-men's clubs, and was a writer on financial reform and trade unions.

[2] Not located.

[3] Probably a reference to a Scottish tax then under review. See the speech of 4 Mar., 1870, *PD*, 3rd ser., Vol. 199, cols. 1321–3, by George Young (1819–1907), the Lord Advocate, introducing a bill to relieve the citizens of Edinburgh of a tax levied to support the Established Church, *PP*, 1870, I, 53–70, subsequently enacted as 33 & 34 Victoria, c. 87 (9 Aug., 1870).

1587B. TO CAROLINE LINDLEY[1]

Blackheath Park
July 29. 1870

DEAR MISS LINDLEY

Since you ask my opinion as to whether it is most advisable that your nephew Robert[2] should go up again for examination, or that he should join his father and brother and commence at once the practical study of his intended profession under the advantageous circumstances of being directly under his father; so far as I am able to judge, this last appears to me greatly preferable. Should he even succeed at the examination, this success if attained in a single year, could probably be only the result of strenuous cramming, and the time so occupied would be almost lost time in respect to his real mental development. Many youths fail at examinations, as examinations are commonly conducted, merely because they are not quick in catching up and recollecting detached points, and cannot give themselves the appearance of knowing a subject unless they know it thoroughly. This may be Robert's case, and if so, he cannot too soon begin to learn that which it is necessary he should know thoroughly, and his knowledge of which can be tested by results instead of by questions on a paper: and if he begins at once, he will probably enter with strong interest upon the new kind of work, and take it up with spirit and vigour. If, on the contrary, he goes up for examination again and should unfortunately suffer a second defeat, the discouragement may be such as to paralyse his energies for a long time to come: while, if he succeeds, the moral consequences may not be at all desirable; for if he is a steady thoughtful youth, he may know very well that he has only succeeded by *coaching*, and may have learnt a lesson not at all conducive to thoroughness and earnestness in the work of life. If the real intellectual advantages of the University education are desired, I am of opinion that several years should be given to attaining them; so that the successful passing through the examination may prove, not readiness of wit, nor power to burthen the memory with a mass of matter for a short time, but thorough and familiar acquaintance with the subjects of the examinations. To have passed the examination is, to my mind, and, I know, in the opinion of many of the examiners, far from a conclusive test of having passed through the really useful discipline of education. The examiners may do what they can to make it so, and yet fail, if parents encourage the system of forcing youths hurriedly on. A thorough and well grounded professional education is of more value to the habits of mind than a hasty and superficial university one. Of course when there is time for both, it is well to

---

[1] MS at Fukuyama University, Japan.
See Letter 1326A above.
[2] Not further identified.

have both; but I think a superficial training of any sort is a distinct disadvantage both to the moral and intellectual progress of a growing mind: and when I speak of hurried and superficial, it must be borne in mind that that which might not be hurried for one character may easily be so for another. I am, Dear Miss Lindley

yours very sincerely

J.S. MILL

1594A. TO THE PEOPLE'S GARDEN COMPANY[1]

Blackheath Park
Kent
Aug. 24. 1870

DEAR SIR

I beg to acknowledge your letter of Aug. 19.

The object of the People's Garden Company[2] is excellent, but I abstain on principle from connecting my name with any enterprise, either philanthropic or pecuniary, the conduct of which, for want of time to attend to it, I am unable to be responsible for. I am, Dear Sir

yours very sincerely

J.S. MILL

1599A. TO CHARLES SHARP[1]

Blackheath Park
Kent
Sept. 15. 1870

DEAR SIR

I beg to acknowledge your letter of the 13th instant.[2]

I feel much interested by what you tell me respecting the Liverpool Institute, and highly honoured by the wish of the Directors that I should take the Chair at their

---

[1]MS in the William R. Perkins Library, Duke University.
[2]Not further identified.

---

[1]MS in the William R. Perkins Library, Duke University.
Charles Sharp has not been identified.
[2]Not located.

annual meeting in November next.³ But the demands on my time and exertions have made it necessary for me, as a rule, to decline invitations of that nature. I am Dear Sir

Yours very sincerely
J.S. MILL

Charles Sharp Esq.

1609A. TO HENRY WENTWORTH ACLAND[1]

Blackheath Park
Kent
Nov. 15. 1870

DEAR SIR

I am much obliged to you for the opportunity of reading your Memoranda.[2] I am glad to find that the Sanitary Commission are likely to report in favour of a comprehensive measure; though I doubt whether the Poor Law Administration should be included in the duties of a Minister of Public Health, as it seems to me quite sufficient in itself to occupy a ministerial department.

I never was more astonished at anything I have read in print about myself, than when I saw the writer against Poor Laws in Macmillan not only claiming me as of his way of thinking, but actually putting forth his proposition for abolishing the Poor Law as taken from me.[3] I am entirely of the opinion expressed in my Political Economy, that a Poor Law, giving the destitute a right to relief (on terms more onerous than the condition of the independent labourer) is a necessary part of a good public administration.[4] I have even been strengthened in this opinion by all

---

[3]In the event, on 15 November, Charles Dilke took the chair and spoke on secondary education. See "Liverpool Institute. Sir Charles W. Dilke and Professor Roscoe on Education," *Liverpool Journal*, 19 Nov., 1870, p. 2. The Liverpool Mechanics' Institute had been established in 1825; at the meeting prizes were awarded to pupils of the high, commercial, and evening classes.

---

[1]MS at the Bodleian Library.
[2]Undoubtedly a reference to Acland's "Memorandum of Duties of Medical Officers of Public Health," printed in "Second Report of the Royal Commission to Inquire into the Operation of the Sanitary Laws in England and Wales," *PP*, 1871, XXXV, 545–54; and probably to his memorandum of the previous year concerning the proper qualifications for candidates seeking employment as medical officers of public health, mentioned in that "Report," p. 269.
[3]Charles Baron Clarke (1832–1906), an Indian civil servant and botanist, "The Existing Poor Law of England," *Macmillan's Magazine*, XXIII (Nov. 1870), 46–52; he attributes his view of the Poor Law (4 & 5 William IV, c. 76 [1834]) to Mill on p. 50.
[4]*Principles of Political Economy*, Bk. II, Chap. xii, Sect. 2; in *CW*, Vol. II, pp. 359–60.

that has come to my knowledge concerning the effects of the public charities in a country where there is no legal right to relief, and where most of the evils produced by our poor law administration when at its worst, flourish exuberantly without the accompanying benefits. I am, Dear Sir

very truly yours
J.S. MILL

Dr Acland

1624A. TO ÉMILE LOUIS VICTOR DE LAVELEYE[1]

Blackheath Park
le 27 Decembre 1870

CHER MONSIEUR

Je ne saurais trop vous remercier pour M. Cairnes et pour moi-même.

Si j'avais eu avec moi mes numéros de la Revue des Deux Mondes, je n'aurais pas eu besoin de m'adresser à votre complaisance; mais malheureusement ces numéros sont à Avignon.[2]

Je vous remercie également de vos renseignements sur les sources à consulter, dont j'ai fait part à M. Cairnes.[3]

Je n'ai pas connaissance du nouveau projet du Cobden Club. Je présume que le Club se propose de publier un volume d'Essais sur les moyens d'empêcher la guerre dans l'état actuel du monde. Sans rien préjuger sur ce qu'il y aurait à dire sur cette question, il me semble qu'elle est loin d'avoir été suffisamment approfondie; et qu'un écrivain qui a étudié autant que vous l'histoire moderne et la politique générale pourrait remplir très utilement le cadre que le Club vous propose.[4]

Agréez, cher Monsieur, l'expression de mon estime et de mon dévouement.

J.S. MILL

---

[1]MS in University of Iowa Library, Iowa City.
Emile Louis Victor, baron de Laveleye (1822–92), Belgian political economist, whose work Mill much admired.

[2]Cairnes, who was preparing "Our Defences: A National or a Standing Army," *Fortnightly Review*, n.s. IX (Feb. 1871), 167–98, had apparently wanted to consult Laveleye's series of articles entitled "L'Allemagne depuis la guerre de 1866," which had appeared in the *Revue des Deux Mondes* (Feb. 1867–Oct. 1869), reprinted as *La Prusse et l'Autriche depuis Sadowa*, 2 vols. (Paris: Hachette, 1870). Laveleye seems to have provided the volume, which Cairnes cited, pp. 175n, 176, and 187–8.

[3]Cairnes also cited articles in *Annales de l'Association Internationale pour le Progrès des Sciences Sociales* (Paris, Brussels, 1866), acknowledging Laveleye's suggestion, p. 189n.

[4]Laveleye contributed "On the Causes of War, and the Means of Reducing Their Number," *Cobden Club Essays*, 2nd ser. (London, Paris, and New York: Cassell, *et al.*, 1872), pp. 1–55.

1627A. TO CHARLES BRADLAUGH[1]

Blackheath Park
Kent
Jan. 2, 1871

DEAR SIR

Should you be able to send me the letter which appeared in the Bury Times?[2] I should then be able to tell you explicitly whether I wrote the letter, and under what circumstances. I am, Dear Sir

yours very truly
J.S. MILL

1631A. TO CHARLES BRADLAUGH[1]

Blackheath Park
Kent
Jan. 7. 1871

DEAR SIR

The letter which you have sent to me, from the Bury Times, was written by me, on the 9th of November last;[2] and is correctly printed, with the exception of the substitution of the word *even* for *ever* in the fourth line; which does not, however, substantially alter the sense. Having referred to the letter from Mr. King to which mine was an answer,[3] I find it says, that the writer had several times, of late, in public meetings, heard my name, and the names of other persons, "Lord Amberley and others," associated with the "Elements of Social Science,"[4] and referred to as

---

[1] MS at the Bishopsgate Foundation, London.
[2] The letter (misdated) is in *CW*, Vol. XVII, p. 1768; see Letter 1631A below.

---

[1] MS at the Bishopsgate Foundation, London.
[2] Mill's letter to the Birmingham evangelist and publisher, David King (1819–94) was included in an undated letter to the editor, signed F.H. Martin, 8 Garden-street, Bury, in the *Bury Times*, 24 Dec., 1870, p. 8; see *CW*, Vol. XVII, p. 1768, where it is surmised to have been written in October 1870.
[3] King's letter has not been located. In the course of a debate with Bradlaugh, later published as *Christianity v. Secularism: Report of a Public Discussion between David King and Charles Bradlaugh, Bury, Lancashire, September 27–30, & October 25 & 26, 1870* (Birmingham: King, 1870), King had questioned Bradlaugh's assumption that Mill approved of the work mentioned below, and had written to ascertain his opinion.
[4] The famous birth-control pamphlet, published anonymously as "By a Student of Medicine," was the work of George R. Drysdale (1825–1904). The first edition was entitled *Physical, Sexual, and Natural Religion* (London: Truelove, 1854), later editions adding the popular title Mill uses.

commending it: and he then asked, whether, when he again heard my name thus used, he should be at liberty to say that the representation is incorrect.

This is the only information I have received that I am represented as commending the book; and I have never heard either yourself or any other person mentioned, either expressly or by implication, as having so represented me. I am, Dear Sir

yours very faithfully
J.S. MILL

Charles Bradlaugh Esq.

1642AA. TO WILLIAM ROSSITER[1]

Blackheath Park
Kent
March 14. 1871

DEAR SIR

I am much obliged by your kind offer of a copy of your book,[2] and have read with pleasure the pages you have sent. I should be happy to see you, but I have so many demands on my time that I do not find it possible at present to fix a time for our meeting. I am Dear Sir

yours very sincerely
J.S. MILL

W. Rossiter Esq.

1654A. TO BENJAMIN WAUGH[1]

Blackheath Park
Kent
April 6. 1871

DEAR SIR

I do not know whether you may have already received a copy of the inclosed protest;[2] but I should be much gratified by being the means of procuring your

---

[1]MS at Kwanseigakuin University, Nishinomiya, Japan.
[2]*An Elementary Handbook of Physics* (London and Edinburgh: Blackwood, 1871).

[1]MS in the Congregational Library, Gordon Square, London.
Benjamin Waugh (1839–1908), Congregational minister and philanthropist.
[2]Presumably against the Contagious Diseases Acts. A Royal Commission had been convened early in January to investigate the operation of 29 Victoria, c. 35 (1866), and 32 & 33 Victoria, c. 96 (1869), and there was much public agitation during the six months of its sitting. Mill's evidence, given on 15 May before this Commission, is in *CW*, Vol. XXI, pp. 349–71.

signature to it. It is particularly wished to obtain the signatures of ministers of religion, and of members of the medical profession; and in the former case, it is desirable to add to the signatures the statement of the denomination to which those signing it belong. If I am under a mistaken impression in believing that your sympathies in this matter are on the same side as my own, I must beg you to excuse the trouble to which I have put you. I am Dear Sir

Yours very truly
J.S. MILL

Rev. B. Waugh

1654B. TO DUNCAN MCLAREN[1]

Blackheath Park
Kent
April 7. 1871

DEAR MR MCLAREN

The Committee for the Scott Centenary had already done me the honour of asking me to be present at the celebration,[2] but I have been obliged to answer them that my occupations and engagements do not allow me to avail myself of the invitation. I am, Dear Mr McLaren

very truly yours
J.S. MILL

1667B. TO AN UNIDENTIFIED CORRESPONDENT[1]

Blackheath Park
Kent
May 28, 1871

DEAR SIR

I have not myself taken any part in editing Mr Buckle's posthumous works, nor have I written, nor do I intend to write, any Memoir of him. His posthumous works

---

[1] MS at the College of Law, Nihon University, Tokyo.
Duncan McLaren (1800–86), merchant, M.P. for Edinburgh 1865–81, was, with other members of his family, a strong supporter of women's causes.
[2] At the celebration of the 100th anniversary of the birth of Sir Walter Scott (1771–1832), when 2000 gathered in the Edinburgh Corn Exchange, Mill's apologies were noted along with others'; see "The Scott Centenary," *The Times*, 10 Aug., 1871, p. 12.

---

[1] MS at Kokugakuin University, Tokyo. The recipient was probably interested in a U.S. edition of Buckle's posthumous writings.

however are being prepared for the press by my step daughter, Miss Helen Taylor, and will probably be published, with a short Memoir, in the course of next year.[2] The publishers will be Messrs Longmans, Green, and Co, who, we understand, have made arrangements with an American publisher.[3] I am, Dear Sir

Yours very faithfully

J.S. MILL

1673A. TO PIERRE AUGUSTIN ROUVIÈRE[1]

Lucerne
Aug. 9 [187]1

MONSIEUR—J'espère arriver à Avignon en quelques jours d'ici et j'ai alors besoin d'un médicament dont je vous envoie copie de l'ordonnance. N'ayant pu obtenir ce médicament en Suisse où il paraît qu'on ne se sert plus du *pareira*[2] je crains qu'il n'en fut peut-être de même à Avignon et dans ce cas je vous engage à vouloir bien en procurer à Paris ou à Marseille. On m'ordonne d'user de ce remède deux fois par jour pendant un temps considérable.

1673B. TO AUGUSTE VON LITTROW[1]

Lucerne
Aug. 9. 1871

DEAR MADAM—I am very happy to learn from your testimony that there is already

---

[2]Helen Taylor wrote a "Biographical Notice" of Henry Thomas Buckle for her edition of his *Miscellaneous and Posthumous Works*, 3 vols. (London: Longmans, Green, 1872), pp. ix–lv.

[3]No American edition appeared.

---

[1]MS draft at the Palais du Roure, Avignon. Published in *MNL*, XV (Summer 1980), 3, edited by Marion Filipiuk.

Pierre Augustin Rouvière (b. ca. 1803), whose last name appears on the back of the draft, was a pharmacist in Avignon 1836–75, at 16 place du Change.

[2]A bitter tonic made of the root of a Brazilian shrub, taken as a diuretic.

---

[1]MS draft at the Palais du Roure, Avignon. In reply to Littrow's letter of 7 July, also at Avignon, signed "Auguste Littrow-Bischoff." Published in *MNL*, XV (Summer 1980), 4, edited by Marion Filipiuk.

Auguste von Littrow (1819–90) (the hyphenated addition to Littrow identifies her as the daughter of a celebrated Viennese physician, Ignaz Rudolph Bischoff), author, and advocate of women's rights. See also Letter 1690A below.

a widely spread interest among German women for the cause of the political & social equality of the sexes. I am much honoured by your wish that some words of approval from myself should be prefixed to the work you have prepared on "die Zukunft der Deutschen Volksschule,"[2] but I have thought it right to lay down to myself as a rule, never to give my public recommendation to any work which I have not read.

1674A. TO HODGSON PRATT[1]

A[vignon]
Aug 23. 1871

DEAR SIR—I beg to acknowledge your letter of July 27 which owing to my absence from England has only just reached me.

Your desire for an organization to give true information to England & France respecting one another & to correct mutual misapprehensions is very laudable.[2] But I believe that the information which it would be possible to supply, especially on the French side, would be, in the vast majority of cases, false information. The monstrous absurdities which have been & still are believed even by highly educated people in France, & the multitude of mere lies which are invented, circulated, & generally credited here respecting what takes place in France itself, would make it impossible for any French Committee to supply England with that authentic information which they themselves would seldom possess. Things are a little better in England, but even if an English Committee were able to lay before the French people the exact truth, no part of it would be believed except what agreed with the national prejudices or party prepossessions of each person. For these reasons, I hope too little from your experiment to be willing to take part in it, though I shd be most highly gratified if it were successful.

---

[2]Not located.

[1]MS draft at the Palais du Roure, Avignon. In reply to Pratt's letter of 27 July, also at Avignon. Published in *MNL*, XV (Summer 1980), 5, edited by Marion Filipiuk.

Hodgson Pratt (1824–1907), a Bengal civil servant and educational reformer, was an active advocate of peace, and was awarded the Nobel Prize for Peace in 1906.

[2]Pratt enclosed a copy of a "Draft Scheme for an Anglo-French Association for the Promotion of International Goodwill."

1676A. TO P.L. MILLS[1]

A[vignon]
Sept. 4. 1871

DEAR SIR—Your note of the 17th ulto has been forwarded to me here. I only received while at Luzern one letter which was not intended for you and this I returned personally to the Luzern post office. I shd add that the letter in question did not bear your name on the cover.

1684A. TO GEORGE GILL[1]

A[vignon]
Oct. 9. 1871

DEAR SIR—I beg to acknowledge your letter of Sept. 28 & your tract on Tenant Right.[2] I have read both of them with interest but it is out of the question that I shd make an application to Mr Gladstone tending to procure for you any pecuniary benefit. I have made it a rule not to use influence with any Govt for such a purpose even if I possessed it, & to this rule I could not make you an exception even if I were competent to judge of the inventions referred to in your letter.

I return the pamphlet as I infer from your letter that you have not at present any other copy.

---

[1]MS draft at the Palais du Roure, Avignon. In reply to Mills' letter of 17 August, also at Avignon. A second version reads: "Dear Sir—Your note of the 17th ulto has been forwarded to me here, and in reply I beg to say that I have not received either at Luzern or elsewhere any letter addressed to you." Published in *MNL*, XV (Summer 1980), 5, edited by Marion Filipiuk.

P.L. Mills, not otherwise identified, was a member of the firm of Mills and Gibb, of New York and Nottingham.

---

[1]MS at the Palais du Roure, Avignon. In reply to Gill's letter of 27 September, also at Avignon. Published in *MNL*, XV (Summer 1980), 6, edited by Marion Filipiuk.

George Gill (b. ca. 1820) identified himself in his letter as a surgeon, aged fifty-one, who had worked to elect Chadwick in 1868.

[2]Gill enclosed a copy (presumably in manuscript) of his "Scheme of Tenant Rights for England as well as Ireland."

1684B. TO AN UNIDENTIFIED CORRESPONDENT[1]

Avignon
le 9 octobre 1871

MONSIEUR

Votre lettre du 18 septembre m'a été envoyée de Londres, mais votre brochure ne m'est pas encore parvenue.[2] Je n'ai pourtant pas besoin d'attendre son arrivée pour vous témoigner ma profonde sympathie pour les opinions dont votre lettre m'apprend qu'elle est l'expression. Rien ne me donne plus d'espérance pour l'avenir de la France, que le mouvement qui se montre pour l'autonomie de la personne humaine et pour le gouvernement républicain, fédératif: et je ne doute pas que je ne trouve dans votre brochure, comme j'ai trouvé dans votre lettre, de nouveaux motifs d'encouragement à ce sujet.

J'apprends avec plaisir que vous avez collaboré à la traduction de mes volumes de Mélanges.[3] Je vous donne à vous et à M. Boirac[4] pleine liberté de vous qualifier de traducteurs autorisés par moi. Seulement je vous prie de vouloir bien avertir le lecteur que je n'ai pas vu la traduction; non pas assurément par méfiance de son mérite, mais parce que, n'ayant pas le loisir de la lire et de l'examiner, je trouve juste d'en laisser l'honneur et la responsabilité à qui de droit.

Agréez, Monsieur, l'assurance de ma considération distinguée et de mes sentiments amicaux.

J.S. MILL

1685A. TO JAMES KEAPPOCH HAMILTON WILLCOX[1]

A[vignon]
Oct. 10. 1871

P.S. as you say that Mr Leverson[2] has printed notes of mine by way of testimonials

---

[1]MS in the Osborn Collection, Yale University.
[2]Neither letter nor brochure has been located.
[3]No French translation of *Dissertations and Discussions* appeared.
[4]Possibly Emile Boirac (1851–1917), later known as a psychologist and philosopher, though he would then have been only twenty years old.

---

[1]MS draft at the Palais du Roure, Avignon. In reply to Willcox's letter of 6 April, also at Avignon. Mill's reply published in the *New York Tribune*, 18 Nov., 1871, p. 5; in *CW*, Vol. XVII, pp. 1840–1, to which this is a postscript. Published in *MNL*, XV (Summer 1980), 7, edited by Marion Filipiuk.
James Keappoch Hamilton Willcox (1842–98), U.S. insurance broker, editor, and politician, prominent in the women's suffrage movement, had visited Mill in Avignon in September 1869.
[2]Montague Richard Leverson (1830–1917), anti-vivisectionist and anti-vaccinationist doctor, had written on copyright before emigrating to the U.S.A. for unknown reasons.

for the office of President of a College,³ it is well you shd know that I never gave him my permission to do so, & moreover that the notes were all written before the occurrences which led to his leaving England. I have no knowledge of those occurrences, nor have I any opinion as to whether they are at all discreditable to him, but I could not have given him anything of the nature of a recommendation for such an office without knowing more about these transactions than I do.

1685B. TO ARTHUR PATCHETT MARTIN[1]

A[vignon]
Oct. 10. 1871

Private:

DEAR SIR—I thank you for your letter of the 22nd of April last. The information it contains relating to the politics of Victoria is very interesting, as to me much of it was new.

I entirely agree with you that compulsory & secular education is the most important of all questions for Australia. If this can be obtained, & successfully worked, all other questions will, in a country like yours, very soon come right of themselves. It is to be feared that the new ministry, having a Catholic though one of the best of Catholics at its head,[2] will do all it can to discourage this movement. As for state-assisted immigration, whether it is desirable or not it clearly ought not to be carried into effect in opposition to the *public opinion* of the colony. But I have always thought that the unoccupied lands of Australia were prematurely given up to the governments of the several colonies, & ought to have been reserved as the property of the empire at large until much greater progress had been made in peopling them. The renunciation of them was by no means a necessary consequence of the introduction of responsible government. The step, however, cannot be retraced & it is to be hoped that the principle of the State being the sole landlord may be adopted in Australia so far as respects unappropriated land while there still remains a great quantity of land in that condition.

I cannot agree with Mr Higinbotham[3] in his idea that the legislature shd consist

---

[3]Willcox's letter identifies the institution as the New York City Free College.

---

[1]MS draft at the Palais du Roure, Avignon. In reply to Martin's letter of 22 April, also at Avignon. Published in *MNL*, XV (Summer 1980), 8–9, edited by Marion Filipiuk.

Arthur Patchett Martin (1851–1902), Australian author, journalist, and civil servant.

[2]Charles Gavan Duffy (1816–1903), a "Young Irelander" who had founded the *Nation* in 1842 and tried to persuade Mill to stand for an Irish constituency in 1851, emigrated to Australia in 1856, where he became prominent politically. He was Chief Secretary (i.e., head of government) of Victoria 1871–72.

[3]Martin had reported this view of George Higinbotham (1826–91), the leading radical politician in Victoria.

of only 40 or 50 members, elected by the whole of the colony as one constituency, & largely remunerated. Forty or fifty are too few for a deliberative assembly, & too many for an administrative board, neither is it desirable that the legislature should administer; & if men are paid two or three thousand a year merely for legislating, they will think themselves bound to earn their salary by legislating a great deal too much. Besides, so long as Hare's system[4] is not adopted, the uniting of the whole electorate as one body would deprive all minorities of even the imperfect representation which the accidents of local opinion give them & the majority alone would be ever heard in the legislature.

As to the question of separation, my conviction is, that it shd rest entirely with the Australian people, & that our Govt & Parlt shd exert no pressure either way. A time will of course come when the Australian colonies, feeling strong enough to defend themselves unassisted against any attack, will think the power of England to involve them in her wars without consulting them, an evil more than equivalent to the advantage of English protection. I confess that I shd reject separation, but I do not think that the federal principle can be worked successfully when the different members of the confederacy are scattered all over the world; & I think the English people would prefer separation to an *equal* federation.

I hope your university will soon follow the example of the university of Sydney & that of Chicago, in the admission of women.[5] At Chicago even the law school has lately been opened to them on exactly the same conditions as to male students.[6] Their admission to serve on juries in the Territory of Wyoming has been, according to the testimony of the Chief Justice who had opposed it,[7] eminently successful.

Pray give my compliments to Mr Rusden.[8] It is very fortunate for Victoria that it contains persons of such enlightened political opinions as yourself, Mr Rusden & Mr Gresham.[9]

[4] See Letter 388A above.

[5] Women were admitted to the Junior and Senior Examinations at Sydney in 1871 (W. Vere Hole and Anne H. Treweeke, *The History of the Women's College within the University of Sydney* [Sydney: Halstead Press, 1953], pp. 30–1).

[6] The first woman student graduated from the Law Department of the University of Chicago in June 1870. (The Department later became the Union College of Law, and relocated as the Law Department at Northwestern University, after the first University of Chicago dissolved in 1886.)

[7] John H. Howe (d. 1873) was quoted to this effect in the new organ of the National American Woman Suffrage Association, *Woman's Journal*, I (23 Apr., 1870), 123. T.A. Larsen, *History of Wyoming* (Lincoln: University of Nebraska Press, 1965), pp. 84–5, says that, following the granting of suffrage to women in 1869, they served on juries in 1870 and 1871, but then were not called, on the ground that the suffrage did not entail such service.

[8] Henry Keylock Rusden (1826–1910), an author and civil servant in Victoria, had corresponded with Mill.

[9] William Hutchison Gresham (1824–75), political writer, was active in the Land Tenure Reform League of Victoria.

1690A. TO AUGUSTE VON LITTROW[1]

A[vignon]
Oct. 25. 1871

DEAR MADAM—I thank you for your pamphlet[2] which I have read with great interest & which seems to me both well argued and well written. You have confined yourself to a single item in the large subject of justice to women; but that one item is of very great importance; & you have the advantage in that instance, of making out what seems to be a case of necessity, since from your statements it appears that unless women are admitted to a large share in the work of public teaching, the popular education which is the glory of Germany is in danger not merely of remaining stationary but even of degenerating. I congratulate you cordially on your valuable contribution to the cause both of women & of education & I hope it is not the only one which they are destined to receive from you as a writer.

1699A. TO MLLE GUILLAUMIN[1]

Avignon
le 10 Decembre 1871

MADEMOISELLE

Il n'y a presque pas de changements dans la dernière (la septième) édition de mes Principes d'Economie Politique.[2] Mais la traduction a été faite, si je ne m'y trompe pas, sur la troisième édition, et il a été fait assez de changements depuis lors pour qu'il me semble désirable que le traducteur en tienne compte.[3]

Ma fille se recommande particulièrement à vos bons souvenirs. Elle a été beaucoup fatiguée, sans quoi elle se serait donné le plaisir d'aller chez vous en passant par Paris.

---

[1]MS draft at the Palais du Roure, Avignon. In reply to Littrow's response to the letter of 9 August above, also at Avignon. Published in *MNL*, XV (Summer 1980), 9, edited by Marion Filipiuk.
[2]See Letter 1673B above.

---

[1]MS in the possession of Mrs. Barbara McCrimmon.
Mlle Guillaumin, daughter of the publisher Gilbert Urbain Guillaumin, had taken over the business.
[2]The 7th ed. appeared in 1871. It is a matter of judgment whether there are almost no changes in it, but there are few compared to those in other editions; see the Textual Introduction, *CW*, Vol. II, pp. lxix ff.
[3]Courcelle-Seneuil (see Letter 136B above) made the necessary revisions for the 3rd French ed. (Paris: Guillaumin, 1873).

Veuillez agréer, Mademoiselle, l'expression de ma considération la plus distinguée.

J.S. MILL

1704A. TO [AUBERON HERBERT][1]

[29 Jan., 1872]

I have read your letter with warm interest and sympathy, & the practical effect on my mind would be to wish that you would pursue the plan that has suggested itself to you, because it would, whatever its result, be one of those moralizing influences of which there are so few & of which the world wants so many; & also because the fact that it has suggested itself to you makes you the fit person to carry it out.

The only point in which I do not agree with you is the impression that the present time is a time of crisis. I have always felt very strongly the truth of St. Paul's saying, "Behold *now* is the acceptable time: behold now is the time of salvation."[2] As every day of our lives is a new year's day, so the more one reads history & watches one's own time, does it appear to me that every time is a time of crisis: & perhaps those times in which it appears the most on the surface are the least so in fact; for it is the silent workings in men's minds which are the true crises of history. Connected with my disagreement, if I have understood you rightly, on this point, is my deep agreement with you on the want now beginning to be felt of new, high, & definite, moral purposes—purposes capable too of inspiring lasting enthusiasm. But I think that it will never be possible to work on any great scale on the minds of the working classes, excepting by the same means & at the same time that we work upon the minds of the earnest & intelligent among other classes. In the present state of education & civilisation, working men of native energy & talent are open to the same influences as other people: & the most lasting effects upon the more commonplace characters in their own rank will be produced by these men, & not by their social superiors, however devoted & earnest.

I look upon it as the great work now to be done, to build up a system of morals capable of inspiring enthusiasm & satisfying the intellect. My own belief is that

---

[1] MS draft in the Mill-Taylor Collection, British Library of Political and Economic Science, in reply to Herbert's of 26 December, 1871, also in the Mill-Taylor Collection. The letter is bound as part of a correspondence between Herbert and Helen Taylor, but is in Mill's hand, as is the letter of 29 January published in *CW*, Vol. XVII, pp. 1869–71, of which this appears to be an earlier draft.

Auberon Edward William Molyneux Herbert (1838–1906), author and political philosopher.

[2] II Corinthians, 6:2.

this will be a developement of Xtianity, properly understood; that it must be a development from the state at which we are now arrived, worked out by many minds, for that it is a task far beyond the powers of any one; & that we are all contributing to it, — bringing stones as it were to the building of the temple, when we attempt to clear up any high point of morals or philosophy or science, inasmuch as truth will be the great object of our new system, & the world is beginning to learn how precious truth is in little things & in great. Thus it seems to me that your plan might do much, as tending both to love of truth & to human sympathy: but that lasting progress in the moral nature of all classes must come by the same means, & that we can only hope for it to come very gradually.

1767A. TO THE JOURNAL DES ÉCONOMISTES[1]

le 20 Decembre 1872

Abonnement au Journal des Economistes pour l'année 1873

de la part de

J. STUART MILL

Avignon

1773A. TO THE HOTEL WINDSOR[1]

Tournon (Ardèche)
le 5 février 1873

M. J.S. Mill prie M. le maître de l'Hotel Windsor[2] de lui garder le petit apartement à l'entresol sur la rue pour vendredi soir le 7 février, ou si cet apartement est pris de lui donner un autre appartement sur la rue. M. Mill compte arriver vendredi vers 6½ h du soir et prie qu'il y ait du feu et qu'un diner fut préparé pour son arrivée.

---

[1] MS in the possession of Professor Satoshi Yamasaki, Kagawa University, Japan.

---

[1] MS draft in the Yale University Library.
[2] At 226 rue de Rivoli, Paris. As Mill was in Dijon on 6 February, and in Montbard, only a few kilometers to the northwest on the 8th (presumably travelling by boat on the Burgundy canal), it would appear that his plans changed, and perhaps this reservation was never made.

1784A. TO LEONARD HENRY COURTNEY[1]

10, Albert Mansions,
Victoria Street S.W.
March 15, 1873

DEAR MR COURTNEY

Will you do us the pleasure of dining with us here at seven o'clock on Friday next, March 21st? I am, Dear Mr Courtney

very truly yours
J.S. MILL

1795A. TO MONCURE DANIEL CONWAY[1]

10 Albert Mansions
Victoria Street. S.W.
[early April 1873]

DEAR MR CONWAY

It would have given my daughter and myself great pleasure to have dined with you and Mrs Conway,[2] and to have met Mr Emerson and his daughter;[3] but we have a long standing engagement to dine with Mr and Mrs Cairnes[4] on the 12th. I am, Dear Mr Conway

very truly yours
J.S. MILL

---

[1] MS in the Pierpont Morgan Library.
Leonard Henry Courtney (1832–1918), later Baron Courtney of Penrith, a lawyer and journalist who favoured reform of endowments, was Professor of Political Economy at University College London.

---

[1] MS in the Houghton Library, Harvard University. Dated by the reference to Emerson and his daughter, who were in London from 5 April to 15 May, and saw Mill during that time.
Moncure Daniel Conway (1832–1907), U.S.-born Unitarian, pastor of South Place Chapel, Red Lion Square, from February 1864, was a frequent contributor to the *Fortnightly Review* and *Fraser's Magazine*.
[2] Ellen Davis Conway (née Dana) (d. 1897).
[3] Ralph Waldo Emerson (1803–82), the American transcendentalist, and his eldest daughter, Ellen Tucker Emerson (1839–1909).
[4] Eliza Charlotte Cairnes (née Alexander).

UNDATED LETTERS

Undated Letters

No. 1. TO HENRY COLE[1]

DEAR COLE

After seeing you I remembered a prior dinner engagement which in an unfortunate hour I made & should have written to you about it, but that from what Grant told me I concluded there was no chance for *this* Wednesday.

It is provoking, but pray try to fix some other day.

Yours ever
J.S. MILL

No. 2. TO HENRY COLE[1]

India House
Wedy.

MY DEAR COLE—I presume this[2] is printed only for private use. If it were to appear in any newspaper or be otherwise published I should wish my name for various reasons to be struck out.

As it stands, I have no correction to make in what you make me say, as I have no objection to the substance of it & it only purports to be your report of a conversation. If I were speaking for myself I should state my opinion in rather different words, but that, if it is sure not to be published, is immaterial.

I have not shewn it to Peacock or Melvill[3] & had rather not to the

---

[1]MS not located; typescript McCrimmon. *Addressed*: Henry Cole Esq. / 4, Adam Street / Adelphi. Probably written in the early 1830s.

---

[1]MS not located; typescript McCrimmon.
[2]Not identified; perhaps the document referred to in No. 3 below.
[3]For Melvill and Peacock, see Letters 290.1 and 237.2 above, respectively.

latter—therefore I should not save you any trouble by becoming your medium of communication with the former.

Yours faithfully
J.S. MILL

No. 3. TO HENRY COLE[1]

I.H.
Wedy.

DEAR COLE

If I were you I would for the sake of apparent fairness *cite* rather than *describe* the "ambiguous" letter from Hume,[2] & I would avoid the words hallucination or monomania. It seems to me that if you also suppressed the whole of the concluding paragraph you would not at all weaken the effect. All which is there said is so completely suggested by the previous paragraph that you do not strengthen the impression by adding anything more.

Perhaps also the short note, which is as it were the "lie direct" had better be omitted.

Yours ever
J.S. MILL

No. 4. TO HENRY COLE[1]

Thursday

DEAR COLE

If the article is to be made up it is I conclude only to save time & not to preclude alterations afterwards. But I shall see all about it today.

Ever yours
J.S. MILL

---

[1]MS not located; typescript McCrimmon. Perhaps dealing with the same document as No. 2 above.

[2]Presumably Joseph Hume.

---

[1]MS not located; typescript McCrimmon. Possibly related to the matter discussed in the two preceding letters, Nos. 2 and 3.

No. 5. TO EDWIN CHADWICK[1]

India House
Monday
[after 1834]

DEAR CHADWICK, It appears that your official frank is of no validity quoad postage to or in India—Even the President of the Board of Control sends his India letters here to be franked by the Chairman, Deputy Chn or Secretary who alone have the power of franking—& whom I hardly like to ask to frank anything larger than a letter since I cannot say that it is for strictly official purposes. Perhaps there may be an opportunity of sending by a private hand.

yours faithfully
J.S. MILL

No. 6. TO JOHN TEMPLE LEADER[1]

DEAR LEADER

I have great pleasure in introducing to you Mr Fox, whom I need not say that you ought to know, & that he ought to know you—I am desirous on every account to make him and you acquainted, & should probably have taken another opportunity, if one had not presented itself on which you may possibly be of use to him. He will explain in what way—

Ever yours truly
J.S. MILL

---

[1]MS at University College London. Between 1834 and 1846, Chadwick, as Secretary to the Poor Law Commission, was the Chief Executive Officer under the Poor Law Amendment Act. In this capacity, his signature was sufficient to send letters free in England. It is reasonable to assume that this request came early in his tenure, before he learned the intricacies of the perquisite system.

---

[1]MS in the Keynes Collection, King's College, Cambridge. *Addressed:* J.T. Leader Esq. M.P. / 8 Stratton Street.

John Temple Leader (1810–1903), one of the active Philosophic Radicals in the post-Reform parliament, was M.P. for Bridgenorth 1835–37 and for Westminster 1837–47. As he had not yet met William Johnson Fox (1786–1864), the Unitarian clergyman, editor and author, an intimate friend of Mill's, one may infer that the letter dates from the earliest days of Leader's parliamentary career.

No. 7. TO NASSAU WILLIAM SENIOR[1]

DEAR SENIOR

I will duly account to Chapman for the cheque.[2]
I go into town daily at the usual time—about ¼ before 9.[3]

yours faithfully
J.S. MILL

No. 8. TO AN UNIDENTIFIED CORRESPONDENT[1]

I.H.
Monday
[Apr. 1836–Mar. 1840]

MY DEAR SIR

The L. & W. review will be published about the end of this month. If there is any little thing which you could do for it there is still room, & it would give me much pleasure.

ever yours
J.S. MILL

No. 9. TO AN UNIDENTIFIED CORRESPONDENT[1]

Ex. Off.
Wedy
[between 1836 and 1846]

MY DEAR SIR

Mr Bonham's[2] application has been received & is with the Financial

---

[1] MS in the Varnhagen von Ense Collection, Jagiellonian Library, Cracow.
[2] Presumably the reference is to Henry Samuel Chapman (1803–81), a journalist who assisted with the financial affairs of the *London Review* after his return from Canada in 1834.
[3] Mill was probably staying at the family's summer residence in Mickleham.

---

[1] MS in the University of Iowa Library, Iowa City. Dated by the reference to the *London and Westminster Review*.

---

[1] MS in the Osborn Collection, Yale University. Dated from Thornton's tenure in the Secretary's Office.
[2] Not identified.

Department (Mr Thornton).³ Nothing has yet been done respecting it.

Yours faithfully
J.S. MILL

No. 10. TO MR. STONE¹

[summer; probably before 1851]

DEAR SIR

I am extremely sorry to hear that you are unwell—and still more sorry that you sat up waiting for me—especially as I was a little behind my time; I was too late partly by being *too* early, and partly by making too much haste—according to the old proverb.

I shall leave town for a few weeks on Friday night—if we *could* finish this matter first it would be better, but if it would task your health or your convenience in the least, we will wait till I return—which I shall regret the less, as it will be somewhat inconvenient to myself to come here tomorrow evening—however I think I *could* come.

Yours ever
J.S. MILL

A note addressed to me at the India House, early tomorrow, will reach me in time. I leave at four.

---

³Possibly Edward Thornton (1799–1875), who would have handled financial matters in his capacity as Assistant in Charge in the Secretary's Office between 1836 and 1846.

---

¹MS in the Mill-Taylor Collection, British Library of Political and Economic Science. Stone has not been identified, nor has the "matter" in question. Mill in general was absent from the India Office for extended periods only in the summer months. The wording also suggests that the letter was written before his marriage in 1851.

No. 11. TO CATHERINE STANLEY[1]

I[ndia] H[ouse]
thursday
[before Aug. 1858]

DEAR MRS STANLEY—I would come to you tomorrow evening with great pleasure but I am engaged, I am afraid for all the evening.

yours ever
J.S. MILL

No. 12. TO AN UNIDENTIFIED CORRESPONDENT[1]

I.H.
Monday
[before Aug. 1858]

MY DEAR SIR

I will certainly have the pleasure of attending the celebration[2] on the 25th July.

Yours truly
J.S. MILL

---

[1] MS at the College of Law, Nihon University, Tokyo. As dated from India House, before August 1858.

Presumably Catherine Stanley (née Leycester) (1792–1862), wife of Edward Stanley (1779–1849), Bishop of Norwich, and mother of Arthur Penrhyn Stanley (1815–81), later Dean of Westminster.

---

[1] MS in the possession of Professor J.R.deJ. Jackson, University of Toronto. As dated from India House, before August 1858.

[2] Not identified.

No. 13. TO WILLIAM CHARLES BONAPARTE WYSE[1]

Saint Véran, Avignon
Saturday.
[after Dec. 1859]

DEAR SIR

Though very busy, I shall be happy to see you and your two friends.[2] I shall be in town this afternoon about three, and will have the pleasure of calling on you then if convenient to you. If not I shall be glad to see you here between two and three o'clock on Monday. I am

yours very truly
J.S. MILL

No. 14. TO AN UNIDENTIFIED CORRESPONDENT[1]

DEAR SIR—I very much recommend writing as an occupation of leisure, & as a means of self-improvement, but not as a profession, or in the hope of making money by it. The very best writers have almost always to wait many years before they attain the reputation which procures lucrative literary employment. If you like to send me your essay, I will willingly read it, but however high my opinion of it may be, I cannot recommend it to editors, from which even in the case of personal friends I find it necessary to abstain. I see no objection to a young writer himself offering his writings to editors or publishers. He must expect to be generally unsuccessful, & will do well to persevere in writing & to be content with such chance successes as may offer themselves.

---

[1] MS at the College of Law, Nihon University, Tokyo.
William Charles Bonaparte Wyse (1826–92), son of Sir Thomas Wyse, whom Mill had met in Athens in 1855, and Laetitia Wyse (daughter of Lucien Bonaparte). W.C.B. Wyse first arrived in Avignon in December 1859, and later, becoming a friend of Frédéric Mistral and a writer in the Provençal dialect, took a house there.
[2] Not identified.

---

[1] MS draft in the Mill-Taylor Collection, British Library of Political and Economic Science. Presumably written no earlier than the 1860s, when Mill reached the height of his reputation as an author.

No. 15. TO AN UNIDENTIFIED CORRESPONDENT[1]

GENTLEMEN—I have received from you an acknowledgment of the receipt of my notice for Policy No. [blank] but no acknowledgment of my Policy No. [blank] & of the fact that you have received the original policies Nos. & all of which came under the same cover as the notice No. [blank] receipt of which you have acknowledged. I shd be obliged therefore by receiving an acknowledgment in form of the original policies of both numbers.

---

[1] MS draft in pencil in the Mill-Taylor Collection, British Library of Political and Economic Science. Nothing is known of Mill's insurance policies.

APPENDICES

Appendix A

LETTERS TO THEODOR GOMPERZ: VARIANT READINGS

THE VARIANT READINGS below result from a collation of the versions of Mill's letters to Theodor Gomperz, already published in Vols. XIV–XVII of the *Collected Works*, and not reprinted above, with copies of the manuscripts in the collection at Kokugakuin University. Differences in salutations and complimentary closings have not been noted. Page and line numbers at the left refer to *Collected Works*, Vols. XIV–XVII. The reading found there is given first; the manuscript reading follows in square brackets.

238.8   I have the   [I have had the]
238.8   20th of July   [20th July]
581.7   could give   [would give]
589.12   post or   [post either in France or]
739.11   Aug. 21   [Aug. 24]
740.8   Avignon where   [Avignon (Saint Véran, près Avignon, Vaucluse) where]
861.21   June 6   [5 or 6 June] [5 or *written in another hand*]
862.11   necessity of   [necessity or utility of]
862.12   of excusing   [or excusing]
862.14   Nobody   [No one]
862.18   could be   [would be]
863.5   unchangeable   [unchangeably]
863.9   anything   [whatever]
863.11   will have   [will always have]
863.13   your feelings   [your friendly feelings]
865.27   July 5   [July 15]
866.3   & will   [and I will]
866.13   pro Archia   [*pro Archia*]
866.14   literature—when   [literature. Whether]
866.17   store   [stores]
866.25   as makes   [as to make]
866.30   chiefly   [cheerfully]
874.31   greatest . . . I   [gravest . . . *I*]
1197.13–14   Rien . . . succès   [*Rien . . . succès*]
1197.29   made. It   [made: it]
1197.33   this year   [the year]
1356.18   Jan. 27   [Jan. 28]
1357.19   were   [was]

1357.24   your publications   [your various publications]
1374.34   P[ark]   [Park / Kent]
1375.3   of Porphyry   [on Porphyry]
1375.7   make sure   [take care]
1391.2   P[ark]   [Park, Kent]
1391.30   out   [down]
1655.22   to yours   [with yours]
1655.32   effective   [effectual]
1655.33   with either good   [with good]
1655.34   cases   [case]
1655.37   grateful   [thankful]

Appendix B

LIST OF FORM LETTERS AT THE INDIA OFFICE LIBRARY AND RECORDS

AS EXAMINER of Indian Correspondence in the East India House, Mill served as Clerk to the Secret Committee of the Court of Directors. In this capacity, he frequently wrote to the responsible official of the Board of Control, Thomas N. Waterfield (Senior Clerk in the Secret Department), to request the release of various secret documents. The form letter on these occasions, prepared by a clerk for Mill's signature, was worded: "I am directed by the Secret Committee to request, that the Right Honorable the Commissioners for the Affairs of India will be pleased to authorize the Committee to communicate to the Court of Directors the undermentioned Secret Papers . . . ." Details of the necessary documents followed.

The list below provides the location of these requests in the India Office Library and Records, the date, and a brief summary of the subject matter of the letter.

LOCATION	DATE	SUBJECT
L/P&S/3/52 (347)	4 May, 1857	Persian Expedition
/54 (525)	29 June, 1857	Disaffection of Bengal Native Troops
(641)	July 1857	Mutinous proceedings of Bengal Native Troops; Application to Lord Elgin (on his way to China) for European troops
/55 (1)	1 Aug., 1857	Mutinies of Bengal Native Troops, N.W.P.
/56 (211)	19 Oct., 1857	Aspect of Affairs and Military resources in Madras
/53 (399)	16 Nov., 1857	Services of Officers employed in Persian Gulf Expedition brought to notice
(535)	18 Dec., 1857	Services of Officers employed in Persian Expedition
/60 (121)	5 Feb., 1858	Addition of 3 Regiments of European Infantry to the Army in India
(129)	6 Feb., 1858	Sentiments of the Sultan respecting the Indian Mutinies; Announcement of Intended Contributions by the Shah of

		Persia and his Prime Minister to the Indian Relief Fund
(173)	19 Feb., 1858	Correspondence between Viscount Canning and the Earl of Elgin on the subject of directing the troops on their way to China to proceed to India
(339)	25 Mar., 1858	Services rendered by Maun Singh and others to fugitive Europeans
(359)	30 Mar., 1858	Application to the Governor General of Australia for Troops
(439)	9 Apr., 1858	Delhi fortifications
(463)	14 Apr., 1858	Annexation of Dhar; Services rendered by Maun Singh to fugitive Europeans
(501)	24 Apr., 1858	Policy to be pursued with regard to Mutineers and others
(529)	20 May, 1858	Affairs of Oude
(545)	27 May, 1858	Annexation of Dhar
(565)	31 May, 1858	Disarming in Guzerat, etc.
/61 (13)	8 June, 1858	Disarming in Guzerat
(103)	21 June, 1858	Disarming of the Population of Guzerat
(119)	6 July, 1858	Services of Maharajah Jung Bahadoor and Nepaul Troops
(275)	22 July, 1858	Services of the Guickwar
(295)	23 July, 1858	Case of Mr. Hudson, Agent of the Rajah of Joudpoor
(375)	3 Aug., 1858	Lord Harding's Minute on Corporal Punishment; Oudh Proclamation
(411)	6 Aug., 1858	Disarming in Guzerat
(525)	23 Aug., 1858	Approval to make the 25th Bombay Native Infantry [a] Light Infantry Regiment

Appendix C

ADDITIONS AND CORRECTIONS TO THE CHECK LIST OF MILL'S INDIAN DESPATCHES IN VOLUME XXX

ONE OPENING of MSS Eur B405 in the India Office Library and Records, the list Mill kept of his Indian Despatches, was unfortunately not recorded in Appendix A of *Writings on India*, Volume XXX of the *Collected Works*. The missing six entries, which fall between those there listed as Nos. 925 and 926, are here given numbers 925/1 to 925/6.

925/1   16 Apr., 1834. PC 1236, Dr 207, D 7: E/4/1057, pp. 793–836; L/P&S/6/289, pp. [231]–[312].
925/2   16 Apr., 1834; affairs of Kathiawar. PC 1215, Dr 176, D 5: E/4/1057, pp. 739–78; L/P&S/6/288, pp. 333–[388].
925/3   2 July, 1834; affairs of the Gaikwar. PC 1309, Dr 360, D 9: E/4/1058, pp. 9–19; L/P&S/6/290, pp. 425–[452].
925/4   26 Sept., 1834; Southern Maratha states and jagirdars. PC 1329, Dr 473, D 11: E/4/1058, pp. 295–355; L/P&S/6/291, pp. 5–[158].
925/5   20 Aug., 1834; Persian Gulf. PC 1339, Dr 435, D 10: E/4/1058, pp. 199–222; L/P&S/6/290, pp. 793–[836].
925/6   5 Nov., 1834. PC 1353, Dr 524, D 12: E/4/1058, pp. 479–537; L/P&S/6/391, pp. 187–[298].

Two corrigenda are also necessary:

722X   For D 16 of 4 July, 1855, substitute D 26 of 10 Oct., 1855.
920X   Affairs of Kathiawar. See full entry at new **925/2** above.

Appendix D

LIST OF LETTERS TO MILL

THIS ALPHABETICAL LIST of those whose letters to Mill are extant gives birth and death dates when known, followed by the dates and the location of the letters in manuscript and printed sources. When all its elements are doubtful, a date is enclosed in square brackets and preceded by a question mark. If only one element is conjectural, the question mark follows that element. If a question mark stands alone, it indicates that no information is available. When non-institutional locations are given, we have used the latest information available, but the phrase "at one time" should be understood. The following abbreviations are used:

A	Palais du Roure, Avignon; summarized in *MNL*, XV (Summer 1980)
BL	British Library
H	Harvard University
Hayek	F.A. Hayek, *John Stuart Mill and Harriet Taylor: Their Friendship and Subsequent Marriage* (London: Routledge and Kegan Paul, 1951)
JH	Johns Hopkins University
MNL	*Mill News Letter*
MT	Mill-Taylor Collection, British Library of Political and Economic Science
NLS	National Library of Scotland
TT	*The Times*
UCL	University College London
Y	Yale University

Acland, Thomas Dyke (1809–98) / 25 Nov., 1868 / JH
Adams, W.O. / 2 Nov., 1865 / JH
Adcroft, George / 10 June, 1870 / JH
Adderley, Charles Bowyer (1814–1905) / 26 Aug., [1853] / MT
Allen, Grant (1848–99) / 4 Sept., 1872 / JH
Allen, John (1810–86) / 22 May, 1867 / JH
   28 May, 1867 / JH

Amalgamated Society of Railway Servants. *See* Shrives
Amberley. *See* Russell
American and Continental Literary Agency / 15 May, 1871 (enclosed with Trübner's of 19 May, 1871) / Y
American Social Science Association. *See* Villard
Amnesty Committee. *See* Sherman
Anon. (an American supporter of women's suffrage) / ? / Y

Appleton & Co. / 28 Mar., 1873 / MT
Argyll. *See* George Campbell
Arlès-Dufour, François Barthélemy
(1797–1872) / 26 Sept., 1870 / JH
    15 Nov., 1870 / JH
Arnold, Edwin (1832–1904) / 8 May,
1872 / Y
Arvers (?), Félix / 18 Feb., 1870 / MT
Ashburton. *See* Baring
Ashworth, Lilias S. (National Society for
Women's Suffrage, Bristol & West
of England Branch) / 27 Jan., 1873 / MT
Aspland, Lindsey Middleton (1843–91) /
19 Feb., 1868 / JH
Austin, John (1790–1859) / 27 June, 1842 /
MT
    25 and 26 Dec., 1844 / Y
Austin, Sarah (1793–1867) / 10 June,
1836 / MT
    3 Mar., 1837 / MT
    7 Nov., [1839?] / MT
Babbage, Charles (1792–1871) / 27 June,
1864 / BL
Baer, Constantino / 12 May, 1856 / JH
    2 Jan., 1872 / Y
    5 June, 1872 / JH
    26 Sept., 1872 / JH
Bailey, Samuel (1791–1870) / 14 Apr.,
1862 / JH
    27 Mar., 1863 / JH
Bain, Alexander (1818–1903) / 14 Mar.,
1859 / NLS
    18 Jan., 1863 / JH
    14 May, 1864 / JH
    27 Oct., 1867 / JH
    30 Nov., 1867 / JH
    28 May, 1869 / JH
    10 July, 1869 / Y
    19 July, 1870 / JH
    16 Aug., 1870 / JH
Balard, Antoine Jérôme (1802–76) / all
MT; and in *MNL*, XXII (Summer 1987)
    27 June, 1822
    July 1824
    4 Apr., 1827
    19 Jan., 1831
Baring, William Bingham (Lord Ashburton) (1774–1848) / 26 May, 1851 /
Y
Barnard, James Munson (1819–1904) / 8
Aug., 1869 / Y
    3 Oct., 1869 / Y
Barnes, A.S., & Co. / 29 Apr., 1873 / MT
Barrett, Thomas Squire (b. 1842) / 8 Feb.,
1872 / JH
    7 Mar., 1872 / JH
    11 Apr., 1872 / JH
    14 May, 1872 / JH
Barry, M. Maltman (1842–1909) / 18
May, 1870 / A
    (Political Refugee Society) / 20 Apr.,
1872 / MT
Barry, William / 27 June, 1872 / MT
Barzelotti, Giacomo / Mar. 1872 / MT
Bates, Frederick / 6 Nov., 1868 / MT; *TT*,
11 Nov., 1868, 5
Beal, James (1829–91) / 4 Mar., 1865 / JH
    12 Apr., 1865 / JH
    9 Dec., 1868 / Y
    2 Feb., 1869 / JH
Beales, Edmund (1803–81) / 2 Mar., 1867
/ JH
Beaumont, Gustave de (1802–66) / 21
Aug., 1835 / MT
Beggs, Thomas (1808–96) / 21 Sept.,
1868 / JH
    19 Nov., 1868 / JH
Benedetti (?) / 16 Oct., 1870 / MT
Bentham, George (1800–84) / 16 June,
1832 / MT
Bentham, Jeremy (1748–1832) / 5 Apr.,
1827 / Y
    18 Apr., 1827 / Y
    24 Apr., 1827 / Y
    24 Apr., 1827 / Y
Bentley, W. / 7 Aug., 1868 / MT
Bernard, Theodore (?) / 30 Oct., 1871 / MT
Bernays, Leopold John (1820–82) / 3 Jan.,
1868 / Y
    21 Jan., 1868 / Y
Bickley, Joseph / 4 Feb., 1873 / MT
Bird, J.S. / 29 Oct., 1868 / MT
Bisset, Andrew (1803–99) / 31 Mar., 1873
/ MT
Black, Euphemia / 29 June, 1867 / MT
Blackwell, Anna (ca. 1817–1900) / 12
Aug., 1851 / JH

Blanc, Jean Joseph Louis (1811–82) / 3 July, 1858 / JH
    1 July, 1864 / Y
    28 Mar., 1865 / Y
Bon Pasteur Monastery. *See* Marie de St. Elie
Booker, Frederick / 30 Oct., 1870 / JH
    18 Nov., 1870 / JH
Bourne, Henry Richard Fox (1837–1909) / 7 Jan., 1872 / MT
    5 May, 1873 / MT
Bouverie, Edward Pleydell (1818–89) / 26 Sept., 1868 / JH; *TT*, 16 Oct., 1868, 10
    13 Oct., 1868 / JH; *TT*, 16 Oct., 1868, 10
    23 Oct., 1868 / *TT*, 24 Oct., 1868, 3
Brace, Charles Loring (1826–90) / 30 June, ? / MT
    11 Dec., 1870 / JH
    4 July, 1871 / JH
Bradford, Gamaliel (1831–1911) / 5 Dec., 1865 / Samuel Jones Loyd, *The Correspondence of Lord Overstone*, ed. D.P. O'Brien, 3 vols. (Cambridge: Cambridge University Press, 1971)
Bradlaugh, Charles (1833–91) / 19 Nov., 1868 / JH
Brandes, Georg Morris Cohen (1842–1927) / 9 Jan., 1872 / JH; *Correspondance de Georg Brandes*, ed. Paul Kruger, 2 vols. (Copenhagen: Rosehilde and Bagger, 1952)
Brandreth, Henry Samuel (1841–1919) / 2 Feb., 1867 / JH
Brentano, Franz Clemens (1838–1917) / 2 Feb., 1871 / H
    before 4 Mar., 1872 / Prof. R.M. Chisholm, Brown University
    29 Nov., 1872 / H
    19 Jan., 1873 / H
    3 May, 1873 / MT
Brewer, William (d. 1881) / 8 July, 1865 / MT
Bridges, John Henry (1832–1906) / 10 Nov., 1867 / JH
Broadhurst, Henry (1840–1911) (Labour Representation League) / 17 Mar., 1873 / MT
    28 Mar., 1873 / MT
Broadwood, John, & Sons / 21 Feb., 1872 / MT
    13 Mar., 1872 / MT
Browning, Oscar (1837–1923) / 14 Oct., 1867 / JH
Brunialti, A. / 6 Aug., 1871 / MT
    30 Aug., 1871 / MT
Bryce, James (1838–1922) / 20 Jan., [1871] / MT
Buckle, John / 31 Dec., 1868 / MT
    9 Jan., 1869 / MT
Buller, Charles (1806–48) / 13 Oct., 1838 / Dominion of Canada, *Report of the Public Archives for the Year 1928* (Ottawa, 1929), App. F, 74–7
    19 Oct., 1838 / MT
Buller, John (1771–1849) / 17 ?, ? / MT
Bundey, William H. / 21 May, 1872 / MT
Bureau de Bienfaisance d'Avignon / 23 May, 1859 / MT
Burnett, E.L. / 26 July, 1870 / MT
Burns, J. Dawson (1828–1909) / 6 Nov., 1868 / *TT*, 10 Nov., 1868, 4; *Falmouth and Penryn Weekly Times*, 14 Nov., 1868
Burton, Samuel Warren / 29 Oct., 1868 / *Morning Star*, 29 Oct., 1868, 2
Cairnes, John Elliott (1823–75) / MS copies in MT unless otherwise noted; some quoted in Mill's *Principles of Political Economy* [*PPE*], *CW*, III
    8 Apr., 1859
    14 May, 1861
    1 Aug., 1861
    25 Aug., 1861
    21 Nov., 1861
    4 Mar., 1862
    8 July, 1862
    8 Dec., 1862
    18 Dec., 1862
    23 Dec., 1862
    4 Feb., 1863
    10 Sept., 1863
    9 Dec., 1863
    21 Dec., 1863
    13 Oct., 1864 / *PPE*
    29 Nov., 1864 / *PPE*
    6 Dec., 1864 / *PPE*
    23 Dec., 1864 / *PPE*
    25 Dec., 1864 / *PPE*

List of Letters to Mill

9 Jan., 1865 / *PPE*
24 Jan., 1865 / *PPE*
5 Feb., 1865 / *PPE*
1 Mar., 1865 / *PPE*
13 Mar., 1865 / *PPE*
17 Mar., 1865
20 Mar., 1865
27 Mar., 1865 / *PPE*
2 June, 1865 / *PPE*
20 Aug., 1865
28 Aug., 1865
9 Jan., 1866
25 Jan., 1866
6 Feb., 1866
10 Feb., 1866
14 Feb., 1866 (2)
29 Mar., 1866
28 June, 1866
7 July, 1866
12 July, 1866
18 July, 1866
20 May, 1867
10 June, 1867
7 July, 1867
26 July, 1867 / JH
29 July, 1867 / Y
2 Aug., 1867
11 Aug., 1867
7 Sept., 1867
15 Feb., 1868
21 May, 1868 / JH
9 Nov., 1868
12 Dec., 1868
13 Apr., 1869
23 May, 1869
9 Nov., 1869 / JH
26 Nov., 1869 / JH
21 Dec., 1869
13 Jan., 1870
28 Feb., 1870
17 Apr., 1870
10 Sept., 1870
22 Sept., 1870
25 Aug., 1871
23 Oct., 1871
24 Dec., 1871
9 Apr., 1872
2 May, 1872 / JH
6 May, 1872
16 June, 1872

20 Dec., 1872
Callerall, P. / 2 Oct., 1868 / JH
Campbell, Alexander D. / 14 Feb., 1870 / JH
   3 Mar., 1870 / Y
Campbell, George Douglas (Duke of Argyll) (1823–1900) / 2 Feb., 1864 / Y
Campbell, John (1779–1861) / 31 Mar., 1866 / JH
   9 Apr., 1866 / JH
Candlish, John (1815–74) / 27 Nov., 1868 / JH
Capel, George / 3 Nov., 1866 / MT
   1 June, 1868 / MT
   12 June, 1868 / MT
Capper, Samuel James / 11 Apr., 1873 / MT
Carlyle, Thomas (1795–1881) / MSS in NLS unless otherwise noted; also in *Collected Letters of Thomas and Jane Welsh Carlyle*, ed. C.R. Sanders, *et al.* (Durham, N.C.: Duke University Press, 1970–), from which the dates are taken
   [5 Oct., 1831]
   [? Oct., 1831] / King's College, Cambridge
   [12 Mar., 1832]
   18 May, 1832
   16 June, 1832
   28 Aug., 1832
   16 Oct., 1832
   19 Nov., 1832
   12 Jan., 1833
   22 Feb., 1833
   21 Mar., 1833
   18 Apr., 1833
   1 May, 1833
   13 June, 1833
   18 July, 1833
   10 Sept., 1833
   24 Sept., 1833
   28 Oct., 1833
   17 Dec., 1833
   24 Dec., 1833
   20 Jan., 1834
   22 Feb., 1834
   18 Apr., 1834
   [18 Aug., 1834]

[5 Sept., 1834]
[ca. 10 Jan., 1835]
[2 Feb., 1835]
[12 Feb., 1835]
[7 Mar., 1835]
[9 Mar., 1835]
[13 Mar., 1835]
17 Mar., [1835]
[27 Mar., 1835]
[20 Apr., 1835]
[3 May, 1835]
[27 May, 1835]
[1 June, 1835]
[10 Sept., 1835]
[ca. late Sept. 1835] / U. of California, Santa Cruz
30 Oct., 1835
[25 Feb., 1836]
[29 Feb., 1836]
2 Mar., 1836
[28 Mar., 1836] / MT
2 May, 1836
[?late May 1836]
[2 June, 1836]
[6 June, 1836]
[25 June, 1836] / Hornel Collection, Kirkcudbright, Scotland
[1 July, 1836]
[12 July, 1836]
[22 July, 1836]
[28 July, 1836]
9 Oct., 1836
[25 Nov., 1836]
[8 Dec., 1836]
[9 Jan., 1837]
[24 Jan., 1837]
[28 Jan., 1837]
[22 Feb., 1837]
[11 Mar., 1837]
[Apr., 1837]
[?10 Apr., 1837]
[27 Apr., 1837]
[19 or 26 May, 1837]
18 July, 1837
10 Aug., 1837
30 Oct., 1837
[10 Nov., 1837]
[8 Dec., 1837]
[late Jan./early Mar. 1838]
[?12 Mar., 1838]

[4 Apr., 1838]
[?11 Apr., 1838]
23 Mar., 1839
[30 Sept., 1839]
[22 Oct., 1839]
6 Dec., 1839
[7 Oct., 1840]
24 Feb., 1841
21 Mar., 1841
11 Apr., 1842
1 Feb., 1843
9 Nov., 1843
[4 July, 1845]
30 Apr., 1852
28 June, 1858
13 Mar., 1866
16 Mar., 1869
Carpenter, Mary (1807–77) / 11 Aug., 1867 / MT
  27 Jan., 1868 / MT
  5 Jan., 1871 / JH
Carpenter, William B. (1813–85) / 17 Jan., 1872 / JH
  31 Jan., 1872 / JH
Cavaignac, Louis Eléonore Godefroi (1801–45) / 3 Nov., 1837 / JH
Cazelles, Emile Honoré (1801–1907) / 3 June, 1869 / JH
  28 May, 1869 / JH
  17 Oct., 1869 / Y
Cecil, Robert Arthur Talbot Gascoyne (Lord Salisbury) (1830–1903), / 14 June, 1869 / Y
Chadwick, Edwin (1800–90) / JH unless otherwise noted
  29 Apr., 1865
  25 May, 1865
  28 Oct., 1867
  15 Aug., 1868
  19 Aug., 1868
  30 Sept., 1868
  4 Oct., 1868
  22 Apr., 1869 (2)
  26 Dec., 1870
  13 Jan., 1871
  26 Apr., 1873 / MT
Chadwick, Marion (1844–1928) / 25 Dec., 1866 / JH
Chadwick, Rachel / 18 Oct., 1868 / JH
  30 Nov., 1868 / JH

Chapé, August Joanny / 10 Oct., 1867 / Y
  18 Jan., 1868 / JH
Chapman, John (1822–94) / 1 Aug., 1861 / Y
  19 Nov., 1868 / Y
  9 May, 1873 / MT
Chelsea Working Men's Parliamentary Electoral Association. *See* Madge
Chément, L. de / 3 Mar., 1873 / MT
Chesney, George (1836–95) / 3 Aug., 1870 / MT
Christie, William Dougal (1816–94) / all Y
  2 Apr., 1868
  7 Apr., 1868
  17 Apr., 1868
  25 Apr., 1868
  6 May, 1868
  9 May, 1868
Clarke, William Branwhite (1798–1878) / 14 Feb., [1872/3] / MT
Clémenceau, Georges (1841–1929) / 27 Apr., 1867 / JH
Cobbe, Frances Power (1822–1904) / 4 June, 1869 / JH
Cole, Henry (1808–82) / both typescripts Mill archive, Toronto
  [6 Mar., 1840]
  15 Nov., 1843
Collier, Robert (1817–86) / 26 Jan., 1870 / JH
  21 Feb., 1870 / JH
Colman, Charles Frederick / 17 June, 1854 / MT
  12 July, 1854 / MT
Colman, Mary Elizabeth (née Mill) (1822–1913) / all MT
  18 July, 1851
  3 Apr., [1854]
  10 Apr., 1854
  [15 Feb., 1858]
  [after 16 Feb., 1858]
  15 Nov., 1858
  [Dec.] 1858
  24 Dec., [1858]
  [17? Jan.,] 1859
  [1873?]
  Feb. 1873
  Apr. 1873 (2)
Colman, Stuart / 14 Feb., 1873 / MT

Commons Preservation Society. *See* Arthur Lankester
Comte, Auguste (1798–1857) / all Maison d'Auguste Comte, Paris, and in *Auguste Comte: Correspondance*, ed. Barrêdo Carneiro and Arnaud (Paris: E.H.E.S.S., 1973–)
  20 Nov., 1841
  17 Jan., 1842
  4 Mar., 1842
  5 Apr., 1842
  29 May, 1842
  19 June, 1842
  22 July, 1842
  24 Aug., 1842
  30 Sept., 1842
  5 Nov., 1842
  30 Dec., 1842
  27 Feb., 1843
  25 Mar., 1843
  16 May, 1843
  28 May, 1843
  29 June, 1843
  16 July, 1843
  28 Aug., 1843
  5 Oct., 1843
  22 Oct., 1843
  14 Nov., 1843
  23 Dec., 1843
  6 Feb., 1844
  1 May, 1844
  22 July, 1844
  15 Aug., 1844
  23 Aug., 1844
  28 Aug., 1844
  21 Oct., 1844
  25 Dec., 1844
  10 Jan., 1845
  28 Feb., 1845
  15 May, 1845
  27 June, 1845
  30 June, 1845
  14 July, 1845 (2)
  8 Aug., 1845
  24 Sept., 1845
  18 Dec., 1845
  21 Jan., 1846
  6 May, 1846
  10 Aug., 1846
  2 Sept., 1846

Appendix D

    3 Sept., 1846
Congreve, Richard (1818–99) / 3 Aug., 1865 / JH
Conway, Moncure Daniel (1832–1907) / 10 Mar., ? / MT
Courcelle-Seneuil, Jean Gustave (1813–92) / 26 Oct., 1853 / MT
Courtney, Leonard Henry (1832–1918) / first two in Courtney Collection, British Library of Political and Economic Science
    17 Sept., 1861
    20 Sept., 1861
    18 Nov., 1870 / JH
Cowper, Thomas Alexander (1819–1902) / all JH
    30 May, 1870
    1 June, 1870
    19 June, 1870
    30 June, 1870
    18 Apr., 1872
Davies, Emily (1830–1921) / 26 Apr., 1872 / JH
    17 Mar., 1873 / MT
De Morgan, Augustus (1806–71) / some in Sophia De Morgan, *Memoir of Augustus De Morgan* (London: Longmans, Green, 1882) [DeM]
    5 Feb., 1864 / DeM
    10 Oct., 1864 / Y; DeM
    23 Oct., 1864 / Y
    16 Nov., 1864 / UCL
    26 Mar., 1865 / Y; DeM
    27 Apr., 1865 / JH; DeM
    3 Aug., 1865 / UCL
    28 Sept., 1865 / UCL
    20 Feb., 1868 / DeM
    3 Sept., 1868 / DeM
Delesau, Raffaele / 28 Oct., 1868 / MT
Deml, Peter / 15 Apr., 1868 / JH
Derby. *See* Edward Stanley
Dervillé & Cie / all MT
    25 Aug., 1859
    25 Oct., 1859
    12 Nov., 1859
    24 Nov., 1859
    27 Nov., 1859
    1 Dec., 1859
    22 Dec., 1859
Dilke, Charles Wentworth (1843–1911) / JH unless otherwise noted

    13 Feb., 1869
    25 Feb., 1870 / Y
    7 May, 1870
    23 May, 1870
    30 May, 1870
    4 June, 1870
    26 Sept., 1870
    16 Jan., 1871 / Y
    3 Aug., 1872
    18 Mar., 1873 / Y
Donovan, C. / [1866] / Y
Duff. *See* Grant Duff
Duffy, Charles Gavan (1816–1903) / ca. 1866–68 / Y
    25 Aug., 1866 / JH
Duignan, William Henry (d. 1914) / 31 Mar., 1873 / MT
Eastwick, Edward Backhouse (1814–83) / Apr. 1873 / MT
Edge, Frederick Milnes / 15 Feb., 1866 / JH
Edwards, James / before 5 Nov., 1868 / JH
Eglise Réformée d'Avignon / 15 May, 1859 / MT
Eichthal, Gustave d' (1804–86) / JH except first two, which are in *John Stuart Mill: Correspondance inédite avec Gustave d'Eichthal, 1828–1842, 1864–1871*, ed. Eugène d'Eichthal (Paris: Alcan, 1898)
    after 7 Nov., 1829
    3 Feb., 1830
    26 June, 1863
    2 May, 1870
    17 May, 1870
    8 Aug., 1870
    16 May, 1871
Elkington & Co. / 15 June, 1871 / MT
    20 June, 1871 / MT
Emancipation Society (London) / 18 Apr., 1864 / A
Emerson, Ralph Waldo (1803–82) / 6 May, 1865 / *More Books*, XV (1940), 436–7
Enderby, Charles / 29 July, 1872 / MT
Enquête sur la circulation monétaire et fiduciaire / 21 Aug., 1869 / MT
Epping Forest Fund. *See* William A. Smith
Era / 14 Sept., 1851 / MT
"Erinna" / 31 July, 1851 / JH

Eurbiglio, S. (?) / 23 Dec., 1869 / MT
Fabre, Jean Henri (1823–1915) / 29 Apr., 1873 / MT
Fawcett, Henry (1833–84) / 23 Dec., 1859 / Leslie Stephen, *Life of Fawcett* (London: Smith, Elder, 1885), 102 n.d. fragment / *ibid.*, 102–3
    ? / Y
    8 Nov., 1865 / JH
    17 July, 1867 / JH
    21 Mar., 1869 / JH
    23 July, 1870 / JH
Fitch, Joshua Girling (1824–1903) / 10 Apr., 1869 / JH
Fletcher, J.H. / 4 Nov., 1868 / JH
Fonblanque, Anthony (1793–1872) / ? / Sir Fredrick Chapman
Fowle, Thomas Welbank (1835–1903) /
    7 Feb., 1867 / JH
    12 Feb., 1867 / JH
Francis, A.M. / 14 Feb., 1869 / JH
Frank, Malvina / 17 July, 1872 / MT
Franks, Henry / 14 July, 1865 / JH
Freeman, Edward Augustus (1823–92) / 26 Dec., 1870 / JH
Friend, Charles J. (b. 1836) / 26 Oct., 1868 / JH
Froude, James Anthony (1818–94) / 15 June, [1868] / JH
Furnivall, Frederick James (1825–1910) /
    13 Nov., [1850] / MT
    23 Nov., [1850] / MT
Gaskell, Elizabeth Cleghorn (1810–65) / all Rutgers University, and in *The Letters of Mrs. Gaskell*, ed. A. Pollard and J.A.V. Chapple (Manchester: Manchester University Press, 1966)
    14 July, 1859
    11 Aug., 1859
George, Henry (1839–97) / 22 Aug., 1869 / MT
    16 July, 1870 / JH
Giles, Joseph (1832–1930) / 10 May, 1870 / JH
    18 May, 1871 / JH
Gill, George (b. ca. 1820) / UCL unless otherwise noted
    20 Oct., 1868
    5 Nov., 1868
    6 Nov., 1868
    9 Nov., 1868
    10 Nov., 1868
    [Nov.] 1868 (2)
    28 Sept., 1871 / A
    27 Oct., 1871 / A
Gilpin, Charles (1815–74) / 7 Sept., 1868 / JH
Gladstone, William Ewart (1809–98) /
    8 Jan., 1864 / BL
    [1865] / UCL
Godkin, Edwin L. (1831–1902) / 1 Apr., 1865 / JH
Godwin, Parke (1816–1904) / 8 Apr., 1865 / JH
    27 June, 1865 / JH
    26 Dec., 1868 / Y
Gomperz, Theodor (1832–1912) /
    20 July, 1854 / MT
    10 Nov., 1858 / JH
    1 Aug., 1861 / JH
    ca. 9 Jan., 1868 / MT
    26 Mar., 1868 / JH
    11 June, 1868 / JH
Gore, George (1826–1908) / 3 Apr., 1873 / MT
Graham, William (1817–85) / 2 Oct., ? / Y
Grant, Horace (1800–59) / 27 July, 1851 / Y
    5 Dec., 1858 / Y
Grant Duff, Mountstuart Elphinstone (1829–1906) / 12 Mar., 1859 / JH
Greene, Arthur W. / 11 Dec., 1861 / MT
    21 Dec., 1861 / MT
    1 Jan., 1862 / MT
Greening, Edward Owen (d. 1911) / 14 Aug., 1865 / A
Gregson, Robert S. / 15 Feb., 1860 / JH
    7 Apr., 1865 / MT
    29 June, 1872 / MT
Grey, Henry George (Earl) (1802–94) / 6 May, 1864 / Y
    23 May, 1864 / JH
    15 May, 1866 / Y
Grosser, Julius / 9 Jan., 1868 / MT
Grosvenor, Chates & Co. / 29 Dec., 1868 / MT
Grote, George (1794–1871) / some excerpts in Harriet Grote, *The Personal Life of George Grote* (London: Murray, 1873) [G]
    Jan. 1845 / G

[3 Oct., 1855] / JH
31 Mar., 1856 / MT
6 Apr., 1856 / MT
Oct. 1857 / G
Jan. 1862 / G
Dec. 1862 / G
June 1865 / G
20 Nov., 1865 / Y; G
6 Nov., 1866 / JH
30 Nov., 1866 / JH
13 Dec., 1866 / G
25 Mar., 1867 / JH
11 Dec., 1868 / G
Grote, Harriet (1792–1878) / 5 Oct., 1867 / MT
Guilbert, Aristide Mathieu (1804–63) / 23 June, 1834 / MT
Gurney, Henry Cecil (1819?–79) / 13 Nov., 1858 / Y
1 Dec., 1858 / Y
Hales, John (b. 1839) / 27 May, 1871 / MT
Halsted, Mrs. M.C. / 29 Dec., 1870 / JH
Hancock, Edward / 4 Mar., 1870 / MT
8 Feb., 1872 / MT
Hardy, Arthur (1817–1909) / 14 Feb., 1859 / Y
20 Jan., 1871 / MT
Hardy de Beaulieu, Charles Le (1816–71) / 16 May, 1870 / JH
6 June, 1870 / JH
Hare, Thomas (1806–91) / 18 Feb., 1860 / MT
Harrison, Robert (1820–97) / 8 Dec., 1864 / JH
Haslam, Thomas Joseph (1825–1917) / 8 Apr., 1873 / MT
Hawtrey, Stephen Thomas (1808–86) / 7 July, 1867 / JH
Hayes, Charles / 12 Feb., 1868 / JH
Hayward, John / 12 Nov., 1868 / JH
4 Dec., 1868 / JH
19 Dec., 1868 / JH
Hazard, Rowland Gibson (1801–88) / 6 Feb., 1865 / Wellesley College, Wellesley, Mass. [W]
[7 Feb., 1865] / W
1 July, 1865 / Rhode Island Historical Society [RIHS]
22 Oct., 1866 / R.G. Hazard, *Two Letters on Causation . . . Addressed to John Stuart Mill* (London: Longmans, *et al.*, 1869) [Hazard]
4 Nov., 1866 / W
25 Nov., 1866 / RIHS
after 25 Nov., 1866 / Hazard
7 Mar., 1873 / MT
Helps, Arthur (1813–75) / 8 Feb., 1870 / Y
Hennessy, Patrick / 25 Aug., 1870 / MT
Herbert, Auberon (1838–1906) / 22 May, 1871 / Y
26 Dec., 1871 / JH; S. Hutchinson Harris, *Auberon Herbert: Crusader for Liberty* (London: Williams and Norgate, 1943)
29 May, [1872?] / MT
Herford, Edward (1815–96) / 19 Oct., 1854 / MT
27 Oct., 1854 / MT
4 Nov., 1854 / MT
Herschel, John Frederick William (1792–1871) / Royal Society of London, unless otherwise noted
10 July, 1845
13 July, 1845 / Y
16 July, 1845
18 July, 1845
22 Dec., 1845
2 Apr., 1846
3 Apr., 1846
after 8 Apr., 1846
Hertz, Fanny / 19 May, 1872 / MT
Hickson, Wilhelmina / 23 Mar., 1870 / JH
29 Mar., 1870 / JH
Hickson, William Edward (1803–70) / 29 Apr., 1865 / JH
Hill, Caroline Southwood / ? / MT
Hobart, Vere Henry (Lord) (1818–75) / 12 Aug., 1853 / Y
Holden, George Kenyon (1806–79) / Feb. 1868 / JH
9 Aug., 1871 / MT
Holyoake, George Jacob (1817–1906) / MT unless otherwise noted
26 Mar., 1856
2 Apr., 1856
5 Apr., 1856
26 Sept., 1856
26 Dec., 1862 / in part Cooperative

Union, Holyoake House, Manchester
  11 Apr., 1864
  4 Aug., 1864
  21 Apr., 1865
  20 May, 1865
  1 Aug., 1869
  25 Mar., 1871
  12 Apr., 1871
  15 May, 1871
  4 Feb., 1872
  27 Mar., 1873
Hooker, Isabella Beecher (1822–1907) / 10 Aug., 1869 / Y; I.B. Hooker, *Womanhood: Its Sanctities and Fidelities* (Boston: Lee and Shepherd, 1874)
Hoskins, James T. / 20 Sept., 1871 / A
Howe, Julia Ward (1819–1910) / 7 May, 1873 / MT
Howell, George (1833–1910) / 19 Dec., 1868 / JH
Hoyle, William (1831–86) / 25 Feb., 1871 / MT
Huxley, Thomas Henry (1825–95) / all JH
  1 Aug., 1865
  14 Aug., 1865
  20 Aug., 1865
  23 Mar., 1866
  7 Mar., 1869
  25 Mar., 1869
International Working Men's Association. *See* Thomas Smith
Institut Impérial de France. *See* Mignet
Ireland, William (1832–1909) / 19 June, 1867 / JH
Irvine, Alexander (1793–1873) / 4 Sept., [1858] / MT
  29 Mar., 1873 / Y
James, Stanley / 19 June, 1872 / MT
Jevons, William Stanley (1835–82) /
  8 May, 1865 / JH; *MNL*, XVIII (Summer 1983)
    20 Apr., 1866 / University of Manchester
Jones, Edward (1823–1908) / 6 Jan., 1869 / JH

Jones, Henry / 8 June, 1868 / JH
Jones, Thomas / 24 Mar., 1865 / JH
Kelsall, Thomas F. (1799–1872) /
  20 Mar., 1871 / JH
Kilburn, Nicholas (1843–1923) / 11 Mar., 1868 / JH
Kilgour, Henry / 10 Aug., 1870 / JH
  18 Aug., 1870 / JH
Kingsley, Charles (1819–75) / 3 June, 1869 / Wilfrid Ward, *William George Ward and the Catholic Revival* (London: Macmillan, 1893) [Ward]
  17 June, 1869 / Ward
  1870 / *Charles Kingsley: His Letters and Memories of His Life*, ed. Frances Eliza Kingsley, 2 vols. (London: King, 1877)
Kinnear, John Boyd (1828–1920) / 7 July, 1865 /JH
  11 Sept., 1865 / JH
  1 June, 1870 / JH
  4 Aug., 1870 / JH
Kyllmann, Max (1832–67) / 22 Apr., 1865 / JH
Labour Representation League. *See* Broadhurst
Ladé (?), E.A. / 11 Nov., 1872 / MT
Lalande, Armande (1820–94) / 16 Apr., 1868 /JH
  15 Apr., 1869 / JH
Lalor, John (1814–56) / 18 June, 1852 / MT
  30 June, 1852 / MT
  5 July, 1852 / MT
Lambert, Elizabeth B. / 20 Nov., 1868 / JH
Land Tenure Reform Association. *See* Reid
Lankester, Arthur (Commons Preservation Society) / 19 Jan., 1866 / JH
Lankester, Edwin Ray (1847–1929) / 8 Jan., 1873 / JH
Lattimer, W. / 19 Mar., 1873 / MT
Lauda, Luigi / 6 Mar., ? / MT
Laurens d'Oisibay, baron et baronne / 31 Oct., 1871 / MT

Laurie, Louis K. / 26 June, 1871 / MT
Laveleye, Emile Louis Victor de (1822–92) / 25 July, 1869 /MT
   7 Aug., 1869 / MT
   27 Nov., 1870 / MT
   5 Nov., 1872 / MT and in E.L.V. de Laveleye, *De la propriété et de ses formes primitives* (Paris: Baillière, 1874)
Lavington, Frederick / 6 Nov., 1872 / MT
Lazzaroni, P. / 17 Nov., 1871 / MT
Leaver, Henry / 18 Mar., 1867 / JH
Leslie, Thomas Edward Cliffe (1826–82) / 15 Mar., ? / MT
   17 Jan., 1869 / JH
   2 May, 1869 / JH
   3 May, 1869 / JH
   31 Aug., 1869 / JH
   20 Sept., 1869 /JH
   4 Mar., 1870 / MT
   22 Jan., 1871 / JH
   7 Feb., 1871 / JH
   23 Mar., 1871 / H
   1 Nov., 1871 / JH
   3 Jan., 1872 / JH
Levey, George / 11 Aug., 1869 / MT
   16 Aug., 1869 / MT
Lewald-Stahr, Fanny (1811–89) /
   10 Nov., 1869 / in her *Für und wider die Frauen* (Berlin: Janke, 1870)
Lewis, Frankland / 21 Oct., ca. 1837–40 / MT
Lewis, George Cornewall (1806–63) / 14 Mar., 1859 / JH
Ley, William / 27 Nov., 1854 / Y
   11 May, 1855 / Y
Littré, Emile (1801–81) / 26 Nov., 1848 / JH
   5 May, 1865 / JH
Littrow, Auguste von (1819–90) / 7 July, 1871 / A
   after 9 Aug., 1871 / A
Liverpool Philomathic Society. *See* Rathbone
Logan, Edward / 23 Jan., 1869 / JH

Longman, William (1813–77) / MT unless otherwise noted
   22 Feb., 1864
   26 Feb., 1864
   4 Nov., 1864
   10 Feb., 1865
   15 Feb., 1865
   28 Apr., 1865
   3 May, 1865
   14 Mar., 1866
   28 Mar., 1866
   20 Apr., 1866
   25 Apr., 1866
   4 Mar., 1867 / Y
   1 June, 1867 / Y
   4 June, 1867 / Y
   12 Dec., 1867
   3 Jan., 1868
   16 Mar., 1871
   20 Mar., 1871
   18 Apr., 1871
   27 Apr., 1871
   15 May, 1871
   19 May, 1871
   26 June, 1871
Longmans, Green & Co. / 24 Mar., 1871 / MT
   23 May, 1872 / MT
   19 Nov., 1872 / MT
Lowe, Louisa / 25 Jan., 1873 / MT
Lyttleton, William Henry (1820–84) / 8 July, 1865 / JH
MacCarthy, John George (1829–92) / 19 Feb., 1870 / MT
MacCormac, Henry (1800–86) / 29 Nov., 1865 / JH
Macdonell, John / 7 Oct., 1871 / MT
McDowell, J.P. *See* Sherman
McLaren, Charles Benjamin Bright (1850–1934) / 23 Apr., 1871 / MT
   10 May, 1871 / MT
McLaren, Duncan (1800–86) / 29 Dec., 1868 / Y
   24 Apr., 1871 / MT
McLaren, Priscilla (1814–1906) (National

Society for Women's Suffrage [Edinburgh Branch]) / 1 Dec., 1868 / JH; *TT*, 23 Dec., 1868, 9
Madge, R.C. (Chelsea Working Men's Parliamentary Electoral Association) / 27 Nov., 1868 / JH
Maine, Henry James Sumner (1822–88) / 1 Nov., 1868 / JH
Malleson, William T. / 14 Jan., 1870 / JH
Manning, Charlotte Speir (1803–71) / 18 Oct., 1869 / JH
Mairie d'Avignon / 16 May, 1859 / MT
Marie de St. Elie (Bon Pasteur Monastery) / 28 Nov., 1862 / Y
Marshall, Richard / 4 Nov., 1868 / JH
    10 Nov., 1868 / JH
Martin, Arthur Patchett (1851–1902) / 22 Apr., 1871 / A
Martin, Louis / 4 Jan., 1861 / Y
Martineau, James (1805–1900) / 4 July, 1866 / JH
Mathison & Co. / ? / MT
Matthew, Patrick / 17 June, 1868 / Y
Maurice, Frederick Denison (1805–72) / 2 May, 1865 / JH
Mawby, J. George / 1866 / *Diplomatic Review* [*DR*], 4 July, 1866, 91
    1 July, 1866 / *DR*, 4 July, 1866, 91
    23 Aug., 1866 / *DR*, 5 Sept., 1866, 116
Mayo, August Frederick (1821–69) / ? / MT
Mazzini, Giuseppe (1805–72) / 29 Dec., 1857 / Y
    10 Apr., 1858 / Y
Michelet, Jules (1798–1874) / 7 Apr., 1840 / MT
Mignet, François Auguste Marie (1797–1884) (Institut Impérial de France) / 26 Apr., 1869 / JH
    9 May, 1869 / JH
    5 Dec., 1869 / JH
Mill, Clara Esther (1810–86) / 3 Mar., [1852] / MT; Hayek
    10 Apr., [1854] / MT; Hayek

Mill, George Grote (1825–53) / 27 May, 1850 / MT
Mill, Harriet (née Burrow) (1782?-1854) / 27 Mar., 1854 / MT
    29 Mar., [1854] / MT
    11 Apr., [1854] / MT
Mill, Harriet Isabella (1812–97) / [9 June, 1854] / MT
    10 June, [1854] / MT
    14 Jan., 1873 / MT
Mill, Harriet Taylor (1807–58) / manuscript letters are listed by item number in the MT catalogue; * means quoted or excerpted in Hayek; "pm", postmarked; "wm", watermarked. *See also* John Taylor

    MT, Vol. II: 313, ?; 314, wm 1837; 316, [Summer 1833]; 317, ?; 318, ?; 319, [1837]; 320, ?; 321, [Sept. 1833]; 322, [27–28 July, 1848]; 323, ?; 324, wm 1831; 325, [?June 1844]; 327 and Box III, item 103, [ca. 1844]; 330, [30 June, 1838] (fragment)

    Vol. XXVIII: 233, [?1840 or earlier], "[1845?]" on MS*; 234, wm 1838*; 235, wm 1833*; 236, [12 July, 1858]*; 237, [13 July, 1858]; 238, wm 1837*; 239, ?; 240, [12 Sept., 1857]; 241, 19 June [1849]; 242, ?

    Vol. L: 3, [Winter 1830/31]*; 4, 6 Sept., 1833*; 5, [20 Feb., 1834]*; 6, wm 1835*; 7, wm 1835*; 8 pm 25 July, 1848*; 9, [15 May, 1849]; 10, [16 May, 1849] or [July 1849]; 11, [17 May, 1849]; 12 [21 May, 1849]*; 13, [mid-May? 1849]; 14, [23 May? 1849]; 15, [25 May? 1849]; 16, [28 May? 1849]*; 17, [early June 1849]*; 18 [May or early June? 1849]*; 19, [3 June? 1849]; 20, [4 June? 1849]; 21, [5 June, 1849]; 22, [mid-June 1849]; 23, [22 June? 1849]; 25, pm 30 June, 1849*; 26, [early June 1849]; 27, [5 or 12 July, 1849]*; 28, pm 6 July, 1849*; 29, [7–8 July,

1849]*; 30, pm 9 July, 1849*; 31, pm
10 July, 1849*; 32, [19 July?
1849]*; 33, [mid-July 1849]; 34, 18
July, [1849]*; 35, pm 19 July, 1849;
36, 19 July, [1849]*; 37, 22 July,
[1849]*; 40, 14 & 15 Feb., [1854?]*
  Vol. LIII: 30, ? (fragment)
Mill, Henry (1820–40) / 30 Sept., 1837 /
  MT
Mills, P.L. / 17 Aug., 1871 / A
Mistral, Frédéric Joseph Etienne (1830–
  1914) / 12 Sept., 1869 / JH
Molesworth, William (1810–55) /
  18 Aug., 1844 / JH
  17 Sept., 1845 / JH
  14 May, 1853 / JH
Morley, John (1828–1923) / 21 Sept.,
  1866 / JH
  11 Nov., 1867 / Y
  17 Nov., 1870 / JH
  30 Nov., 1870 / JH
  3 Jan., 1871 / JH
  28 Apr., 1872 / Y
  1 May, 1872 / Y
  6 May, 1872 / Y
  14 May, 1872 / Y
  2 Mar., 1873 / MT
  21 Mar., 1873 / MT
  15 Apr., 1873 / JH
Motley, John Lothrop (1814–77) /
  28 Sept., 1862 / H
Muston, Alexis (1810–88) / 4 Oct., 1870 /
  JH
National Republican Brotherhood /
  27 Mar., 1873 / MT
National Society for Women's Suffrage.
  See Ashworth (Bristol) and McLaren
  (Edinburgh)
New York Liberal Club. *See* Willcox
Nichol, John Pringle (1804–59) / 12 July,
  1868 / UCL
  20 July, 1869 / JH
  26 Dec., 1870 / JH
  7 Jan., 1871 / JH
Nicholson, Robert (Royal Institution) /
  22 Dec., 1868 / JH

Nightingale, Florence (1820–1910) / first
  three Boston University; in BL, in copy
  or draft; in *Hospitals*, X (July 1936),
  and summarized in Sue Goldie, *A Calendar of the Letters of Florence Nightingale*
  (London: Oxford Microform, 1983)
  5 Sept., 1860
  12 Sept., 1860
  28 Sept., 1860
  29 Sept., 1860
  11 Aug., 1867 / BL draft
  30 Jan., 1868 / BL draft not in F.N.'s
    hand
Norton, Charles Eliot (1827–1908) /
  10 Apr., 1868 / JH
  29 Aug., 1868 / JH
  17 Sept., 1868 / JH
  17 June, 1870 / JH
Nunn, M. / 5 Apr., 1873 / MT
O'Connell, J. / 6 Jan., 1870 / MT
Odger, George (1820–77) / 19 May, 1871
  / MT
O'Grady, Standish (1846–1928) / 9 Jan.,
  1869 / JH
Ollivier, Robert Wilby / 2 July, 1867 / JH
O'Neill, Henry / 8 Oct., 1871 / MT
Palma, Luigi / 21 Nov., 1869 / MT
Partridge, J. Arthur (d. 1891) / 1 Aug.,
  1866 / MT
Pascal, Eugène / MT unless otherwise
  noted
  10 Feb., 1859
  14 May, 1859
  16 July, 1859
  14 Sept., 1859
  17 Sept., 1859
  29 Sept., 1859
  26 Oct., 1859
  1 Nov., 1859
  17 Nov., 1859 / Y
  18 Nov., 1859 / Y
  16 Dec., 1859 / Y
  12 Apr., 1860 / Y
Paull, Samuel / 19 Nov., 1861 / MT
Peirce, Charles Saunders (1839–1914) /
  ca. 1865–68 / Y

Pharazyn, Robert (1833–96) / 14 Apr., 1866 / *National Reformer*, 28 Sept., 1884, 213–14
Philosophical Institution (Edinburgh) / May 1865 / MT
Phin, John / 10 Apr., 1865 / Y
Picard, Nancy / 14 Sept., 1869 / MT
Place, Francis (1771–1854) / 10 Feb., 1837 / BL; Graham Wallas *The Life of Francis Place* (London: Longmans, Green, 1898)
Plummer, John (ca. 1831–1914) / ? / MT
    4 Mar., 1873 / MT
Political Refugee Society. *See* Barry
Poore, R. / 23 Sept., 1866 / JH (enclosed with D. Urquhart, 27 Sept., 1866)
Pope, Frederick / 17 Oct., 1854 / JH
Possnikoff, Alexander / 22 Mar., 1873 / MT
Potonié (?), Ed. / 25 Oct., 1865 / MT
Pratt, Hodgson (1824–1907) / 27 July, 1871 / A
Pratten, William Sims / 8 June, 1868 / JH
    11 June, 1868 / JH
    (Westminster Liberal Registration Society) / 4 Apr., 1873 / MT
Prescott, Grote & Co. / 23 Oct., 1861 / A
    24 Oct., 1872 / Y
Quain, Richard (1800–37) / 11 June, [1854] / MT
Rae, John (1796–1872) / 5 Dec., 1853 to 9 Jan., 1854 / MT
Raisky, W. / 2 Jan., 1873 / JH
Ramadge, Francis Hopkins (1793–1867) / 25 Aug., 1855 / MT
Rathbone, Philip Henry (1828–95) (Liverpool Philomathic Society) / 22 Dec., 1868 / JH
    31 Dec., 1868 / JH
Redpath, James / 14 Apr., 1873 / MT
Reeve, Henry (1813–95) / 17 Mar., 1869 / MT
    19 Mar., 1869 / MT
Reid, Andrew (Land Tenure Reform Association) / 29 Sept., 1869 / JH
    14 Oct., 1869 / JH

Revans, John / 18 May, 1854 / Y
    6 June, 1854 / Y
Rey, Louis (1837–1939) / 13 Apr., 1873 / MT
    22 Apr., 1873 / MT
Riddle, William / 4 Feb., 1873 / MT
Robertson, George Croom (1842–92) / 2 July, 1869 / JH
    24 Jan., 1872 / JH
    30 July, 1872 / UCL
    28 Oct., 1872 / MT
    9 Dec., 1872 / UCL
Robinson, William L. (d. 1870) / 28 Sept., 1871 / JH
    21 Oct., 1871 / JH
Rolland, Stewart Erskine / 21 Sept., 1866 / JH (enclosed with D. Urquhart, 27 Sept., 1866)
Rose, D.C. / 22 Apr., 1871 / MT
Roth, Mme N. de / 6 May, 1870 / Kwansei Gakuin, Osaka; *MNL*, IX (Summer 1974)
Rows, R.G. / 6 Feb., 1873 / MT
Roy, Rakhal (?) Chandra / 25 Nov., 1871 / MT
Rusden, Henry Keylock (b. 1826) / 21 May, 1870 / Y
    9 Sept., 1870 / MT
Russell, John (Lord) (1792–1878) / 22 July, 1867 / JH
Russell, John (Viscount Amberley) (1842–76) / 18 Nov., 1868 / Y
    23 Mar., 1869 / JH
    22 Jan., 1870 / JH
Russell, Katherine Louisa (Viscountess Amberley) (1842–74) / 9 June, 1869 / MT
Russell, Richard / 4 Mar., 1867 / JH
    29 Mar., 1867 / JH
Salisbury. *See* Cecil
Sandwith, Humphrey (1822–81) / 15 Nov., 1872 / MT
Saville, Edwards & Co. / 1 Jan., 1869 / MT
    5 Jan., 1869 / MT
    24 Feb., 1873 / MT

Schaeffer, J. de / 26 Feb., 1873 / Y
Sergeant, Lewis (1841–1902) / 14 Sept., 1872 / JH
   12 Oct., 1872 / JH
Sewell, Sarah Ann / 17 Oct., 1868 / MT
Sharp, G.W. / 27 May, 1867 / JH
Shaw, James Johnston (1845–1910) / 1869 / summarized in M.G. Woods' Introduction to J.J. Shaw, *Occasional Papers* (Dublin: Hodges, Figgis, 1910)
Sherman, Josiah (Amnesty Commission) / 1 Feb., 1869 / JH
Shrives, C. (Amalgamated Society of Railway Servants) / 16 Apr., 1873 / MT
Sidgwick, Henry (1838–1900) / 28 July, 1867 / JH
Sigerson, George / 1 Jan., 1869 / MT
Smalley, George W. (1833–1916) / 31 Dec., 1868 / JH
Smith, F. Wickings / 11 Oct., 1871 / A
Smith, Goldwin (1823–1910) / 7 Aug., 1867 / Y
   29 Apr., 1868 / Y
   2 May, 1868 / Y
   27 May, 1868 / Y
Smith, J. Dunn / 10 Nov., 1872 / MT
Smith, Sydney (1771–1845) / 1 May, 1843 / MT
Smith, Thomas (International Working Men's Association) / 27 Aug., 1872 / JH
Smith, William A. (Epping Forest Fund) / 24 Mar., 1873 / MT
Soden, Henry / 25 Feb., 1867 / JH
South London Working Men's Institute / 28 Mar., 1873 / MT
Spalding, Douglas A. / 5 Feb., 1873 / MT
   13 Mar., 1873 / MT
Spencer, Herbert (1820–1903) / 29 July, 1858 / H. Spencer, *Autobiography*, 2 vols. (New York: Appleton, 1904) [S]
   27 Nov., 1858 / Y; David Duncan, *Life and Letters of Herbert Spencer*, 2 vols. (New York: Appleton, 1908) [D]
   17 Feb., 1859 / this and following manuscript letters are at Northwestern University unless otherwise noted; D
   25 Mar., 1859 / part in D
   24 Feb., 1863 / part in S, and in Alexander Bain, *Mental and Moral Science*, 3rd ed. (London: Longmans, 1872)
   25 Feb., 1863
   1 Mar., 1863 / D
   20 Mar., 1863
   2 Apr., 1864
   8 Apr., 1864 / D
   7 Dec., 1864 / S
   28 Feb., 1865
   5 Mar., 1865
   13 Mar., 1865 / D
   26 May, 1865 / D
   21 Aug., 1865 / D
   11 Oct., 1865 / D
   7 Feb., 1866 / S
   6 Feb., 1867
   28 May, 1867 / extracts in D
   5 June, 1867
   9 Aug., 1867 / D
   8 May, 1868
   26 May, 1868
   19 Nov., 1868
   9 June, 1869 / extract in D
   27 Feb., 1872 / BL
   8 Apr., 1873 / JH
Stanley, Arthur Penrhyn (1815–81) / 3 Jan., 1866 / JH
   22 Jan., 1866 / JH
Stanley, Edward George Geoffrey Smith (14th Earl Derby) (1799–1869) / 20 Aug., 1866 / Y
   15 July, 1867 / Y
Stapleton, John / 19 Aug., 1871 / JH
   18 Oct., 1871 / JH
   10 Nov., 1871 / JH
Stephen, James (1789–1859) / 3 May, 1845 / MT
   13 May, 1845 / MT
Stephen, James Fitzjames (1829–94) /

all Cambridge University Library; and
summarized in *MNL*, XXII (Winter 1987)
- 9 Apr., 1864
- 14 Apr., 1864
- May 1865
- 24 Apr., 1869
- 3 Aug., 1871

Sterling, John (1806–44) / King's College, Cambridge, unless otherwise noted; printed or excerpted in Anne Kimbell Tuell, *John Sterling: A Representative Victorian* (New York: Macmillan, 1941) unless noted as "not in T"
- 31 Mar., 1830
- 14 June, 1830
- 21 June, 1830
- 8 Mar., 1832
- 18 June, 1832
- 18 Sept., 1832
- 10 June, 1833
- 15 May, 1835 / MT
- [1 Jan., 1836?]
- 22 Feb., 1838
- 14 July, 1838
- [?Aug. 1838] (2) / not in T
- 4 Sept., 1838 / not in T
- 18 Mar., 1840 / untraced; referred to in T
- 10 June, 1840
- 16 June, 1840
- 21 Sept., 1840
- 20 Nov., 1840
- 9 Dec., 1840
- 4 Jan., 1841
- 6 Jan., 1841
- 11 Mar., 1841 / not in T
- 15 Mar., 1841
- 18 Mar., 1841
- 1 Aug., 1841
- 4 Oct., 1841 / not in T
- 6 Dec., 1841 / not in T
- 5 Jan., 1842
- 10 Jan., 1842 / not in T
- 22 Jan., 1842 / not in T
- 2 Feb., 1842 / not in T
- 17 July, 1842
- 30 Aug., 1842
- 24 Oct., 1842
- 21 Nov., 1842
- 29 Apr., 1843
- 11 Aug., 1843
- 28 Dec., 1843
- 1 Feb., 1844 / not in T
- June 1844
- 2 June, 1844
- 8 Sept., 1844 / Y; not in T

Stern, John S. / 16 Apr., 1873 / MT
Sterne, Simon / 16 June, 1872 / MT
Steward (?), Joanna / 24 Mar., 1871 / MT
Steward, W. / 23 May, ? / MT
Stewart, George C. / 9 Sept., 1871 / MT
- 30 Sept., 1871 / MT

Stiguard (?), Helen / ? / MT
Tabor, J.A. / 8 Mar., 1878 [*sic*; 1873?] / MT
Taine, Hippolyte (1828–93) / 2 Apr., 1870 / JH
- 13 Apr., 1870 / JH
- 15 July, 1870 / JH

Tauchnitz, Christian Bernard von / 24 Dec., 1872 / Y
Taylor, Clementia (1811–1908) / 10 Feb., 1870 / MT
Taylor, Helen (1831–1907) / all MT
- 1 Nov., 1858 (telegram)
- [May 1867]
- 12 Nov., 1868
- 16 Nov., 1868
- 19 Nov., 1868
- [19 Nov., 1868]
- [20 Nov., 1868]

Taylor, Henry (1800–86) / 6 Jan., 1831 / MT
- 28 May, 1861 / *The Works of Sir Henry Taylor*, 5 vols. (London: King, 1877–78)

Taylor, Henry R. / 19 June, 1872 / MT
- 25 June, 1872 / MT

Taylor, John (1796–1849), and Harriet / 28 Jan., [1831?] / MT

Taylor, Peter Alfred (1819–91) / 14 May, 1869 / JH
   25 May, 1869 / JH
   21 Aug., 1870 / JH
Thatcher, George / 21 Sept., 1868 / MT
   8 Oct., 1868 / MT
Thompson, George W. / 30 Aug., 1869 / MT
Thornton, William Thomas (1813–80) / 27 Nov., [1852] / *The Correspondence of Lord Overstone*, ed. D.P. O'Brien, 3 vols. (Cambridge: Cambridge University Press, 1971)
   19 Sept., 1860 / Alexander Bain, *John Stuart Mill: A Criticism* (London: Longmans, 1882)
   26 Oct., 1867 / JH
   8 Jan., 1868 / JH
   10 Oct., 1869 / JH
   22 Sept., 1872 / Y
Tocqueville, Alexis Clérel de (1805–59) / all JH; and in *Correspondance anglaise*, ed. J.-P. Mayer (Paris: Gallimard, 1954), Vol. VI of *Oeuvres*
   June 1835
   26 June, 1835
   12 Sept., 1835
   3 Dec., 1835
   10 Feb., 1836
   10 Apr., 1836
   5 June, 1836
   10 Nov., 1836
   24 June, 1837
   14 Nov., 1839
   3 May, 1840
   18 Dec., 1840
   28 Mar., 1841 / in Mayer as 18 Mar., 1841
   9 Feb., 1843
   12 Mar., 1843
   27 Oct., 1843
   23 Apr., 1847
   22 June, 1856
   19 Dec., 1856
   9 Feb., 1859

Train, George Francis (1829–1904) / both in *Irishman*, 16 July, 1868
   29 June, 1868
   after 29 June, 1868
Trant, William / all MT
   2 Aug., 1870
   12 Sept., 1870
   30 Oct., 1870
   13 Nov., 1870
   18 Nov., 1870
   24 Sept., 1872
Trask, James / 20 Apr., 1868 / Y
   25 Apr., 1868 / Y
Trevelyan, Charles Edward (1807–86) / 8 Mar., 1854 / JH
   11 May, 1854 / MT
   24 May, 1854 / MT
   30 May, 1854 / JH
   2 June, 1854 / JH
Trübner & Co. / 15 May, 1871 / Y; enclosed with Trübner, 19 May, 1871
Trübner, John Nicolaus (1817–84) /
   1 June, 1867 / Y
   4 June, 1867 / Y
   19 May, 1871 / Y
   2 June, 1871 / Y
University of Munich / 19 Aug., 1872 / MT
Urquhart, David (1805–77) / 27 Sept., 1866 / JH
   29 Sept., 1866 / JH
   18 Oct., 1866 / JH
Urquhart, Harriet / [1866] / JH; copy enclosed with D. Urquhart, 29 Sept., 1866
Villard, Henry (American Social Science Association) / 21 Dec., 1868 / JH
Villari, Pasquale (1826–1917) / 15 Apr., 1857 / JH
   10 Apr., 1858 / Y
   12 Mar., 1869 / JH
   18 Oct., 1869 / JH
   31 Dec., 1871 / JH
   5 Jan., 1872 / Y
   9 Apr., 1872 / JH

Wakeman, Maurice (1801–70) / 29 Sept., 1865 / JH
    17 Nov., 1865 / JH
    23 Nov., 1865 / JH
Ward, William George (1812–82) / Nov. 1848 / excerpt in Wilfrid Ward, *William George Ward and the Catholic Revival* (London: Macmillan, 1893) [W]
    6 Nov., 1859 / JH
    28 Apr., 1865 / W
    17 July, 1865 / W
    Feb. 1867 / W
    7 Feb., 1867 / W
    24 Mar., 1869 / W
Was, H. / ? / MT
Watson, David McBurnie (d. 1902) / 1 Sept., 1869 / JH
Watson, Hewett Cottrell (1804–81) / 14 Jan., 1869 / JH
    6 Feb., 1869 / JH
Westlake, John (1823–1913) / 3 Sept., 1870 / JH
Westminster Liberal Registration Society. *See* Pratten
Whewell, William (1794–1866) / 15 May, 1865 / JH
White, Horace (1834–1916) / 3 Nov., 1865 / JH
    23 Nov., 1869 / Y
White, Joseph Blanco (1775–1841) / all in *The Life of Joseph Blanco White*, ed. John Hamilton Thom (London: Chapman, 1845)
    20 Apr., 1835
    25 May, 1835
    10 June, 1835
    27 June, 1835
    [after 28 Aug., 1835] / dated 25 Aug. in Thom
    7 Feb., 1836
    14 Feb., 1836
    4 Apr., 1836
    26 June, 1836
    16 Nov., 1837
    15 Dec., 1837
Wikelas, W. / 13 Apr., 1869 / MT
Wilkinson, Charles W. / 18 Oct., 1869 / JH
    28 Oct., 1869 / JH
Wilkinson, J.J. Garth (1812–99) / 19 Mar., 1873 / MT
Willcox, J.K. Hamilton (1842–98) (New York Liberal Club) / 8 Oct., 1870 / JH
    11 Oct., 1870 / JH
    1 Apr., 1871 / A
    6 Apr., 1871 / A
Wilson, Mr. / 11 June, [1854] / MT
Wilson, John / 11 Sept., 1834 / Prof. Akira Tada, Chiba, Japan
Wood, William / 20 May, 1867 / JH
    28 Dec., 1870 / MT
Wragg, William A. / 20 Jan., 1873 / MT
Wrightson, Henry A. / 1 Feb., 1873 / MT
Youmans, Edward Livingstone (1821–87) / 10 Dec., 1868 / Y
Young, E.W. / 23 Oct., 1867 / JH

Appendix E

INDEX OF CORRESPONDENTS

THIS INDEX includes the names of all recipients of letters included in this volume, and is a supplement to the Indexes in Vol. XIII, pp. 780–4, and Vol. XVII, pp. 2078–83, of the *Collected Works*. Amalgamated lists are entered as "Letters to" under individuals' names in the Index of Persons and Works in *Indexes*, *Collected Works*, Vol. XXXIII. References here are to the first page of a letter; when two letters appear on the same page, that fact is recorded thus: 782 (2).

Acland, Henry Wentworth: 158, 223
Alves, Henry Scott: 29
Arnold, Edwin: 160
Austin, John: 69, 71
Austin, Sarah: 12, 14, 30
Bain, Alexander: 155
Barry, M. Maltman: 219
Beal, James: 168, 176
Bentley, Richard: 62
Blanqui, Jérôme Adolphe: 18
Booth, Edwin Carton: 182
Bordère, Henri: 120
Bowring, John: 7, 8, 11, 25
Bradlaugh, Charles: 206, 225 (2)
Burnett, Alfred W.: 178
Butler, Josephine Elizabeth: 204
Cabell, William: 13, 17, 22, 24, 28, 29, 33, 34, 36, 37, 38, 39 (2), 40, 41, 48, 49, 51, 55, 57, 58, 59 (2), 60, 61
Calvert, John Mitchinson: 51, 53
Campbell, George: 209, 214, 215
Carlyle, John Aitken: 43
Carlyle, Thomas: 48, 57, 66
Carpenter, Mary: 199, 212
Chadwick, Edwin: 75, 83, 135, 243
Chapman, John: 80, 202
Christie, William Dougal: 150, 165, 192, 195
Clay, Walter Lowe: 171

Index of Correspondents

Clerk, George Russell: 102, 104, 107
Cochut, Pierre André: 126
Cöhn, Gustav: 188
Cole, Henry: 15, 16 (2), 17, 18, 26, 33, 38, 46, 49, 50, 56, 62, 241 (2), 242 (2)
Conway, Moncure Daniel: 237
Cooper, James Alfred: 155
Corrie, William: 163
Courcelle-Seneuil, Jean Gustave: 82
Courtney, Leonard Henry: 237
Crestadoro, Andrea: 174
Crompton, Joseph William: 169
Dall, Caroline Wells (née Healey): 127
Dohrn, Anton: 186, 208
Elliott, John Arthur: 191
Empson, William: 67
Finance and Home Committee of the East India Company: 68, 83, 84 (2) 85 (2), 86 (2), 87, 89, 90, 92, 95, 96, 97, 102, 105 (2), 106, 107, 109 (2), 110, 111, 112, 113, 114
Fox, Robert Were: 58
Furnivall, Frederick James: 81
The Gardeners' Chronicle and Agricultural Gazette: 146
Gill, George: 230
The Glasgow Herald, reporter of: 173
Gomperz, Theodor: 90, 91 (2), 108, 115, 117, 118, 119, 123, 125, 131 (2), 133, 136, 140 (2), 143, 149, 152, 205
Gordon, Robert: 42
Graham, George John: 175
Grant, Horace: 44
Grant Duff, Mountstuart Elphinstone: 138, 180, 186, 187, 192, 203
Grote, George: 1, 147
Grote, Harriet: 1
Guillaumin, Gilbert Urbain: 128
Guillaumin, Mlle: 234
Hare, Thomas: 196
Harrison, Robert: 193
Harvey, G.: 166
Haslam, Thomas Joseph: 182
Havlin, Thomas: 160
Herbert, Auberon Edward William Molyneux: 235
Hill, Frank Harrison: 217
Hodges, J.H.: 198
Holmes, Oliver Wendell: 166, 168
Holyoake, George Jacob: 171
Hotel Windsor (Paris): 236
Hughes, Thomas: 190
Hutchinson, James: 73
International Working Men's Association, General Council of: 220

Jevons, William Stanley: 153
Johnston, Henry: 210
Le Journal des Economistes: 236
Kemble, John Mitchell: 45, 66, 69
Lankester, Phebe: 157
Laveleye, Emile Louis Victor: 224
Leader, John Temple: 243
Lindley, Caroline: 200 (2), 221
Littrow, Auguste von: 228, 234
Longman, William: 156, 162, 170
Lucas, Samuel: 121
Ludlow, John Malcolm Forbes: 173, 174, 178, 179, 216
McLaren, Duncan: 227
Mahaffy, John Pentland: 183
Malleson, Elizabeth: 172
Martin, Arthur Patchett: 232
Masters, Maxwell Tylden: 148
Mignet, François Auguste Marie: 122, 123, 139
Mills, P.L.: 230
Mitchell, Henry: 197
Morley, John: 173
Naville, Jules Ernest: 159, 187
Nicholson, Edward Williams Byron: 213
Osborne, Ralph Bernal: 162
Owens College, Trustees of: 164
Parker, John William: 64, 65, 74, 80 (2), 117, 129, 138
Passy, Frédéric: 181
Paulin, J.B. Alexandre: 32
Pearson, Charles Henry: 139
People's Garden Co.: 222
Phillips, Henry Wyndham: 177
Plummer, John: 145
Potter, Thomas Bayley: 141
Prandi, Fortunato: 22
Pratt, Hodgson: 229
Prescott, Grote & Co.: 151
Rae, William Fraser: 211
Reeve, Henry: 73
Robertson, John: 35
Roebuck, John Arthur: 26
Rogers, James Edwin Thorold: 137, 141, 219
Rossiter, William: 184, 193, 194, 210, 226
Rouvière, Pierre Augustin: 228
Russell, John: 151
Russell, Katherine Louisa: 177
Say, Jean Baptiste: 9

Scott, Edward: 44
Secretary to the Board of Control, The: 87, 94, 101, 112
Senior, Nassau William: 47, 124, 244
Sharp, Charles: 222
Shaw, James Johnston: 207
Sidgwick, Henry: 180, 185
Smalley, George Washburn: 201
Smith, Joshua Toulmin: 167
Smith, William: 170
The Spectator, editor of: 136
Spedding, Thomas Story: 74
Spence, Catherine Helen: 126
Spencer, Herbert: 122
Stanley, Catherine: 246
Stark, Hugh: 79
Stebbing, William: 116
Stephen, James: 41
Stephen, James Fitzjames: 148, 154, 206
Stone, Mr.: 245
Tabouelle, R. Henry: 189
Taylor, Peter Alfred: 196
Theobald, Henry Studdy: 176
Thibaudeau, Adolphe Narcisse: 27
Thom, John Hamilton: 72
Trant, William: 220
Trevelyan, Charles Edward: 130
Trübner, John Nicholas: 164
Unidentified Correspondents: 49, 59, 64, 72, 136, 161, 162, 190, 197, 199, 208, 227, 231, 244 (2), 246, 247, 248
Villard, Henry: 211, 213
Waley, Jacob: 116
Waterfield, Thomas Nelson: 63, 67, 79, 92, 93, 94, 98 (2), 99, 100, 103, 110, 113
Watkins, John: 156
Waugh, Benjamin: 226
Webb, Richard Davis: 189
Wertheimstein, Josephine von: 142
Willcox, James Keappoch Hamilton: 231
Williams, Arthur John: 158
Wilson, Effingham: 23
Wilson, Horace Hayman: 23, 30
Wyse, William Charles Bonaparte: 247

Appendix F

INDEX OF PERSONS, AND WORKS CITED,
With Variants and Notes

THIS APPENDIX is an index of names and titles of works, which do not appear in the subject Index. Also included here (at the end of the appendix and listed chronologically) are references to official documents and to statute laws. The material otherwise is arranged in alphabetical order, with an entry for each correspondent, and each person or work quoted or referred to. Anonymous articles are entered in order of date under the newspaper or journal in which they appear. References to mythical and fictional characters are excluded. The following abbreviations are used: *ADB* (*Allgemeine Deutsche Biographie*), *AusDB* (*Australian Dictionary of Biography*), *DAB* (*Dictionary of American Biography*), *DBF* (*Dictionnaire de biographie française*), *DIB* (*Dictionary of Indian Biography*), *DNB* (*Dictionary of National Biography*), *EB* (*Encyclopaedia Britannica*, 11th ed.), EIC (East India Company), *GDU* (Larousse, *Grand dictionnaire universel du XIXe siècle*), *MEB* (Boase, *Modern English Biography*), *PD* (*Parliamentary Debates*), *PP* (*Parliamentary Papers*), SC (JSM's library, Somerville College, Oxford), *WWG* (*Who Was Who in the Greek World*), *WWBMP* (*Who's Who of British Members of Parliament*).

The entries take the following form:
  1. Identification of persons: birth and death dates and a source of further biographical information are given whenever possible; otherwise "fl." with a date or an identifying phrase appears.
  2. Identification of works: author, title, etc., in the usual bibliographic form.
  3. Notes (if required) giving information about JSM's use of the source, indication if the work is in his library, Somerville College, Oxford, and any other relevant information.
  4. Lists of the pages where works are quoted or referred to.
  5. In the case of quotations, a list of substantive variants between Mill's text and his source, in this form: Page and line reference to the present text. Reading in the present text] Reading in the source (page reference in the source). Quoted passages are placed in context by giving beginnings and endings of sentences.

ACLAND, HENRY WENTWORTH (1815–1900; *DNB*). Letters to: 158, 223
—— *The Harveian Oration*. London: Macmillan, 1865.
REFERRED TO: 158

ADAMS, WILLIAM BRIDGES (1797–1872; *DNB*). Referred to: 36
—— "Dr. Arnott, On Warming and Ventilation," *London and Westminster Review*, VI & XVIII (Jan. 1838), 345–67.
REFERRED TO: 36

AKBAR II (King of Delhi; ruled 1806–37). Referred to: 61

Index of Persons and Works 279

ALFRED (of England) (849–901 A.D.; *DNB*). Referred to: 147

ALVES, HENRY SCOTT (d. before Nov. 1859).
NOTE: see *Gentleman's Magazine* (1859), 546.
LETTER TO: 29

ALVES, NATHANIEL.
NOTE: a Political Agent of the EIC.
REFERRED TO: 36–7

AMBERLEY. See Russell.

AMOS, ANDREW (1791–1860; *DNB*). Referred to: 21

ANDREW, F.P. (fl. 1850s). Referred to: 99

Annales de l'Association Internationale pour le Progrès des Sciences Sociales. 4ième sess., Congrès de Berne (1865). Paris and Brussels, 1866.
REFERRED TO: 224

ARANGIO, DIEGO (fl. 1830s).
NOTE: a refugee.
REFERRED TO: 42

ARNAND RAO (Gaikwar of Baroda) (ruled 1800–19). Referred to: 63

ARNOLD, EDWIN (1832–1904; *DNB*). Letter to: 160

ATKINS, AARON.
NOTE: Assistant Registrar in Book Office of the EIC.
REFERRED TO: 106, 107, 114

AUCKLAND, LORD. See George Eden.

AUSTIN, CHARLES (1799–1874; *DNB*). Referred to: 4, 11, 197

AUSTIN, JOHN (1790–1859; *DNB*).
LETTERS TO: 69, 71
REFERRED TO: 3–4, 12, 13, 21, 30–1, 65

——— "Periodical Literature: *Edinburgh Review*, Number XL, Art. IV—Disposition of Property by Will [and] Primogeniture," *Westminster Review*, II (Oct. 1824), 503–53.
REFERRED TO: 6

AUSTIN, LUCIE (later Duff-Gordon) (1821–69; *DNB*). Referred to: 13, 15

AUSTIN, SARAH (1793–1867; *DNB*).
NOTE: see also Cousin and Raumer.
LETTERS TO: 12, 14, 30
REFERRED TO: 3–4, 23

AYRTON, ACTON SMEE (1816–86; *DNB*). Referred to: 168, 176

BABINGTON, CHARLES CARDALE (1808–95; *DNB*). Referred to: 148

BACON, FRANCIS (Lord Verulam) (1561–1626; *DNB*). Referred to: 159

——— *Novum Organum* (1620). In *Works*. Ed. James Spedding, *et al.* 14 vols. London: Longman, *et al.*, 1857–74, I, 119–365 (Latin); IV, 38–248 (English).
NOTE: in SC.
QUOTED: 159
159.27 *axiomata media*] Duae viae sunt, atque esse possunt, ad inquirendam et inveniendam veritatem. Altera a sensu et particularibus advolat ad axiomata maxime generalia, atque ex iis principiis eorumque immota veritate judicat et invenit axiomata media; atque haec via in usu est. (I, 159; sect. xix)

Appendix F

BAIN, ALEXANDER (1818–1903; *DNB*).
LETTER TO: 155
REFERRED TO: 75–6, 205

——— *The Emotions and the Will* (1859). 2nd ed. London: Longmans, *et al.*, 1865.
REFERRED TO: 205

——— *On the Applications of Science to Human Health and Well-being. Being a Lecture, Introductory to a Course, "On the Application of Physics to Common Life," Delivered at the Edinburgh Philosophical Institute in June, 1847*. London and Glasgow: Griffin, 1848.
REFERRED TO: 75–6

——— *The Senses and the Intellect* (1855). 3rd ed. London: Longmans, Green, 1868.
REFERRED TO: 205

BAIN, FRANCES A. (née Wilkinson) (d. 1892). Referred to: 205

BAJI RAO II (Peshwa of the Marathas) (1775–1851?). Referred to: 63

BAKER, THOMAS.
NOTE: a labourer at the EIC.
REFERRED TO: 86

BARRÈRE, PIERRE (fl. 1860s).
NOTE: a professor.
REFERRED TO: 147, 170

BARRY, M. MALTMAN (1842–1909). Letter to: 219

BAYLEY, WILLIAM BUTTERWORTH (1782–1860; *DNB*). Referred to: 51, 58

BEAL, JAMES (1829–91; *MEB*).
LETTERS TO: 168, 176
REFERRED TO: 174, 179

BEAUMONT, THOMAS WENTWORTH (1792–1848; *DNB*). Referred to: 46, 47

BEAUMONT DE LA BONNINIÈRE, GUSTAVE AUGUSTE DE (1802–66; *DBF*). Referred to: 73

BEGGS, THOMAS (1808–96; *MEB*). Referred to: 169

BELL, CHARLES.
NOTE: a writer in the Judicial Dept. of the EIC.
REFERRED TO: 87, 110

BENSON, RALPH AUGUSTUS (1828–86; *MEB*). Referred to: 217–18

BENTHAM, GEORGE (1800–84; *DNB*). Referred to: 11

BENTHAM, JEREMY (1748–1832; *DNB*). Referred to: 15, 66

——— *Rationale of Judicial Evidence, Specially Applied to English Practice*. Ed. John Stuart Mill. 5 vols. London: Hunt and Clarke, 1827.
REFERRED TO: 7

——— *Traité des preuves judiciaires*. Ed. Pierre Etienne Louis Dumont. 2 vols. Paris: Bossange, 1823.
REFERRED TO: 4

BENTLEY, RICHARD (1794–1871; *DNB*). Letter to: 62

BIBLE. Referred to: 53

——— II Corinthians. Quoted: 235

BICKERSTETH, HENRY (Baron Langdale) (1783–1851; *DNB*). Referred to: 31

BINGHAM, PEREGRINE (1788–1864; *DNB*). Referred to: 4

───── "Periodical Literature: The *Quarterly Review*, No. LVIII—Faux's Memorable Days in America," *Westminster Review*, I (Jan. 1824), 250–68.
REFERRED TO: 5

───── "Travels of Duncan, Flint and Faux," *Westminster Review*, I (Jan. 1824), 101–20.
REFERRED TO: 5

BINGMANN, DR. (fl. 1860s).
NOTE: a translator.
REFERRED TO: 205

BIRKBECK, GEORGE (1776–1841; *DNB*). Referred to: 200

BLACK, JOHN (1783–1855; *DNB*). Referred to: 6–7

BLACKWOOD, FREDERICK TEMPLE HAMILTON-TEMPLE (1st Marquis Dufferin and Ava) (1826–1902; *DNB*). Referred to: 216

BLAKE, JOHN ALOYSIUS (1826–87; *MEB*). Referred to: 183

BLANC, JEAN JOSEPH LOUIS (1811–82; *DBF*). Referred to: 140

BLANQUI, JÉRÔME ADOLPHE (1798–1854; *DBF*). Letter to: 18

BLIGNIÈRES, CÉLESTIN LE BARBIER DE (1822–1905; *DBF*). Referred to: 128

BOIRAC, EMILE (1851–1917). Referred to: 231

BONHAM, MR. (fl. ca. 1840). Referred to: 244

BOOLE, GEORGE (1815–64; *DNB*). Referred to: 153

───── *An Investigation of the Laws of Thought, on Which Are Founded the Mathematical Theories of Logic and Probabilities*. London: Walton and Maberley, 1854.
REFERRED TO: 153

BOOTH, EDWIN CARTON (ca. 1827–78; *AusDB*). Letter to: 182

BOOTH, JAMES (1796–1880; *DNB*). Referred to: 11

BORDÈRE, HENRI (1825–89).
NOTE: see *Biographical Notes upon Botanists*.
LETTER TO: 120

BORTHWICK, W.
NOTE: Political Agent of the EIC.
REFERRED TO: 56

BOURDILLON, EDMUND D.
NOTE: retired from the EIC in June 1867.
REFERRED TO: 97

BOURKE, RICHARD SOUTHWELL (6th Earl of Mayo) (1822–72; *DNB*). Referred to: 199

BOUVERIE, EDWARD PLEYDELL (1818–89; *DNB*). Referred to: 201

───── Letters to Mill (25 Sept. and 13 Oct., 1868), *The Times*, 16 Oct., 1868, 10.
REFERRED TO: 201

BOWRING, JOHN (1792–1872; *DNB*).
NOTE: see also *PP* (1834, 1835).
LETTERS TO: 7, 8, 11, 25

BRADLAUGH, CHARLES (1833–91; *DNB*). Letters to: 206, 225 (2)

BREWER, WILLIAM (d. 1881; *MEB*). Referred to: 194

BRIGHT, JOHN (1811–98; *DNB*). Referred to: 178

The British and Foreign Review. Referred to: 46

British Controversialist and Literary Magazine. Referred to: 155, 156

———"Modern Logicians: John Stuart Mill," n.s. XII (Mar. and Apr. 1865), 161–73 and 241–56.
REFERRED TO: 156

BROUGHAM, HENRY PETER (Lord) (1778–1868; *DNB*). Referred to: 66

BROWN, FRANCIS.
NOTE: a warehouse pensioner of the EIC.
REFERRED TO: 86

BROWN, THOMAS (1778–1820; *DNB*). Referred to: 8

——— *Lectures on the Philosophy of the Human Mind*. 4 vols. Edinburgh: Tait, 1820.
REFERRED TO: 8

BUCHEZ, PHILIPPE JOSEPH BENJAMIN, and PROSPER CHARLES ROUX, eds. *L'histoire parlementaire de la révolution française, ou Journal des assemblées nationales depuis 1789 jusqu'en 1815*. 40 vols. Paris: Paulin, 1834–38.
REFERRED TO: 32

BUCKLE, HENRY THOMAS (1821–62; *DNB*). Referred to: 127

——— *Miscellaneous and Posthumous Works of Henry Thomas Buckle*. Ed. with a Biographical Notice by Helen Taylor. 3 vols. London: Longmans, Green, 1872.
REFERRED TO: 227–8

BULLER, CHARLES (1806–48; *DNB*). Referred to: 11, 27, 28, 31, 64

BULLMORE, FREDERICK CHARLES (1801–96).
NOTE: physician in Falmouth who attended Henry Mill in his last illness.
REFERRED TO: 52

BULWER, EDWARD GEORGE EARLE LYTTON (later Bulwer-Lytton, later Lord Lytton) (1803–73; *DNB*). Referred to: 15

——— *Pelham; or, The Adventures of a Gentleman*. 3 vols. London: Colburn, 1828.
REFERRED TO: 15

BURIDAN, JEAN (ca. 1290–ca.1358; *DBF*). Referred to: 1

BURNES, ALEXANDER (1805–41; *DNB*). Referred to: 66

BURNETT, ALFRED W. (fl. 1867). Letter to: 178

BURTON, RICHARD FRANCIS (1821–90; *DNB*). Referred to: 104–5

The Bury Times. Referred to: 225

BUTLER, JOSEPHINE ELIZABETH (1828–1906; *DNB*). Letter to: 204

CABELL, WILLIAM (1786–1853).
NOTE: Senior Clerk and later Assistant Secretary to the Board of Control.
LETTERS TO: 13, 17, 22, 24, 28, 29, 33, 34, 36, 37, 38, 39 (2), 40, 41, 48, 49, 51, 55, 57, 58, 59 (2), 60, 61

CAIRNES, ELIZA CHARLOTTE (née Alexander; Mrs. John Elliot). Referred to: 237

CAIRNES, JOHN ELLIOT (1823–75; *DNB*). Referred to: 118, 218, 224, 237

——— "Essay towards an Experimental Solution of the Gold Question (Part I)," *Fraser's Magazine*, LX (Sept. 1859), 267–78.
REFERRED TO: 118

——— "Essay towards an Experimental Solution of the Gold Question (Part II)," *Fraser's Magazine*, LXI (Jan. 1860), 38–53.
REFERRED TO: 118

——— "The Laws, According to Which a Depreciation of the Precious Metals Consequent upon an Increase of Supply Takes Place, Considered in Connection with the Recent Gold Discoveries," *Journal of the Dublin Statistical Society*, Pt. XIII (Jan. 1859), 236–69.
NOTE: read before the British Association, September 1858.
REFERRED TO: 118

——— "Our Defences: A National or a Standing Army," *Fortnightly Review*, n.s. IX (Feb. 1871), 167–98.
REFERRED TO: 224

——— "Political Economy and Land," *Fortnightly Review*, n.s. VII (Jan. 1870), 41–63.
REFERRED TO: 218

——— *The Slave Power; Its Character, Career, and Probable Designs: Being an Attempt to Explain the Real Issues Involved in the American Contest*. London: Parker, Son, and Bourne, 1862.
REFERRED TO: 132

CALVERT, JOHN MITCHINSON (1801–42).
NOTE: see Caroline Fox, *Memories*, and Thomas Carlyle, *Life of Sterling*.
LETTERS TO: 51, 53
REFERRED TO: 43, 58

CAMERON, CHARLES HAY (1795–1880; *DNB*).
NOTE: see also his "Report," *PP* (1831–32).
REFERRED TO: 31

CAMPBELL, GEORGE (1824–92; *DNB*). Letters to: 209, 214, 215

——— *The Irish Land*. London: Trübner; Dublin: Hodges, Foster, 1869.
REFERRED TO: 209, 214–15

——— "The Irish Land Question," *Daily News*, 30 Nov., 1869, 5.
QUOTED: 215

——— "The Tenure of Land in India." In *Systems of Land Tenure in Various Countries*. London: Macmillan, 1870, 145–227.
NOTE: a Cobden Club volume.
REFERRED TO: 209

CAMPBELL, GEORGE DOUGLAS (8th Duke of Argyll) (1823–1900; *DNB*). Referred to: 212

CANNING, STRATFORD (Viscount Stratford de Redcliffe) (1786–1880; *DNB*). Referred to: 99

CARLILE, RICHARD (1790–1843; *DNB*). Referred to: 6

CARLYLE, JANE BAILLIE (née Welsh) (1801–66; *DNB*). Referred to: 57

CARLYLE, JOHN AITKEN (1801–79; *DNB*). Letter to: 43

CARLYLE, THOMAS (1795–1881; *DNB*).
LETTERS TO: 48, 57, 66
REFERRED TO: 32, 44

——— *Chartism*. London: Fraser, 1840.
REFERRED TO: 48

——— *The French Revolution: A History*. 3 vols. London: Fraser, 1837.
REFERRED TO: 44

―――― "Occasional Discourse on the Negro Question," *Fraser's Magazine*, XL (Dec. 1849), 670–9.
REFERRED TO: 80

―――― "Parliamentary History of the French Revolution," *London and Westminster Review*, V & XXVII (Apr. 1837), 233–47.
REFERRED TO: 32

―――― *Sartor Resartus* (1833–34). 2nd ed. Boston: Munroe; Philadelphia and Pittsburgh: Kay, 1837.
NOTE: in SC.
QUOTED: 55
55.6–7 "An unknown condiment named Point."] Their [the Irish "Drudges" or "Poor Slaves"] universal sustenance is the root named Potato, cooked by fire alone; and generally without condiment or relish of any kind, save an unknown condiment named *Point*, into the meaning of which I have vainly inquired; the victual *Potatoes-and-Point* not appearing, at least not with specific accuracy of description, in any European cookery-book whatever. (285; Bk. III, Chap. x.)

CARNAC, JAMES RIVETT (1785–1846; *DNB*). Referred to: 29, 37, 38, 63

CARPENTER, MARY (1807–77; *DNB*). Letters to: 199, 212

―――― *Suggestions on Prison Discipline and Female Education in India*. Bristol: Arrowsmith, 1867.
REFERRED TO: 199

CARR, WILLIAM OGLE (1802/3–56).
NOTE: see *Annual Register*, 1856.
REFERRED TO: 11

CARREL, JEAN BAPTISTE NICOLAS ARMAND (1800–36; *DBF*). Referred to: 28, 32–3

CASSAL, HUGUES CHARLES STANISLAS (1818–85; *DBF*). Referred to: 147

CHADWICK, EDWIN (1800–90; *DNB*).
LETTERS TO: 75, 83, 135, 243
REFERRED TO: 15, 124, 180, 201

―――― "Life Assurances," *Westminster Review*, IX (Apr. 1828), 384–421.
REFERRED TO: 83

CHAPMAN, HENRY SAMUEL (1803–81; *DNB*). Referred to: 244

CHAPMAN, JOHN (1821–94; *DNB*). Letters to: 80, 202

CHEDZOY, CHARLES.
NOTE: a warehouse pensioner of the EIC.
REFERRED TO: 86

CHESSON, FREDERICK WILLIAM (ca. 1833–88; *MEB*). Referred to: 179

CHEVALIER, MICHEL (1806–79; *DBF*). Referred to: 181

CHRIST. See Jesus.

CHRISTIE, WILLIAM DOUGAL (1816–74; *DNB*). Letters to: 150, 165, 192, 195

―――― "Amendment of Election Petitions and Corrupt Practices at Elections Bill," *Pall Mall Gazette*, 29 Apr., 1868, 5.
REFERRED TO: 192

―――― *The Brazil Correspondence in the Case of the "Prince of Wales" and the Officers of the "Forte," Reprinted from Papers Laid before Parliament*. London: Ridgway, 1863.
REFERRED TO: 150

────── *Electoral Corruption and Its Remedies*. London: National Association for the Promotion of Social Science, 1864.
REFERRED TO: 165

────── *Notes on Brazilian Questions*. London and Cambridge: Macmillan, 1865.
REFERRED TO: 150

────── *Suggestions for an Organization for the Restraint of Corruption at Elections*. London: National Association for the Promotion of Social Science, 1864.
REFERRED TO: 165

CLARENDON. See Villiers.

CLARK, WILLIAM HENRY.
NOTE: member of Reform Club 1847–71.
REFERRED TO: 150

CLARKE, CHARLES BARON (1832–1906; *DNB*). Referred to: 223

────── "The Existing Poor Law of England," *Macmillan's Magazine*, XXIII (Nov. 1870), 46–52.
REFERRED TO: 223

CLARKE, WILLIAM STANLEY.
NOTE: Chairman of the Court of Directors of the EIC 1835–36.
REFERRED TO: 29

CLAY, WALTER LOWE (1833–75).
NOTE: see *Alumni Cantab*.
LETTER TO: 171

CLERK, GEORGE RUSSELL (1800–89; *DNB*).
LETTERS TO: 102, 104, 107
REFERRED TO: 87, 94, 112

CLERK, GODFREY (b. 1835; *DIB*).
NOTE: Lieutenant in the army of the EIC.
REFERRED TO: 107

COBBE, FRANCES POWER (1822–1904; *DNB*). Referred to: 182

COCHRANE, JOHN GEORGE (1781–1852; *DNB*). Referred to: 14

COCHUT, PIERRE ANDRÉ (1812–90; *DBF*). Letter to: 126

COGHLAN, WILLIAM M. (1803–85; *DIB*). Referred to: 100, 104

CÖHN, GUSTAV (1840–1919; *NDB*). Letter to: 188

COLE, HENRY (1808–82; *DNB*). Letters to: 15, 16 (2), 17, 18, 26, 33, 38, 46, 49, 50, 56, 62, 241 (2), 242 (2)

────── "Uniform Penny Postage," *London and Westminster Review*, VII & XXIX (Apr. 1838), 225–64.
REFERRED TO: 38–9

COLMAN, MARY ELIZABETH (née Mill; one of JSM's sisters) (1822–1913). Referred to: 17, 52

COMTE, AUGUSTE (1798–1857; *DBF*). Referred to: 152, 159

COMTE, FRANÇOIS CHARLES LOUIS (1782–1837; *DBF*). Referred to: 21

CONOLLY, JOHN (1794–1866; *DNB*). Referred to: 21

CONWAY, ELLEN DAVIS (née Dana; Mrs. Moncure Daniel) (d. 1897; *DAB*). Referred to: 237

CONWAY, MONCURE DANIEL (1832–1907; *DAB*). Letter to: 237

COOPE, WILLIAM JOHN (1809–70).
NOTE: rector of Falmouth. See *Bibliotheca Cornubiensis* (1874).
REFERRED TO: 52, 53

COOPER, JAMES ALFRED (1822–98; *MEB*). Letter to: 155

The Cooperator. Referred to: 188

CORRIE, WILLIAM (1806–81; *MEB*). Letter to: 163

COULSON, WALTER (1794–1860; *DNB*). Referred to: 11

COURCELLE-SENEUIL, JEAN GUSTAVE (1813–92; *DBF*).
LETTER TO: 82
REFERRED TO: 234

——— *Traité théorique et pratique des opérations de banque.* Paris: Guillaumin, 1853.
REFERRED TO: 82

The Courier and Evening Gazette. Quoted: 6

COURTNEY, LEONARD HENRY (later Baron Courtney of Penrith) (1832–1918; *DNB*). Letter to: 237

COUSIN, VICTOR (1792–1867; *DBF*). *Report on the State of Public Instruction in Prussia.* Trans. Sarah Austin. London: Wilson, 1834.
REFERRED TO: 23

COWLEY, LORD. See Henry Wellesley.

COX, SAMUEL SULLIVAN (1824–89; *DAB*). Referred to: 164

CRAWLEY, FRANCIS EDWARD (1803–32). Referred to: 12, 14

CRESTADORO, ANDREA (1808–79; *DNB*). Letter to: 174

———, ed. *Manchester Public Free Libraries. Index-Catalogue of the Hulme Lending Branch.* Manchester, 1867.
REFERRED TO: 174

CROMPTON, JOSEPH WILLIAM (fl. 1850s).
NOTE: classmate of James Bentham Mill.
LETTER TO: 169

CUNNINGHAM, HENRY FRANCIS (fl. 1837–49).
NOTE: an artist at Falmouth who did portraits of JSM and his brother.
REFERRED TO: 52

CURRIE, FREDERICK (1799–1875; *DNB*).
NOTE: the references are to him as a member of the Secret Committee in his capacity as Deputy Chairman of the Court of Directors of the EIC 1857–58, and Chairman April–August 1858.
REFERRED TO: 102–3, 104–5, 107, 110–11, 112, 113

The Daily News. Referred to: 150, 201–2, 217–18

——— Leader on the case of Constable William Smith, 18 Jan., 1870, 4–5.
REFERRED TO: 217–18

The Daily Telegraph. Referred to: 160–1, 202

——— "The Negro Insurrection," 29 Nov., 1865, 3.
REFERRED TO: 160

——— "Governor Eyre," 30 Nov. 1865, 3.
REFERRED TO: 160

Index of Persons and Works

DALL, CAROLINE WELLS (née Healey) (1822–1912; *DAB*). Letter to: 127

——— *Woman's Rights under the Law: In Three Lectures Delivered in Boston, January, 1861*. Boston: Walker, Wise, 1861.
REFERRED TO: 127–8

DANVERS, FREDERICK CHARLES (1833–1906; *DNB*). Referred to: 87

DAVIS, DAVID DANIEL (1777–1841; *DNB*). Referred to: 21

DE MORGAN, AUGUSTUS (1806–71; *DNB*). Referred to: 153

——— *Formal Logic; or, The Calculus of Inference, Necessary and Probable*. London: Taylor and Walton, 1847.
REFERRED TO: 153

DICEY, EDWARD JAMES STEPHEN (1832–1911; *DNB*). Referred to: 132

——— *Rome in 1860*. London: Macmillan, 1861.
REFERRED TO: 132

——— *Six Months in the Federal States*. London and Cambridge: Macmillan, 1863.
REFERRED TO: 132

DIGWEED, CLARA ESTHER (née Mill; one of JSM's sisters) (1818–86). Referred to: 17, 52

DISRAELI, BENJAMIN (1804–81; *DNB*). Referred to: 195

DOANE, RICHARD (1805–48). Referred to: 5, 7

DOHRN, ANTON (1840–1909).
NOTE: see *Der Grosse Brockhaus*.
LETTERS TO: 186, 208

DOLLFUS, JOHANN HEINRICH (1800–87; *EB*). Referred to: 181

DOWNTON, JOHN.
NOTE: a writer at the EIC.
REFERRED TO: 109–10

DREW, HENRY THOMAS.
NOTE: a messenger at the EIC.
REFERRED TO: 89

DRUMMOND, HENRY (1786–1860; *DNB*). Referred to: 19

DRYSDALE, GEORGE R. (1825–1904). *Physical, Sexual, and Natural Religion*. London: Truelove, 1854.
REFERRED TO: 225–6

DUFF, MOUNTSTUART ELPHINSTONE GRANT. See Grant Duff.

DUFFERIN, LORD. See Frederick Blackwood.

DUFFY, CHARLES GAVAN (1816–1903; *DNB*). Referred to: 232

DUNDAS, ROBERT SAUNDERS (2nd Viscount Melville) (1771–1851; *DNB*). Referred to: 20

DUPONT-WHITE, CHARLES BROOK (1807–78; *DBF*).
NOTE: see also J.S. Mill, *Considerations on Representative Government*, trans. Dupont-White.
REFERRED TO: 128

——— *La centralisation: suite à L'individu et l'état*. Paris: Guillaumin, 1860.
REFERRED TO: 129

——— *L'individu et l'état* (1857). 2nd ed. Paris: Guillaumin, 1858.
REFERRED TO: 129

DUSSARD, HIPPOLYTE (1798–1876; *DBF*). Referred to: 27

EASTWICK, WILLIAM JOSEPH (1808–89; *MEB*).
  NOTE: the references are to him as a member of the Secret Committee in his capacity as Deputy Chairman of the Court of Directors of the EIC from April to August 1858.
  REFERRED TO: 112, 113

EDEN, GEORGE (Earl of Auckland) (1784–1849; *DNB*). Referred to: 55–6, 59

EDGAR (of England) (944–75 A.D.; *DNB*). Referred to: 147

Edinburgh Review. Referred to: 6, 65

EDMONSTONE, NEIL BENJAMIN (1765–1841; *DNB*). Referred to: 56, 57, 59

EICHTHAL, GUSTAVE D' (1804–86; *DBF*). Referred to: 176

ELLICE, EDWARD (1810–80; *DNB*). Referred to: 4, 5

ELLIOTT, JOHN ARTHUR (fl. 1868). Letter to: 191

ELLIS, WILLIAM (1800–81; *DNB*). Referred to: 4, 5, 6, 8

—————— "Charitable Institutions," *Westminster Review*, II (July 1824), 97–121.
  REFERRED TO: 5

—————— "Political Economy," *Westminster Review*, II (Oct. 1824), 289–310.
  REFERRED TO: 5

ELPHINSTONE, JOHN (Baron) (1807–60; *DNB*). Referred to: 104

ELPHINSTONE, MOUNTSTUART (1779–1859; *DNB*). Referred to: 22, 121

EMERSON, ELLEN TUCKER (1839–1909).
  NOTE: daughter of Ralph Waldo Emerson.
  REFERRED TO: 237

EMERSON, RALPH WALDO (1803–82; *DAB*). Referred to: 237

EMPSON, WILLIAM (1791–1852; *DNB*).
  LETTER TO: 67
  REFERRED TO: 12

—————— "Jeremy Bentham," *Edinburgh Review*, LXXVIII (Oct. 1843), 460–516.
  REFERRED TO: 67

ERSKINE, JAMES.
  NOTE: an employee of the EIC.
  REFERRED TO: 34

The Examiner. Referred to: 32

—————— Review of JSM's *England and Ireland*, 22 Feb., 1868, 116.
  REFERRED TO: 190

EYRE, EDWARD JOHN (1815–1901; *DNB*). Referred to: 160–1

—————— "Despatch to the Rt. Hon. Edward Cardwell, M.P." (20 Oct., 1865), *PP*, 1866, LI, 151–60.
  REFERRED TO: 161

FALCONER, THOMAS (1805–82; *DNB*). Referred to: 26, 32

FAURIEL, CLAUDE CHARLES (1772–1844; *DBF*). Referred to: 32

—————— *Histoire de la Gaule méridionale sous la domination des conquérants germains*. 4 vols. Paris: Paulin, 1836.
  REFERRED TO: 32

FAWCETT, HENRY (1833–84; *DNB*). Referred to: 140, 167

FAWCETT, MILLICENT (née Garrett; Mrs. Henry) (1847–1929; *DNB*). Referred to: 182

FERRABOSCHI, JANE STUART (née Mill; one of JSM's sisters) (1816?–83). Referred to: 17, 52

FEUGUERAY, HENRI ROBERT (1813–54; *DBF*). *L'association ouvrière, industrielle et agricole*. Paris: Havard, 1851.
REFERRED TO: 81

FIDLER, W.C.
NOTE: a temporary writer at the EIC.
REFERRED TO: 111

FINANCE AND HOME COMMITTEE OF THE EAST INDIA COMPANY. Letters to: 68, 83, 84 (2), 85 (2), 86 (2), 87, 89, 90, 92, 95, 96, 97, 102, 105 (2), 106, 107, 109 (2), 110, 111, 112, 113, 114

FINLAISON, JOHN (1783–1860; *DNB*). Referred to: 83

FISCHER, ERNST KUNO BERTHOLD (1824–1907; *EB*). Referred to: 184

——— *A Commentary on Kant's Critick of Pure Reason*. Trans. John Pentland Mahaffy, London: Longmans, Green, 1866.
REFERRED TO: 184

FONBLANQUE, ALBANY WILLIAM (1793–1872; *DNB*). Referred to: 17, 18

FONBLANQUE, JOHN SAMUEL MARTIN DE GRENIER (1787–1865; *DNB*). Referred to: 11

FONBLANQUE, MRS. (née Keane; Mrs. Albany). Referred to: 17

FORSTER, WILLIAM EDWARD (1818–86; *DNB*). *The Speech . . . on the Slaveholders' Rebellion; and Professor Goldwin Smith's Letter on the Morality of the Emancipation Proclamation*. Manchester: Union and Emancipation Society, 1863.
REFERRED TO: 142

FOX, ANNA MARIA (sister of Robert Barclay Fox) (1816–97; *DNB*). Referred to: 52, 57

FOX, CAROLINE (sister of Robert Barclay Fox) (1819–71; *DNB*). Referred to: 52, 57

FOX, MARIA (née Barclay; mother of Robert Barclay Fox) (1786–1858; *DNB*). Referred to: 52, 57

FOX, ROBERT BARCLAY (1817–55; *DNB*). Referred to: 52, 57

FOX, ROBERT WERE (father of Robert Barclay Fox) (1789–1877; *DNB*).
LETTER TO: 58
REFERRED TO: 52, 57

FOX, WILLIAM JOHNSON (1786–1864; *DNB*). Referred to: 243

——— "Men and Things in 1823," *Westminster Review*, I (Jan. 1824), 1–18.
REFERRED TO: 5

Fraser's Magazine for Town and Country. Referred to: 80, 118, 129, 154

FURNIVALL, FREDERICK JAMES (1825–1910; *DNB*). Letter to: 81

GALLOWAY, ARCHIBALD (1780–1850; *DNB*). Referred to: 79

The Gardeners' Chronicle and Agricultural Gazette. Letter to: 146

GARIBALDI, GIUSEPPE (1807–82; *EB*). Referred to: 132–3

GILCHRIST, JAMES (1783–1835). Referred to: 8

GILCHRIST, JOHN BORTHWICK (1759–1841; *DNB*). Referred to: 8

GILL, GEORGE (b. ca. 1820). Letter to: 230

GILLRAY, JAMES (1757–1815; *DNB*).
NOTE: JSM uses the spelling Gilray.
REFERRED TO: 35–6

GLADSTONE, WILLIAM EWART (1809–98; *DNB*). Referred to: 165, 195, 198–9, 230

—— Speech on the Representation of the People Bill (12 Mar., 1866; Commons), *PD*, 3rd ser., Vol. 182, cols. 18–60.
REFERRED TO: 165

The Glasgow Herald. Letter to reporter of: 173

—— Account of JSM's Inaugural Address, 2 Feb., 1867, 6.
REFERRED TO: 173

The Globe and Traveller. Referred to: 27

GLYDE, LAVINGTON (1823–90; *AusDB*). Referred to: 127

GOMPERZ, PHILIPP (father of Theodor) (1782–1857). Referred to: 108

GOMPERZ, THEODOR (1832–1912; *EB*).
LETTERS TO: 90, 91 (2), 108, 115, 117, 118, 119, 123, 125, 131 (2), 133, 136, 140 (2), 143, 149, 152, 205
REFERRED TO: 137

—— *Die Apologie der Heilkunst. Eine griechische Sophistenrede des fünften vorchristlichen Jahrhunderts bearbeitet, übersetzt, erläutert und eingeleitet.* In *Sitzungsberichte der Kaiserliche Akademie der Wissenschaften. Philosophisch-historische Classe.* Vol. 120. Vienna, 1890.
REFERRED TO: 108

—— *Griechische Denker. Eine Geschichte der antiken Philosophie.* 3 vols. Leipzig: Veit, [1893]–1909.
REFERRED TO: 108, 115

—— *Herkulanische Studien. Erstes Heft: Philodem über Induktionsschlüsse, nach der Oxforder und Neapolitaner Abschrift.* Leipzig: Teubner, 1865.
REFERRED TO: 152

—— *Philodemi Epicurei de ira liber.* Leipzig and London: Teubner, 1864.
REFERRED TO: 149

—— "Zu den griechischen Tragikern," *Rheinisches Museum*, XIII (1858), 477–9.
REFERRED TO: 108, 115

—— "Zu Euripides," *Rheinisches Museum*, XI (1857), 470–1.
REFERRED TO: 108, 115

GORDON, ROBERT (1791–1847; *DNB*).
LETTER TO: 42
REFERRED TO: 40

GOWAN, GEORGE EDWARD (d. 1865; *MEB*).
NOTE: Political Commissioner of the EIC.
REFERRED TO: 40

GRAHAM, GEORGE JOHN (1801–88).
LETTER TO: 175
REFERRED TO: 4, 14–15, 16

—— "Law Abuses: Pleadings," *Westminster Review*, IV (July 1825), 60–88.
REFERRED TO: 7

────── "Law Abuses: Pleading—Practice," *Westminster Review*, VI (July 1826), 39–62.
REFERRED TO: 7

GRANT, HORACE (1800–59).
LETTER TO: 44
REFERRED TO: 12, 16, 27, 241

GRANT, JOHN PETER (1807–93; *DNB*). Referred to: 214

GRANT DUFF, MOUNTSTUART ELPHINSTONE (1829–1906; *DNB*). Letters to: 138, 180, 186, 187, 192, 203

GRATRY, AUGUSTE JOSEPH ALPHONSE (1805–72; *GDU*). Referred to: 181

GRAY, JOHN (1816–75; *DNB*). Referred to: 183

GREEN, M.S.
NOTE: Captain in the army of the EIC.
REFERRED TO: 92

GREENING, EDWARD OWEN (1836–1923). Referred to: 188–9

GREENWOOD, FREDERICK (1830–1909; *DNB*). Referred to: 192

GRESHAM, WILLIAM HUTCHISON (1824–75; *AusDB*). Referred to: 233

GREY, GEORGE (1799–1882; *DNB*). Referred to: 60

GRIEVE, JAMES JOHNSTON (1810–91; *MEB*). Referred to: 195

GROTE, GEORGE (1794–1871; *DNB*).
LETTERS TO: 1, 147
REFERRED TO: 136, 142, 152, 205

────── *Plato and the Other Companions of Sokrates*. 3 vols. London: Murray, 1865.
REFERRED TO: 152

GROTE, HARRIET (1792–1878; *DNB*).
LETTER TO: 1
REFERRED TO: 147

GUILLAUMIN, GILBERT URBAIN (1801–64; *DBF*).
LETTER TO: 128
REFERRED TO: 126

GUILLAUMIN, MLLE.
NOTE: daughter of the publisher Gilbert Urbain Guillaumin; she took over his business.
LETTER TO: 234
REFERRED TO: 129

GUROWSKI, ADAM (1805–66).
NOTE: see *Polski Slownik Biograficzny*.
REFERRED TO: 163

────── *Diary*. 3 vols. Boston: Lee and Shepard, 1862 (Vol. I); New York: Carleton, 1864 (Vol. II); New York: Morrison, 1866 (Vol. III).
NOTE: the third volume appeared in early April 1866. There was no English edition of this or the two previous volumes.
REFERRED TO: 163

HAJEE KULEEL KHAN (d. 1802).
NOTE: the Persian Ambassador to Bombay.
REFERRED TO: 41

HAMILTON, WILLIAM (1788–1856; *DNB*). Referred to: 207

HAMMOND, ANTHONY (1758–1838; *DNB*). Referred to: 1–2

HAMMOND, EDMUND (later Lord Hammond) (1802–90; *DNB*). Referred to: 93, 98

HARDY, JOHN BRAITHWAITE.
NOTE: Lieutenant in the army of the EIC.
REFERRED TO: 107

HARE, KATHERINE (daughter of Thomas Hare). Referred to: 182–3

HARE, THOMAS (1806–91; *DNB*).
LETTER TO: 196
REFERRED TO: 118, 127, 159, 122

——— *A Treatise on the Election of Representatives, Parliamentary and Municipal.* London: Longman, *et al.*, 1859.
REFERRED TO: 118, 127, 151, 159, 233

HARE, WILLIAM.
NOTE: a labourer at the EIC.
REFERRED TO: 86

HARFIELD, JAMES (fl. 1824). Referred to: 4–5

HARRISON, ROBERT (1820–97; *MEB*). Letter to: 193

HARVEY, G. (fl. 1866). Letter to: 166

HASLAM, ANNA MARIA (née Fisher; wife of T.J. Haslam) (ca. 1830–after 1918). Referred to: 183

HASLAM, THOMAS JOSEPH (1825–1917).
LETTER TO: 182
REFERRED TO: 189

——— ["OEdipus"]. *The Marriage Problem. By Oedipus. Printed for Gratuitous Circulation amongst Adult Readers Only.* Dublin: n.p., 1868.
REFERRED TO: 183

HAVLIN, THOMAS (fl. 1866). Letter to: 160

HAWKINS, JOHN ABRAHAM FRANCIS.
NOTE: retired as Assistant Examiner from the EIC in January 1866.
REFERRED TO: 110

HAYWARD, ABRAHAM (1801–84; *DNB*). Referred to: 11

HECKENS, MR.
NOTE: member of a deputation from Heligoland.
REFERRED TO: 192

HELPS, ARTHUR (1813–75; *DNB*). Referred to: 127

HENNELL, SAMUEL.
NOTE: Lieutenant-Colonel in the army of the EIC.
REFERRED TO: 93

HERBERT, AUBERON EDWARD WILLIAM MOLYNEUX (1838–1906; *DNB*). Letter to: 235

HETZENDORF, DR. (fl. 1869). Referred to: 204

HICKSON, WILLIAM EDWARD (1803–70; *DNB*). Referred to: 50, 59

HIGINBOTHAM, GEORGE (1826–92; *DNB*). Referred to: 232

HILL, DAVID (1786–1866).
NOTE: see C.C. Prinsep, *Record of . . . Civil Servants in the Madras Presidency.*
REFERRED TO: 110

Index of Persons and Works

HILL, FRANK HARRISON (1830–1910; *DNB*). Letter to: 217
HILL, JANE DALZELL (née Finlay; Mrs. Frank) (d. 1904; *DNB*). Referred to: 218
HIPPOCRATES (ca. 460–380 B.C.; *WWG*). Referred to: 108
HOBHOUSE, JOHN CAM (Baron Broughton de Gyfford) (1786–1869; *DNB*). Referred to: 37
HODGES, J.H. (fl. 1868). Letter to: 198
HOGARTH, WILLIAM (1697–1764; *DNB*). Referred to: 36
HOLMES, OLIVER WENDELL (1841–1935; *DAB*). Letters to: 166, 168
HOLYOAKE, GEORGE JACOB (1817–1906; *DNB*). Letter to: 171
HOPPUS, JOHN (1789–1875; *DNB*). Referred to: 21
HOTEL WINDSOR (Paris). Letter to: 236
HOWE, JOHN H. (d. 1873).
NOTE: see *Who Was Who in America*.
REFERRED TO: 233
HOWELL, A.
NOTE: son of a messenger at the EIC.
REFERRED TO: 86
HOWELL, JOHN (d. 1856).
NOTE: a messenger at the EIC.
REFERRED TO: 84, 86
HUGHES, THOMAS (1822–96; *DNB*).
LETTER TO: 190
REFERRED TO: 157
HUME, DAVID (1711–76; *DNB*). *The History of England from the Invasion of Julius Caesar to the Revolution in 1688*. 8 vols. London: Cadell, Rivington, *et al.*, 1823.
REFERRED TO: 147
HUME, JOSEPH (1777–1855; *DNB*). Referred to: 1, 2, 242
HUTCHINSON, JAMES (fl. 1847). Letter to: 73
HUTTON, RICHARD HOLT (1826–97; *DNB*). Referred to: 136–7

The Industrial Partnership Record. Referred to: 189
INTERNATIONAL WORKING MEN'S ASSOCIATION, GENERAL COUNCIL. Letter to: 220
IRVINE, ALEXANDER (1793–1873; *DNB*).
NOTE: the identification is conjectural.
REFERRED TO: 120–1
——— *The Illustrated Handbook of the British Plants*. London: Nelson, 1858.
NOTE: the identification is conjectural. Work formerly in SC.
REFERRED TO: 120–1

JAMESON, ANNA BROWNELL (1794–1860; *DNB*). Referred to: 199
——— *Communion of Labour: A Second Lecture on the Social Employments of Women*. London: Longman, *et al.*, 1856.
REFERRED TO: 199
JENKINS, RICHARD (1785–1853; *DNB*). Referred to: 51, 58
JENKINSON, ROBERT BANKS (Lord Liverpool) (1770–1828; *DNB*). Referred to: 20

JESUS. Referred to: 53

JEVONS, WILLIAM STANLEY (1835–82; *DNB*).
LETTER TO: 153
REFERRED TO: 164

———— *The Coal Question: An Enquiry Concerning the Progress of the Nation, and the Probable Exhaustion of Our Coal Mines.* London and Cambridge: Macmillan, 1865.
REFERRED TO: 165

———— *Pure Logic; or, The Logic of Quality Apart from Quantity, with Remarks on Boole's System and on the Relation of Logic to Mathematics.* London: Stanford, 1864.
REFERRED TO: 153, 165

———— *A Serious Fall in the Value of Gold Ascertained, and Its Social Effects Set Forth.* London: Stanford, 1863.
REFERRED TO: 164

JOHN, RICHARD EDUARD (1827–89; *ADB*). Referred to: 119

JOHNSTON, HENRY (1842–1919). Letter to: 129

JONES, RICHARD (1790–1855). Referred to: 19

Le Journal des Débats. Referred to: 129

Le Journal des Economistes.
LETTER TO: 128–9
REFERRED TO: 236

KAYE, JOHN WILLIAM (1814–76; *DNB*). Referred to: 85, 121

———— "Mountstuart Elphinstone. In Memoriam," *Once a Week*, I (10 Dec., 1859), 502–4.
REFERRED TO: 121

KEMBALL, ARNOLD BURROWS (b. 1820; *DIB*). Referred to: 99

KEMBLE, JOHN MITCHELL (1807–57; *DNB*). Letters to: 45, 66, 69

———— "The State of the Nation," *British and Foreign Review*, IX (July 1839), 273–319.
NOTE: written with the assistance of the proprietor, T.W. Beaumont.
REFERRED TO: 46

KINDERSLEY, RICHARD TORIN (1792–1879; *DNB*). Referred to: 71

KING, DAVID (1819–94). Referred to: 225

———— *Christianity v. Secularism: Report of a Public Discussion between David King and Charles Bradlaugh, Bury, Lancashire, September 27–30, & October 25 & 26, 1870.* Birmingham: King, 1870.
REFERRED TO: 225

KING, WILHELMINA FORBES (née Mill; one of JSM's sisters) (1808–61). Referred to: 17, 52

KINGSLEY, CHARLES (1819–75; *DNB*). Referred to: 141

KINGSTON, MRS.
NOTE: member of a musical family friendly with the Mills in the early 1830s.
REFERRED TO: 18

KYLLMANN, MAX (1832–67). Referred to: 138, 151

LABOUCHERE, HENRY (later Baron Taunton) (1798–1869; *DNB*). Referred to: 100

LANG, JAMES STRACHAN.
  NOTE: Political Agent of the EIC.
  REFERRED TO: 61
LANGLEY, JOHN BAXTER (fl. 1868). Referred to: 198
LANKESTER, PHEBE (née Pope) (d. 1900; *DNB*). Letter to: 157
LAVELEYE, EMILE LOUIS VICTOR, BARON DE (1822–92; *GDU*). Letter to: 224
——— "On the Causes of War, and the Means of Reducing Their Number," *Cobden Club Essays*, 2nd ser., 1871–72. London, Paris, and New York: Cassell, *et al.*, 1872, 1–55.
  REFERRED TO: 224
——— *La Prusse et l'Autriche depuis Sadowa*. 2 vols. Paris: Hachette, 1870.
  REFERRED TO: 224
LAWFORD, EDWARD (n.d.; *MEB*).
  NOTE: solicitor to the EIC 1826–54.
  REFERRED TO: 17
LAWRENCE, JOHN LAIRD MAIR (Baron) (1811–79; *DNB*). Referred to: 199
LEADER, JOHN TEMPLE (1810–1903; *DNB*). Letter to: 243
LECHEVALIER-SAINT-ANDRÉ, ANDRÉ LOUIS JULES (fl. 1850s). Referred to: 81
——— *Five Years in the Land of Refuge: A Letter on the Prospects of Co-operative Associations in England*. London: Richardson, 1854.
  REFERRED TO: 81
LECKY, WILLIAM EDWARD HARTPOLE (1838–1903; *DNB*). *The History of European Morals from Augustus to Charlemagne*. 2 vols. London: Longmans, Green, 1869.
  REFERRED TO: 206
LEVERSON, MONTAGUE RICHARD (1830–1917). Referred to: 231
LIEBIG, GEORG VON (Baron) (1827–1903). Referred to: 108
LIEBIG, JUSTUS VON (Baron) (1803–73; *ADB*). Referred to: 108
LINDLEY, CAROLINE (fl. 1860s).
  NOTE: a friend of Helen Taylor.
  LETTERS TO: 200 (2), 221
LINDLEY, JOHN (1799–1865; *DNB*). Referred to: 146
LITTRÉ, MAXIMILIEN PAUL EMILE (1801–81; *GDU*). Referred to: 129, 150
LITTROW, AUGUSTE VON (née Bischoff) (1819–90).
  NOTE: see *Deutscher Biographischer Index*.
  LETTERS TO: 228, 234
LIVERPOOL, LORD. See Robert Jenkinson.
LOCH, JOHN (1781–1868; *MEB*). Referred to: 23–4, 30
London and Westminster Review.
  NOTE: references include those to the *London Review*; see also *Westminster Review*.
  REFERRED TO: 26, 31, 32, 35–6, 46, 46–7, 48, 49, 49–50, 50, 244
LONGFIELD, MOUNTIFORT (1802–84; *DNB*). Referred to: 19
LONGMAN, WILLIAM (1813–77; *DNB*).
  NOTE: the references are all to the publishing firm, headed by Longman.
  LETTERS TO: 156, 162, 170
  REFERRED TO: 174, 189, 194, 227
LONGMAN, MRS. (wife of William). Referred to: 162

LOWE, ROBERT (1811–92; *DNB*). Referred to: 217

LOYSON, CHARLES (Père Hyacinthe) (1827–1912; *GDU*). Referred to: 181

LUCAS, MARGARET (née Bright) (1818–90; *DNB*). Referred to: 182–3

LUCAS, SAMUEL (1818–68; *DNB*). Letter to: 121

LUDLOW, JOHN MALCOLM FORBES (1821–1911; *DNB*). Letters to: 173, 174, 178, 179, 216

LUNFORD, MR (fl. 1840s).
NOTE: a legal associate of W.E. Hickson.
REFERRED TO: 59

LUSHINGTON, JAMES LAW (1779–1859; *DNB*). Referred to: 37, 38

LUSK, ANDREW (1810–1909; *DNB*). Referred to: 195

LUSK, ROBERT (brother of Andrew). Referred to: 195

MCCULLOCH, JOHN RAMSAY (1789–1864; *DNB*). Referred to: 2, 6, 10, 18, 20, 21

―――― "Complaints and Proposals Regarding Taxation," *Edinburgh Review*, LVII (July 1833), 434–48.
REFERRED TO: 20

―――― "Disposal of Property by Will—Entails—French Law of Succession," *Edinburgh Review*, XL (July 1824), 350–75.
REFERRED TO: 6

―――― "Price of Foreign Corn—Abolition of the Corn-Laws," *Edinburgh Review*, XLI (Oct. 1824), 55–78.
REFERRED TO: 2

―――― "Prussian Commercial Policy, Pts. I and II," *Foreign Quarterly Review*, IX (May 1832), 455–70, and XI (Apr. 1833), 403–6.
REFERRED TO: 20

―――― "Ricardo's *Political Economy*," *Edinburgh Review*, XXX (June 1818), 59–87.
REFERRED TO: 20

―――― "Wine Trade of France," *Foreign Quarterly Review*, III (Jan. 1829), 636–49.
REFERRED TO: 20

MCDOWELL, WILLIAM (b. 1794).
NOTE: an undertaker in Falmouth.
REFERRED TO: 52, 53

MCKENNIE, THOMAS.
NOTE: assistant fire-lighter at the EIC.
REFERRED TO: 86

MCLAREN, DUNCAN (1800–86; *DNB*). Letter to: 227

MACLEAN, ALEXANDER.
NOTE: an employee of the EIC in Madras.
REFERRED TO: 79

MACNAUGHTEN, ELLIOT (1807–88; *DIB*). Referred to: 95

MAGINN, WILLIAM (1793–1842; *DNB*). Referred to: 5

―――― "Letters to Timothy Tickler, Esq. (No. XVII): To Christopher North, Esq., on the last *Westminster Review*," *Blackwood's Edinburgh Magazine*, XVI (Aug. 1824), 222–6.
REFERRED TO: 5

MAGUIRE, JOHN FRANCIS (1815–72; *DNB*). Referred to: 183

MAHAFFY, JOHN PENTLAND (1839–1919; *DNB*).
NOTE: see also Fisher.
LETTER TO: 183

MALLESON, ELIZABETH (née Whitehead) (1828–1916). Letter to: 172

MALTHUS, THOMAS ROBERT (1766–1834; *DNB*). Referred to: 5–6, 20

———— *The Measure of Value Stated and Illustrated, with an Application of It to the Alterations in the Value of the English Currency since 1790.* London: Murray, 1823.
REFERRED TO: 6

———— "Political Economy," *Quarterly Review*, XXX (Jan. 1824), 297–334.
REFERRED TO: 6

MANGLES, FRANK.
NOTE: a clerk at the EIC.
REFERRED TO: 111

MANGLES, ROSS DONNELLY (1801–77; *DNB*).
NOTE: the references are to him as a member of the Secret Committee in his capacity as Deputy Chairman of the Court of Directors of the EIC 1856–57, and Chairman 1857–58.
REFERRED TO: 87, 92, 93, 94–5, 98–9, 100, 101, 102–3, 104–5, 107

MARINELLI, GAETANO (1754–1820).
NOTE: see *New Grove Dictionary of Music and Musicians*.
REFERRED TO: 16

MARRAST, ARMAND (1801–52; *GDU*). Referred to: 65

MARTIN, ARTHUR PATCHETT (1851–1902).
NOTE: see *Who Was Who*, I.
LETTER TO: 232

MARX, KARL (1818–83; *ADB*). Referred to: 220

———— "Working Men and the War" (23 July, 1870), *Pall Mall Gazette*, 28 July, 1870, 3.
REFERRED TO: 220

MASSON, CHARLES, *pseud.* of James Lewis (fl. 1830s). Referred to: 24

MASSON, DAVID (1822–1907; *DNB*). Referred to: 69

MASTERS, MAXWELL TYLDEN (1833–1907; *DNB*). Letter to: 148

MAZZINI, GIUSEPPE (1805–72; *EB*). Referred to: 41–2

MELVILL, JAMES COSMO (1792–1861; *DNB*). Referred to: 57, 99, 241

MELVILLE, LORD. See Robert Dundas.

The Memorial to the Government Concerning a Chair of Political Economy in the University of Edinburgh. BL Add. MSS 38746, f. 219.
REFERRED TO: 20

MÉRIC-LILANDE, HENRIETTE (1798–1867). Referred to: 15

MERIVALE, CHARLES (1808–93; *DNB*). Referred to: 154

MERIVALE, HERMAN (1806–74; *DNB*). Referred to: 47, 100

METCALFE, CHARLES THEOPHILUS (1785–1846; *DNB*). Referred to: 214

MIGNET, FRANÇOIS AUGUSTE MARIE (1796–1884; *GDU*). Letters to: 122, 123, 139

MILL, CLARA ESTHER. See Digweed.

MILL, GEORGE GROTE (one of JSM's brothers) (ca. 1825–53). Referred to: 68–9

MILL, HARRIET (née Burrow; JSM's mother) (1782?–1854). Referred to: 17, 52
MILL, HARRIET ISABELLA (one of JSM's sisters) (1812–97). Referred to: 17, 52
MILL, HARRIET TAYLOR (née Hardy; JSM's wife) (1807–58). Referred to: 23, 91, 108, 115, 128
——— "Enfranchisement of Women," *Westminster and Foreign Quarterly Review*, LV (July 1851), 289–311. In *Dissertations and Discussions*, II, 411–49; *CW*, XXI, 393–415.
REFERRED TO: 128
MILL, HENRY (one of JSM's brothers) (1820–40). Referred to: 52–3
MILL, JAMES (1773–1836; *DNB*). Referred to: 1–7 *passim*, 9, 17, 21, 26, 31, 33, 66, 67
——— *Analysis of the Phenomena of the Human Mind* (1829). 2nd ed. Ed. John Stuart Mill, with notes by Alexander Bain, Andrew Findlater, and George Grote. 2 vols. London: Longmans, *et al.*, 1869.
REFERRED TO: 205, 206–7
——— *Elements of Political Economy* (1821). Rev. ed. London: Baldwin, Cradock, and Joy, 1824.
REFERRED TO: 5
——— "Periodical Literature: *Edinburgh Review*" (Pt. I), *Westminster Review*, I (Jan. 1824), 206–49.
REFERRED TO: 5
——— "Periodical Literature: The *Quarterly Review*," *Westminster Review*, II (Oct. 1824), 463–503.
REFERRED TO: 5
——— "Southey's *Book of the Church*," *Westminster Review*, III (Jan. 1825), 167–212.
REFERRED TO: 6
MILL, JAMES BENTHAM (one of JSM's brothers) (1814–62). Referred to: 31
MILL, JANE STUART. See Ferraboschi.
MILL, JOHN STUART. "Affairs of the Guicowar [Gaikwar]" (2 July, 1840). In part in *PP*, 1852–53, LXIX, 259. See *CW*, XXX, App. A, No. 979.
REFERRED TO: 54
——— *Auguste Comte and Positivism*. London: Trübner, 1865.
REFERRED TO: 152, 164
——— "Bain's On the Application of Science to Human Health and Well-being," *Examiner*, 2 Sept., 1848, 565. In *CW*, XXV, 1118–20.
REFERRED TO: 75–6
——— "Bentham," *London and Westminster Review*, VII & XXIX (Aug. 1838), 467–506. In *CW*, X, 75–115.
REFERRED TO: 54
——— "Blessings of Equal Justice," *Morning Chronicle*, 20 Aug., 1823, 2. In *CW*, XXII, 43–6.
REFERRED TO: 7
——— "Brodie's *History of the British Empire*," *Westminster Review*, II (Oct. 1824), 346–402. In *CW*, VI, 1–58.
REFERRED TO: 5
——— "The Case of William Smith," *CW*, XXV, 1221–2.
REFERRED TO: 217

——— "Coleridge," *London and Westminster Review*, XXXIII (Mar. 1840), 257–302. In *CW*, X, 117–63.
REFERRED TO: 54

——— *Considerations on Representative Government*. London: Parker, Son, and Bourne, 1861. In *CW*, XIX, 371–577.
REFERRED TO: 123, 124, 125, 129–30, 163, 174–5

——— (in French) *Le gouvernement représentatif*. Trans. Charles Brook Dupont-White. Paris: Guillaumin, 1862.
REFERRED TO: 128, 129

——— "The Contest in America," *Fraser's Magazine*, LXV (Feb. 1862), 258–68. In *CW*, XXI, 125–42.
REFERRED TO: 129, 134

——— "The Corn Laws," *Westminster Review*, III (Apr. 1825), 394–420. In *CW*, IV, 45–70.
REFERRED TO: 2

——— "Disputes between the Rao of Cutch and Certain Wagur [Wagher] Chiefs" (8 July, 1840). See *CW*, XXX, App. A, No. 980.
REFERRED TO: 54

——— *Dissertations and Discussions*. London: Parker, 1859 (Vols. I–II); Longman, 1867 (Vol. III); Longman, 1875 (Vol. IV).
REFERRED TO: 54, 128, 175, 231

——— "Duveyrier's Political Views of French Affairs," *Edinburgh Review*, LXXXIII (Apr. 1846), 435–74. In *CW*, XX, 295–316.
REFERRED TO: 69

——— *England and Ireland*. London: Longmans, *et al.*, 1868. In *CW*, VI, 505–32.
REFERRED TO: 189, 190, 194, 209, 215

——— *An Examination of Sir William Hamilton's Philosophy and of the Principal Philosophical Questions Discussed in His Writings*. London: Longmans, *et al.*, 1865. *CW*, IX.
REFERRED TO: 149–50, 152, 153, 174–5, 207

——— "Free Discussion [Letters I, II, III]," *Morning Chronicle*, 28 Jan., 8 and 12 Feb., 1823. In *CW*, XXII, 9–12, 12–15, 15–18.
REFERRED TO: 6

——— "The Game Laws," *Westminster Review*, V (Jan. 1826), 1–22. In *CW*, VI, 99–120.
REFERRED TO: 8

——— *Gesammelte Werke*. Ed. Theodor Gomperz. 12 vols. Leipzig: Fues, 1869–80.
REFERRED TO: 90, 119, 134, 208

——— *Inaugural Address, Delivered to the University of St. Andrews*. London: Longmans, *et al.*, 1867. In *CW*, XXI, 215–57.
REFERRED TO: 173, 174–5, 208

——— (in German) *Rectoratsrede, gehalten an der St. Andrews Universität am 1. Februar 1857*. Trans. Adolf Wahrmund (1827–1913). In *Gesammelte Werke*, I, 203–63.
REFERRED TO: 186

——— "The Later Speculations of Auguste Comte," *Westminster and Foreign Quarterly Review*, LXXXIV (July 1865), 1–42. In *CW*, X, 328–68.
REFERRED TO: 152

"Letter to the Editor of the *Edinburgh Review* on James Mill," *Edinburgh Review*, LXXIX (Jan. 1844), 267–71. In *CW*, I, 533–8.
REFERRED TO: 67

"The Metropolitan Government Bill" (7 Aug., 1867), *PD*, 3rd ser., Vol. 189, cols. 1040–1. In *CW*, XXVIII, 230–1.
REFERRED TO: 177, 178–9

"Mignet's French Revolution," *Westminster Review*, V (Apr. 1826), 385–98. In *CW*, XX, 1–14.
REFERRED TO: 123

"Mrs. Austin's Translation of M. Cousin's Report." See "Reform in Education."

"The Municipal Corporations Bill" (21 May, 1867), *PD*, 3rd ser., Vol. 187, cols. 882–5, 891. In *CW*, XXVIII, 162–5.
REFERRED TO: 177

"The Negro Question," *Fraser's Magazine*, XLI (Jan. 1850), 25–31. In *CW*, XXI, 85–95.
REFERRED TO: 80

On Liberty. London: Parker, 1859. In *CW*, XVIII, 213–310.
REFERRED TO: 108, 117, 119–20, 163, 174–5

(in German) *Über die Freiheit*. Trans. Theodor Gomperz. In *Gesammelte Werke*, I, 1–123.
REFERRED TO: 119–20, 125

(in German) *Über die Freiheit*. Trans. F. Pickford. Frankfurt: Sauerländer, 1860.
REFERRED TO: 124, 125

"Periodical Literature: *Edinburgh Review*" (Pt. II), *Westminster Review*, II (Apr. 1824), 505–41. In *CW*, I, 291–325.
REFERRED TO: 5

"The Positive Philosophy of Auguste Comte," *Westminster and Foreign Quarterly Review*, LXXXIII (Apr. 1865), 339–405. In *CW*, X, 261–327.
REFERRED TO: 152

Principles of Political Economy, with Some of Their Applications to Social Philosophy. 2 vols. London: Parker, 1848. *CW*, II–III.
REFERRED TO: 74, 116, 126, 130, 163, 174–5, 223

(in French) *Principes d'économie politique* (1854). Trans. Hippolyte Dussard and Jean Gustave Courcelle-Seneuil. 2 vols. 3rd ed. Paris: Guillaumin, 1873.
NOTE: in SC.
REFERRED TO: 82, 234

"Recent Writers on Reform," *Fraser's Magazine*, LIX (Apr. 1859), 489–508. In *CW*, XIX, 341–70.
REFERRED TO: 118

"Reform in Education," *Monthly Repository*, n.s. VIII (July 1834), 502–13. In *CW*, XXI, 61–79.
REFERRED TO: 23

"The Rules of the Booksellers' Association [2]." In *Opinions of Certain Authors on the Bookselling Question*. London: Parker, 1852, 47. In *CW*, XXV, 1189.
REFERRED TO: 80

――― "Securities for Good Government," *Morning Chronicle*, 25 Sept., 1823, 2. In *CW*, XXII, 62–4.
REFERRED TO: 7

――― "The Slave Power," *Westminster Review*, n.s. XXII (Oct. 1862), 489–510. In *CW*, XXI, 143–64.
REFERRED TO: 132

――― *The Subjection of Women*. London: Longmans, *et al.*, 1869. In *CW*, XXI, 259–340.
REFERRED TO: 207, 208

――― *A System of Logic, Ratiocinative and Inductive*. 2 vols. London: Parker, 1843. *CW*, VII–VIII.
REFERRED TO: 64–5, 65, 90, 91, 115, 116, 130, 134–5, 156, 205, 207

――― (a part in German) *Die inductive Logik*. Trans. J. von Schiel. Braunschweig: Vieweg, 1849.
NOTE: see also next entry.
REFERRED TO: 133

――― (in German) *System der deductiven und inductiven Logik*. Trans. J. von Schiel. 2 vols. Braunschweig: Vieweg, 1862–63.
NOTE: see also previous entry.
REFERRED TO: 133

――― (in German) *System der deductiven und inductiven Logik*. Trans. Theodor Gomperz. Vols. II–IV of *Gesammelte Werke*.
REFERRED TO: 90, 91, 114, 134–5, 205

――― *Thoughts on Parliamentary Reform* (1859). 2nd ed. London: Parker and Son, 1859. In *CW*, XIX, 311–39.
REFERRED TO: 118, 138

――― *Utilitarianism*. London: Parker, Son, and Bourne, 1863. In *CW*, X, 203–59.
REFERRED TO: 138, 139, 144, 205

――― (in German) *Das Nützlichkeits-princip*. Trans. Adolph Wahrmund. In *Gesammelte Werke*, I, 125–200.
REFERRED TO: 144, 205

――― "Ware's Letters from Palmyra," *London and Westminster Review*, VI & XXVIII (Jan. 1838), 436–70. In *CW*, I, 431–61.
REFERRED TO: 36

――― "The Westminster Election of 1865" [1] (3 July, 1865), *Daily Telegraph*, 4 July, 1865, 3. In *CW*, XXVIII, 13–18.
REFERRED TO: 155

――― "The Westminster Election of 1865" [2] (5 July, 1865), *Morning Star*, 6 July, 1865, 2. In *CW*, XXVIII, 18–28.
REFERRED TO: 155

――― "The Westminster Election of 1865" [3] (6 July, 1865), *Daily News*, 7 July, 1865, 3. In *CW*, XXVIII, 28–31.
REFERRED TO: 155

――― "The Westminster Election of 1865" [4] (8 July, 1865), *Daily Telegraph*, 10 July, 1865, 2. In *CW*, XXVIII, 31–40.
REFERRED TO: 155

——— "The Westminster Election of 1865" [5] (10 July, 1865), *Morning Star*, 11 July, 1865, 2. In *CW*, XXVIII, 40–2.
REFERRED TO: 155

——— "The Westminster Election of 1865" [6] (10 July, 1865), *Daily Telegraph*, 11 July, 1865, 4. In *CW*, XXVIII, 42–3.
REFERRED TO: 155

——— "The Westminster Election of 1865" [7] (12 July, 1865), *Morning Star*, 13 July, 1865, 2. In *CW*, XXVIII, 43–5.
REFERRED TO: 155

——— "Whately's Introductory Lectures on Political Economy," *Examiner*, 12 June, 1831, 373. In *CW*, XXII, 327–9.
REFERRED TO: 19

——— "Whewell on Moral Philosophy," *Westminster Review*, LVIII (Oct. 1852), 349–85. In *CW*, X, 165–201.
REFERRED TO: 115

MILL, MARY ELIZABETH. See Colman.

MILL, WILHELMINA FORBES. See King.

MILLS, CHARLES.
NOTE: Director of the EIC in 1856.
REFERRED TO: 95

MILLS, P.L. (fl. 1870s). Letter to: 230

MILNES, RICHARD MONCKTON (1st Baron Houghton) (1809–85; *DNB*). Referred to: 48, 64

——— "American Philosophy: Emerson's Works," *London and Westminster Review*, XXXIII (Mar. 1840), 345–72.
REFERRED TO: 48

MITCHELL, GEORGE.
NOTE: a pensioner messenger of the EIC.
REFERRED TO: 86

MITCHELL, HENRY (1830–1902; *DAB*). Letter to: 197

MOOSHERRAF BEGUM (of Joura). Referred to: 56

MORGAN, H.
NOTE: a writer at the EIC.
REFERRED TO: 95

MORLEY, JOHN (Viscount Morley of Blackburn) (1838–1923; *DNB*). Letter to: 173

Morning Chronicle. Referred to: 6

——— "Suicide," 29 Jan., 1830, 3.
REFERRED TO: 9

Morning Star. Unheaded leading article on the bill for municipal reform, 19 July, 1867, 4.
REFERRED TO: 179

MOZART, WOLFGANG AMADEUS (1756–91; *EB*). *Don Giovanni*.
NOTE: first performed in 1787.
REFERRED TO: 15

MOZLEY, ANNE (1809–91; *DNB*). Letter to?: 208

——— "Mr. Mill On the Subjection of Women," *Blackwood's Magazine*, CVI (Sept. 1869), 309–21.
REFERRED TO: 208

MURCHISON, MR.
NOTE: an employee of the EIC.
REFERRED TO: 13

MURRAY, CHARLES AUGUSTUS (1806–95; *DNB*). Referred to: 107, 113

MUSHET, MARGARET (1799–1885). Referred to: 8

MUSHET, ROBERT (1782–1828; *DNB*). Referred to: 8

NAPIER, MACVEY (1776–1847; *DNB*). Referred to: 20, 67

NAPIER, WILLIAM FRANCIS PATRICK (1785–1860; *DNB*). Referred to: 35

——— "The Duke of Wellington," *London and Westminster Review*, VI & XXVIII (Jan. 1838), 367–436.
REFERRED TO: 35

NAPOLEON III (of France) (1808–73; *GDU*). Referred to: 132–3

NASIR-UD-DAULA (Nizam of Hyderabad) (ruled 1829–57). Referred to: 60, 67–8

NASIR-UD-DIN HAIDAR (King of Oudh) (d. 1837). Referred to: 37

NASR-ED-DIN [Nasirud-Din] (Shah of Persia) (1829–96; *EB*). Referred to: 101

National Review. Referred to: 138, 139

NAVILLE, JULES ERNEST (1816–1909).
NOTE: see *Dictionnaire historique et biographique de la Suisse*.
LETTERS TO: 159, 187

——— *Conseil de l'Association Réformiste [de Genève]. Séance du 21 novembre 1865. Réforme du système électoral*. [*Rapport du président, E. Naville*.] Geneva: printed Vaney, 1865.
REFERRED TO: 159

——— *La question électorale en Europe et en Amérique: Rapport présenté à l'Association Réformiste de Genève*. Geneva: Georg, 1867.
REFERRED TO: 187

NEATE, CHARLES (1806–79; *DNB*). Referred to: 161

NEWMAN, JOHN HENRY (1801–90; *DNB*). Referred to: 154

NEWMARCH, WILLIAM (1820–82; *DNB*). "Commercial History and Review of 1865," "Supplement" to the *Economist*, XXIV (10 Mar., 1866), 1–64.
REFERRED TO: 164

NICHOL, JOHN PRINGLE (1804–59; *DNB*). Referred to: 21, 25, 58, 62

——— "Incidence of Tithes," *Tait's Edinburgh Magazine*, I (May 1832), 224–8.
REFERRED TO: 21

——— "Political Economy for Farmers," *Tait's Edinburgh Magazine*, III (May 1833), 191–8.
REFERRED TO: 21

——— "Rae's *New Principles of Political Economy, in Refutation of Adam Smith*," *Foreign Quarterly Review*, XV (July 1835), 241–66.
REFERRED TO: 26

NICHOLSON, EDWARD WILLIAMS BYRON (1849–1912; *DNB*). Letter to: 213

NORRIS, EDWIN.
NOTE: a messenger at the EIC.
REFERRED TO: 89

North American Review. "Miscellaneous Notices, No. 11. *Westminster Review*," n.s. IX (Apr. 1824), 419–26.
REFERRED TO: 5

O'BEIRNE, JAMES LYSTER (b. 1820; *WWBMP*). Referred to: 183

OLIPHANT, JOHN STEWART.
NOTE: a clerk at the EIC.
REFERRED TO: 111

OLIPHANT, MARGARET (née Wilson) (1828–97; *DNB*). Letter to?: 208

—— "Mill's *The Subjection of Women*," *Edinburgh Review*, CXXX (Oct. 1869), 572–602.
REFERRED TO: 208

OSBORNE, RALPH BERNAL (1811–82; *WWBMP*). Letter to: 162

OUTRAM, JAMES (1803–63; *DNB*). Referred to: 99, 113

OWENS COLLEGE, TRUSTEES OF. Letter to: 164

PACINI, GIOVANNI (1796–1867; *GDU*). *La Niobé*.
NOTE: first performed in 1826.
REFERRED TO: 28

Pall Mall Gazette. Referred to: 192

PARKER, JOHN WILLIAM (1792–1870; *DNB*).
LETTERS TO: 64, 65, 74, 80 (2), 117, 129, 138
REFERRED TO: 91, 118–19, 127–8, 139

PARKES, HENRY (1815–96; *AusDB*). Referred to: 126

PARRY, CLIVE, *et al.*, eds. "Deed of Cession of the Kuria Muria Islands between Great Britain and the Imam of Muscat (Oman). Signed at Muscat, 14 June, 1854." In *The Consolidated Treaty Series.* Dobbs Ferry, N.Y.: Oceana Publications, 1969–86, Vol. 112, pp. 39–40.
REFERRED TO: 100

PASSY, FRÉDÉRIC (1822–1912; *GDU*). Letter to: 181

PATTEN, GEORGE (1801–65).
NOTE: either George, the painter, who studied at the Royal Academy after 1816, or John Wilson-Patten (1802–92), later Baron Winmorleigh, who went up to Magdalen College, Oxford, in 1821.
REFERRED TO: 4

PAUL, ST. Quoted: 235

PAULIN, J.B. ALEXANDRE (1796–1859).
NOTE: Parisian publisher, bookseller, and editor.
LETTER TO: 32

PAYENS, MR.
NOTE: member of a deputation from Heligoland.
REFERRED TO: 192

PEACOCK, THOMAS LOVE (1775–1866; *DNB*). Referred to: 39, 64, 241

PEARSON, CHARLES HENRY (1830–94; *DNB*).
LETTER TO: 139
REFERRED TO: 138

Penny Newsman. Referred to: 145

PEOPLE'S GARDEN CO. Letter to: 222

PETERS, WILLIAM.
NOTE: a writer at the EIC.
REFERRED TO: 90, 113, 114

PETTY-FITZMAURICE, HENRY (3rd Marquis of Lansdowne) (1780–1863; *DNB*). Referred to: 66

PETTY-FITZMAURICE, HENRY THOMAS (Earl of Shelburne, later 4th Marquis of Lansdowne) (1816–66; *DNB*). Referred to: 87

PHILLIPS, HENRY WYNDHAM (1820–68; *MEB*). Letter to: 177

PICARD, AUGUSTE (fl. 1850–60s). Referred to: 128

PICO DELLA MIRANDOLA, GIOVANNI (1463–94; *EB*). Referred to: 6

PIGEARD, JEAN CHARLES EDOUARD (b. 1818). Referred to: 88, 95, 103

PITMAN, HENRY (1826–1909). Referred to: 188–9

PLACE, FRANCIS (1771–1854; *DNB*). Referred to: 7

PLATO (427–437 B.C.; *WWG*). Referred to: 152

PLUMMER, JOHN (1831–1914; *AusDB*).
LETTER TO: 145
REFERRED TO: 193, 194

———— *Our Colonies: An Essay on the Advantages Accruing to the British Nation, from Its Possession of the Colonies, Considered Economically, Politically and Morally.* London, Kettering, and Sydney, 1864.
REFERRED TO: 145

PLUMMER, MARY ANN (née Jenkinson; Mrs. John). Referred to: 146

POLLARD-URQUHART, WILLIAM (1815–71; *DNB*). Referred to: 183

Post-Office London Court Guide. London: Kelly, [1866–68].
REFERRED TO: 198

The Post-Office London Directory. Issued annually.
REFERRED TO: 198

POTTER, JOHN PHILLIPS (1793–1861). "The Philosophy of Socrates," *British and Foreign Review*, XIV (Feb. 1843), 289–333.
REFERRED TO: 66

POTTER, THOMAS BAYLEY (1817–98; *DNB*). Letter to: 141

PRANDI, FORTUNATO (d. 1868).
NOTE: see *Wellesley Index*, II.
LETTER TO: 22

PRATT, HODGSON (1824–1907; *DNB*). Letter to: 229

PRESCOTT, GROTE & CO. Letter to: 151

PRESCOTT, WILLIAM GEORGE (1800–65; *MEB*). Referred to: 3, 7

PRIDEAUX, FRANCIS WILLIAM (d. 1871). Referred to: 90, 113, 114

Prospective Review. "The White Lady and Undine," I (May 1845), 275–82.
REFERRED TO: 72

PROTAGORAS (ca. 490–420 B.C.; *WWG*). Referred to: 108

PRYME, GEORGE (1781–1868; *DNB*). Referred to: 19

———— *A Syllabus of a Course of Lectures on the Principles of Political Economy*. Cambridge: printed Smith, 1816.
REFERRED TO: 19

PULLING, ALEXANDER (1813–95; *DNB*). Referred to: 192

———— "The Law of England Relating to Purity of Elections," *Law Magazine and Law Review*, 3rd ser., XXI (1866), 54–68, and 274–82.
REFERRED TO: 192

RAE, WILLIAM FRASER (1835–1905; *DNB*).
LETTER TO: 211
REFERRED TO: 211

———— "The Future of Reform," *Westminster Review*, n.s. XXXII (July 1867), 161–88.
REFERRED TO: 211

———— "The Hopes and Fears of Reformers," *Westminster Review*, n.s. XXXI (Apr. 1867), 472–502.
REFERRED TO: 211

———— "Reform and Reformers," *Westminster Review*, n.s. XXXI (Jan. 1867), 171–90.
REFERRED TO: 211

———— *Westward by Rail: The New Route to the East*. New York: Appleton, 1870.
REFERRED TO: 218

RAGHUJI III (Raja of Nagpur) (1818–53). Referred to: 60

RATTAZZI, URBANO (1808–73; *EB*). Referred to: 133

RAUMER, FRIEDRICH LUDWIG GEORG (1781–1873; *EB*). *England in 1835*. Trans. Sarah Austin. 3 vols. London: Murray, 1836.
REFERRED TO: 31

REEVE, HENRY (1813–95; *DNB*). Letter to: 73

La République. Referred to: 82

REYNELL, CHARLES WETHERBY (1798–1892; *MEB*). Referred to: 35, 49

RICARDO, DAVID (1772–1823; *DNB*). Referred to: 10

RICKETTS, MORDAUNT.
NOTE: an employee of the EIC.
REFERRED TO: 17

RIDDELL, THOMAS ALEXANDER.
NOTE: a clerk at the EIC.
REFERRED TO: 104

RING, W.I.
NOTE: Captain in the army of the EIC.
REFERRED TO: 92

RITTER, KARL (1779–1859; *ADB*). *Die Erdkunde im Verhältnis zur Natur und zur Geschichte des Menschen oder allgemeine vergleichende Geographie, als sichere*

Grundlage des Studiums und Unterrichts in physicalischen und historischen Wissenschaften. 19 vols. in 21. 2nd ed. Enlarged. Berlin: Reimer, 1822–59.
REFERRED TO: 32

——— (in French) *Géographie générale comparée, ou Etude de la terre dans ses rapports avec la nature et avec l'histoire de l'homme, pour servir de base à l'étude et à l'enseignement des sciences physiques et historiques.* Trans. E. Buret and Edouard Desor. 3 vols. Paris: Paulin, 1835–36.
REFERRED TO: 32

ROBERTSON, JOHN (ca. 1811–75; *MEB*).
LETTER TO: 35
REFERRED TO: 46–7

——— "Caricatures," *London and Westminster Review,* VI & XXVIII (Jan. 1838), 261–93.
REFERRED TO: 35–6

ROCK, EDWARD.
NOTE: assistant fire-lighter at the EIC.
REFERRED TO: 86

ROEBUCK, JOHN ARTHUR (1801–79; *DNB*).
LETTER TO: 26
REFERRED TO: 14, 16

ROGERS, JAMES EDWIN THOROLD (1823–90; *DNB*). Letters to: 137, 141, 219

——— *The History of Agriculture and Prices in England, from the Year after the Oxford Parliament, 1259, to the Commencement of the Continental War, 1793. Compiled Entirely from Original and Contemporaneous Records.* 7 vols. Oxford: Clarendon Press, 1866–1902.
REFERRED TO: 137

ROMILLY, CHARLES (1808–87; *DNB*). Referred to: 11, 14

ROSS, ALEXANDER (b. 1777; *DIB*). Referred to: 40, 41

ROSSI, PELLEGRINO LUIGI EDOARDO (Count) (1787–1848; *EB*). Referred to: 21

ROSSITER, WILLIAM (d. 1897; *MEB*). Letters to: 184, 193, 194, 210, 226

——— *An Elementary Handbook of Physics.* London and Edinburgh: Blackwood, 1871.
REFERRED TO: 226

ROUVIÈRE, PIERRE AUGUSTIN (b. ca. 1803). Letter to: 228

ROY, RAM MOHUN (1774–1833; *EB*). Referred to: 66

ROYLE, JOHN FORBES (1799–1858; *DNB*). Referred to: 64

RUGE, ARNOLD (1802–80; *EB*). Referred to: 91

RUNDALL, WHARTON.
NOTE: a temporary writer in the EIC.
REFERRED TO: 86, 92, 102, 109, 111

RUSDEN, HENRY KEYLOCK (1826–1910; *AusDB*). Referred to: 233

RUSSELL, JOHN (Earl Russell) (1792–1878; *DNB*). Referred to: 8, 88

——— *Memoirs of the Affairs of Europe from the Peace of Utrecht.* 2 vols. London: Murray, 1824–29.
REFERRED TO: 8

Russell, John (Lord Amberley) (1842–76; *DNB*).
LETTER TO: 151
REFERRED TO: 178, 225

Russell, Katherine Louisa (Lady Amberley; née Stanley) (1842–74; *DNB*). Letter to: 177

Said Ibn Sultan (of Oman) (ruled 1804–56).
NOTE: known as the Imaum of Muscat.
REFERRED TO: 100

Say, Jean Baptiste (1767–1832; *GDU*).
LETTER TO: 9
REFERRED TO: 21

——— *Cours complet d'économie politique pratique, ouvrage destiné à mettre sous les yeux des hommes d'état, des propriétaires fonciers et des capitalistes, des savans, des agriculteurs, des manufacturiers, des négocians, et en général de tous les citoyens, l'économie des sociétés.* 7 vols. Paris: Rapilly, 1828–29.
NOTE: the quotation is not exact.
QUOTED: 10
REFERRED TO: 9–10

Say, Julie (née Gourdel-Deloche) (d. 1830). Referred to: 9

Sayaji Rao (Gaikwar of Baroda) (ruled 1819–47). Referred to: 38

Schiel, J. von.
NOTE: see JSM, *System of Logic*, trans. von Schiel.
REFERRED TO: 133

Schröder-Devrient, Wilhelmine (1804–60; *ADB*). Referred to: 15

Scotsman. Leading article on secular education in Ireland, 29 Jan., 1866, 2.
REFERRED TO: 161

Scott, Benjamin (1814–92; *DNB*). Referred to: 174, 179

Scott, Edward (1752/3–1842). Letter to: 44

Scott, Louisa Mary (née Anwyl) (d. 1812). Referred to: 45

Scott, Walter (1771–1832; *DNB*). Referred to: 227

Séances et Travaux de l'Académie des Sciences Morales et Politiques. Paris: au bureau du Moniteur Universel, *et al.*, 1842–1935.
REFERRED TO: 130

Secretan, John James (fl. 1824).
NOTE: author on commercial subjects.
REFERRED TO: 4

Secretary to the Board of Control. Letters to: 87, 94, 101, 112

Selby, W.B.
NOTE: Commander in the Indian Navy.
REFERRED TO: 93

Senior, Nassau William (1790–1864; *DNB*).
LETTERS TO: 47, 124, 244
REFERRED TO: 17, 19

——— *Correspondence and Conversations of Alexis de Tocqueville with Nassau William Senior from 1834–1859.* Ed. M.C.M. Simpson. 2 vols. London: King, 1872.
REFERRED TO: 124

Index of Persons and Works 309

———— *An Introductory Lecture on Political Economy Delivered before the University of Oxford, the 6th of December, 1826.* London: Mawman, 1827.
REFERRED TO: 19

———— *Suggestions on Popular Education.* London: Murray, 1861.
REFERRED TO: 124–5

———— *Three Lectures on the Cost of Obtaining Money, and on Some Effects of Private and Government Paper Money; Delivered before the University of Oxford, in Trinity Term, 1829.* London: Murray, 1830.
REFERRED TO: 19

———— *Three Lectures on the Transmission of the Precious Metals from Country to Country and the Mercantile Theory of Wealth, Delivered before the University of Oxford, in June, 1827.* London: Murray, 1828.
REFERRED TO: 19

———— *Two Lectures on Population, Delivered before the University of Oxford in Easter Term 1828 . . . to Which Is Added a Correspondence between the Author and the Rev. T.R. Malthus.* London: Murray, 1831.
REFERRED TO: 19

SEVERN, JOSEPH (1793–1879; *DNB*). Referred to: 43

SEYMOUR, HENRY DANBY (1820–77; *DIB*). Referred to: 87

SHAH SHUJA (King of Afghanistan) (1780–1842; *EB*). Referred to: 60–1

SHARP, CHARLES (fl. 1870s). Letter to: 222

SHAW, JAMES JOHNSTON (1849–1910; *DNB*). Letter to: 207

SHEIL, JUSTIN (1803–71; *DNB*). Referred to: 101

SHEPHERD, JOHN (d. 1859; *MEB*). Referred to: 79

SIDGWICK, HENRY (1838–1900; *DNB*). Letters to: 180, 185

———— *The Ethics of Conformity and Subscription.* London: Williams and Norgate, 1870.
REFERRED TO: 180, 185

SINDHIA, DAULAT RAO (Maharaja of Sind) (1780–1827). Referred to: 28

SLATER, PHILIP.
NOTE: a warehouse pensioner of the EIC.
REFERRED TO: 86

SMALLEY, GEORGE WASHBURN (1833–1916; *DAB*). Letter to: 201

SMITH, ADAM (1723–90; *DNB*). *An Inquiry into the Nature and Causes of the Wealth of Nations.* Ed. James Edwin Thorold Rogers. 2 vols. Oxford: Clarendon Press, 1869.
REFERRED TO: 219

———— *The Theory of Moral Sentiments . . . to Which Is Added a Dissertation on the Origin of Language* (1759). 6th ed. 2 vols. London: Strahan and Cadell; Edinburgh: Creech and Bell, 1790.
NOTE: in SC.
REFERRED TO: 193

SMITH, GOLDWIN (1823–1910; *DNB*). Referred to: 145

———— *The Empire: A Series of Letters Published in the Daily News, 1862, 1863.* Oxford and London: Henry and Parker, 1863.
REFERRED TO: 145

———— *War Ships for the Southern Confederacy: Report of Public Meeting in the*

Free-Trade Hall, Manchester; with Letter from Professor Goldwin Smith to the "Daily News." Manchester: Union and Emancipation Society, 1863.
REFERRED TO: 142

SMITH, JOSHUA TOULMIN (1816–69; *DNB*). Letter to: 167

SMITH, WILLIAM (1813–93; *DNB*). Letter to: 170

SMITH, WILLIAM.
NOTE: a police constable.
REFERRED TO: 217–18

SMYTHE, MR. (fl. 1850s).
NOTE: a correspondent of J.W. Parker.
REFERRED TO: 118

SOCRATES (469–399 B.C.; *WWG*). Referred to: 66

SOUTHEY, ROBERT (1774–1843; *DNB*). Referred to: 6

——— *The Book of the Church.* 2 vols. London: Murray, 1824.
REFERRED TO: 6

——— *A Vision of Judgement.* London: Longman, *et al.*, 1821.
REFERRED TO: 6

SPANKIE, SERJEANT.
NOTE: standing counsel to the EIC.
REFERRED TO: 60

Spectator.
LETTER TO: 136
REFERRED TO: 214

——— "Mr. Mill on the Irish Land Question," 22 Feb., 1868, 216–18.
REFERRED TO: 190

SPEDDING, THOMAS STORY (1800–70).
NOTE: see *Alumni Cantab.*
LETTER TO: 74

——— *Letters on the Poor-Laws.* London: printed Odell, 1847.
REFERRED TO: 74–5

SPENCE, CATHERINE HELEN (1825–1910; *AusDB*). Letter to: 126

——— *A Plea for Pure Democracy: Mr. Hare's Reform Bill Applied to South Australia.* Adelaide: Rigby, 1861.
REFERRED TO: 126–7

——— "Representation of Minorities" (letter to the editor; signed "C.H.S."), *South Australian Gazette and Colonial Register*, 31 Aug., 1861, 3.
REFERRED TO: 127

——— "Representation of Minorities" (letter to the editor; signed "C.H.S."), *South Australian Gazette and Colonial Register*, 9 Sept., 1861, 3.
REFERRED TO: 127

SPENCE, WILLIAM.
NOTE: Assistant Messenger in the Book Department of the EIC.
REFERRED TO: 114

SPENCER, HERBERT (1820–1903; *DNB*).
LETTER TO: 122
REFERRED TO: 168

——— *First Principles*. London: Williams and Norgate, 1862.
REFERRED TO: 122

STANGER, MARY (née Calvert) (1804–90).
NOTE: sister of John Mitchinson Calvert.
REFERRED TO: 58

STANLEY, CATHERINE (née Leycester) (1792–1862; *DNB*). Letter to: 246

STANLEY, EDWARD HENRY (Lord Stanley; later 15th Earl of Derby) (1826–93; *DNB*). Referred to: 115

STANSFELD, JAMES (1820–98; *DNB*). Referred to: 196

STARK, HUGH.
NOTE: Assistant Secretary and Senior Clerk in the Revenue Department of the EIC.
LETTER TO: 79
REFERRED TO: 67

STEBBING, WILLIAM (1832–1926).
NOTE: see *Wellesley Index*, I.
LETTER TO: 116

——— *An Analysis of Mr. Mill's System of Logic*. London: Longman, *et al.*, 1864.
REFERRED TO: 116–17

STEPHEN, JAMES (1789–1859; *DNB*). Letter to: 41

——— "Works of the Author of *The Natural History of Enthusiasm*," *Edinburgh Review*, LXXI (Apr. 1840), 220–63.
REFERRED TO: 54–5

STEPHEN, JAMES FITZJAMES (1829–94; *DNB*). Letters to: 148, 154, 206

——— "Dr. Newman's *Apologia*," *Fraser's Magazine*, LXX (Sept. 1864), 265–303.
REFERRED TO: 154

——— "Dr. Pusey and the Court of Appeal," *Fraser's Magazine*, LXX (Nov. 1864), 644–62.
REFERRED TO: 154

——— *Essays by a Barrister*. London: Smith, Elder, 1862.
REFERRED TO: 207

——— "Merivale's Sermons on the Conversion of the Roman Empire," *Fraser's Magazine*, LXXI (Mar. 1865), 363–82.
REFERRED TO: 154

——— "The Privy Council and the Church of England," *Fraser's Magazine*, LXIX (May 1864), 521–37.
REFERRED TO: 154

——— "The Study of History" (Nos. I and II), *Cornhill Magazine*, III (June 1861), 666–80, and IV (July 1861), 25–41.
REFERRED TO: 148

——— "What Is the Law of the Church of England?" *Fraser's Magazine*, LXXI (Feb. 1865), 225–41.
REFERRED TO: 154

——— "Women and Scepticism," *Fraser's Magazine*, LXVIII (Dec. 1863), 679–98.
REFERRED TO: 154

STERLING, ANTHONY CONINGHAM (1805–71; *DNB*). Referred to: 43

STERLING, CHARLOTTE (née Baird) (d. 1863; *DNB*). Referred to: 43

STERLING, JOHN (1806–44; *DNB*). Referred to: 11, 43, 52, 53–4

STEWART, DUGALD (1753–1828; *DNB*). Referred to: 20

———*Collected Works*. Ed. William Hamilton. 11 vols. Edinburgh: Constable, 1854–60.
REFERRED TO: 19–20

STOLDT, MR.
NOTE: member of a deputation from Heligoland.
REFERRED TO: 192

STONE, MR. (fl. 1850s?).
NOTE: an acquaintance of JSM's.
LETTER TO: 245

STRUTT, EDWARD (Lord Belper) (1801–80; *DNB*). Referred to: 15

SUTHERLAND, JAMES.
NOTE: Political Agent of the EIC.
REFERRED TO: 61

SWIFT, JONATHAN (1667–1745; *DNB*).
NOTE: the quotation has not been identified.
QUOTED: 54

Sydney Morning Herald. Referred to: 145

SYKES, WILLIAM HENRY (1790–1872; *DNB*).
NOTE: the references are to him as a member of the Secret Committee in his capacity as Chairman of the Court of Directors of the EIC 1856–57.
REFERRED TO: 87, 90, 92, 93, 94–5, 98–9, 100, 101

TABOUELLE, R. HENRY (fl. 1868).
NOTE: a French translator.
LETTER TO: 189

TARRANT, JAMES.
NOTE: a messenger at the EIC.
REFERRED TO: 89

TAYLOR, CLEMENTIA (1811–1908; *DNB*). Referred to: 182, 206

TAYLOR, HELEN (1831–1907; *DNB*). Referred to: 117, 129, 131–3, 140, 143, 144, 145, 146, 147, 149, 152, 155, 173, 200, 205, 211, 212, 218, 228, 234, 237

——— "Biographical Notice." In *Miscellaneous and Posthumous Works of Henry Thomas Buckle*. Ed. Helen Taylor. 3 vols. London: Longmans, Green, 1872, ix–lv.
REFERRED TO: 228

——— "A Few Words on Mr. Trollope's Defence of Fox-Hunting," *Fortnightly Review*, n.s. VII (Jan. 1870), 63–8.
REFERRED TO: 218

TAYLOR, HENRY (1800–86; *DNB*). Referred to: 31

——— *The Statesman*. London: Longman, *et al.*, 1836.
REFERRED TO: 31

TAYLOR, ISAAC (1759–1829; *DNB*). Referred to: 54

TAYLOR, PETER ALFRED (1819–91; *DNB*). Letter to: 196

TAYLOR, PHILIP MEADOWS (1808–76; *DNB*). Referred to: 73

TAYLOR, R.S.
  NOTE: Major in the army of the EIC.
  REFERRED TO: 107
TAYLOR, RICHARD (1781–1858; *DNB*). Referred to: 66
TEMPLE, HENRY JOHN (3rd Viscount Palmerston) (1784–1865; *DNB*). Referred to: 66
THEOBALD, HENRY STUDDY (1847–1934).
  NOTE: a law student; later a writer of legal treatises.
  LETTER TO: 176
THIBAUDEAU, ADOLPHE NARCISSE, COMTE (1795–1856; *GDU*). Letter to: 27
THOM, JOHN HAMILTON (1808–94; *DNB*). Letter to: 72
THOMMEREL, J.P. (fl. 1840).
  NOTE: a writer on English literature.
  REFERRED TO: 69
THOMPSON, THOMAS PERRONET (1783–1869; *DNB*). Referred to: 20–1
——— "Absenteeism in Ireland," *Westminster Review*, X (Jan. 1829), 237–43.
  REFERRED TO: 21
——— "Archbishop of Dublin on Political Economy," *Westminster Review*, XVI (Jan. 1832), 1–22.
  REFERRED TO: 19
——— "Property Tax," *Westminster Review*, XIX (July 1833), 1–9.
  REFERRED TO: 21
THOMSON, ANTHONY TODD (1778–1849; *DNB*). Referred to: 21
THORNTON, EDWARD (1799–1875; *DNB*). Referred to: 245
THORNTON, WILLIAM THOMAS (1813–80; *DNB*). Referred to: 97, 188, 198
The Times.
  NOTE: anonymous articles follow chronologically.
  REFERRED TO: 132, 202
——— Paragraph reporting W.E. Tooke's suicide, 28 Jan., 1830, 2.
  REFERRED TO: 9
——— "The Civil War in America," 8 Sept., 1862, 9.
  REFERRED TO: 132
——— "Royal Horticultural Society," 22 Jan., 1864, 5.
  REFERRED TO: 146
——— Leader on foreign policy, 14 July, 1864, 8.
  REFERRED TO: 150
TITE, WILLIAM (1798–1873; *DNB*). Referred to: 198
TOCQUEVILLE, ALEXIS HENRI CHARLES MAURICE CLÉREL, COMTE DE (1805–59; *GDU*). Referred to: 124
——— *L'ancien régime et la révolution*. Paris: Lévy, 1856.
  REFERRED TO: 124
——— "Political and Social Condition of France," *London and Westminster Review*, III & XXV (Apr. 1836), 137–69.
  REFERRED TO: 124
TOOKE, THOMAS (1774–1858; *DNB*). Referred to: 3, 9, 122

TOOKE, WILLIAM EYTON (1806–30).
NOTE: see *Alumni Cantab*.
REFERRED TO: 3, 9, 10

────── "*Memoirs of the Affairs of Europe*," *Westminster Review*, IV (July 1825), 178–83.
REFERRED TO: 8

TOWNSEND, MEREDITH WHITE (1831–1911; *DNB*). Referred to: 136–7

TRANT, WILLIAM (fl. 1870s).
NOTE: associated with the working men's clubs movement.
LETTER TO: 220

TREVELYAN, CHARLES EDWARD (1807–86; *DNB*).
NOTE: see also *PP* (1854).
LETTER TO: 130

TRÜBNER, JOHN NICHOLAS (1817–84; *DNB*). Letter to: 164

TUCKER, HENRY ST. GEORGE (1771–1851; *DNB*). Referred to: 25

TURGOT, LOUIS FÉLIX ETIENNE, MARQUIS DE (1796–1866; *GDU*). Referred to: 88

TURNER, JOHN LEE.
NOTE: a messenger at the EIC.
REFERRED TO: 89

UPTON, RICHARD.
NOTE: a clerk in the Secret Department of the EIC.
REFERRED TO: 111

UPTON, W.I.
NOTE: a temporary writer at the EIC.
REFERRED TO: 92, 102, 109, 111

USIGLIO, ANGELO (1803–75).
NOTE: see *Dizionario del Risorgimento Nazionale*.
REFERRED TO: 41–2

VARNHAGEN VON ENSE, KARL AUGUST (1785–1858; *EB*). Referred to: 66

VENN, JOHN (1834–1923; *DNB*). Referred to: 153

VILLARD, HENRY (1835–1900; *DAB*). Letters to: 211, 213

VILLARI, PASQUALE (1826–1917; *EB*). Referred to: 130–1

────── *La storia di Girolamo Savonarola e de' suoi tempi narrata da Pasquale Villari con l'aiuto di nuovi documenti*. 2 vols. Florence: Le Monnier, 1859–61.
REFERRED TO: 131

VILLIERS, GEORGE WILLIAM FREDERICK (4th Earl of Clarendon) (1800–70; *DNB*). Referred to: 93, 98, 99

WADDILOVE, ALFRED (1806–90; *MEB*). Referred to: 158

────── "Is It Expedient to Remove Any and What of the Remaining Restrictions on the Admissibility of Evidence in Civil and Criminal Cases?" In *Transactions of the National Association for the Promotion of Social Science*. Sheffield Meeting, 1865. Ed. George W. Hastings. London: Longman, *et al.*, 1866.
REFERRED TO: 158

Index of Persons and Works

WADE, CLAUDE MARTINE (1794–1861; *DNB*). Referred to: 61

WALEY, JACOB (1818–73; *DNB*). Letter to: 116

WARD, ALEXANDER.
NOTE: a writer (retired) at the EIC.
REFERRED TO: 109–10

WATERFIELD, THOMAS NELSON (1799–1862).
LETTERS TO: 63, 67, 79, 92, 93, 94, 98 (2), 99, 100, 103, 111, 113
REFERRED TO: 101

WATKINS, JOHN (fl. 1865).
NOTE: a London photographer.
LETTER TO: 156

WATSON, DAVID MCBURNIE (d. 1902).
NOTE: see also *CW*, XVII, 1638n–9n.
REFERRED TO: 213

WAUD, CHRISTOPHER.
NOTE: Registrar in the Examiner's Office of the EIC.
REFERRED TO: 84, 85, 86, 89

WAUGH, BENJAMIN (1839–1908; *DNB*). Letter to: 226–7

WEBB, RICHARD DAVIS (d. 1872).
NOTE: Dublin printer and anti-slavery writer.
LETTER TO: 189
REFERRED TO: 182

WELLESLEY, HENRY RICHARD CHARLES (1st Earl Cowley) (1804–84; *DNB*). Referred to: 88

WELSH, DAVID (1793–1845; *DNB*).
NOTE: JSM uses the spelling Welch.
REFERRED TO: 8

———— *An Account of the Life and Writings of Thomas Brown, M.D., Late Professor of Moral Philosophy in the University of Edinburgh*. Edinburgh: Tait, 1825.
REFERRED TO: 8

WERTHEIMSTEIN, CARL (1847–66). Referred to: 205

WERTHEIMSTEIN, JOSEPHINE VON (née Gomperz) (1820–94).
LETTER TO: 142
REFERRED TO: 108, 115, 145, 152, 205

WESSEL, EDUARD (1822–79).
NOTE: journalist and teacher.
REFERRED TO: 140, 142, 143, 145, 152, 205

WESTERTON, CHARLES (1813–72; *MEB*). Referred to: 155

Westminster Review.
NOTE: see also *London and Westminster Review*; one anonymous article follows.
REFERRED TO: 2, 6, 7, 8, 20–1, 56, 81, 202

———— "Political Economy [by Nassau Senior]," VIII (July 1827), 177–89.
REFERRED TO: 19

WHATELY, RICHARD (1787–1863; *DNB*). Referred to: 19

———— *Introductory Lectures on Political Economy; Being Part of a Course Delivered in Easter Term, MDCCCXXXI*. London: Fellowes, 1831.
REFERRED TO: 19

WHATMOUGH, JOHN.
NOTE: a messenger at the EIC.
REFERRED TO: 105–6

WHEWELL, WILLIAM (1794–1866; *DNB*). Referred to: 115, 207

WHITE, I.
NOTE: a labourer at the EIC.
REFERRED TO: 86

WHITMORE, WILLIAM (fl. 1824).
NOTE: cousin of the following.
REFERRED TO: 2

WHITMORE, WILLIAM WOLRYCHE (1787–1858; *MEB*). Referred to: 2

———— *A Letter on the Present State and Future Prospects of Agriculture*. London: Hatchard, 1822.
NOTE: reviewed by Mill in his "Corn Laws," *q.v.*
REFERRED TO: 2–3

WILBERFORCE, ROBERT ISAAC (1802–57; *DNB*). Referred to: 53

WILBERFORCE, SAMUEL (1805–73; *DNB*). Referred to: 53

WILLCOX, JAMES KEAPPOCH HAMILTON (1842–98). Letter to: 231

WILLIAMS, ARTHUR JOHN (1836–1911; *WWBMP*). Letter to: 158

WILLIAMS, JAMES.
NOTE: a Political Commissioner of the EIC.
REFERRED TO: 33–4, 38

WILLIAMS, WILLIAM FENWICK (1800–83; *DNB*). Referred to: 93

WILLOCK, HENRY (1788/9–1858; *MEB*). Referred to: 56

WILLOCK, JOHN HENRY.
NOTE: a clerk at the EIC.
REFERRED TO: 103

WILSON, EFFINGHAM (1783–1868; *MEB*). Letter to: 23

WILSON, HORACE HAYMAN (1786–1860; *DNB*). Letters to: 23, 39

———— "Education of the Natives of India," *Asiatic Journal and Monthly Register of British and Foreign India, China and Australasia*, n.s. XIX (Jan.–Apr. 1836), 1–16.
REFERRED TO: 30

WILSON, JOHN (fl. 1834–66).
NOTE: editor, and Factory and Poor Law Commissioner.
REFERRED TO: 27

WITTUL ROW DEWANJEE (fl. 1830s).
NOTE: Indian administrator.
REFERRED TO: 39

WOLFF, JOSEPH (1795–1862; *DNB*). Referred to: 43

WORDSWORTH, WILLIAM (1770–1850; *DNB*). Referred to: 12

The Working Man; a Weekly Record of Social and Industrial Progress.
NOTE: ran from 6 Jan. to 22 Dec., 1866.
REFERRED TO: 171

WYSE, WILLIAM CHARLES BONAPARTE (1826–92; *DNB*). Letter to: 247

YOUNG, GEORGE (1819–1907; *DNB*). Speech on Introducing a Bill to Abolish the Annuity Tax (4 Mar., 1870; Commons), *PD*, 3rd ser., Vol. 199, cols. 1321–3.
REFERRED TO: 220

YOUNG, JOHN.
NOTE: a warehouse pensioner of the EIC.
REFERRED TO: 86

PARLIAMENTARY PAPERS

"Treaty between the East India Company and the Peshwa; Concluded at Bassein, the 31st December, 1802," *PP*, 1803–04, XII, 90–3.
REFERRED TO: 63

"Treaty with the Peishwa, Dated 13th June, 1817," *PP*, 1818, XI, 346–50.
REFERRED TO: 63

"Report from the Select Committee on the Criminal Law of England" (2 Apr., 1824), *PP*, 1824, IV, 39–405.
REFERRED TO: 2

"Minutes of Evidence Taken before the Select Committee on the Affairs of the East India Company; and also an Appendix and Index," *PP*, 1831–32, XIV.
REFERRED TO: 25

"Report of Charles H. Cameron, Esq., . . . upon the Judicial Establishments and Procedure in Ceylon" (31 Jan., 1832), *PP*, 1831–32, XXXII, 119–42.
REFERRED TO: 51

"First Report on the Commercial Relations between France and Great Britain, Addressed to the Right Honourable the Lords of the Committee of Privy Council for Trade and Plantations, by George Villiers and John Bowring, with a Supplementary Report by John Bowring," *PP*, 1834, XIX, 1–257.
REFERRED TO: 25

"Second Report on the Commercial Relations between France and Great Britain. Silks and Wine. By John Bowring," *PP*, 1835, XXXVI, 441–697.
REFERRED TO: 25, 26

"Report on the Affairs of British North America, from the Earl of Durham," *PP*, 1839, XVII, 1–690.
REFERRED TO: 43

"Report on the Organisation of the Permanent Civil Service, together with a Letter from the Rev. B. Jowett," *PP*, 1854, XXVII, 1–31.
NOTE: prepared by Sir Charles Edward Trevelyan (*q.v.*) and Sir Stafford Northcote.
REFERRED TO: 130

"Return to an Order of the Honourable House of Commons, Dated 24 August 1857; for, a Selection of Papers Showing the Measures Taken since 1847 to Promote the Cultivation of Cotton in India," *PP*, 1857 (II), XXXI.
REFERRED TO: 113–14

"Miscellaneous Statistics of the United Kingdom (Part IV)," *PP*, 1862, LX, 443–783.
REFERRED TO: 135

"Correspondence Respecting the Plunder of the Wreck of the British Barque *Prince of Wales*; and the Ill-treatment of Officers of Her Majesty's Ship *Forte*," *PP*, 1863, LXXIII, 121–277.
REFERRED TO: 150

"Brazil. Further Correspondence Respecting the Plunder of the Wreck of the British Barque *Prince of Wales*; and the Ill-treatment of Officers of Her Majesty's Ship *Forte*," *PP*, 1863, LXXIII, 279–89.
REFERRED TO: 150

"Brazil. Further Correspondence Respecting the Plunder of the Wreck of the British Barque *Prince of Wales*," *PP*, 1863, LXXIII, 291–4.
REFERRED TO: 150

"Brazil. Further Correspondence Respecting the Ill-treatment of Officers of Her Majesty's Ship *Forte*," *PP*, 1863, LXXIII, 297–302.
REFERRED TO: 150

"Return of the Order in Council of the 7th Day of January, 1864, and the 29th Day of February, 1868, as to the Government of Heligoland," *PP*, 1890, XLIX, 503–9.
REFERRED TO: 186, 187, 192

"A Bill to Extend the Right of Voting at Elections of Members of Parliament in England and Wales," 29 Victoria (13 Mar., 1866), *PP*, 1866, V, 87–100.
REFERRED TO: 165, 169

"First Report from the Select Committee on Metropolitan Local Government, etc.; together with the Proceedings of the Committee, Minutes of Evidence, and Appendix" (16 Apr., 1866), *PP*, 1866, XIII, 171–315.
REFERRED TO: 168

"Second Report from the Select Committee on Metropolitan Local Government, etc.; together with the Proceedings of the Committee, Minutes of Evidence, and Appendix" (30 July, 1866), *PP*, 1866, XIII, 317–628.
REFERRED TO: 168

"Second Report from the Select Committee on Metropolitan Local Government, etc.; together with the Proceedings of the Committee, and Appendix" (6 May, 1867), *PP*, 1867, XII, 435–41*.
REFERRED TO: 176

"Third Report from the Select Committee on Metropolitan Local Government, etc.; together with the Proceedings of the Committee, Minutes of Evidence, and Appendix" (20 May, 1867), *PP*, 1867, XII, 443–660.
REFERRED TO: 174, 176

"A Bill for the Establishment of Municipal Corporations within the Metropolis," 30 Victoria (21 May, 1867), *PP*, 1867, IV, 447–66.
REFERRED TO: 177, 216

"A Bill for the Better Government of the Metropolis," 30 & 31 Victoria (6 Aug., 1867), *PP*, 1867, IV, 215–56.
REFERRED TO: 177, 178, 179, 216

"A Bill for Amending the Laws Relating to Election Petitions, and Providing More Effectually for the Prevention of Corrupt Practices at Elections," 31 Victoria (13 Feb., 1868), *PP*, 1867–68, II, 267–86.
REFERRED TO: 190–1, 192, 195

"A Bill for the Amendment of the Representation of the People in Scotland," 31 Victoria (17 Feb., 1868), *PP*, 1867–68, IV, 579–614.
REFERRED TO: 193, 194

"A Bill to Repeal Certain Tests and Alter Certain Statutes Affecting the Constitution of the Universities of Oxford and Cambridge," 31 Victoria (18 Feb., 1868), *PP*, 1867–68, III, 589–92.
REFERRED TO: 196

"Report from the Select Committee on Extradition, together with the Proceedings of the Committee, Minutes of Evidence, and Appendix" (6 July, 1868), *PP*, 1867–68, VII, 129–338.
REFERRED TO: 171, 196

"A Bill to Amend the Act Twenty-third and Twenty-fourth Victoria Chapter Fifty, Intituled 'An Act to Abolish the Annuity Tax in Edinburgh and Montrose etc.,'" 33 & 34 Victoria (11 July, 1870), *PP*, 1870, I, 53–70.
REFERRED TO: 220

"Second Report of the Royal Commission to Inquire into the Operation of the Sanitary Laws in England and Wales," *PP*, 1871, XXXV.
REFERRED TO: 223

STATUTES

20 Henry III, Statutes of Merton, c.9. "He is a Bastard That is Born before the Marriage of His Parents" (1235).
REFERRED TO: 42

7 & 8 George IV, c. 27. An Act for Repealing Various Statutes in England Relative to the Benefit of the Clergy, and to Larceny and Other Offences Connected Therewith, and to Malicious Injuries to Property, and to Remedies against the Hundred (21 June, 1827).
REFERRED TO: 2

7 & 8 George IV, c. 28. An Act for Further Improving the Administration of Justice in Criminal Cases in England (21 June, 1827).
REFERRED TO: 2

7 & 8 George IV, c. 29. An Act for Consolidating and Amending the Laws in England Relative to Larceny and Other Offences Connected Therewith (21 June, 1827).
REFERRED TO: 2

7 & 8 George IV, c. 30. An Act for Consolidating and Amending the Laws in England Relative to Malicious Injuries to Property (21 June, 1827).
REFERRED TO: 2

7 & 8 George IV, c. 31. An Act for Consolidating and Amending the Laws in England Relative to Remedies against the Hundred (21 June, 1827).
REFERRED TO: 2

4 & 5 William IV, c. 76. An Act for the Amendment and Better Administration of the Laws Relating to the Poor in England and Wales (14 Aug., 1834).
REFERRED TO: 223

29 Victoria, c. 35. An Act for the Better Prevention of Contagious Diseases at Certain Naval and Military Stations (11 June, 1866).

Appendix F

NOTE: superseded the first Contagious Diseases Act, 27 & 28 Victoria, c. 85 (29 July, 1864).
REFERRED TO: 226

29 & 30 Victoria, c. 121. An Act for the Amendment of the Law Relating to Treaties of Extradition (10 Aug., 1866).
REFERRED TO: 171

30 & 31 Victoria, c. 102. An Act Further to Amend the Laws Relating to the Representation of the People in England and Wales (15 Aug., 1867).
REFERRED TO: 178, 180, 188, 213

31 & 32 Victoria, c. 48. An Act for the Amendment of the Representation of the People in Scotland (13 July, 1868).
REFERRED TO: 193

32 & 33 Victoria, c. 96. An Act to Amend the Contagious Diseases Act, 1866 (11 Aug., 1869).
REFERRED TO: 226

33 & 34 Victoria, c. 87. An Act to Amend the Act Twenty-third and Twenty-fourth Victoria Intituled "An Act to Abolish the Annuity Tax in Edinburgh and Montrose, etc." (9 Aug., 1870).
REFERRED TO: 220

SOUTH AUSTRALIA

14 & 15 Victoria, 1861, No. 20. "An Act to Provide for the Election of Members to Serve in the Parliament of the Province of South Australia" (29 Nov., 1861).
REFERRED TO: 127

Index

Aspects of Mill's personal life are indexed under Mill, John Stuart. For specific laws and parliamentary documents, as well as people and writings, see App. F. Geographical names and constituencies mentioned incidentally are not indexed. Abbreviations: *ER* (*Edinburgh Review*), JSM (John Stuart Mill), HTM (Harriet Taylor Mill), *LWR* (*London and Westminster Review*), *WR* (*Westminster Review*).

ACADÉMIE DES SCIENCES MORALES ET POLITIQUES (Institut de France): JSM becomes correspondent of, 122–3; JSM sends writings to, 123, 139; mentioned, 130
Africa, slave trade in, 150
Agra, 40–1
Agriculture and distribution of produce, 137
America. *See* United States
Anglo Indian College (Hindu College), choice of headmaster for, 23–4, 30
Annuities, JSM investigates, 83
Aristocracy, *ER* and English, 5
Artists' General Benevolent Institution, 177
Association of ideas, importance of, 207
Athenaeum Club, 11
Australia: proportional representation in, 127; education and land policy in, 232; question of its separation from England, 233; mentioned, 130. *See also* Victoria
Austria: at war with France over Italy, 118, 119; JSM visits, 131–2; mentioned, 137
Avignon, JSM's life at, 144

BALLOT, in other countries, 213–14
Baroda: Resident of, removed, 33–4; mentioned, 39
Bengal Presidency: pensions for officers in, 68; mentioned, 35
Berbera, 104
Birkbeck Schools, 200
Birth control, Drysdale's book on, 225–6
Board of Control: receives and alters draft despatches from JSM, 13–14, 17, 25, 33–41, 48–9, 51, 55–61, 63, 67–8, 79; keeps copies of documents from India, 96
Bombay Presidency, letters from, 35
Botany: JSM practises, 120; would be adversely affected by planned contest of herbaria, 146–7, 148

Brazil, Christie's controversy over slavery in, 150–1
Bribery at elections: JSM's work against, 190, 192–3, 195; whether restrained by use of ballot, 213–14
Brutality, domestic, and P.C. Smith case, 217–18

CAMBRIDGE UNIVERSITY, political economy at, 19
Causes, Comte on final, 159
Centralization, a French error, 204
Christianity: meaning of, 53; effect of philosophy on belief in, 53; future morality as development of, 236
Church rates, 220
Civilization, potential and actual, 74–5
Coal, 165
Cobden Club, publications of, 209, 224
Codification of English law, proposed, 2
Colonies, British: policy of federation for, 145–6; question of their separation, 233
Colonization of Australia, 232
Contagious Diseases Acts, protest against, 226–7
Contradiction, principle of, 134, 135
Co-operation, progress of, 81, 126, 188–9
Corn Laws, agitation against, 2–3, 62
Cornwall, JSM's tour of, 27, 55
Cotton, from India, 113–14
Council of India, JSM declines a seat on, 115
Credit, role of, 82

DEFINITION, 135
Discussion, value of, 139
Dublin, 189

EAST INDIA COMPANY: its civil service, 17–18; its system of written reports from India,

34–5; patronage in, 40; JSM's attitude to his work at, 54; disposition of its records, 85, 86, 89, 96, 106; Secret Committee business of, 87–9, 92–5, 98–105, 110–13; army of, 98; restrictions on employment of foreigners in, 108; franking of letters in, 243

Examiner's Office of: correspondence regarding drafts of despatches from, 13–14, 17, 25, 33–41, 48–9, 51, 55–61, 63, 67–8, 79; searches for documents by, 22, 28, 38, 113–14; JSM's concerns with premises of, 83–5, 107; JSM's concerns with staff of, 84, 86, 87, 90, 92, 95, 97, 102, 105–6, 109–14

Education: Cousin's report on, 23; in India, 24, 30, 108; in Italy, and question of public examinations, 130; of women, 137, 233; JSM's advice on practical *vs.* university, 221–2; in Australia, 232; in Germany, 234; mentioned, 124

Elections: need for reform of, 165–6; payment of expenses of by public, 167; JSM's work against bribery at, 190, 192–3, 195; use of ballot in, 213–14. *See also* Proportional representation

England and France, misunderstanding between, 229

Evidence, exclusion of judicial, 158

Examinations: competitive, 130; matriculation, should be open to girls, 137; limitations of, as tests of knowledge, 221–2

Experience, philosophical school of, 115

Extradition, 171–2, 196

FALLACIES, 134

Falmouth, Henry Mill's grave at, 52–3

France: choice of a correspondent in, for *Globe and Traveller*, 27; under Louis Napoleon, 82, 141; Indian possessions of, 87–9, 94–5, 102–3, 112; interference of in Italy, 118, 119, 132–3; tone of writers in, 132; over-centralized, 204; censorship by Post Office of, 218; arbitrary government and deviousness in, 218; misunderstanding between England and, 229; outlook of, in 1871, 231; mentioned, 43

Franco-Prussian War, 220

Free trade, political economists generally favour, 20

French (language), 147

French Revolution (1789), *LWR* article on, 32

Friendly societies, 216

GAME LAWS, JSM's article on, 8

Germany: intellectual liberty in, 108; universities in, 186; women in, 229, 234; mentioned, 149, 152, 204

Glasgow, 210

Gold: effect of recent discoveries on value of, 117–18; Jevons on value of, 164

Government, and size of legislature, 232–3

Greece (ancient), Gomperz's work on philosophy of, 115, 152

Greece (modern): JSM visits, 129–31; needs of, 136

Greenock, Christie as candidate for, 195

Greenwich, Gladstone as candidate for, 198–9

HAILEYBURY COLLEGE, political economy in, 20

Happiness as end of moral actions, 185

Heligoland, discontent in, 186–7, 192

Herat, 92, 107, 113

History and times of crisis, 235

Hong Kong, 98

House of Commons, JSM obtains passes to Speaker's gallery of, 162; hours of, 177

Hyderabad: revenue from villages in, 60; pensions for officers in, 67–8

IMPROVEMENT OF MANKIND: as necessary goal, 74–5; and position of women, 207

Inconceivable, meaning of, 207

India: education in, 23–4, 30, 108; titles in, 60–1; and question of Resident of Shorapore, 73; proposed exchange of French and English territory in, 87–9, 94–5, 102–3, 112; customs laws in, 101; cotton from, 113–14; public works in, 198; prisons in, 199; land tenure in, comparable to Irish, 209, 214, 216; visitors from, 212; postal communications with, 243; mentioned, 31 *See also* Council of India, East India Company, Native States

India House. *See* East India Company

India Office, JSM receives pension from, 151

Institut de France. *See* Académie des Sciences Morales et Politiques

International School, JSM recommends candidate to head Parisian, 170

International trade, effect of improvements on, 116

International Working Men's Association, 220

Ireland: migrant labourers from, 3; agriculture in, 137; women's suffrage movement in, 182–3; land tenure in, 209, 214–16

Italy: exiles from, 41–2; JSM visits, 43–4; English interest in, 130–1; unification of, 132–3

JAMAICA: punishment of rebellion in, 160–1; much of suffering in, avoidable, 203
Joke, contributor to *LWR* praised for inserting a, 36
Juries, women on, 233
Jurisprudence, Austin's lectures on, 12, 14, 21
Jyepore [Jaipur], 55

KATTYWAR [Kathiawar], 34, 39–40
Kedah, 13
King's College London, political economy in, 18–19
Kuria Muria Islands, 100–1

LABOURING CLASSES: attitude to American Civil War, 141–2; JSM and, 171; improvement of their minds, 235
Lake District, JSM visits, 12
Land: absolute ownership of, a modern notion, 167; tenure of, in different countries, 209; tenure of, in Ireland, 214–16; management of colonial, 232
Landlords, favoured class in England, 216
Law, English: reform of, 1–2; defects of, 7; popular study at University of London, 21; and legitimacy, 42
Law, Roman, in Europe, 43
Liberty: ideas of JSM's essay on, 108, 120; defence of, JSM's motive in his writing, 191
Ligue Internationale de la Paix, 181
Liverpool Mechanics' Institute, JSM invited to preside at, 222–3
Logic: Stebbing's analysis of JSM's work on, 116–17; Boole's and De Morgan's systems of, 153; JSM's discussed, 155–6; formal, 165
London, reform of government of: JSM's work on Select Committee on, 168–9, 176–7; B. Scott's views on, 173–4; JSM's bill for, 177, 178–9; J.M. Ludlow's contribution to, 216
London National Society for Women's Suffrage, 182–3, 208
Lucerne, JSM at, 228, 230
Lymington, JSM to visit, 16

MACARONI, JSM's diet of, 44
Madras Presidency, army in, 98
Magistrates, Black's criticisms of, 7
Malta, 42
Manchester Public Free Libraries, 174–5
Mauritius, possible disturbances in, 203
Medicine, popular study in University of London, 21

Metaphysics, 8
Metropolitan Board of Works, 198
Mill, John Stuart: his early circle, 1–7; on Eyton Tooke's death, 9; his arrangements for brother's grave, 52–3; sends autographs of the famous, 66; his memories of his wife, 128; donates books, 138, 163, 174–5, 194; worries about Gomperz, 142–4, 149; his photograph, 156–7, 160; dislikes general society, 175; responds to requests for recommendations, 183–4, 216–17, 229, 231–2, 247; declines to exert influence with government, 230
Finances of, 69–71, 83, 151, 248
Health of, 44, 200–1, 228
Journalism of: helps to edit *WR*, 7–8, 56; solicits a French correspondent for the *Globe and Traveller*, 27; closes Parisian agency of *LWR*, 32; edits *LWR*, 35, 38–9, 48, 49; sells *LWR*, 45–7, 49–50; declines payment for article, 80; reflections on *WR*, 202
Parliamentary career of: election of 1865, 155, 157, 160; admits visitors to Speaker's gallery, 162; dines with Sheriffs of London, 163; serves on Select Committee, 168–9, 176–7; other work, 177–9, 190, 192, 193–4, 196–7; declines another constituency, 178; stands for re-election, 194
Publishers, relations with, 64–5, 129–30, 138, 156
Trips: to Lake District, 12; to Lymington, 16; to Italy, 43–4; to Greece and Europe, 129–32
See also East India Company
Miracles, belief in, 53
Monarchy, 120
Morality: utilitarian, defended against Whewell, 115; and limits of duty of truth, 185; task of building a new, 235–6
Myhee Caunta [Mahi Kantha], 33–4, 63
Mysore, 51

NAGPORE [Nagpur], 60
National Association for the Promotion of Social Science, meetings of, 158, 171–2
National Society for Women's Suffrage, 206
Native States (of India), 55–6, 60
New York City Free College, 231–2

OUDE [Oudh], 37, 56, 59
Owens College, 165
Oxford: JSM invited to, 137, 141; JSM's visits to, 219
Oxford University, Drummond Chair of political economy in, 19

PARIS: JSM visits, 32; *LWR* closes agency in, 32
Parks for children of poor, 210
Parliament, JSM as member of, 178. *See also* Westminster
Patent Laws, 211
People's Garden Company, 222
Persia: British relations with, 93, 98–9, 101; mentioned, 41, 113
Philology, 8, 108
Philosophy: and religion, 53; ancient Greek, 115, 152; and *axiomata media*, 159–60; Mahaffy's contribution to, 184
Plants, extirpation of rare British, 146–7
Pleading (legal): Graham on, 7; mentioned, 2
Political economy: Say's work on, 9–10; English school of, 10; state of, in Great Britain, 18–21; Courcelle-Seneuil's book on, 82; progress of, 219
Political Economy Club, meetings of, 47, 64, 126, 154, 166–7
Pondicherry, 87–9, 94–5, 103
Poor Law, New, principle of, 74–5, 223–4
Population: society's need to control, 75; mentioned, 3, 4
Postal services to the East, 98–9, 243
"Potatoes and point," 55
Primogeniture, articles about, 6
Prisons in India, 199
Progress, JSM and, 207
Proportional representation: progress of Hare's plan for, 126–7; importance of, 159; movement for in Switzerland, 188; and 1867 Reform Act, 188; recommended for Victoria, Australia, 233; mentioned, 151
Public health, Sanitary Commission's recommendations for, 223

RADICALS: views of, 20; *LWR* as organ of, 46
Rampore [Rampur], Rohilla jageer in, 57, 59
Reform, parliamentary: 1866 Bill for, and Gladstone, 165–6; 1867 Act for, and representation of minorities, 188; mentioned, 169
Religion, question of outward comformity to, 180–1, 185
Riding, JSM practises, 44
"Right to work" possible in future, 75
Roman Catholic Church and Canon Law on legitimacy, 42–3
Royal Geographical Society, 104–5
Royal Horticultural Society, JSM opposes its plan of a contest of herbaria, 146–7, 148
Russia: Asiatic or European? 101–2; mentioned, 188

SCIENCE: teaching of in India, 108; social now more important than physical, 122–3
Scotland: political economy seldom taught at universities of, 19–20; mentioned, 43
Slavery: and American Civil War, 132; British attitude to, in Brazil, 150–1; JSM's opposition to, 191
Social Science Association. *See* National Association for the Promotion of Social Science
Socialism, its erroneous notions regarding credit, 82
Society of French Teachers, 147
Somaliland, British relations with, 104–5
South London Working Men's College, 184, 193–4
Specialization, dangers of narrow, 186
Sterling Club, 53
Style, JSM's thoughts on revising his own, 54
Suffrage, JSM's idea of just, 151
Suffrage, women's: JSM's motion for, 178; Society for, 182–3; petitions for, 206; mentioned, 127

TENANT RIGHT, 214–15, 230
Tests, religious, question of, 180–1, 185
Tories: beliefs of, 20; mentioned, 5
Translation: JSM's troubles with unauthorized, 125; and copyright, 144–5
Truth: moral limits of obligation to, 185; as goal, 236
Turkey, Asiatic or European? 101–2

UNION AND EMANCIPATION SOCIETY, 142
United States: Civil War in, 132, 141–2, 201; JSM writes letter of introduction for traveller to, 211; ballot in, 213–14; progress of women in, 233; mentioned, 5
Universities: German, compared to English, 186; not necessarily best training for life, 221–2
University College London, JSM recommends Examiner for, 147
University of Chicago, 233
University of Dublin, political economy in, 19
University of Edinburgh, political economy in, 19–20
University of London: political economy in, 18; state of (1833), 21; JSM invited to represent in Parliament, 178; parliamentary representation of, 180; mentioned, 217
University of Sydney, 233
Utilitarianism, not popular in French Académie des Sciences, 139
Utilitarians, activities of, in 1820s, 1–7
Utility as standard in morality, 115

VALUE, Malthus on measure of, 6
Victoria (Australia), political prospects of, 232–3
Vienna, 131, 144

WAR, means of avoiding, 224
Westminster: 1865 election at, 155, 157, 160; JSM as member for, 178; JSM's election campaign for (1868), 194; JSM's defeat in (1868), 201
Whigs: *ER* as supporter of, 5; views of, 20; mentioned, 31
Women: HTM and rights of, 128; education of, 137, 233; freedom of employment for, 199–200; political rights basic to improvement in condition of, 204; improvement of human race depends on condition of, 207; in India, 209; in Germany, 229, 234
suffrage of: manhood suffrage an unacceptable substitute for, 151; JSM's motion for, 178; movement for, 182–3, 206; mentioned, 127
Working Women's College, 172
Writing: JSM's advice on, 148–9; JSM's aim in his own, 191; not recommended as a career, 247

ZURICH, proportional representation association in, 188

DATE DUE

HIGHSMITH 45-220